D1738889

A Choctaw Reference Grammar

STUDIES
IN THE ANTHROPOLOGY OF
NORTH AMERICAN INDIANS

Editors
Raymond J. DeMallie
Douglas R. Parks

A CHOCTAW REFERENCE GRAMMAR

George Aaron Broadwell

Published by the University of Nebraska Press
Lincoln and London

In cooperation with the American Indian Studies Research
Institute, Indiana University, Bloomington

Library of Congress Cataloging-in-Publication Data
Broadwell, George Aaron.
A Choctaw reference grammar / George Aaron Broadwell.
p. cm.—(Studies in the anthropology of North American Indians)
"In cooperation with the American Indian Studies Research Institute,
Indiana University, Bloomington."
Includes bibliographical references and index.
ISBN-13: 978-0-8032-1315-9 (cloth: alk. paper)
ISBN-10: 0-8032-1315-8 (cloth: alk. paper)
1. Choctaw language—Grammar.   2. Choctaw language—Phonology.
3. Choctaw language—Morphology.   I. Indiana University, Bloomington.
American Indian Studies Research Institute.   II. Title.   III. Series.
PM872.B76   2006
2005033764

Contents

Tables

Acknowledgments

This book could not have been written without the help of many people. First and foremost, I would like to thank the Choctaw speakers who have patiently helped me understand their language. My primary teachers were the late Gus Comby, of Pearl River, Mississippi; the late Josephine Wade, of Los Angeles, California; Henry Willis, of Moore, Oklahoma; and Edith Gem, of Long Beach, California. I also learned valuable things from many other Choctaw speakers, including Thallis Lewis, Roseanne Tubby, Henry Williams, Loretta York, and the late Henry Tubby. Thanks are also due to Catherine Willmond, a native speaker of Chickasaw who gave me valuable comparisons between Choctaw and Chickasaw.

I also thank all those on the Choctaw reservation who made it possible for me to do my research there. Thallis Lewis, director of the Bilingual Education Project of the Mississippi Band of Choctaw Indians from 1983 to 1986, was invaluable in introducing me to speakers and made much of my early work on the Choctaw language possible. Gene Franks, director of the project from 1986 to 1988, continued the tribe's strong support for research on the Choctaw language. My coworkers during the summers of 1986 and 1987, Nellie Steve, Annie Pearl Bell, Doris Billie, Emilee Denson, and Nelda Lewis, provided good company and answered my endless questions. Cillo Cotton and Henry Williams, administrators at Bogue Chitto and Conehatta, introduced me to many speakers, and I thank them. Thanks are also due to Phillip Martin, chief of the Mississippi Band of Choctaw Indians, for his progressive leadership in encouraging the study and maintenance of the Choctaw language.

Acknowledgments are also due to the late Harry Folsom, Father Bob Goodyear, Dr. and Mrs. Shaw Gaddy, Brother Theodore Jurdt, Father Walter O'Donnell, and Don Sharp for their friendship and hospitality during the summers of 1984 and 1986. I thank Harry and Geri Harm for providing me with valuable materials from their Choctaw Bible Translation Committee.

This book is an outgrowth of my doctoral dissertation at the University of California, Los Angeles. I thank the members of my committee, Hilda Koopman, Pamela Munro, and Tim Stowell, for valuable guidance on the dissertation. I began work on Choctaw as an undergraduate in 1982, and I thank Jeff Heath for providing me with early guidance in its study. I also thank Marcia Haag, Jack Martin, Pamela Munro, and Carson Schütze for their helpful comments and suggestions on subsequent revisions to the analyses found there. Matthew Dryer carefully read a nearly final version of this grammar and provided extensive and careful comments that greatly improved the end product. Special thanks to Peter Marino for many hours of help in editing this manuscript for publication, and to Anastasiya Forin, Mulan Mo, and Sibel Cakir, undergraduate work-study students who entered Choctaw data into databases and double-checked citations for me.

My research on Choctaw has been supported by the Choctaw Bilingual Education Program of the Mississippi Band of Choctaw Indians; the Phillips Fund of the American Philosophical Society; a National Science Foundation graduate fellowship; the Department of Linguistics, UCLA; the Department of Anthropology, University of Oklahoma; the Department of Anthropology of the University at Albany, State University of New York; and a Faculty Research Awards Program grant from University at Albany, State University of New York. I completed the bulk of this manuscript while on sabbatical; I thank the University at Albany for releasing me from teaching obligations for that year and also thank the Department of Linguistics at UCLA for graciously hosting me.

Abbreviations and conventions

1	first person
2	second person
ABL	ablative
AC	accusative
AC2	accusative 2 (Choctaw -*ano*)
Acts	Acts of the Apostles
ADV	adverb
AFF	affected
AFFIRM	affirmative
BEN	benefactive
CAUS	causative
CBTC	Choctaw Bible Translation Committee
CERT	certainty
CON	contrastive
COMPAR	comparison
COMIT	comitative
COMP	complementizer
CONCESS	concessive
COP	copula
Cor.	Corinthians
D:AC	demonstrative accusative
DEM	demonstrative
DIM	diminutive
DISTR	distributed
D:NM	demonstrative nominative
DPAST	distant past
DS	different subject
DS2	different subject 2 (Choctaw -*no*)
DU	dual
EMPH	emphatic
EVID	evidential
EXCLAM	exclamatory
EXHORT	exhortation
FOC:NM	focus nominative
FOC:AC	focus accusative

G	g-grade
Gen.	Genesis
H	h-grade
Heb.	Hebrews
HN	hn-grade
HSAY	hearsay
I	agreement class I
II	agreement class II
III	agreement class III
IMP	imperative
INSTR	instrumental
INT	interrogative
INTR	intransitive
IRR	irrealis
IRR2	irrealis 2 (Choctaw -*ahii*)
Josh.	Joshua
Judg.	Judges
L	l-grade
LINK	linker
LOC	locative
Matt.	Matthew
MP	multiple plural
N	n-grade
N	negative agreement class
NEG	negative
NM	nominative
NM2	nominative 2 (Choctaw -*ato*)
NML	nominalizer
OBL	oblique
P	plural (in person-number affixes)
PLOBJ	plural object
PL(UR)	plural
PART	participial
PEJOR	pejorative
POT	potential
PREV	previous mention
PROHIB	prohibitive
PROV	pro-verb
PT	past

Q	question
RCP	reciprocal
RFL	reflexive
Rom.	Romans
S	singular (in person-number affixes)
Sam.	Samuel
SG	singular
SS	same subject
SS2	same subject 2
TNS	default tense
TR	transitive
WARN	warning
VOC	vocative
Y	y-grade

Except in person-number affixes, a colon (:) is used in glosses to connect words or abbreviations that gloss a single Choctaw morpheme. An equals sign (=) connects Choctaw words that receive a single gloss.

Glosses for person-number affixes in examples from Muskogean languages follow the order PERSON-NUMBER-AGREEMENT CLASS; thus "1SI" is 'first person singular, I agreement class'; 2PIII is 'second person plural, III agreement class', and so on.

Verbs in Muskogean languages which reflect internal aspectual modification have the name of the aspectual grade following the gloss. Thus "see:H" is the h-grade of the verb 'see', "leave:L" is the l-grade of the verb 'leave', and so on.

An asterisk (*) before an example indicates unacceptability; one or more question marks before an example indicates doubtful acceptability. The sign % before an example indicates that speakers differ as to whether it is acceptable.

Angle brackets < > with roman type indicate the original orthography of a source. Angle brackets within a morpheme enclose infixes.

1. The Choctaw language

1.1. Locations and numbers of speakers, past and present

Choctaw is a Muskogean language originally spoken in Mississippi, Alabama, and Louisiana. The majority of the Choctaw tribe was forcibly relocated to Oklahoma between 1831 and 1833, but a substantial number resisted removal and remained in Mississippi. There are now four main groups of Choctaw speakers: Mississippi Choctaws, Oklahoma Choctaws, Louisiana Choctaws, and Mississippi Choctaws of Oklahoma.

In total there are probably between 9,000 and 11,000 speakers of Choctaw. The 1990 United States census estimated 9,211 for Choctaw and Chickasaw together[1] This figure may be somewhat too low, for reasons discussed by Broadwell (1995).

1.1.1. Mississippi Choctaw

There are approximately 5,000 speakers of Mississippi Choctaw. There are two sources for estimating the number of speakers of Mississippi Choctaw. First, the 1990 United States census figures show 4,410 speakers of Choctaw and 124 speakers of an unspecified "American Indian language" in the state of Mississippi.

A second source of information is a tribal census reported by Fortune (1986), who gives the number of Choctaws on the Mississippi reservation as 4,478. In response to questionnaires, 82.2 percent indicated that they spoke Choctaw "very well," 6.4 percent that they speak "some" Choctaw, and 11.4 percent that they speak "hardly any" Choctaw. There are probably several hundred speakers of Mississippi Choctaw living off the reservation in Mississippi communities including Philadelphia, and Jackson. In addition, perhaps as many as 100 speakers of Mississippi Choctaw now live in Ripley, Tennessee, where they relocated in the 1950s (Kenaston 1972).

The Choctaw language is spoken by people of all ages on the Choctaw reservation, and there are many children acquiring Choctaw as their first language, though there are troubling indications that the percentage of children acquiring Choctaw is declining (P. Kwachka, p.c.).

---

1. Chickasaw is a language closely related to, but distinct from, Choctaw. United States census figures unfortunately combine these two languages, making it difficult to estimate numbers of speakers for each. However, there are far fewer speakers of Chickasaw, perhaps in the range of a few hundred (Munro, p.c. 1995), and the majority of those included in the census figure of 9,211 must be Choctaw speakers.

A significant number of Choctaw children are monolingual in Choctaw when they arrive at kindergarten, and the tribal education department employs specialists in English as a Second Language for helping Choctaw children learn English. Kwachka (1981) discusses some of the issues involved in the acquisition of English by Choctaw-speaking children.

1.1.2. Oklahoma Choctaw and Mississippi Choctaw of Oklahoma

There are probably between 4,000 and 6,000 speakers of Oklahoma Choctaw, and perhaps a few hundred speakers of Mississippi Choctaw of Oklahoma. It is rather difficult to be sure of these figures, however. The 1990 census reports only 3,467 speakers of Choctaw (including Chickasaw) in the state of Oklahoma, but I suspect the true number is somewhat higher than this.

Unlike Mississippi Choctaw, there are few, if any, children acquiring Oklahoma Choctaw, and speakers of Choctaw under the age of thirty-five are unusual; I have heard of a few cases where younger people speak the language because they have been raised by Choctaw-speaking grandparents. R. S. Williams (1995) provides a more detailed study of language obsolescence in Oklahoma Choctaw.

The Mississippi Choctaw of Oklahoma dialect (MCO) is spoken by some Choctaws who live in the Chickasaw nation. According to the 1980 census, the counties of Oklahoma which contain significant numbers of both Choctaws and Chickasaws are Atoka, Bryan, Coal, Hughes, and Pontontoc. In these counties live 2,150 Choctaws and 1,765 Chickasaws, and if we make the estimate that 30 percent of the Choctaws speak MCO that would imply about 600 speakers. There is some reason to believe that the speakers of MCO may represent the descendents of about 300 Mississippi Choctaws who were relocated to Oklahoma from 1903 to 1907, some seventy years after the main migration (Debo 1961:274-275; Roberts 1986). Ulrich (1986) and Broadwell (1992) discuss some linguistic features of this group.

1.1.3. Louisana Choctaw

Choctaw is spoken in two communities in Louisiana. There are a few speakers living among the Koasati in Elton and there is also a group of ethnic Choctaws with a few speakers in Jena. There were at one time more speakers of Choctaw in Louisiana.

Kimball (1991:9) reports that in the late nineteenth century there was a Choctaw community on the Calcasieu River near Indian Town, Louisana, and that most of these Choctaws relocated to Oklahoma in 1908. The speakers of Choctaw currently living among the Koasati are apparently the descendants of this community.

Bushnell (1909) discussed a group of Choctaws living just north of New Orleans at Bayou Lacomb, Tammany Parish, Louisiana and included a vocabulary of about sixty words. According to Bushnell, at one time "more than a hundred Choctaw lived in the vicinity of Bayou Lacomb, Bayou Castine, and near the Chefuncte river; but by act of Congress of July 1, 1902, they were persuaded to remove to the Indian Territory and receive an allotment of land" (1909:3). Bushnell worked with a few members of this group who remained in Louisiana after this date. There are apparently no longer speakers of Choctaw in this area.

Swanton (1946:123) reports that the 1910 United States census showed 115 Choctaws living in Louisiana, and the 1930 census showed 190. The 1990 census lists 6 speakers of Choctaw in Louisiana.

1.1.4. Other Choctaw groups

In addition to the groups just discussed, there are also a few other groups in the southeast who claim full or partial Choctaw ancestry. In some cases, these claims are the subject of controversy.

Within Louisiana, the Apache-Choctaw are centered around Ebarb and Zwolle, Sabine Parish (Roche 1982); the Clifton Choctaw in nearby Mora, Natchitoches Parish; and there are also a number of ethnic Choctaws in the Baton Rouge area. To the best of my knowledge there are no speakers of Choctaw among these groups.[2]

Certain other historically attested tribes in Louisiana may also have spoken Choctaw. Bushnell (1909) suggests that the Choctaw of Bayou Lacomb were the descendants of the Acolapissa, a Choctaw-speaking group politically distinct from the main body of the Choctaw tribe. Swanton (1946) also suggests that the Acolapissa, as well as the Chakchiuma, spoke Choctaw. There is also a band of ethnic Choctaws in Western Alabama, known as the Mowa Choctaw. There were apparently some speakers of Choctaw in this group until the last decade, but nothing of this dialect was ever recorded.

Nicklas (1974) mentions the existence of a group of Choctaw speakers near Tallahassee, Florida, but I have not been able to confirm this.

1.2. Orthography and glossing conventions

1.2.1. Orthography

Choctaw has been written in a variety of orthographies, and the choice of a writing system has been controversial, with different groups favoring

---

2. I thank Dayna Lee, a graduate student in the Department of Anthropology, University of Oklahoma, for providing me with information about these groups (p.c.).

different orthographies. The orthographies vary from each other primarily in the way vowels are written and in the representation of /ɬ/, /š/, and /č/.

1.2.1.1. Traditional orthography

The earliest orthography, which we can call the "traditional orthography," was that used by nineteenth century missionaries, who produced translations of many books of the Bible and other religious works.

The missionaries failed to recognize vowel length as significant in Choctaw, and designed an orthography that reflects distinctions between tense and lax vowel quality. In this orthography, vowel length can sometimes, but not always, be inferred from the spelling of a word. The vowel symbols, along with their phonemic interpretation, are shown in table 1.1.

Table 1.1. Traditional orthography of vowels and phonemic equivalents

ORTHOGRAPHIC SYMBOL	PHONEMIC EQUIVALENT
<a>	/a/, /aa/
<ʊ>	/a/
<i>	/i/, /ii/
<e>	/ii/
<o>	/o/, /oo/
<u>	/o/

Both short and long vowels tend to be tense in open syllables, while short vowels are usually lax in closed syllables. The orthography reflects this allophonic alternation, with the symbols <ʊ> and <u> being used primarily in short closed syllables. Some examples showing uses of the traditional orthography are shown in table 1.2.

Table 1.2. Examples of traditional orthography of vowels

TRADITIONAL	PHONEMIC	GLOSS
<nushkobo>	/noškóboʔ/	'head'
<ohoyo>	/ohooyoʔ/	'woman'
<ahalʊlli>	/aahalálliʔ/	'handle'
<peni>	/píiniʔ/	'boat'
<kostini>	/kostiinih/	'obedient'
<chekusi>	/čiikosih/	'very soon'
<iti>	/ittiʔ/	'tree'

The distinction between final /h/ and final /ʔ/ is not generally represented in the traditional orthography. Vowel nasalization is sometimes indicated by underlining and sometimes by writing a homorganic nasal consonant. As the last example in this list shows, the traditional orthography is also sometimes unreliable on consonant gemination.

The phonemes /š/ and /č/ are written as digraphs <sh> and <ch> respectively, as shown in the preceding examples. The phoneme /ł/ was written <lh> before a consonant and <hl> before a vowel, as in table 1.3.

Table 1.3. Examples of traditional orthography of /ł/

TRADITIONAL	PHONEMIC	GLOSS
<ilhkoli>	/iłkolih/	'to go (pl.)'
<a̱hli>	/ã́łih/	'true'

Unfortunately, the spelling <hl> also represents the frequent cluster /hl/ in Choctaw (e.g., <mʊhli> /mahli/ 'wind'), and thus some words in the traditional orthography can be difficult to interpret.[3]

A final noteworthy feature of the traditional orthography is its practice of breaking long words up into shorter orthographic units, for example:

(1)   <ʊlla chipunta yʊt ʊm ʊla hi a̱ hʊsh im ahni . . .>
        /allaʔ čipõta-yat am-al-ahii-yã̄
        child small:PL-NM 1sIII-come-IRR-DS
        haš-im-ahni . . ./
        2PI-III-allow
        'Suffer the little children to come unto me . . .' (Matt. 19:14)

As this example shows, the orthographic units do not always correspond to morphemes.

1.2.1.2. Mississippi Choctaw orthography

A second orthography was designed by the staff of the Bilingual Education program of the Mississippi Band of Choctaw Indians in the mid-1970s, and was used in producing many of the materials used in the

3. To complicate matters even more, the editors of Byington (1915) changed several aspects of the traditional orthography. They indicated nasal vowels by a superscript n (e.g.,<aⁿ>), and replaced Byington's <ʊ> with <a̱> (<a> with a subscript dot). Furthermore, they replaced all instances of <hl> with <®>, despite the fact that most medial instances of <hl> represent the sequence /hl/, and not /ł/, introducing more difficulties into the orthography. This yields an unfortunate situation in which this, the largest dictionary of Choctaw, is written in an orthography which does not match any of the orthographies in general use.

reservation schools.

The Mississippi Choctaw orthography uses the phonetic symbols <š>, <č>, and <ł> for /š, č, ł/ and uses hooks to represent vowel nasalization. Vowel length is somewhat irregularly indicated by either an acute accent or a macron. The following sentence is written in Mississippi Choctaw orthography:

(2)   <Alla čipǫta amalahíyą hašimahni . . .>.
        /allaʔ čipōta-yat am-al-ahii-yā
        child small:PL-NM 1sIII-come-IRR-DS
        haš-im-ahni . . ./
        2PI-III-allow
        'Suffer the little children to come unto me . . .' (Matt. 19:14)

1.2.1.3. Modified traditional orthography

The orthography used in this grammar is what we may call "modified traditional orthography." This orthography is the one most frequently used by linguists in discussions of the language. It uses the digraphs *sh* and *ch* as in the traditional orthography, and consistently uses *lh* for /ł/. The modified traditional orthography also uses underlining to represent vowel nasalization, but uses only three of the vowel symbols: *a*, *i*, and *o*, which are doubled when long.

Word divisions in the modified traditional orthography reflect those found in spoken Choctaw. The following sentence is written in modified traditional orthography:

(3)   Alla' chipotayat amalahiiya hashimahni . . .
        /allaʔ čipōta-yat am-al-ahii-yā
        child small:PL-NM 1sIII-come-IRR-DS
        haš-im-ahni . . ./
        2PI-III-allow
        'Suffer the little children to come unto me . . .' (Matt. 19:14)

The modified traditional orthography found in this work also marks pitch accent (indicated with an acute accent) and glottal stop (indicated with an apostrophe). Pitch accent is only marked when it occurs on a nonfinal syllable.

1.2.1.4. Choctaw Bible Translation Committee orthography

In recent work on a new Mississippi Choctaw Bible translation, a fourth orthography has appeared. It is similar to the modified traditional orthography used in this work in using <sh>, <ch>, and <lh> and the three vowel symbols <a>, <i>, <o>. It differs in two respects: it uses the acute accent to mark vowel length, and it approximates the traditional orthography in breaking up long words into shorter orthographic units. It does not represent glottal stop or pitch accent.

The following sentence is written using this orthography:

(4)   <Alla chip<u>o</u>ta yat am ala hí y<u>a</u> hash im ahni . . .>
/alla^ʔ čip<u>ō</u>ta-yat am-al-ahii-yā
child small:PL-NM 1SIII-come-IRR-DS
haš-im-ahni . . ./
2PI-III-allow
'Suffer the little children to come unto me . . .' (Matt. 19:14)

1.2.2. Glossing conventions

Choctaw words are cited in morphologically segmented forms, and there is a one-to-one match between items in the Choctaw and items in the gloss line. When a Choctaw word is glossed by more than one English word, the English words are separated by a colon, as in the following example:

(5)   *Okmocho̱-t   hilha-h!*
close:eyes-PART dance-TNS
'Close your eyes and dance!'

Colons are also used for portmanteau morphemes and for stems which appear in a derived grade (chapter 6) as in the following examples:

(6)   *Hattak-mat pisokpolo-h.*
man-D:NM   ugly-TNS
'That man is ugly.'

(7)   *Oh<u>ó</u>ba-na   nittak pókkooli-h oshta-ttook.*
rain:HN-DS day   ten-TNS   four-DPAST
'It kept on raining for forty days.'

When a Choctaw compound corresponds to a single English gloss, the parts of the compound are separated by =, as in the following example:

(8)   *Holisso'=pisáachi' si-ya-h.*
teacher   1SII-be-TNS
'I am a teacher.'

Outside the examples, Choctaw words and morphemes are cited in italics.

1.3. Sources of information

The primary source of my data is my own field notes on Mississippi and Oklahoma Choctaw. My primary consultants were Henry Willis, of Moore, Oklahoma; Edith Gem, originally of Battiest, Oklahoma (who lived in Long Beach, California, at the time of this research); the late Josephine Wade, originally of Eagletown, Oklahoma (who lived in Los Angeles during all of this research); and the late Gus Comby of the Pearl River community, Choctaw reservation, near Philadelphia, Mississippi.

In addition to these consultants, I have also worked with several dozen additional speakers, mainly gathering lexical material. Their names and home communities (all in Mississippi) are: Ann Bell, Nellie Bell, Dolphus Henry, Claude Jackson, Claude Joe, Archie Mingo, Charlie Steve, Gerald Steve, Nellie Steve, Nellie Willis, and Steven Willis of Bogue Chitto; John Jim, Melvin Nickey, Riley Thomas, Austin Wallace, and Loni Wallace of Bogue Homa; Angela Farve, Eddie Gibson, Mary Lou Jefferson, Roseanne Tubby, Henry Williams, and Jimson Williams of Conehatta; Isa Bell, Dullie Billy, Herbert Comby, Theron Denson, Sarah Dixon, Calvin Gibson, Laura John, Thallis Lewis, Daniel Tubby, Estelline Tubby, Henry Tubby, Lewis Tubby, Lynn Tubby, Robert Tubby, Marcella Vaughn, and Loretta York of Pearl River; Beatrice Steve and Eugene Tubby of Red Water; Charlie Denson of Standing Pine; and Nelda Lewis of Tucker. The speakers from whom I obtained significant amounts of grammatical information were Roseanne Tubby, Nelda Lewis, Loretta York, and Henry Tubby. Data from my notes have no special indication.

In addition to my notes, I have also used several sources of Choctaw textual material, dating back over one hundred and fifty years.

1.3.1. Early and middle nineteenth century materials

We are fortunate to have at least two thousand to three thousand pages of Choctaw textual material. Many Choctaws were literate in the nineteenth century, and newspapers, almanacs, political advertisements, and religious tracts were printed in the language.

By far the largest source of information comes from religious materials, and in particular from the Choctaw translation of the Bible. There are translations of all the books of the New Testament, and also translations of many books of the Old Testament. The New Testament is readily available from the American Bible Society, but the books of the Old Testament are all out of print and difficult to obtain. I consulted copies of several books of the Old Testament in the Widener and Andover Libraries at Harvard University. The entire New Testament was published in 1848, though translations of the Gospels appeared separately in 1845. The books of Genesis, Exodus, Leviticus, Deuteronomy, and Numbers were published in 1867, and the books of Joshua, Judges, Ruth, 1 and 2 Samuel, and 1 and 2 Kings were published in 1852. References to the Choctaw Bible are by book, chapter, and verse.

Most of these translations were completed by Cyrus Byington or Alfred Wright or both, two missionaries to the Choctaw. Both also published other religious pamphlets: a set of questions on the books of Luke and Mark (Alfred Wright 1852a, b), and a Choctaw spelling book with grammatical exercises and reading passages (Byington 1827).

L. S. Williams (1835) is a fifty-page discourse on Christian child-raising, probably translated from a contemporary English original.

Byington also devoted himself to the study of the grammar and lexicon of Choctaw, and Byington (1852) is a short "English and Choctaw Definer." Byington had extensive notes for a grammar and a larger dictionary of the Choctaw language at his death in 1868, and both were published posthumously.

Byington (1870) is a grammatical sketch of about fifty pages, edited by Daniel Brinton.

Byington (1915) is an extensive dictionary of Choctaw. The dictionary includes some syntactic information, mostly in the form of illustrative passages in the Bible.

1.3.2. Late nineteenth and early twentieth century materials

There are several sources from this period. Allen Wright (1880) and Watkins (1892) are dictionaries of the language written by native speakers.[4]

There are also additional religious materials from this period. I have consulted Ketcham (1916), a Choctaw catechism of about two hundred pages. References to the catechism (signaled as "Catechism") are by page number.

An additional source is Broadwell (1991b), "The Divorce of Amos and Molsey Yale." This text is a Choctaw transcription of the court testimony during an 1897 divorce trial in the Choctaw Nation of Oklahoma. The original is in the archives of the Oklahoma Historical Society. References to this text are preceded by "Yale" and are to section and line number.

1.3.3. Modern sources of textual information

Several examples are taken from Broadwell (1990b), a collection of Choctaw jokes and folktales. Many of these folktales were originally recorded by the staff of the bilingual education program of the Mississippi Band of Choctaw Indians. I reelicited these texts with the late Mrs. Josephine Wade, and refer to them by text and line number. I use the following system of text numbers:

T1	"Why the owl lives alone"
T2	"The grasshopper and the ant"
T3	"The rabbit tricks the women"
T4	"How the bear got a short tail"
T5	"Possum tricks wolf"

4. It is important to distinguish Alfred Wright, the Presbyterian missionary who translated several books of the bible, from Allen Wright, the author of a Choctaw dictionary. Allen Wright was a native speaker of Choctaw who was chief of the Choctaw nation from 1866–1870.

T6	"Why possum has a hairless tail"
T7	"Newlywed confessions"
T8	"Turkey and turtle race"

Another source of information is a new Mississippi Choctaw Bible translation project which is now in progress, directed by the Choctaw Bible Translation Committee. I consulted their new translations of several parts of the Bible. Examples from this work are cited by book, chapter and verse, and followed by the abbreviation "CBTC."

1.4. Interpretations of textual material

A problem in the use of some of the texts just cited is that they are unreliable in indicating certain phonological distinctions. Since the religious texts use the traditional orthography, it is sometimes difficult to determine vowel or consonant length.

For the most part, the nineteenth century Biblical materials appear to be grammatically reliable, though they contain material that is difficult for modern speakers to understand. The Bible translators appear to have relied heavily on the King James Version of the Bible, and the Choctaw translation is extremely faithful to the English. This sometimes appears to yield unidiomatic results, and I have noted a few examples where this appears to be the case.

Despite potential problems in the Bible materials, these materials provide many useful examples of morphemes and constructions from nineteenth century Choctaw. Whenever possible, I have included both modern and nineteenth century examples that illustrate the grammatical issues under discussion.

In all citations from the Bible and catechism, I give the example in its original orthography in the text (marked by angled brackets) with my reconstruction of the phonemics and morphological segmentation on a following line. One difficulty is that a single Choctaw sentence in these materials may correspond to several independent sentences in the English translation. In citations of such material, lack of an initial capital letter or final punctuation mark shows that the Choctaw material has been taken from a longer passage. The English translation receives an initial capital and ordinary final punctuation if it constitutes an independent sentence on its own. In some cases, I have adjusted the English translation so as to make the sense of the Choctaw clearer.

When I have reelicited portions of the Bible speakers, I list these with no special notation, since these can be reliably interpreted as acceptable sentences of modern Choctaw.

1.5. Choctaw dialects

Dialect differences in modern Choctaw are fairly minor, and appear to be primarily restricted to a few lexical items. I am not aware of any data pointing to the existence of social dialects in Choctaw, but there some forms that vary according to region. However, caution must be applied in attempting to identify regional dialects of Choctaw. One of the complications of such inquiry is that speakers often have difficulty distinguishing idiolectal variation from dialectal variation.

In my own fieldwork in Mississippi, I spent some time trying to identify words that varied according to community, and often encountered situations like the following. I asked a speaker of Choctaw who lives in Pearl River the word for 'one', and she replied *acháffah*. When asked about the pronunciation *cháffah*, she said that this is what people say in Conehatta. The next day in Conehatta, I asked the word for 'one', and my consultant said *acháffah*. The pronunciation *cháffah*, he said, is what people say in Pearl River. Clearly both speakers could not be right.

After asking people in several communities, I found that the pronunciations *cháffah* and *acháffah* are not correlated with community of residence at all, but are a matter of idiolectal variation. This sort of situation turned out to be extremely common.

There is a tendency among Choctaw speakers to attribute any form they regard as unusual to some other community of speakers. But without going to that other community and confirming the facts, it is not possible to take individual speaker statements about dialect differences as reliable evidence.[5]

Given these concerns, there is not much good evidence for regional dialects of Oklahoma Choctaw. Nicklas (1974) often refers to variation among speakers in Oklahoma as dialectal, but he does not relate any of this variation to particular regions of the Oklahoma Choctaw-speaking territory. I believe that most of the variation he discusses is better regarded as idiolectal or possibly familial in nature.

Dialect distinctions that can be confirmed and tied to particular communites are most evident in Mississippi Choctaw, where there seem to be three primary dialects: Northern, spoken in the community of Bogue Chitto; Central, spoken in Pearl River, Standing Pine, Red Water, and Tucker; and Southern, spoken in Conehatta and Bogue Homa. There also seem to be certain forms that are unique to Pearl River, the largest of the communities and the center of the tribal government.

Mississippi Choctaw speakers are highly conscious of dialect differences, and will often give examples of lexical isoglosses that distinguish one Choctaw community from another. Examples of some of the variants are presented in table 1.4.

---

5. Of course, this is true of English speakers as well. Native speakers of a language often have little detailed knowledge of dialects other than their own.

Table 1.4. Examples of lexical differences between dialects

GLOSS	FORM	COMMUNITY
'to be small (pl.)'	*chipįtah*	Pearl River
	chipǫtah	others
'onion'	*naakosooma'*	Bogue Chitto
	shachonna'	other Mississippi Choctaw
	hatofaláaha'	Oklahoma Choctaw
'tail'	*halįbis*	Pearl River
	hasįbis	others
'head'	*nishkóbo'*	Bogue Chitto
	noshkóbo'	others
'railroad train'	*kochcha balíili'*	Bogue Chitto
	píinih or *píini'*	others
'to comb'	*shifih*	Conehatta
	shillih	others
'wasp'	*chanáshshik*	Bogue Chitto
	cháshshik	others

There is also a fair amount of idiolectal variation which does not seem correlated with community of origin. The examples in (9) show that initial short vowels are dropped in some words by some speakers. Those in (10) show alternations between *sh* and *s* in syllable-final position. Those in (11) show a tendency of *h* to assimilate to a following consonant, and (12) shows some variation in short vowels in the first syllable of a word.

(9)   'horse'   *issóbah/sóbah*
      'money'   *iskali'/skali'*
      'one'   *acháffah/cháffah*

(10) 'blood'   *issish/issis*
      'short'   *yoshkoloolih/yoskoloolih*

(11) 'Choctaw'   *chahta'/chatta'*
      'bag'   *báhta'/bátta'*

(12) 'short'   *kowaashah/kawaashah*
      'short'   *yoshkoloolih/yishkoloolih*

Byington (1915) recorded some information about dialectal variation, primarily words that were peculiar to the Sixtowns dialect, which was formerly spoken in the southern part of the Choctaw nation. At this point it is not clear if there might be a connection between the old Sixtowns dialect and one of the modern dialects of Mississippi Choctaw.

1.6. Related Muskogean languages

Although the primary focus of this work is Choctaw, in some cases the Choctaw data are compared with data from other Muskogean languages, especially Chickasaw. The Muskogean family is made up of four groups of languages, as shown in figure 1.1. Higher-level classification within the family is controversial.

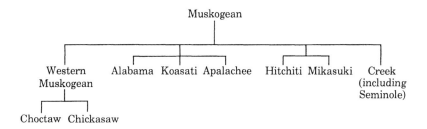

Figure 1.1.

Choctaw is closely related to Chickasaw, and the two languages form the group Western Muskogean.[6] The two languages are perhaps as closely related as Spanish and Portuguese. While they show many similarities, many Choctaws report that they cannot understand Chickasaw. Because Choctaw is more widely spoken, and because many Chickasaws have been exposed to Choctaw through Bible translations, Chickasaws are more often able to understand Choctaw. Chickasaw syntax has been extensively investigated by Pamela Munro, and her analyses are frequent points of reference. The Chickasaw dictionary of Munro and Willmond (1994) is also an important point of comparison for discussions of the various contributions of lexical information to Choctaw syntax.

The other Muskogean languages currently spoken are Alabama, Koasati (also known as Coushatta), Mikasuki, and Creek, including its Florida and Oklahoma Seminole dialects. Several other Muskogean languages are extinct: Apalachee (Kimball 1987, 1988), Hitchiti, and Mobilian, a Muskogean-based lingua franca of the southeast (Crawford 1978; Drechsel 1979).

My information on Creek is primarily based on my own work with Margaret Mauldin, of Okemah, Oklahoma. Information also comes from Nathan (1977), Hardy (1988), and Martin (1991).

Information for other Muskogean languages comes from Kimball (1985, 1991) on Koasati; Lupardus (1982) and Sylestine, Hardy, and

6. See Munro (1987a) for arguments that Chickasaw is not merely a dialect of Choctaw, as suggested by Haas (1941a).

Montler (1993) on Alabama; Boynton (1982) and Derrick-Mescua (1980) on Mikasuki; and Booker (1980) on comparative Muskogean. In citations from other Muskogean languages, I use the orthographic conventions of the source unless otherwise noted.

Haas (1951, 1952) has suggested that Muskogean is a member of the Gulf stock, which also includes four extinct language isolates formerly spoken on the lower Mississippi: Natchez, Tunica, Atakapa, and Chitimacha. These relationships seem promising, but have not yet been rigorously established.

2. Phonology

2.1. Phonemic inventory

2.1.1. Consonantal phonemes and their allophones

The phonemic inventory of consonants in Choctaw is presented in table 2.1.

Table 2.1. Consonant phonemes

p	t	č	k	ʔ
b				
f	s	š		h
m	n			
	l			
	ɬ			
w		y		

NOTE: In the modified traditional orthography employed in most of this book, /č ɬ š ʔ/ are spelled *ch lh sh* '.

The voiceless stops are pronounced much as in English. /t, n, l/ are alveolars, much like the same consonants in English. The alveopalatal affricate /č/ is similar to English *ch* as in *cheese*; glottal stop /ʔ/ is like the break between the syllables of English *uh-oh*. Voiceless stops are sometimes lightly aspirated when word initial; they are unaspirated elsewhere. Nicklas (1974:15) notes that for some speakers, the voiceless stops may be partially voiced between vowels.[1] I have personally observed intervocalic voicing only for /k/, not for other voiceless stops.

For some speakers, voiced /k/ further lenites to [ɣ] (voiced velar fricative). This is particularly noticeable in the suffix *-akilih* 'indeed', as in the following example:

(1) *im-ofi-akilih*   [ɪmofiyəɣẽ:lih]
     III-dog-indeed
     'his own dog'

---

1. He also notes that such voicing is more prominent in the speech of men than that of women. My own observations of intervocalic voicing agree with Nicklas on this point.

/ł/ is a voiceless lateral fricative (no close English equivalent), spelled *lh* in the orthography used in this work.[2] Some younger speakers of Oklahoma Choctaw have shifted from a lateral to an interdental articulation for this sound, which is then pronounced [θ]. I have not observed this pronunciation among Mississippi Choctaws.

/f/ is labiodental for speakers I have worked with, but Nicklas (1974:16) describes a voiceless bilabial fricative [ɸ] for some speakers.

The contrast between /s/ and /š/ (the latter like English *sh* as in *ship*, and so spelled in the orthography used in this work) is weak in syllable final position. As mentioned in chapter 1, there is a consider-able amount of interspeaker variation in words like *hasibish/hasibis* 'tail'.

/h/ frequently has [ç] (a voiceless palatal fricative) as an allomorph before /č/, as in examples like the following:

(2)   *katihchish*   [katIçčIš]   'how'

When /k/ and /h/ are followed by a voiced consonant, an epenthetic vowel breaks up the cluster. The quality of the vowel is schwa-like, perhaps slightly colored by the quality of the preceding vowel:

(3)   *ahnih*   [ahənih]   'to think'
       tohbih   [tohəbih]   'white'
       bohlih   [bohəlih]   'to place'
       yohmih   [yohəmih]   'to do so'
       akni'   [akəni?]   'oldest sibling'
       takbah   [takəbah]   'bitter'
       toklih   [tokəlih]   'to push'
       hokmih   [hokəmih]   'to burn'

The status of glottal stop as a phoneme in Choctaw is controversial. See section 2.3 below for discussion.

2.1.2. Vowel phonemes and their allophones

The vowel inventory is presented in table 2.2.

Table 2.2. Vowel phonemes

i,ii,ĩ	o,oo,õ
a,aa,ã	

NOTE: In the modified traditional orthography employed in most of this book, nasalization is indicated by an underline; thus /ã ĩ õ/ are spelled *a i o*.

2. Clusters of /l/ plus /h/ are very rare in Choctaw. In the few cases where they occur, they are written with a separating period. For example, some speakers pronounce the word *asil.hah* 'to request' as [asilhah] (not [asiłah]).

The vowels vary somewhat in tenseness. Long vowels (indicated by doubling) are generally tense. Short /i/, /a/, and /o/ vary between between tense [i], [a], and [o] and lax [ɪ], [ə], and [ʊ] respectively. The lax variants are more common in closed syllables.

Nasal vowels are probably derived from underlying /VN/ clusters by rule (Ulrich 1986:60–67). Length is not contrastive for nasal vowels, but they are phonetically long, thus [ĩ:], [ã:], and [õ:]. Rules that distinguish between monomoraic and bimoraic syllables (e.g., rhythmic lengthening) treat syllables with a nasal vowel as bimoraic syllables.

2.2. Suprasegmental phenomena

Choctaw is a pitch accent language, but there seem to be almost no pairs which are distinguished by pitch alone. Ulrich (1986:68) cites the following example, which is the only minimal pair for accent that I am aware of:

(4)   *tanáp*   'war'
      tánap   'turnip'

But this pair is weakened by the fact that the second word cited is a borrowing from English. There are, however, other near-minimal pairs for accent:

(5)   *Chahtá'*   'Choctaw'
      báhta'   'bag'
(6)   *naníh*   'hill'
      náni'   'fish'

For nearly all Choctaw nouns, accent falls on either the final or the penultimate syllable. Ulrich (1986) cites one noun, *tíshkilah* 'bluejay', which has antepenultimate accent.

For nearly all underived verbs, the accent is predictable.[3] It is placed on the tense marker (in the case of the tense markers *-tok* or *-ttook*) or on the syllable immediately preceding the tense marker (in the case of the tense marker *-h*).

(7a)   *Taloowá-h.*   'She/he sings.'
       sing-TNS

(7b)   *Taloowa-tók.*   'She/he sang.'
       sing-PT

(7c)   *Taloowa-li-tók.*   'I sang.'
       sing-1SI-PT

---

3. Ulrich (1986:68) cites *achólih* 'to sew', *yókpah* 'to laugh', and *áyyokah* 'each' as examples of verbs with unpredictable accent.

In these simple cases, one could say that the accent appears on the final syllable, but this is not true when other morphemes follow the tense markers:

(8a)   *Taloowá-h-o̱?*   'Does she/he sing?'
       sing-TNS-Q

(8b)   *Taloowa-tók-chi.*   'I wonder if she/he sang?'
       sing-TNS-WONDER

The rule for the placement of accent in verbs might be simplified to final syllable in some domain if we were to posit a fairly strong boundary between the tense markers and following markers.

Verbs in the aspectual grades have an accent on either the penult or the antepenult, depending on the grade. See chapter 10 for further discussion.

Deverbal nouns have a predictable accent on the penult:[4]

(9)   *talóowa'*   'singer'

However, the accent on underived nouns is not predictable.

In this work, pitch accent is written when it occurs on a nonfinal syllable.

2.3. Syllable structure and phonotactics

2.3.1. Possible syllables

Choctaw syllables must contain a vowel (long, short, or nasalized), and in general have no more than one consonant in the onset and no more than one consonant in the coda. (Some exceptions with contractions will be discussed shortly). Table 2.3 (based on Ulrich 1986:12) shows the range of possible syllable types.

Table 2.3. Possible syllable types

LIGHT SYLLABLES		
V	**a**.*bih*	'to kill'
CV	**no**.*sih*	'to sleep'
HEAVY SYLLABLES		
VV	**ii**.*chih*	'to drive'
CVV	**pii**.*ni'*	'boat, train'
<u>V</u>	**a̱**.*chi'*	'quilt'

---

4. This book adopts the convention that for long vowels, pitch accent is written only on the first vowel of the double vowel sequence.

CV	*ta*.*chi'*	'corn'
VC	*ish*.*ki'*	'mother'
CVC	ha.*bish*.ko'	'nose'

SUPERHEAVY SYLLABLES

VVC	*óok*.cha-cha	'she/he woke up and . . .'
CVVC	*náaf*.ka'	'dress'
VC	*at*	'come and'
CVC	ok.*hish*	'medicine'

Some superheavy syllables of the shape (C)VCC appear in the contracted participles ending in -*t*. For most of these forms a noncontracted version is also possible:

(10a) *tabli-t* ~ *tap-t*
       cut-PART
       'cutting'

(10b) *ishi-t* ~ *ish-t*
       take-PART
       (instrumental applicative)

Syllables of this shape are only found in word-final position.

There are a few cases where syllables appear to begin with consonant clusters. In casual speech initial *i* may be deleted before *sC* or *shC*:

(11a) *Iskitiini-h.* ~ *Skitiini-h.*
       small-TNS
       'It's small.'

(11b) *isht-pɪha-'* ~ *ishpɪha'* ~ *shpɪha'*
       INSTR-dig-NML
       'shovel' (noun)

There is one example of a borrowed word with an initial *bl* cluster, *bliasis* [blæsɪs] 'molasses, syrup'.

2.3.2. Possible onsets and rimes

Syllables may begin with any vowel or with any consonant other than glottal stop. As noted above, a syllable generally begins with at most one consonant, but there are a small number of cases where words begin with consonant clusters.

Noun roots must end with one of the following consonants: *p, t, k, '*, *f, s, sh, h, m, n, l.* The only consonants that do not end words are *b, lh, w, y* and *ch. Ch,* however, requires some special discussion. Although no native Choctaw nouns end in *ch*, there is at least one borrowed noun, *kalaach* 'collards', which does have this final consonant. Some Mississippi Choctaw personal names also end in *ch*:

(12) *Laach*   (a man's name)
      Tiich   (a man's name)
      Naach   (a woman's name)

Verb roots must end with a vowel, but every verb root must be followed by at least one suffix, so the final vowel of the verb root is never in word-final position.

Nominal and verbal affixes may end with either a consonant or a vowel, as is shown by the examples in table 2.4.

Table 2.4. Final segments of affixes

C-FINAL		
Verbal prefixes	*ish-*	'second person singular, class I'
Verbal suffixes	*-tok*	'past tense'
Nominal prefixes	*am-*	'first person singular , class III'
Nominal suffixes	*-at*	'nominative'
V-FINAL		
Verbal prefixes	*chi-*	'second person singular, class II'
Verbal suffixes	*-cha*	'same subject'
Nominal prefixes	*sa-*	'first person singular , class II'
Nominal suffixes	*-ba*	'only'

2.3.3. Minimal words

The minimal word in Choctaw is bimoraic; it contains either two short vowels or one long vowel:

(13) *ofi'*   'dog'
      waak   'cow'

There are no Choctaw words that contain only a single short vowel, thus there are no words like **fi'* or **wak*.

However, there may be some verb roots (the so-called "short verbs") that are shorter than the minimal word. For example, the underlying form of the verb 'to kill' is probably *bi:*

(14) *ish-bi-h*
      2SI-kill-TNS
      'you kill'

When no prefix is present, an epenthetic *a* appears.

(15a)   *abi-h*
         kill-TNS
     `   'she/he/it/they kill'

(15b)   **bi-h*

We can view this insertion of this *a* as a device that ensures that the verb stem meets the minimal length requirements for a word. See chapter 9 for more details on short verbs.

2.4. General rules of Choctaw phonology

Nicklas (1974) and Ulrich (1986) are the principal sources for a detailed discussion of Choctaw phonology. My remarks here summarize the work of Ulrich, which should be consulted for further information. In the present section, I discuss general ("postlexical") phonological rules of the language. Rules which apply only in the derivational morphology are treated in section 2.5–2.6. For the purposes of these sections, underlying forms (preceding the application of the phonological rules discussed) are represented in the phonemic orthography of tables 2.1 and 2.2, between slashes / /.

2.4.1. Rhythmic lengthening

2.4.1.1. General description

Choctaw has a pervasive rule of rhythmic lengthening, which lengthens even-numbered nonfinal CV syllables, as in the following example:

(16)   /salaha–tok / → [sala:hatok]
         slow+PT
         'He was slow.'

Ulrich (1986:53) claims that rhythmically lengthened vowels are phonetically shorter in duration than underlying long vowels. A similar rule applies in Chickasaw, and Gordon, Munro, and Ladefoged (1997) provide instrumental evidence for shorter duration of lengthened vowels in that language. No similar study has been done for Choctaw.

There are several areas in which the rule of rhythmic lengthening is more complex than just described. Since the rule affects even-numbered nonfinal CV syllables, it is necessary to determine where the syllable count begins. Some of the prefixes that precede a noun or verb stem are within the scope of rhythmic lengthening, while other prefixes are not within the scope of the rule.

For verbs, the II prefixes (see chapter 6) are always within the scope of the rule:

(17)   /sa-salaha-tok/ → [sasa:laha(:)-tok][5]
       1sII-slow-PT
       'I am slow.'

However, I prefixes and most III prefixes are not within its scope:

(18)   /ish-ačifa-tok/ →   [Išači:fatok]
       2sI-wash-PT   *[iša:čifatok]
       'You washed it.'

(19)   /im-ačifa-tok/ →   [Imači:fatok]
       III-wash-PT   *[ima:čifatok]
       'He washed it for her.'

There is an exception for verbs of the shape VCV, however. For these verbs, III prefixes are within the scope of the rule:

(20)   /im-abi-tok/ → [Ima:bitok]
       III-kill-PT
       'He beat them.'[6]

The pattern for rhythmic lengthening in nouns is similar. In general, III prefixes on nouns are not within the scope of rhythmic lengthening:

(21)   /im-abooha?/ → [Iməbo:ha?]
       III-room   *[Ima:bo:ha?]
       'his/her room'

However, as with the verbs, nouns with the shape VCV exceptionally do show rhythmic lengthening for many speakers:

(22)   /im-ofi?/ → [Imo:fi?]
       III-dog
       'his/her dog'[7]

(23)   /am-afo?/ → [ama:fo?]
       1sIII-grandfather
       'my grandfather'[8]

Speakers vary on whether rythmic lengthening applies after II prefixes in nouns. For some speakers, the rule is not applicable in cases like the following:

5. As discussed below, speakers vary in whether rhythmic lengthening applies before -tok.

6. Imabi, literally 'kill to him/her/them', is an idiom meaning 'beat, defeat'.

7. Some speakers also seem to have a nasal vowel in the possessed form of ofi', which is then imófi'. So far as I know, this is an irregularity confined to this single word.

8. Since this noun obligatorily appears with a possessive III prefix, the vowel in the stem is almost always long. However, some speakers have a vocative form afo', providing evidence for a short vowel in the underlying representation.

(24)   /sa-hatãbiš/ → [sahatã:biš]
       1sII-navel
       'my navel'

However, other speakers do allow rhythmic lengthening in this context:

(25)   /sa-hatãbiš/ → [saha:tã:biš]

The latter form seems to be more common among Mississippi Choctaws, while Oklahoma Choctaws show both forms.[9]

    Another prefix sometimes within the scope of the rhythmic lengthening rule is the plural imperative. This prefix has idiolectal variants: some speakers have *hoo* ~ *ooh*, others have invariable *hoo-*, and still others have *ho-* ~ *oh-*.[10] For speakers using *ho-* ~ *oh-*, the prefix causes rhythmic lengthening of a following CV syllable:

(26a) /ho-yiłipah/ → [hoyi:łipah]
       PL-run:PL
       'Y'all run!'

(26b) /oh-akammih/ → [oha:kammih]
       PL-close
       'Y'all close it!' (Ulrich 1986:282)

    At the right edge of the word, there is variation in what counts as the end of the word. Recall that the rule of rhythmic lengthening only affects syllables that are non-final in some domain. For some speakers of Choctaw, the tense suffix -*tok* is outside the scope of this rule, and an even-numbered CV syllable will not be lengthened before it:

(27)   /nokowa-či-tok/ → [noko:wačitok]
       angry-CAUS-PT
       'He angered her.'

Other speakers do allow rhythmic lengthening before -*tok*:

(28)   /nokowa-či-tok/ → [noko:wači:tok]
       angry-CAUS-PT

    It is difficult to generalize about the distribution of these two patterns, but the latter seems more frequent with Mississippi Choctaws. Oklahoma Choctaws show both patterns.

2.4.1.2. The reanalysis of rhythmic lengthening

Since a verb stem of the shape /CVCVCV/ very frequently appears

---

    9. Nicklas (1974:120) gives [hači-no:takfa] 'y'all's jaws' as an example, demonstrating that such forms are possible for the Oklahoma Choctaws he consulted. See chapter 4 for more discussion.
    10. For speakers with two variants of this morpheme, *ho(o)-* appears before consonants and *o(o)h-* appears before vowels.

phonetically as [CVCV:CV], it is perhaps not surprising that many speakers have reanalysed the penultimate vowel as underlyingly long, thus /CVCVVCV/.

Consider the following words taken from two different speakers of Mississippi Choctaw:

(29)   Speaker 1 /salaaha-tok/ → [sala:hatok]
       Speaker 2 /salaha-tok/ → [sala:hatok]
       'He was slow.'

Despite having different underlying forms, the two speakers pronounce the form in the same way.

However, the two speakers diverge in their pronunciation of forms with a II prefix:

(30)   Speaker 1 /sa-salaaha-tok/ → [sasa:la:hatok]
       Speaker 2 /sa-salaha-tok/ → [sasa:laha:tok]
       'I was slow.'

Thus it is only possible to determine the underlying form of a word with the phonetic pattern [CVCV:CV] by comparing this word to a form with a II prefix. If the penultimate vowel is an underlying short vowel, it will revert to short in the II prefix forms.

In investigating the phonology of Mississippi Choctaw, I have found that speakers vary from word to word according to whether the phonetic pattern [CVCV:CV] corresponds to an underlying form /CVCVCV/ or /CVCV:CV/.[11] Since there is little agreement between speakers about which words have underlying long vowels, it seems that much of the variation is idiolectal.

This raises a problem for the orthography. Three options seem possible:

(a) Write every word of the shape [CVCV:CV] as if its underlying form were /CVCVCV/. This is the approach adopted by nearly all the previous work on the language, but it seems to me to misrepresent the variation in speakers' knowledge of such words. Consider speaker 1 above. Since the penultimate vowel of *salaahatok* is always long for him, he must have a long vowel in his underlying representation of the word. Given the formulation of rhythmic lengthening above, there is no other way to explain his pronunciation of *sasalaahatok*. To write the word *salahatok* only represents one of the idiolectal variants of this word.

This option also involves a certain number of arbitrary decisions. A

---

11. Nicklas (1974:120) discusses similar speaker alternations in rhythmic lengthening, which he treats as instances of multiple application of the rule. For example, [sa-mi:ta:fah] 'I was cut' contains two long vowels. In Nicklas's approach, the rhythmic lengthening rule applies first to the verb stem, then expands to include the II prefix in a second application of the rule. On this approach, dialects differ on whether the rule applies first to the stem.

certain number of words contain long vowels which might be the result of the rhythmic lengthening rule, but for phonological or morphological reasons, one cannot compare another form to determine this. Consider the following words:

(31)   [ano:litok]   'He told.'
        [achi:fatok]   'She washed.'

Should the first word be written *anolitok* or *anoolitok*? We cannot determine which is the underlying form because the verb is vowel- initial and it is not possible to construct a context in which the [o:] will be in an odd-numbered syllable. The object of this verb is indicated with a III prefix, and such prefixes are outside the scope of rhythmic lengthening.

From the point of view of constraining the abstractness of phonological representations, it seems difficult to justify positing short vowels in such forms in the lack of any evidence for them.

(b) The second option is to represent the idiolectal variation in underlying forms in the orthography. Clearly this is the most correct approach, but it involves so many difficulties that it is impractical to carry out in a work of this size.

Under this option, every word of the shape [CVCV:CV] must be compared with a prefixed form to determine its underlying form before its orthographic representation can be determined. Furthermore, the representation arrived at for one speaker will not necessarily be the same as that for another speaker. Thus, to know how to write a speaker's utterance correctly, the writer must elicit additional morphological information from that speaker for each ambiguous verb.

The data in this grammar come from several different speakers of the language, some of whom are now deceased. Other data come from historical texts in the language, where the speaker is unknown. For these reasons it is impossible to recheck every ambiguous form with the original speaker to determine what the representation of the word should be.

(c) The third option, that which I will adopt in this work, is to write all phonetically long vowels within the verb stem as long in the orthography. In this respect, the orthography is sub-phonemic for some words for some speakers, but it avoids the misrepresentations of the first option and the impracticality of the second.

Lengthened vowels outside the verb stem (primarily in the causative *-chi* and the first person *-li*) can still be written as short in the orthography since there is no evidence that any speakers have reanalyzed the vowels in these affixes as long.[12] Since speakers uniformly

---

12. No doubt this is because these suffixes appear in both even-numbered and odd-numbered syllables with sufficient frequency that speakers have no difficulty in assigning them an underlying representation.

have short vowels in the underlying forms of these suffixes, they can be orthographically represented this way without a problem.

2.4.2. Vowel deletion

In general, when two short vowels occur at a morpheme boundary, the first deletes (Ulrich 1986:151) in a rule we might formalize as follows:

(32)   Short vowel deletion
      $V \rightarrow \emptyset / \_\_\_ V$

This is shown in the following example:

(33)   /baliili-aačị̄-h/ → *baliilaachị̄h*
      run-IRR-TNS
      'She/he will run.'

However, the class II prefixes are a lexical exception. They always retain their vowel and trigger deletion of a following short vowel:

(34)   /sa-ibaa-wašoohah/ → *sabaawashoohah*
      1sII-with-play
      'Play with me!'

2.5. Rules applying in derivational morphology

2.5.1. Assimilations with *-li*

The verbal suffix *-li* (discussed in chapter 8) is associated with a somewhat idiosyncratic set of assimilations. Ulrich (1986) contains a comprehensive discussion of the subject, and should be consulted for details.

    The /l/ of this suffix assimilates to a preceding /f, ł, h, m, n, w/ for all speakers:

(35a) /kobaf-a-h/ → *kobaafah*
      break-INTR-TNS
      'to be broken'

(35b) /kobaf-li-h/ → *kobaffih*
      break-TR-TNS
      'to break'

For many speakers, /l/ also assimilates to a stem final /b/, but there is some variability on this point:

(36)   /atob-li-h/ → *atoblih, atobbih*
      pay-TR-TNS
      'to pay'

Stem-final /p/ assimilates in voicing to the following /l/:

(37)   /tap-li-h/ → *tablih*
        cut:off-TR-TNS
        'to cut off'

Stem-final /t/ assimilates to /l/:

(38)   /palhat-li-h/ → *palhallih*
        split-TR-TNS
        'to split'

2.5.2. Rules applying in grades

There are also some rather complex morphophonological rules associated with the verbal grades, treated in detail by Nicklas (1974) and Ulrich (1986). See chapter 10 for a description of the phonology of grade formation.

2.6. The status of *h* and glottal stop

2.6.1. The standard view of glottal stop insertion

I follow Ulrich (1986, 1993) in regarding the glottal stop as an additional consonantal phoneme of Choctaw, but the issue is controversial.

There is a two-way phonetic distinction between final vowels which are followed by glottal stop and those which are not, as shown in the following two nouns:

(39)   [koni]   'skunk'
        [ofiʔ]   'dog'

The final vowel in [koni] has a breathy quality, and might sometimes be best represented as [konih]. When a suffix such as the nominative case marker -*at* is added, an [h] is clearly audible:

(40)   [konih-at] 'skunk (nominative)'

No such [h] is present when a case marker is added to a form ending in glottal stop. Some speakers retain glottal stop in this context, but there are two other options: (a) insert an epenthetic *y*, or (b) delete the second vowel and lengthen the first:

(41)   [ofiʔ-at]   'dog (nominative)'
        [ofi-yat]
        [ofi-it]

The most widespread view of Choctaw phonology (implicit, for example, in Nicklas [1974] and Davies [1981]) holds that the two types of nouns just cited correspond to the following underlying representations:

(42)   /konih/ → [koni ~ konih] 'skunk'
       /ofi/ → [ofiʔ] 'dog'

This view of Choctaw phonology holds that there are (at least) two rules affecting these forms. First, a glottal stop is added by rule to all final vowels:[13]

(43)   ∅ → ʔ / V __ #

Second, /h/ is deleted in word-final position for some speakers:

(44)   h → ∅ / __# (optional)

2.6.2. Problems with the standard view

This view of Choctaw phonology is quite appealing in eliminating the glottal stop as a phoneme, but unfortunately the rules fail to account for the full range of data. Determiners and complementizers, in particular, show behavior that is not consistent with this analysis.

The determiner suffix -ba is generally translated as 'only', as in the following example:

(45)   *John-ba   pɪsa-li-tok.*
       John-only   see:N-1SI-PT
       'I only saw John.'

If the rule adding a glottal stop to any final vowel were correct, we would expect **John-ba'* here instead of the attested *John-ba.*

It would be problematic to claim that the correct underlying form is /-bah/ (and that the /h/ is deleted or inaudible), since when case-markers follow this determiner, the forms are -baat (nominative) and -ba̲ (accusative):

(46)   *Hattak-mak-ba-at a̲ya-h-o̲   pɪsa-li-tok.*
       man-DEM-only-NMgo:along-TNS-PART:DSsee-1SI-PT
       'I saw only that man going along.'

(47)   *John-ba̲   pɪsa-li-tok.*
       John-only:AC see:N-1SI-PT
       'I saw only John.'

We know from ordinary nouns that when a case marker is added to a stem ending in /h/, the /h/ is always present:

---

13. Actually, since some speakers have glottal stop before the case endings (e.g. *ofi 'at* 'dog (nominative)'), the rule probably needs to be modified to insert glottal stop before some other morphological boundaries as well.

(48a) [konih-at]   'skunk (nominative)'

(48b) [konih-a̱]   'skunk (accusative)'

Like -ba, the emphatic determiner -akịlih is not followed by a glottal stop when it appears in word-final position.

(49)   *Ilaap im-ofi-akịlih abi-tok.*
        self   III-dog-EMPH kill-PT
        'He killed his own dog.'

However, in contrast to -ba, -akịlih shows /h/ when it appears before other suffixes:[14]

(50)   *Oklah hachishn-akịlih-oosh itti' hash-ahoochich-ahịla-h.*
        PLUR   y'all-EMPH-PART:SS   tree   2PI-find-IRR-TNS
        'Y'all should find a tree for yourselves.'

It seems that the contrast between -akịlih and -ba needs to be represented as final /h/ versus final ∅. But in this case, the rule adding glottal stop to word final vowels does not work.

Most determiners and complementizers in Choctaw are vowel-final, and so far as I know none of them show the predicted glottal stop in word final position. The majority show behavior like -ba: no glottal stop when word final, no *h* when followed by another subject.

In this respect they are different from nominal stems. We can articulate the difference as follows:

(a) Every Choctaw noun ends in a consonant.

(b) Other parts of speech (in particular, determiners and complementizers) may end in vowels.

The contrasts between nouns like *ofi'* 'dog' and *konih* 'skunk' are now to be represented as follows:

(51a) /ofiʔ/   [ofiʔ]
       'dog'

(51b) /ofiʔ-at/   [ofiʔət ~ ofiyət]
       dog-NM
       'dog (nominative)'

(52a) /konih/   [konih ~ koni]
       'skunk'

---

14. See chapter 5 for further discussion of noun phrases with -akịlih. There I suggest that the final /h/ may be the tense affix. The phonological issue is the same, however, whether -akịlih is monomorphemic or bimorphemic.

(52b)   /konih-at/   [konihət]
         skunk-NM
         'skunk (nominative)'

2.6.3. Vowel lowering as an argument for glottal stop

An additional argument for a three-way distinction between final *h*, Ø, and ˀ comes from the pronunciation of /iː/. When /iː/ appears in word-final position, it is often pronounced [eː], as a result of a rule like the following:

(53)   /iː/ → [eː]/__#

This is shown in the following examples:

(54)   *Chahta' hapiy-a-h-okii!*   [hapiːyahokeː]
        Choctaw 1MPII-be-TNS-indeed
        'We are Choctaws!'

(55)   <. . .himak a ish ithʋnashke . . .>
        himmaka ish-ithána-shkii. [ɪšɪthãːnəške:]
        now   2sI-know:N-EXHORT
        'Know now . . .' (Gen. 37:32)

The suffixes *-okii* and *-shkii* are generally affected by this rule, and this is reflected in their spelling in traditional orthography, where they are written <oke> and <shke> respectively.

Since every noun must end in a consonant, and every verb must be followed by a tense marker (all of which end in consonants), these two suffixes are among the few forms in the language that undergo the rule.[15] It would be quite unattractive to posit an /e/ phoneme to account for these suffixes; there is no evidence elsewhere in the language for such a phoneme. The proposed rule neatly accounts for this pronunciation.

In contrast, words that end in /iː/ followed by /h/ or glottal stop are not affected by the rule:

(56)   *tii'*   [tiːˀ]   *[teːˀ]   'tea'
        hiihiih [hiːhiːh]   *[hiːheːh]   'to sing "hiih! hiih!" in a high voice, as
        Choctaw women do during certain dances'

In a model of Choctaw phonology that does not recognize a three-way final distinction between *h*, Ø, and ˀ, it is difficult to write the rule of vowel lengthening in such a way that it correctly picks the right contexts.

---

15. In fact, there is a small exception to the statement that every verb must be followed by a tense marker, found in cases of coordination, as discussed in section 3.2.1.4.

2.6.4. Glottal stop and compensatory lengthening

When nouns ending in glottal stop appear before a consonant-initial suffix, the glottal stop is generally deleted, with compensatory lengthening of the preceding vowel, as discussed in Ulrich (1986):

(57)   /ofiʔ-ma/ → [ofi:ma]
        dog-DEM
        'that dog'

The same effect is seen in compounds:

(58)   /tóbiʔhómmaʔ/ → [tobi:hómmaʔ]
        bean red
        'pinto beans'

2.6.5. Glottal stops in Mississippi Choctaw of Oklahoma

Finally, the occurrence of glottal stop in Mississippi Choctaw of Oklahoma (MCO) is somewhat more complex than that just described for other Choctaw varieties. As mentioned in chapter 1, MCO is a dialect spoken by some Choctaws who live in the Chickasaw Nation of Oklahoma. MCO shows some instances of word internal glottal stops, primarily in the derived grade and valence forms:

(59)   *Hiʔlha-cha . . .*   (MCO)
        dance:L-SS
        'He danced and . . .'

In Mississippi Choctaw and Oklahoma Choctaw, such forms contain a long vowel (thus the name 'lengthened grade'):

(60)   *Hiilha-cha . . .*
        dance:L-SS
        'He danced and . . .'

For this variety of Choctaw, phonetic glottal stops are not restricted to word-final position. Ulrich (1986, 1993) has suggested that other varieties of Choctaw may also have underlying glottal stops in word-medial positions, but that they are deleted in the course of the phonological derivation. Although this analysis is promising, it requires underlying representations that are more distant from their surface realizations, and has not been widely adopted. In this grammar I retain a more conservative representation in which glottal stop only appears in word-final position.

3. Basic syntactic typology

Choctaw is a configurational language with consistent head-final constituent ordering. It shows a mix of head-marking and dependent-marking patterns. This chapter gives an overview of the structure of simple sentences and discusses its place in syntactic typology.

3.1. An overview of simple sentence types

3.1.1. Sentences with only third person arguments

The simplest sentences in Choctaw consist of a verb plus a tense marker, as in the following examples:

(1) *Oba-tok.*
rain-PT
'It rained.'

(2) *Niya-h.*
fat-TNS
'She is fat.'

(3) *Písa-tok.*
see:N-PT
'She saw them.'

The verb plus tense marker *h* is used as the citation form of verbs in this work. As these examples show, there are no obligatory noun phrases in a Choctaw sentence, nor is there any overt indication of a third person subject or object. When there is an overt NP subject, it is marked for case:

(4) *John-at niya-h.*
John-NM fat-TNS
'John is fat.'

Subject NPs are obligatorily marked with the nominative case *-at*. Object NPs are optionally marked with the accusative *-a*:

(5) *John-a písa-tok.*
John-AC see:N-PT
'He saw John.'

(6) *Ahi' honni-tok.*
potatoes boil-PT
'He boiled the potatoes.'

32

(7) *Ahi-ya̱*   *honni-tok.*
     potatoes-AC   boil-PT
     'He boiled the potatoes.'

The conditions under which accusative marking appears are discussed in chapter 5.

3.1.2. Sentences with first and second person arguments

Sentences that contain a first or second person argument show more complex morphology. Intransitive verbs fall into three classes (I, II, and III), according to the type of agreement shown with the subject:

(8) *Baliili-li-tok.*
     run-1sI-PT
     'I ran.'

(9) *Sa-niya-h.*
     1sII-fat-TNS
     'I am fat.'

(10) *A̱-ponna-h.*
     1sIII-skilled-TNS
     'I am skilled.'

As discussed in chapter 9, the III prefixes are probably best treated as dative applicatives. Transitive verbs also fall into several classes (I/II, I/III, II/II, II/III, III/II), depending on the sort of agreement with subjects and objects:

(11) *Chi-písa-li-h.*   (I/II)
     2sII-see:N-1sI-TNS
     'I see you.'

(12) *Chi̱-pa̱ya-li-h.*   (I/III)
     2sIII-call-1sI-TNS
     'I call you.'

(13) *Chi-sa-banna-h.*   (II/II)
     2sII-1sII-want-TNS
     'I want you.'

(14) *Chi̱-sa-yimmi-h.*   (II/III)
     2sIII-1sII-believe-TNS
     'I believe you.'

(15) *Chi-am-ahchiba-h.*   (III/II)
     2sII-1sIII-tired-TNS
     'I'm tired of you.'

Verb agreement is discussed in more detail in chapter 9.

3.1.3. Equational, locational, and possessive sentences

3.1.3.1. Equational sentences

Equational sentences are those in which the identity of two noun phrases is asserted. These correspond to English sentences with a copula and a predicate nominal. As mentioned above, Choctaw uses zero copulas in the third person in the present tense, as the following examples show:

(16)   *Pam-at   holisso'=pisáachi'.*
      Pam-NM teacher
      Pam is the teacher.'

(17)   *Holisso'=pisáachi'-mat Pam.*
      teacher-D:NM   Pam
      'The teacher is Pam.'

When the subject is first or second person, the copula *a* must appear:

(18)   *Holisso'=pisáachi' si-ya-h.*
      teacher   1sII-be-TNS
      'I am the teacher.'

It is ungrammatical to omit the copula in such examples:

(19)   **An-akoosh holisso'=pisáachi'.*
      I-CON:NM   teacher
      ('I am the teacher.')

The overt copula *a* also appears when the sentence is in the past or distant past or when the sentence appears with a modal.

(20)   *Hattak-mat Bill aa-tok.*
      man-D:NM   Bill be-PT
      'That man was Bill.'

(21)   *Hattak-mat Bill a-ttook.*
      man-D:NM   Bill be-DPAST
      'That man was Bill (long ago).'

(22)   *Hattak-mat Bill a-ahila-h.*
      man-D:NM   Bill be-POT-TNS
      'That man might be Bill.'

For reasons that are unclear, the copula appears as a long *aa* before the tense ending *-tok*, but as *a* before *-ttook* or when preceded by a II prefix (e.g., *siyah* 'I am'). Since the minimal verb in Choctaw is bimoraic, perhaps the unusual lengthening in these cases is needed to bring the phonologically aberrant **atok* into conformity with the metrical structure of the language.[1] Unfortunately, the copula is the only verb showing such

---

1. Nicklas (1974:36) cites the example *Nakni a tok* 'He was a man' with a short *a* before the tense marker, but the vowel is clearly long for speakers I consulted.

an alternation, so it is hard to be sure.

Question particles may appear directly on nouns in copular sentences:

(23)   *Ilamm-at Pam i̠-kook-o̠?*
       that-NM   Pam III-coke-Q
       'Is that Pam's Coke?'

The determiner -*ak* (discussed in more detail in chapter 5) frequently occurs on the predicate nominal in copular constructions:

(24)   <Haknip a̠ i pʊla hʊt nishkin ak oke.>
       Haknip-a̠ i̠-palah-at   nishkin-ak okii.
       body-AC   III-light-NM eye-OBL   indeed
       'The light of the body is the eye.' (Matt. 6:22)

(25)   *Nashóoba'-mat chishn-ak a-ttook-o̠?*
       wolf-D:NM   you-OBL   COP-DPAST-Q
       'Was the wolf you?' (said in discussing a school play)

(26)   *Nashóoba'-m-akoosh alla' nakni'-m-ak   a-ttook.*
       wolf-DEM-CON:NM   child male-DEM-OBL COP-DPAST
       'The wolf was that boy.'

(27)   *An-ak aa-tok.*
       I-OBL   be-PT
       'It was me.'

(28)   *An-ak Ø-aachi̠-h.*
       I-OBL   be-IRR-TNS
       'It will be me.'

3.1.3.2. Locational and possessive sentences

Locational sentences are those in which the location of some noun phrase is specified. Sentences of this type do not use the copula as in English, but instead use a small class of verbs of position.

(29)   *Holisso'-mat aa-ípa-'   ittóla-h.*
       book-D:NM   LOC-eat-NML   lie:N-TNS
       'The book is on the table; the book lies on the table.'

(30)   **Holisso'-mat aa-ípa-'   pákna' aa-tok.*
       book-D:NM   LOC-eat-NML   top   be-PT
       ('The book was on the table.')

Sentences that show possessive relationships typically use the same small class of verbs of position along with III-agreement (dative) on the verb:

(31)   *Holisso'-mat am-ittóla-h.*
        book-D:NM   1sIII-lie:N-TNS
        'I have a book.' (Lit., 'The book lies to me.')

There are some complex selectional restrictions between the verb of position and the type of object possessed. These are discussed in more detail in chapter 19.

3.1.4. Applicative prefixes

Choctaw has applicative prefixes that allow the addition of dative, instrumental, benefactive, comitative, superessive, locative, or ablative noun phrases to the sentence. The morphophonology of these prefixes is discussed at length in Ulrich (1986).

    Table 3.1 shows the various applicative prefixes. The following sentences show some examples of these prefixes:

Table 3.1. Applicative prefixes

DATIVE	*im-*
INSTRUMENTAL	*isht-*
BENEFACTIVE	*imi̱-*
COMITATIVE	*ibaa-*
SUPERESSIVE	*on-*
LOCATIVE	*aa-*
ABLATIVE	*imaa-*

(32)   *Itti' iskífa' isht-cha̱ya-tok.*
        wood axe   INSTR-chop-PT
        'He chopped the wood with an axe.'

(33)   *Sa-baa-washooha-t hilha-t   taloowa-h!*
        1sII-COMIT-play-SS dance-SS sing-TNS
        'Sing, dance, and play with me!' T2:7

(34)   *Illípa' kaniimi-ka̱   lowak apákna' aa-nonáachi-cha* . . .
        food   some-COMP:DS fire   top   LOC-cook:L-SS
        'She cooked some food on the fire and . . .' (T1:26)

(35)   *Oklah si-o̱-hilha-tok.*
        PLUR 1sII-on-dance-PT
        'They danced on top of me.'

Applicative prefixes are described in more detail in chapter 9.

3.1.5. Postpositional phrases and other adjuncts

Sentences may also contain various postpositional phrases which are not accompanied by an applicative prefix on the verb:

(36) *Ofi-yat aa-ípa-'   nóta' ittóla-h.*
      dog-NM LOC-eat-NML under lie:N-TNS
      'The dog lies under the table.'

Postpositional phrases are discussed in more detail in chapter 15.
    Occasionally bare NP adjuncts appear in Choctaw sentences:

(37) *Tamáaha'-ma Chahta-at   lawa-h.*
      town-D:AC   Choctaw-NM many-TNS
      'In that town, there are many Choctaws.' (Nicklas 1974:242)

(38) *Ninak si-alhpowa-tok miya-h*
      night 1SII-born-PF   say-TNS
      'They say that I was born at night.'

More frequently, however, such adjuncts require some sort of verbal morphology. For example, in the following sentence, *onnakma* 'tomorrow' appears with irrealis different subject morphology:

(39) *Onna-kma   tamaaha' iya-l-aachi-h.*
      dawn-IRR:DS town   go-1SI-IRR-TNS
      'Tomorrow I'm going to town.'

3.1.6. Causatives

Choctaw has a productive morphological causative *-chi*, as shown in the following examples:

(40) *Nowa-lih.*
      walk-1SI
      'I walked.'

(41) *Sa-nowa-chi-tok.*
      1SII-walk-CAUS-PT
      'He made me walk.'

Causatives are discussed in more detail in chapter 8.

3.1.7. Questions

3.1.7.1. Wh-questions

In general wh-questions may be formed by merely leaving an appropriate interrogative in situ. No special verbal morphology or word order is necessary:

(42) *John-at   kátah-o̱   písa-tok?*
      John-NM who-FOC:AC see:N-PT
      'Who did John see?'

(43) *Hashshok is-sa-chạli-kat   kátihmi-h*
      grass   2sI-1sIII-cut-COMP:SS how:much-TNS
      is-sam-apiis-ahiina-h?
      2sI-1sIII-charge-POT-TNS
      'How much will you charge me to cut the grass for me?'

Choctaw also has optional fronting of interrogatives in the syntax; thus sentences like the following are acceptable:

(44) *Kátah-o̱   John-at   písa-tok?*
      who-FOC:AC John-NM see:N-PT
      'Who did John see?'

Interrogatives are discussed in more detail in chapter 7.

3.1.7.2. Yes-no questions

Yes-no questions in Choctaw are formed by suffixing a question particle -o̱ to the verb, as in the following example:

(45) *John ish-písa-h-o̱?*
      John 2sI-see:N-TNS-Q
      'Do you see John?'

Markers of illocutionary force are discussed in more detail in chapter 12.

3.2. Configurationality

Choctaw is configurational language. The distinction between configurational and nonconfigurational languages is due to Hale (1983, 1989), but the notion has been extended by other researchers (Speas 1990; Baker 1991) as well. As a result, the set of properties said to characterize nonconfigurational languages differs somewhat from source to source. Here I will look at the following properties: nonexistence of a verb phrase, discontinuous constituency, extensive use of null anaphora, and extensive use of agreement morphology.

3.2.1. Configurationality and verb phrases

There are several potential arguments for the existence of a verb phrase (VP) in Choctaw. Since the existence of a verb phrase implies a configurational difference between subjects and objects (with object inside the verb phrase and subject outside it), arguments for verb phrases translate into arguments for configurationality. All the arguments for verb phrases are somewhat theory-internal, but taken as a group they are convincing. I will consider arguments from word order, adverb placement, proforms, coordination, placement of certain VP-internal items, and binding theory.

3.2.1.1. Word order

The normal word order of Choctaw is subject-object-verb. Subjects obligatorily receive nominative case, but overt accusative case is optional for objects.

(46)   *John-at   tákkon(-a)   chopa-h.*
       John-NM   peach(-AC)   buy-TNS
       'John bought a peach.'

However, the orders object-subject-verb and subject-verb-object are also possible (generally accompanied by intonational breaks). In these instances, accusative case is obligatory on the object:

(47)   *Tákkon-a/?*Tákkon, John-at   chopa-h.*
       peach-AC/?*peach   John-NM   buy-TNS
       'John bought a peach.'

(48)   *John-at   chopa-h, tákkon-a/?*tákkon.*
       John-NM   buy-TNS   peach-AC/?*peach
       'John bought a peach.'

There are several ways that these facts might be accounted for, but perhaps the simplest is the following:

(49)   Accusative case is optional for objects that are in situ; obligatory for moved objects.

But this formulation implies that subject-object-verb is the most basic order and that other orders are derived via movement. That follows naturally from positing a verb phrase.

3.2.1.2. Adverb placement

As is shown in more detail in chapter 18, an external temporal adverb like *piláashaash* 'yesterday' may occur sentence-initially, sentence-finally, or between the subject and any objects. However, it may not appear between the verb and the object:

(50a) *Piláashaash Mary-at   sholosh chopa-tok.*   (best order)
       yesterday   Mary-NM shoe   buy-PT
       'Yesterday Mary bought shoes.'

(50b) *Mary-at   piláashaash sholosh chopa-tok.*
       Mary-NM yesterday   shoe   buy-PT

(50c) *Mary-at   sholosh chopa-tok piláashaash.*
       Mary-NM shoe   buy-PT   yesterday

(50d) *Mary-at   sholosh piláashaash chopa-tok.
     Mary-NM shoe   yesterday   buy-PT

We can account for this distribution if we posit a structure like that in figure 3.1.

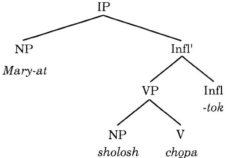

Figure 3.1.

In this structure, an external temporal adverb occurs as a daughter of IP, but is freely ordered with respect to other daughters of IP.

3.2.1.3. Proforms

There are proforms which correspond to a verb plus its object, but not to a verb plus its subject. *Yohmih* is a pro-verb that means 'be so' or 'do so'. It replaces a VP, and it is not possible to leave VP-internal material behind, as the following examples show:

(51a) *John-at   sa-yoppáchi-kma, Bill-ak-kia   yohmi-h.*
     John-NM 1sII-like:N-IRR:DS Bill-OBL-too do:so-TNS
     'John likes me and Bill does too.'

(51b) **John-at   a-yoppáchi-kma, Bill-ak-kia   sa-yohmi-h.*
     John-NM 1sII-like:N-IRR:DS Bill-OBL-too 1sII-do:so-TNS
     ('John likes me and Bill does me too.')

(52) *John-at   niya-kma, hattak-mak-kia yohmi-h.*
     John-NM fat-IRR:DS man-DEM-too   be:so-TNS
     'John is fat and that man is too.'

While there is a pro-verb that corresponds to a verb plus its object, there are no comparable pro-verbs that correspond to a verb plus its subject. If we make the assumption that anaphoric elements refer to constituents, then we have evidence that the verb plus object forms a constituent, while the verb plus subject does not.

3.2.1.4. Coordination

It is possible to coordinate verb phrases, as in the following example:

(53) [[_VP_*Ipa*] *anoti* [_VP_*oka' ishko*]]-*li-tok.*
       eat   and   water drink-1SI-PT
       'I ate and drank water.'

If only constituents may be coordinated, then sentences of this type show that the verb and its object form a constituent. Such sentences also give evidence for some degree of syntactic independence for the verbal suffixes as well, and are the only examples in which a verb is not immediately followed by a tense marker.

3.2.1.5. VP-internal elements

While the order of elements within the VP is relatively free, there are some sentence elements that only appear within VP. These include the plural preverb *oklah*, and the adverb *piih* 'just, merely'. The former is discussed in chapter 14, the latter in chapter 18.

Oklah is both a noun meaning 'people' and a preverb indicating the plurality of an animate subject. In texts, the most natural position for the preverb *oklah* is after any object and immediately before the verb.

(54) *Hitokoosh chókfi' oklah falaama-tok.*
       and:then   rabbit PLUR meet-PT
       'And then they met a rabbit.' (T3:3)

(55) <Holhpokuna ho falamʋt Helot a okla ik im ono ka hi a, Chihowa hʋt
       i̱ miha hatuk o, . . .>
       Holhpokonna-h-o   falaama-t   Herod-a   oklah
       dream-TNS-PART:DS   return-PART Herod-AC PLUR
       ik-im-oon-ok-ahii-ya   Chihoowah-at
       N-III-arrive:L-NEG-IRR-COMP:DS God-NM
       i̱-miha-haatoko . . .
       III-say-because:DS
       'Because God warned them in a dream that they should not return to
       Herod . . .' (Matt. 2:12)

Oklah may also appear before the direct object:

(56) *Oklah Amazing Grace o̱t   taloow-aachi̱-h.*
       plur   Amazing Grace go:and sing-IRR-TNS
       'They're gonna go sing Amazing Grace.'

(57) *Alla' nakni-it oklah tachi' apa-tok.*
       child male-NM PLUR corn   eat-PT
       'The boys ate all the corn.'

However, it may not appear before the subject:

(58)   *Oklah alla' nakni-it t̲achi' apa-tok.
       PLUR   child male-NM corn   eat-PT
       ('The boys ate the corn.')

Similarly, the adverb piih 'just, merely' may appear either before or after
any objects, but not before the subject:

(59)   <. . . peh ikkishi ak o̲ isso mᴜt . . .>
       . . . piih ikkishi-yako̲   isso-hmat . . .
       just   chest-CON:AC hit-when:SS
       'He [just] hit himself on the chest and . . .' (Luke 18:13)

(60)   Na-chap̲óli-'   piih pisa-li-tok.
       thing-sweet-NML just see-1SI-PT
       'I just looked at the cake.'

(61)   *Piih John-at   na-chap̲óli-'   pisa-tok.
       just   John-NM thing-sweet-NML see-PT
       ('John just looked at the cake.')

It is completely ungrammatical for either piih or oklah to appear after
the verb:

(62)   *John-at na-chap̲óli-'   pisa-tok piih.
       John-NM thing-sweet-NML see-PT   just
       ('John just looked at the cake.')

(63)   *Alla' nakni-it t̲achi' apa-tok oklah.
       child male-NM corn   eat-PT   PLUR
       ('The boys ate the corn.')

   A simple way of accounting for the position of piih and oklah is to say
that they occur in a nonfinal position within the VP. But this
generalization requires reference to VP as a constituent.

3.2.1.6. Binding theory

Another argument for the existence of VP was originally developed by
Whitman (1982) for Japanese. In English, we find the following
paradigm:

(64)   *[$_{IP}$ He$_i$ [$_{VP}$ loves John$_i$'s mother]].

(65)   [$_{IP}$ John$_i$'s mother [$_{VP}$ loves him$_i$]].

If we assume that binding theory is formulated in terms of syntactic
constituency, then we may say that (64) is ungrammatical because he c-
commands John, and this is a violation of condition C of the binding
theory (Chomsky 1981). Note, however, that (65) is grammatical. This is
because him does not c-command John, due to the intervening VP node.
If this node were absent, then we would predict (65) to be ungrammatical
for the same reasons that (64) is.

In Choctaw, the paradigm of grammaticality is exactly the same as it is in English:

(66)   *[$_{IP}$ pro$_i$ [$_{VP}$ *John$_i$ ishki' i-hollo-h*]].
       John   mother III-love-TNS
       ('He loves John's mother.')

(67)   [$_{IP}$ *John$_i$ ishki-it* [$_{VP}$ pro$_i$ *i-hollo-h*]].
       John   mother-NM   III-love-TNS
       'John's mother loves him.'

Therefore, by the same reasoning, there must be a VP in Choctaw, or both of these sentences would be ungrammatical. However, if binding theory is not stated over constituent structure, but is based on something like argument structure, then this does not constitute a valid argument.

3.2.1.7. Conclusion

Taken as a whole, the evidence supports the existence of a verb phrase in Choctaw, and consequently a phrase-structural distinction between subject and object positions. This is strong evidence that Choctaw is a configurational language.

3.2.2. Configurationality and discontinuous constituency

Another property associated with nonconfigurationality, discontinous constituency, is not found in Choctaw. For example, it is ungrammatical to separate parts of an NP from each other; as (68b)–(68d) show, breaking up either of the NPs in (68a) results in unacceptability:

(68a) *Alikchi' cháaha-'-mat ofi' lósa-y-a   písa-tok.*
       doctor   tall-NML-D:NM dog black-NML-AC see:N-PT
       'That tall doctor saw the black dog.'

(68b) **Alikchi' ofi' lósa-y-a   písa-tok cháaha-'-mat.*
       doctor   dog black-NML-AC see:N-PT tall-NML-D:NM

(68c) **Alikchi'-mat ofi' lósa-y-a   písa-tok cháaha-'-mat.*
       doctor   dog black-NML-AC see:N-PT tall-NML-D:NM

(68d) **Alikchi' cháaha-'-mat ofi' písa-tok   lósa-y-a.*
       doctor   dog black-NML-AC see:N-PT tall-NML-D:NM

This fact strengthens the conclusion that Choctaw is a configurational language.

3.2.3. Configurationality and null anaphora

Extensive use of null anaphora is often also cited as a property of nonconfigurational languages. Choctaw also shows extensive use of null anaphora; all nominal arguments may be omitted:

(69) *John-at Mary-a̱ holisso' im-aa-tok.*
      John-NM Mary-AC book   III-give-PT
      'John gave Mary a book.'

(70) *Im-aa-tok.*
      III-give-PT
      'She/he gave it to him/her.'

Given the evidence in the preceding sections that Choctaw is configurational, these data show that extensive use of null anaphora is not sufficient to establish a language as configurational.

3.2.4. Configurationality and agreement morphology

Choctaw has extensive verbal agreement morphology, as discussed in more depth in chapter 9. Verbs agree with the subject and direct object, as well as with various kinds of applicative objects (dative, instrumental, comitative, benefactive, ablative, superessive, and locative).

Despite all this agreement morphology, the language is nevertheless configurational by the arguments given above. Once again, it seems that the presence of extensive agreement morphology is not sufficient to establish a language as non-configurational.

3.2.5. Choctaw is not a pronominal argument language

Related to the issue of configurationality is the idea that some languages are "pronominal argument" languages (Jelinek 1984), in that verbal agreement markers occupy the argument positions in the clause, while overt NPs appear in adjunct positions. Jelinek (1989) has argued that Choctaw should be treated as a pronominal argument language.

The evidence for VP that has been discussed above presents a real problem for Jelinek's argument. Since all overt NPs are supposed to be in adjunct positions, why should phenomena such as adverb ordering be sensitive to the VP boundary?

Two other sorts of facts also present problems for the pronominal argument hypothesis. They are the omissibility of some agreement markers and the possibility of extraction from NPs.

3.2.5.1. Omissibility of agreement markers

As originally noted by Ulrich (1986), II agreement markers, those typically used with the objects of verbs, can be omitted in the presence of an emphatic pronoun.

Example (71) is the normal way of expressing a sentence with a second person singular object, but (72) shows that it is grammatical to omit the verbal prefix *chi-* when the pronoun *chishnako̱* is present.

(71) *Chi-písa-li-h.*
      2SII-see:N-1SI-TNS
      'I see you.'

(72) *Chisn-ako̱   písa-li-h.*
      you-CON:AC see:N-1SI-TNS
      'I see *you*; it was you that I saw.'

These examples present a difficulty for the pronominal argument analysis. Jelinek (1984, 1989) makes the assumption that all true arguments are pronominal in such languages. But if this is so, where is the object of 'see' in (72)?

3.2.5.2. The possibility of extraction from NP

It is possible to extract items from noun phrases, as in the following example:

(73) *Kata-h-o̱ᵢ   John-at [tᵢ i-nákfi'] haksichi-tok?*
      who-TNS-FOC:AC John-NM III-brother   trick-PT
      'Whose brother did John trick?' (Lit., 'Who did John trick her brother?')

In the pronominal argument treatment, all overt NPs are in adjunct positions. However, extraction of material from adjuncts is generally forbidden crosslinguistically (due to the Empty Category Principle [Chomsky 1981] or its equivalent in other theories.)

Examples of this sort cannot be reanalyzed as cases of discontinuous constituency, since we have seen that in general Choctaw does not allow discontinuous constituency. Instead, it seems preferable to give this example the structure in figure 3.2.

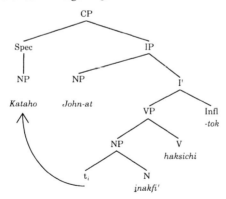

Figure 3.2.

I will take the bulk of the evidence to show that Choctaw is not a pronominal argument language.

3.3. Constituent ordering

Choctaw is a consistently head-final language. In the following sections, I survey a number of syntactic environments where final position of the head is seen.

3.3.1. Word order at the sentential level

As mentioned above, the basic word order of the language is subject-object-verb. Verb phrases are head final, and when there are multiple objects, there is considerable freedom in their order.

(74)   *Charles-at   báshpo' nípi' isht-bashli-h.*
       Charles-NM knife   meat INSTR-cut-TNS
       'Charles cut the meat with a knife.'

(75)   *Charles-at   nípi' báshpo' isht-bashli-h.*
       Charles-NM meat   knife   INSTR-cut-TNS
       'Charles cut the meat with a knife.'

In elicitation contexts, it is generally acceptable to extrapose one constituent after the verb, but it is not possible to extrapose more than one constituent:

(76a) *John-at Mary-a   písa-tok.*
       John-NM Mary-AC see:N-PT
       'John saw Mary.'

(76b) *Mary-a písa-tok, John-at.*

(76c) *John-at písa-tok, Mary-a.*

(76d) **Písa-tok, John-at, Mary-a.*

(76e) **Písa-tok, Mary-a. John-at.*

However, sentences with ordinary NPs positioned after the verb are never volunteered by speakers, and are very rare in texts.

Extraposition of NP objects to clause-initial position is more common, though clearly a marked option. As noted above, extraposed objects must have overt accusative case:

(77)   *Takkon-a, John-at apa-tok.*
      apple-AC   John-NM eat-PT
      'John ate the apple.'

For clausal objects, both right and left extraposition are possible and relatively frequent. Left extraposition appears to be more frequent with verbs of saying, while right extraposition is more common with other verbs.

(78) Clausal object in situ:

> *John-at* [_{CP} *alikchi-it   Bill   lhakoffichi-tok̲a̲*]
> John-NM . doctor-NM Bill cure-PT:COMP:DS
> *anokfilli-h.*
> think-TNS
> 'John thinks that the doctor cured Bill.'

(79) Clausal object extraposed to the right:

> *John-at   anokfilli-h* [_{CP} *alikchi-it   Bill*
> John-NM think-TNS   doctor-NM   Bill
> *lhakoffichi-tok̲a̲*)
> cure-PT:COMP:DS
> 'John thinks that the doctor cured Bill.'

(80) Clausal object in situ:

> *Bonnie-at* [_{CP} *issi-it   bookoshi'-ma̲ attah miya-h-o̲*]_e
> Bonnie-NM   deer-NM creek-D:AC   be   say-TNS-PART:DS
> *am-anooli-tok.*
> 1sIII-tell-PT
> 'Bonnie told me that the deer was at the creek.'

(81) Clausal object extraposed to the left:

> [_{CP} *Issi-it bookoshi'-ma̲ a̲ttah miya-h-o̲*]
> deer-NM   creek-D:AC   be   say-TNS-PART:DS
> *Bonnie-at   am-anooli-tok.*
> Bonnie-NM 1sIII-tell-PT
> 'Bonnie told me that the deer was at the creek.'

It is unclear whether there are any verbs in Choctaw that allow clausal subjects. See section 16.2.4 for discussion of a potential case of a clausal subject.

3.3.2. Predicate nominal + copula

The copula follows the predicate nominal, as is typical in head-final languages. There is no overt copula in third person default tense examples with predicate nominals:

(83) *John-at   Chahta'.*
> John-NM Choctaw
> 'John is a Choctaw.'

However, the copula *a* appears when the subject is not third person, or when the copula would be followed by either a marked tense or modal morphemes:

(84) *Chahta' si-ya-h.*
> Choctaw 1sII-be-TNS
> 'I'm a Choctaw.'

(85) *Pushmataha-yat Chahta' a-ttook.*
Pushmataha-NM Choctaw be-DPAST
'Pushmataha was a Choctaw.'

Adjectives act in many ways like a subclass of verbs in Choctaw, and do not use the copula. Nevertheless, the morphology and semantics of adjectives diverge in some ways from those of ordinary verbs. See chapter 14 for more discussion.

Sentences that express location, possession, and existence do not use the copula, but instead use verbs of posture, such as *biniilih* 'to sit', *hikiiyah* 'to stand', and so on. Sentences of this type are discussed in chapter 19.

3.3.3. Main verb + auxiliary

There are several classes of auxiliary verbs, discussed in more detail in chapter 13. All of them follow the main verb, as is typical in head-final languages. Consider the following representative example, where *tahlih* 'complete' is an auxiliary following the main verb *apah* 'to eat':

(86) *Tạchi' apa-t   tahli-li-tok.*
corn   eat-PART complete-1SI-PT
'I finished eating the corn.'

3.3.4. Sentence + question particle

Yes-no questions are generally formed by suffixing the question particle -*ọ* to the final element of the sentence. Typically the final element is the verb:

(87) *John ish-písa-h-ọ?*
John 2SI-see:N-TNS-Q
'Do you see John?'

(88) *John ish-písa-tok-ọ?*
John 2SI-see:N-PT-Q
'Did you see John?'

(89) *John ish-pís-aachi-h-o?*
John 2SI-see:N-IRR-TNS-Q
'Will you see John?'

However, when a sentence ends with a noun, as in a third person default tense copular sentence, the question particle appears directly on the predicate nominal:

(90) *Ilamm-at Pam i-kook-ọ?*
that-NM   Pam III-coke-Q
'Is that Pam's Coke?'

Chapter 12 discusses a few other question particles also used in Choctaw.

3.3.5. Noun + postposition

Choctaw probably has a distinct lexical class of postpositions, though in many cases they are similar to body part nouns. See chapter 15 for more discussion.

(91) *Ofi-yat chokka' nọta' taláya-h.*
      dog-NM house   under lie:N-TNS
      'The dog is lying under the house.'

(92) *Hoshi-yat itti' pakna' binịli-h.*
      bird-NM tree on   sit:N-TNS
      'The bird is sitting on the tree.'

When the object of a postposition is a non-third person pronoun, there is agreement morphology on the postposition:

(93) *Ofi-yat chi-nọta'   taláya-h.*
      dog-NM 2SII-under lie:N-TNS
      'The dog is lying under you.'

3.3.6. Possessor + possessed

The possessor must precede the possessed within a noun phrase:

(94a) *John   ị-katos*
      John   III-cat
      'John's cat'

(94b) **ị-katos John*

The possessed noun shows agreement with the possessor, divided roughly along alienable-inalienable lines:

(95a) *a-katos*
      1sIII-cat
      'my cat'

(95b) *chị-katos*
      2sIII-cat
      'your cat'

(95c) *ị-katos*
      III-cat
      'his/her/its/their cat'

(96a) *sa-shki'*
      1sII-mother
      'my mother'

(96b) *chi-shki'*
      2sII-mother
      'your mother'

(96c) *ishki'*
mother
'his/her/its/their mother'

(96d) *Mary ishki'*
Mary mother
'Mary's mother'

The ordering facts are discussed in more detail in chapter 5; possessor agreement is discussed in chapter 4.

3.3.7. Noun phrase + determiner

Determiners are usually suffixes in Choctaw, but in some instances a separate word is used. In such cases, the determiner comes at the end of the phrase.

(97) *Ofi' hómma'-mat baliili-h.*
dog red-D:NM   run-TNS
'That red dog is running.'

(98) *Ofi' hómma' yamm-at baliili-h.*
dog red   that-NM   run-TNS
'That red dog is running.'

This order is consistent with head-finality if we take the determiner to be the head of a determiner phrase. It would not be consistent with head-finality if we treated these as noun phrases.

3.3.8. Some noncorrelations

Certain constituent orders typical of other head-final languages do not appear in Choctaw, generally because Choctaw lacks the construction or the part of speech element involved.

3.3.8.1. Internally headed relative clauses

Choctaw has internally headed relative clauses. Since the head of the relative clause appears inside the clause that modifies it, there is no clear ordering relation between the two:

(99) *Hattak-mat ofi' chopa-tok-ma písa-li-tok.*
man-D:NM   dog buy-PT-D:AC   see:N-1SI-PT
'I saw the dog that the man bought.'
'I saw the man that bought the dog.'

As this example shows, relative clauses are potentially ambiguous with respect to their head. Relative clauses are discussed in more detail in chapter 16.

3.3.8.2. Noun + adjective

Choctaw probably does not have a distinct lexical class of adjectives; their meanings are conveyed by stative verbs. When used adnominally, such stative verbs follow the noun, and often show morphology that appears to be nominalization:

(100) *Hattak-at chaaha-h.*
     man-NM   tall-TNS
     'The man is tall.'

(101) *Hattak cháaha-'-at baliili-h.*
     man   tall-NML-NM run-TNS
     'The tall man is running.'

Prima facie, this appears to be a case of a constituent whose head is not final. However, it is best to treat cases like those in (100) as involving internally headed relative clauses (for which, see chapter 16). So the more accurate translation of (100) is something like 'The man who is tall is running.'

    Despite the fact that adjectives are subtype of verb, it is convenient to retain the label "adjective" because words of this class show peculiarities not shared by other verbs. This is discussed in more detail in chapter 14.

3.3.8.3. Comparatives

Comparatives are expressed by means of an auxiliary verb *i-shahlih/ i-shahlichih* 'to exceed':

(102) *John-at Mary chaaha-kat i-shahli-h.*
     John-NM Mary tall-COMP:SS III-exceed-PT
     'John is taller than Mary.'

The ordering follows the general order "main verb + auxiliary." There is no Choctaw element corresponding to English 'than'. The comparative auxiliary is discussed in chapter 13.

4. Noun phrases: Derivation and possession

4.1. Derived nominals

Choctaw shows a moderately productive process of deriving nouns from verbs. Derived nominals may be derived by omitting the tense marker from a verb and suffixing a glottal stop. Consider the following examples:

(1a) *hilha-h*
      dance-TNS
      'to dance'

(1b) *hílha-'*
      dance-NML
      'dance; dancer'

(2a) *asilhha-h*
      beg-TNS
      'to beg'

(2b) *asílhha-'*
      beg-NML
      'beggar; begging'

Derived nominals like those in (1b) and (2b) are also distinguished from verbs by a penultimate pitch accent. As Haag (1995:117–18) shows, the most frequent and predictable meanings of such nominalizations are 'agent' and 'instance of the verbal action'.

Verbs with applicative prefixes are a rich source of nominalizations. *aa-* 'locative' and *isht-* 'instrumental' are particularly frequent on nominalizations:

(3a) *aa-biniilih*
      LOC-sit
      'to sit at/on'

(3b) *aabiníili'*
      'chair'

(4a) *isht-ipah*
      INSTR-eat
      'to eat with'

(4b) *ishtípa'*
      'spoon'

Another type of nominalization uses the morpheme *nan-* ~ *naa-* 'thing' before a verb.[1] These nominalizations refer either to the agent of the verb or to the result of the action of the verb. Some nominalizations of this type are ambiguous between the two readings, but in other cases the result seems to be lexicalized (Haag 1995:118):

(5a)   nan-óffo-'
       thing-plant-NML
       'plant'

(5b)   nan-illi-'
       thing-die-NML
       'dead person/dead thing'

(5c)   naa-hóoyo-'
       thing-hunt-NML
       'hunter', *'prey'

(5d)   nan-ípa-'
       thing-eat-NML
       'food', ?'eater'

As discussed in chapter 14, many adjectives also appear with nominalization morphology:

(6)   hattak cháaha-'
       man tall-NML
       'tall man'

4.2. Possessive prefixes on nouns

4.2.1. Alienably and inalienably possessed nouns

Choctaw has agreement with the possessor which is expressed by a set of prefixes. There are two types of agreement, which are labelled II and III (Munro and Gordon 1982); these are presented in table 4.1 (below).[2] To some extent the two types of agreement correlate with the traditional notions alienable and inalienable, but the facts are somewhat more complicated, as discussed. Nearly all of the nouns that take II agreement are body parts or kinship terms. However, not all body parts or kinship terms take II agreement. There are several cases of nouns with nearly identical semantics that nevertheless differ in the sort of agreement morphology they occur with:

(7a)   sa-shki'
       1sII-mother
       'my mother'

1. The variation appears to be idiolectal.
2. These affixes are also used with verbs, where III typically marks a dative argument and II typically marks a stative subject or the object of a transitive verb. The facts are considerably more complex, however. See chapter 9 for more discussion.

(7b) *sa-háyya'*
      1sII-BrWi
      'my brother's wife'

(7c) *a̱-hokni'*
      1sIII-FaSi
      'my paternal aunt'

(7d) *a̱-ki'*
      1sIII-father
      'my father'

(8a) *sa-hakchin*
      1sII-penis
      'my penis'

(8b) *am-isht   hoshǫwa'*
      1sIII-INSTR urinate
      'my penis [euphemistic]'

(8c) *a̱-talop*
      1sIII-testicle
      'my testicle'

Note that in (8a)–(8c) that the two different words for 'penis' show different agreement types.

Table 4.1. Possessor agreement prefixes

	II	III
1S	sa-*	am-†
2S	chi-	chim-
3	—	im-
1P	pi-	pim-
2P	hachi-	

* This prefix becomes *si-* before a vowel-initial stem. For some speakers, *si-* is also used before stems beginning with *h*, as in *si-haksobish* 'my ear'. I have only heard *si-* used in this way in Oklahoma Choctaw.

† When the III prefixes occur before a consonant-initial stem, they have an allomorph ending in a nasal vowel rather than *Vm-*.

It is unclear whether there were once semantic factors which motivated these differences, but at any rate the choice is highly lexicalized in modern Choctaw.

The following nouns take II agreement with possessors (Byington 1870, 1915; Nicklas 1974; Broadwell 1987b).

(9)
ani'	'fruit'
ayocholóoli'	'descendant'
choshshak	'back of the neck'
hakchin	'penis'
haknip	'flesh, body'
hakshish	'tendon'
haksobish	'ear'
hanaali'	'leg'
hapóllo'	'buttocks'
hási'	'vagina'
hatabish	'navel'
hattip	'thigh, small of the back'[3]
háyya'	'brother's wife, mother's brother's wife'
híshi'	'body hair, feather, leaf'[4]
ibbak	'arm, hand'
ibbakóshi'	'finger'
ibbayyi'	'[a man's] sister's son, [a woman's] brother's son'
ibbi' tiik'	[a man's] sister's daughter, [a woman's] brother's daughter'
ibiilhakla'	'genitals [of either sex]'
ibiishákni'	'nose'
ibílhkan	'snot, nasal mucus'
ichaapa'	'partner, mate'
iffoka'	'stomach, belly'
ikkishi'	'chest'
ikkóla'	'neck'
ippaf	'dog'[5]
ippok	'grandchild'
isso'	'son'[6]
issish	'blood'

3. Nicklas (1974) cites this as *-hhatip,* suggesting some dialectal or idiolectal variation.

4. For many speakers it is awkward or ungrammatical to use a possessive prefix directly on the word *híshi'.* These speakers prefer or require that the name of a body part precede the word: *sabbak híshi'* 'the hair on my arm', *sahanaali híshi'* 'the hair on my leg', and so on.

5. This is an obsolete possessive form of the ordinary word for dog, *ofi',* which now takes ordinary III possessive marking. This form appears to have become obsolete relatively recently, since it is listed in Byington (1915). Two consultants recalled having heard the word *ippaf,* though both confirmed that it is no longer in use.

6. This word is judged obsolete by modern Choctaws, but occurs frequently in Choctaw translations of the Bible.

issolash	'tongue'
ishki'	'mother'
ishkish	'buttocks, anus'
itakha'	'mouth'
itiálbi'	'lips, mouth'
ittáhchi'	'shoulder'
iyyi'	'foot, leg'
iyyop	'daughter's husband or niece's husband'
nakfish	'younger sibling [of the same sex]'
nakshoka'	'face'
nishkin	'eye'
noshkóbo'	'head'
notakfish	'beard, moustache'
obaalaka'	'behind, posterior'
olbal	'behind'
oshi'	'son'
oshi' tiik	'daughter'
pishókchi'	'milk'
-tikba'	'older brother or sister'
tiik	'sister [of a man]'
tokchi'	'saliva'

Although the following items fall into the semantic category of kinship terms and body parts, they nevertheless take III agreement:

(10)

afo'	'grandfather [vocative]'[7]
-aalak	'sister's husband'
-aalakósi'	'wife's brother' (variant and vocative *lakos*)
-anni'	'older brother [of a man], older sister [of a woman]'
-hokni'	'paternal aunt'
kanóomi'	'kinsman, relative'
-ki'	'father'
-lakos ohooyo'	'wife's sister'
-nákfi'	'brother [of a woman]'
noti'	'tooth'
-oksini'	'clitoris'
-osáana'	'forehead'
-oshi'	'mother's brother'
shokáni'	'elbow'
talop	'testicle'
tashka'	'family'

Two of the kinship terms listed above have irregular first person singular forms, though the regular forms are also frequently used. They are:

---

7. As mentioned in chapter 2, rhythmic lengthening exceptionally applies in the possessive forms.

(11)   *hashki'/sashki'*   'my mother'
       happókni'/sappókni'   'my grandmother'

Nicklas (1974:46) lists these forms as *ashki* and *appókni* respectively, suggesting that there may be some dialect variation in the presence of initial *h*.[8]

III marking for possessives is far more common, and there is evidence from loans that it is the productive agreement affix. In the following example, a speaker used a III affix on the English word 'nose', even though the corresponding Choctaw word requires a II prefix:

(12)   *Chi̱-nose . waypa-h!*
       2sIII-nose wipe-TNS
       'Wipe your nose!'

(13)   *chi-bishákni'*
       2sII-nose
       'your nose'

The more productive status of III prefixes is probably related to the observation by R. S. Williams (1995:68) that younger speakers of Oklahoma Choctaw show tendencies towards leveling the possessive paradigm to favor III prefixes over II prefixes.

The nouns in table 4.2 (below) show variation between II and III marking for possessor (Nicklas 1974:48; Broadwell 1987b); they are shown with their alternative first person possessive forms. In some cases the form of the noun has an extra initial geminate consonant in the form with II possession. Section 4.3 discusses the problematic status of this initial consonant.

4.2.2. Obligatory possession

Certain nouns, such as body parts and relatives, only exist in relationship to a particular possessor. A consequence of this is that many nouns in Choctaw cannot be used without some sort of possessive prefix. Consider the following examples:

(14a)   *am-o̱shi'*
        'my mother's brother'

(14b)   *im-o̱shi'*
        'his/her mother's brother'

(14c)   *?*o̱shi'*
        'mother's brother'

---

8. Hitchiti also has an irregular first person form for 'my mother', *ahki* (cf. *iki* 'his mother'). (Munro et al. 1992).

Table 4.2. Nouns with variation between II and III possessor marking

aayokla'	'kinsman, relation'	*(siaayokla'/amaayokla')*
chǫkash	'heart'	*(sahchǫkash/achǫkash)*[9]
fóni'	'bone'	*(sahfóni'/afóni')*
hákshop	'skin,bark'	*sahakshop/ahakshop)*
hokni'	'father's sister'	*(sahokni'/ahokni')*
ippókni'/-pokni'	'grandmother'	*sappókni'/apókni'*
issǫlash	'tongue'	*(sassǫlash/amissǫlash)*
issalakha'/-salakha'	'liver'	*(sassalakha'/asalakha')*
issish	'blood'	*(sassish/amissish)*
lapish	'horn'	*(salapish/alapish)*[10]
shiloppa'	'lung'	*(sashshiloppa'/ashiloppa')*
tikchi'	'wife'	*(sattikchi'/atikchi')*

We can refer to such nouns as obligatorily possessed. In Choctaw, I assume that such nouns can take either II or III agreement. However, the third person II agreement is null:

(15a) *sa-nakfish*
       'my younger brother' (male speaker)

(15b) *chi-nakfish*
       'your younger brother' (male addressee)

(15c) *Ø-nakfish*
       'his younger brother'

Thus for obligatorily possessed nouns with II agreement, we do find the noun stem occurring with no overt prefix. This differs from the situation with obligatorily possessed nouns with III agreement, in which the noun stem never occurs alone.

---

9. Byington (1915:111) lists *ichǫkash*; Nicklas (1974:45) has *-hchǫkash*.

10. First person inalienable forms of 'horn' will, of course, be unusual. However, the distinction between II and III possession can be seen in a phrase like 'the cow's horn', where speakers vary between *waak lapish* and *waak ilapish*.

Such obligatorily possessed nouns occasionally pose a problem of analysis. Column A of table 4.3 shows the noun stems according to Nicklas (1974:46), while column B shows the analysis followed here.

Table 4.3. Obligatorily possessed nouns

A	B	Gloss
maafo'	*-afo'*	'grandfather'
moshi'	*-oshi'*	'mother's brother'
maalak	*-aalak*	'sister's husband'
maalakosi'	*-aalakosi'*	'wife's brother'*
manni'	*-anni'*	'older same sex sibling'†

* Nicklas glosses this word 'spouse's husband', but for speakers I consulted it can only mean 'wife's brother' and not 'husband's brother.' Both *-osi'* and *-oshi'* are diminutives in Choctaw; the difference between my recording and that of Nicklas suggests some dialect variation in the form of this word.

† Nicklas notes that some speakers have a possessive form *samanni'*. I have only recorded *amanni'*, and this appears to be the more conservative form historically (cf. Byington 1915:190). For speakers who say *samanni'*, it seems correct to say that they have reanalysed the stem as *-manni'*.

Nicklas argues that while these nouns historically had underlying forms like those in column B, they have been reanalysed in modern Choctaw as having the underlying forms in column A.

These nouns have paradigms like the following:

(16a) *am-oshi'*
      'my mother's brother'

(16b) *chim-oshi'*
      'your mother's brother'

(16c) *im-oshi'*
      'his/her/their mother's brother'

(16d) *pim-oshi'*
      'our mother's brother'

(16e) *hachim-oshi'*
      'y'all's mother's brother'

The problem arises in elicitation settings when speakers are asked for the noun stems corresponding to an unpossessed 'mother's brother'. Sometimes speakers do produce forms like *moshi'* when asked. However, there is little evidence that these forms have any real currency in the language. They do not seem to appear in texts, and they may be artifacts of the elicitation context.

An additional problem posed by this analysis is that it requires alterations to the set of possessive prefixes, as shown below:

(17a) *a-moshi'*
       'my mother's brother'

(17b) *chi-moshi'*
       'your mother's brother'

(17c) *i-moshi'*
       'his/her/their brother'

What are *a-* and *i-* in this paradigm?

Nicklas suggests that they are variants of the regular set of II prefixes. Let us call them set IIb prefixes for clarity, as in table 4.4. A problem for this analysis is that IIb prefixes, if they exist, have an extremely limited distribution. In Nicklas's account there are only seven nouns that take such prefixes. I therefore prefer the analysis sketched in this chapter which treats them as nouns taking obligatory III possession.

Table 4.4. Possession prefixes according to Nicklas (1974)

SET	II	IIB	III
1S	*sa-*	*a-*	*am-*
2S	*chi-*	*chi-*	*chim-*
3S	∅	*i-*	*im-*

4.3. Nouns with the prefix *iC-*

A problem for the analysis of noun prefixes arises with the following group of nouns (Nicklas 1974:45, Broadwell 1987b):

(18) *ippókni'*   'grandmother'
      ittahchi'   'shoulder'
      innoti'   'tooth'
      innali'   'back'
      ippashi'   'hair (of the head)'
      ittakha'   'mouth'
      ittissópi'   'cheek'
      ikkíshi'   'chest'
      ittakóbba'   'stomach (of an animal)'
      ippochi'   'father-in-law'
      ittikchi'   'wife'

Many or most of these nouns also appear without the initial *iC-*, as in the following examples:

(19)   *pókni'*   'grandmother'
       noti'   'tooth'
       nali'   'back'
       p̲ashi'   'hair'
       tikchi'   'wife'

The difference between the two forms is difficult to determine. It is not related to whether the noun is possessed or not. Ulrich (1986:244) notes that all of the following forms are acceptable, though (20a) and (21a) were preferable:

(20a) *cho̲kash*   'hearts'

(20b) *ichcho̲kash*   'hearts'

(21a) *waak ichcho̲kash*   'beef hearts'

(21b) *waak cho̲kash*   'beef hearts'

Ulrich suggests that the variation is phonological in origin. Choctaw has an optional rule of initial *i* -deletion, which he formulates (approximately) as follows:

(22) $i \rightarrow \emptyset$ / [___

    Condition: Application does not strand melodic material

This is followed by a rule of Stray Erasure, which deletes unsyllabified material. Thus Ulrich suggests the following phonological derivation for forms like those in (19):

(23)   *ippókni'*   Underlying Representation
       ppókni'   Initial *i* -deletion
       pókni'   Stray Erasure

Ulrich notes that similar variation occurs in nouns like *issíto'/síto'* 'pumpkin', where it is independent of whether the noun is possessed or not.

However, positing this phonological rule does not explain why a large number of Choctaw body parts and kinship terms happen to begin with *iC-*. Ulrich suggests that

> one might posit a non-productive prefix of the shape iC-, whose empty C-slot would be filled by leftward spread from the root-initial consonant. This prefix might originally have indicated a possessor, or it might have simply meant "body part." That is, it might or might not have been omissible when the body part was thought of as unpossessed. The current situation can be analyzed as involving either an optional iC- which is losing its meaning of possession, or a non-optional iC- whose deletion by independently motivated rules is being reanalyzed as indicating an unpossessed body part. [1986:245]

The identity of this *iC*- prefix is still uncertain. However, it is interesting to note that other Muskogean languages show similar behavior.

Koasati has a number of body part and kinship terms that contain an initial *iC*- (Kimball 1991:436–37):

(24)   *iccomí*   'anus'
       ittipí   'shoulder joint'
       ittilhí   'eye'
       ittolhpí   'knee *innoti*   'tooth'
       ippokí   'daughter-in-law'

Kimball notes that "in words of three syllables or longer in which the initial syllable is of the shape V or VC, apheresis can take place, in which only the vowel, or the vowel and consonant both are deleted. Thus doublets occur such as *ataffó/taffó* 'grasshopper' and *iccomí/commí* 'anus'" (1991:36). From Kimball's description, the facts sound remarkably like those in Choctaw.

Further complications arise when we attempt to determine the underlying form of this prefix. Ulrich suggests *iC*-, but Nicklas (1974:45) cites some data which is problematic for this assumption. According to Nicklas, some speakers have a prefix *ih*- when the noun stem begins with a fricative:

(25)   *ihfóni'*   'bone'
       ihshakba'   'arm'
       ihhatip   'hip'
       ihshakha'   'top of the back across the shoulders'
       ihhayínchi'   'kidney'
       ihhanaali'   'leg'

The words above show the same alternations as those just discussed:

(26)   *hanaali'*   'leg'
       fóni'   'bone'

According to Nicklas, these forms show assimilation of *h* to the following consonant in some dialects:

(27)   *iffóni'*   'bone'
       ishshakba'   'arm'

Nicklas (1984:45) says "/h/ may assimilate to the following fricative or sibilant. This happens in all words in some dialects. In one dialect, it is optional in [the words above], but occurs in *chchoshshak* 'back of the head', *-ssonlash* 'tongue', *ssish* 'blood', *shshilombish* 'soul', and *ssanáhchi* 'wing'" (1974:45).

Nicklas speculates that the underlying form of the prefix might be *il*-, with the following rules:

(28) $l \rightarrow$ C / ___   C
     [αF]   [αF]
               [-cont]

(29) $l \rightarrow h$ / ___   C
               [+ cont]

Since *l* never surfaces, this is a quite abstract analysis. Ulrich (1986:296) correctly notes that neither of the rules above is independently motivated, and I agree that there is little merit in positing *il-* as the underlying form of this morpheme.

However, these forms raise problems for *ih-* as an underlying form as well. If we take *ih-* as the underlying form, then we are forced to posit the following rule, which is otherwise unmotivated in Choctaw phonology:

(30) $h \rightarrow$ C $\emptyset$ ___
     [α F]   [α F]
              [-cont]

However, there are many words that are counterexamples to such a rule:

(31) *tóhbi'*   'white'
     Chahta'   'Choctaw'
     ahnih   'to think'

There might be fewer problems with the reverse rule:

(32) C $\rightarrow h$ / ___ C (optional)
     [αF]   [αF]
            [+cont]

That is, a geminate fricative degeminates to *hC*.

The problem of the meaning and underlying representation of this element is best regarded as still open.

5. Noun phrases: Order, case marking, and determiners

5.1. Order within the noun phrase

Within the noun phrase (NP), the order of constituents is:

(1)   (possessor NP/complement NP) + noun + (quantifier, adjective) + (determiner) + (case-marker)

The following examples show nouns with preceding possessors:

(2)   *Ishki' i̱-chokka-yo̱   ishi-t   ona-hma̱, . . .*
       mother III-house-FOC:AC take-PART arrive-when:DS
       'When he took her to his mother's house . . .'

(3)   *John im-ofi-it   homma-h.*
       John III-dog-NM red-TNS
       'John's dog is red.'

The agreement morphology that possessors trigger on the following noun is discussed in chapter 4.

As examples (2) and (3) show, possessor NPs typically show no overt case marking. Accusative case marking is also sometimes found on possessor NPs, typically when the possessor is focussed, as discussed in section 5.2.1.

It is ungrammatical for a possessor NP to follow the possessed noun:

(4a)   *Bonnie   i̱-nákfi-it   chaaha-h.*
       Bonnie   III-brother-NM tall-TNS
       'Bonnie's brother is tall.'

(4b)   **I̱-nákfi-it   Bonnie chaaha-h.*
       III-brother-nm Bonnie tall-TNS

(4c)   **I̱-nákfi'   Bonnie-at   chaaha-h.*
       III-brother Bonnie-NM tall-TNS

A small number of nouns may appear with a preceding NP complement. *Holbatoba'* 'picture' is one such noun. For this noun, an NP complement can be distinguished from an NP possessor by the agreement morphology that appears on the head noun:

(5)   *John hólbatóba' pí̱sa-li-tok.*   (NP complement)
       John picture   see:N-1SI-PT
       'I saw a picture of John.'

64

(6)   *John i̱-hólbatóba' pi̱sa-li-tok.*   (NP possessor)
       John III-picture   see:N-1sI-PT
       'I saw John's picture (i.e., the picture that belongs to John).'

When a nonpronominal NP appears as complement to a noun, there is no agreement morphology present, as seen in example (5). A possessor NP, however, triggers the prefix *i̱-*, as shown in (6).

When a NP complement is pronominal, a II prefix appears on the head noun. A NP possessor, however, triggers III agreement:

(7)   *John-at   sa-hólbatóba' pi̱sa-tok.*   (pronominal complement)
       John-NM   1sII-picture   see:N-PT
       'John saw a picture of me.'

(8)   *John-at   a̱-hólbatóba' pi̱sa-tok.*   (pronominal possessor)
       John-NM   1sIII-picture see:N-PT
       'John saw my picture.'

The contrast between (7) and (8) is parallel to a more widespread contrast between alienable and inalienable possession discussed in chapter 4, and NP complements show the agreement typical of inalienable possession.

It is unclear whether NP possessors and NP complements occupy different positions within the noun phrase. The clearest evidence would come from examples that contain both kinds of phrases, but these turn out to be ungrammatical in Choctaw:

(9)   **John Mary hólbatóba' pi̱sa-li-tok.*
       John   Mary   picture   see:N-1sI-PT
       ('I saw John's picture of Mary.')[1]

The equivalents to English noun phrases like (9) require a relative clause, as in the following example:

(10)   *Mary-at   [John-at hólbatóba' aa-hobaachi-tok-ma̱]*
       Mary-NM   John-NM picture   LOC-draw-PT-DS
       ik-ayoppáach-o-tok.
       N-like:L-NEG-PT
       'Mary didn't like the picture of her that John drew.'

The ungrammaticality of examples like (9) may indicate that possessors and NP complements do in fact occur in the same phrase structure position.

Another type of noun complement appears when the measure nouns *alhiiha'* and *yoomi'*, both meaning 'group (of animates)', take a second noun as their complement:

---

1. There is an irrelevant reading in which this is grammatical, meaning 'I saw a picture of John and Mary.'

(11) *Issi' alhiiha-mat ano'.*
      deer group-D:NM mine
      'That bunch of deer is mine.'

The equivalents of adjectives and quantifiers follow the noun. As discussed in chapter 14, it is probably best to treat adjectives and quantifiers as stative verbs, and the following examples as internally headed relative clauses :

(12) *Himmona-ka ohooyo' oshta-h-oosh   hilha-t   ilhkoli-sh*
      once-DS   woman four-TNS-FOC:NM dance-PART go:PL-PART:SS
      ittanohówa-ttook miyah.
      walk:PL:HN-DPAST HSAY
      'Once upon a time, four women were walking to a dance.'

(13) *Chokka' bika-h-o   áyyaasha-h.*
      house   both-TNS-FOC:AC live:Y:PL-TNS
      'They live in both houses.'

(14) *Ofi' sipókni' yamm-at achokma-h.*
      dog old   that-NM good-TNS
      'That old dog is good.'

Choctaw speakers prefer not to use both an adjective and a quantifier within the same NP. Constructed examples of this sort were judged acceptable, if a bit odd. There was some preference for the adjective before the quantifier:

(15a) ?*Ofi' hochiito-'   tóchchiina-' a-máya-h.*
      dog   big:PL-NML three-NML   1PIII-exist:PL-TNS
      'I have three big dogs.'

(15b) ??*Ofi' tóchchiina-' hochiito-'   a-máya-h.*
      dog   three-NML   big:PL-NML 1PIII-exist:PL-TNS
      'I have three big dogs.'

However, more natural than either of these alternatives is one in which there is an additional clause:

(16) *An-ato ofi' hochiito-'   a-máya-h   anóti' tóchchiina-h.*
      I-NM2 dog big:PL-NML 1sIII-exist:PL-TNS and   three-TNS
      'I have big dogs, and there are three of them.'

It is possible that the peculiarity of examples in (15a)–(15b) is due to the fact that they involve relative clauses, so that the English translation is more literally 'I have dogs which are big, which are three', with one relative clause inside the other.

   Most determiners in Choctaw are suffixes to the noun phrase, and are discussed in section 2.3.2 below.

In addition to the suffixal forms of the demonstratives, there are also independent forms *yamma* 'that', and *ilappa* 'this'.[2] The independent demonstratives are occasionally used with a noun phrase, but are most frequently found when a demonstrative is used as an independent pronoun.

(17) Yamma iit   *am-a-h!*
      DEM   toward 1sIII-give-TNS
      'Give that to me!'

Within the noun phrase, determiners are the last items before the case marker:

(18) *Ofi' sipókni' yamm-at achokma-h.*
      dog old   that-NM   good-TNS
      'That old dog is good.'

A apparent variant of the determiner *yamma* serves as a vocative in older styles of Choctaw. Mrs. Edith Gem pronounces this as *ma'*, with final glottal stop. It is thus distinguished in her speech from the determiner, which does not end in glottal stop. It is not clear whether the vocative and demonstrative functions of the determiner have distinct pronunciations for all speakers.

(19) <Hatak okishko shali hvchia ma!>
      Hattak ok-íshko-'   *shahli hachi-ya-h ma'!*
      man   water-drink-NML exceed 2PII-be-TNS VOC
      'Oh, ye drunkards!' (Byington 1827:57)

This only seems to persist in a few fixed phrases, such as *Chiisas ma'!* 'Oh, Jesus!' for modern speakers, and does not seem to be used productively.

(20) *Chiisas ma'!*
      Jesus   VOC
      'Oh, Jesus!'

(21) *?John ma'!
      John VOC
      ('Oh, John!')

There are a few isolated occurrences of demonstratives in other than final position. The temporal demonstrative *himak* 'this (temporal)' regularly precedes the noun.

---

2. There are variant forms for the independent demonstratives in some dialects, including *yappa* 'this' and *ilamma* 'that'. In Chickasaw, there are no suffixal forms of the demonstratives, only independent ones.

(22) *himak nittak*
    this   day
    'today'

(23) *himak ninak*
    this   night
    'tonight'

In the Choctaw Bible, *mih* 'same' also precedes temporal nouns:

(24) <Micha mih ninak a̱ i̱ki ya̱ oka pa̱ki ipetʋt okla tok>
    Micha mih ninak-a̱ i̱-ki-ya̱   oka' pa̱kki' ipiita-tokla-ttook.
    and:SS same night-AC III-father-AC water grape gave-DU-DPAST
    'And on the same night, they gave their father wine to drink.' (Gen.
    19:33)

However, speakers I consulted did not recognize this use of *mih*.

    The following example seems to show *ma* 'that' in a position preceding the noun:

(25) *Ma ninak, ik-oklhilúk-ok-i̱sha-h-o̱* . . .
    DEM night N-dark:L-NEG-yet-TNS-PART:DS
    'That night, when it wasn't dark yet . . .' (T1:16)

Although this order appears in one text, I was unable to confirm this example with other speakers, suggesting that there may be some error here.

5.2. Case markers

5.2.1. Introduction

There are two overt cases in Choctaw: nominative and accusative. Surface structure subjects receive nominative case, and other arguments of the verb optionally receive accusative case, as in the following example:

(26) *Ópah tíkchi-it alla(-ya̱) i̱-pa̱ya-ttook.* ·
    owl   wife-NM child(-AC) III-call-DPAST
    'The owl's wife called the children.'

Nonsubject nouns frequently appear with no overt case marking. This is true for objects (27) and possessors (28):

(27) *John-at Oklahoma iya-ttook.*
    John-NM Oklahoma go-DPAST
    'John went to Oklahoma.'

(28) *John im-ofi-it   illi-tok.*
    John III-dog-NM die-PT
    'John's dog died.'

Possessives may also receive overt accusative case, but this is far less common. Accusative is best in such cases if the possessor is focussed in some way.

(29) *Katah-o̱*   *im-ofi-it*   *illi-h?*
     who-PART:AC III-dog-NM die-TNS
     'Whose dog died?'

(30) *An-ako̱*   *a̱-katos-aash*   *illi-tok, Pam-ano kiiyo-h.*
     I-CON:AC 1sIII-cat-PREV die-PT   Pam-AC2 NEG-TNS
     '*My* cat died; Pam's didn't.'

(31) <Haknip a̱ i pʊla hʊt nishkin ak oke>.
     Haknip-a̱ i̱-palah-at   nishkin-ak-okii.
     flesh-AC   III-light-NM eye-OBL-indeed
     'The light of the body is the eye.' (Matt. 6:2)

NPs are never overtly marked for case in at least three contexts: in certain idiomatic insults (32); in predicate nominal positions (33); and in elliptical answers to questions as in answer (iii) in (34).

(32) *Ishkish(*-at/*-a̱) losa-h!*
     buttocks(-NM/AC) black-TNS
     'Black ass!'

(33) *Pam-at holisso=pisáachi'(*-at/*-a̱).*
     Pam-NM teacher(-NM/AC)
     'Pam is a teacher.'

(34) Q: *Kata-sh*   *apa-tok?*
        who-PART:NM eat-PT
        'Who ate it?'

     A: (i)   *John-at apa-tok.*
               John-NM eat-PT
               'John ate it.'
          (ii)   *John-ak   aa-tok.*
               John-OBL be-PT
               'It was John.'
          (iii) *John.*
               John
               'John.'
          (iv)   **John-at*
               John-NM
               ('John [nominative].')

There are several morphological variants of the case markers, discussed in the following sections.

5.2.1.1. -*at* and -*a̱*

The most neutral case endings are -*at* (nominative) and -*a̱* (accusative).[3]
After a noun ending in a glottal stop, there are three options: the glottal
stop is deleted and epenthetic *y* is added (35a); the glottal stop deletes
and the initial vowel of the case marker assimilates to the preceding
vowel (35b); or the case marker is added to the noun with no phonological
change (35c).[4]

(35a) *ofi-yat*
       dog-NM
       'dog (nom.)'

(35b) *ofi-it*[5]
       dog-NM

(35c) *ofi'-at*
       dog-NM

Below are some textual examples of NPs with the neutral nominative
and accusative markers.

(36) *Chókfi-yat   iit   taloowa-hma̱, okla-hilha-ttook.*
      rabbit-NM toward sing-when:DS PLUR-dance-DPAST
      'When Rabbit sang, they danced.' (T3:10)

(37) *Shaki̱li-it   i̱-yoppa-tok.*
      grasshopper-NM III-laugh-PT
      'The grasshopper laughed at them.' (T2:6)

(38) *Makaatokoosh ihasi̱bis-ma̱ takaachi-ttook miyah.*
      and:then:SS tail-D:AC hang-DPAST HSAY
      'And then he hung it on his tail, they say.' (T3:25)

Overt accusative marking also occurs on some temporal adjuncts:

(39) <Himak a̱ ish ia cha, Amalek a̱ issot ish kanchashke . . .>
      Himak-a̱ ish-iiya-cha Amalek-a̱   isso-t   ish-kanch-ashkii . . .
      now-AC 2SI-go:L-SS Amalek-AC hit-PART 2SI-completely-EXHORT
      'Go now and smite Amalek (completely).' (1 Sam. 15.3)

There is also another set of case markers, which is discussed in the
following section.

---

3. In section 5.2.4 below, I argue against the hypothesis that the case markers
are -*t* and -*n*, preceded by a morpheme -*a*-.
4. This is the option that is most frequent in the speech of Mr. Henry Willis, but
it does not seem to be possible for all varieties of Choctaw. Ulrich (1986) discusses only
the first two options.
5. Nicklas (1974) generally writes cases of this sort *ofi't*, which seems to imply a
short vowel (see, e.g., Nicklas 1974:190). However, the vowel is long for all speakers
I have consulted.

5.2.1.2. -*ato* and -*ano*

Case markers -*ato* (nominative) and -*ano* (accusative) are glossed 'NM2' and 'AC2' respectively, and are used when the noun phrase bears contrastive focus.[6] They differ phonologically from the unmarked nominative and accusative in the following way. When they are suffixed to a noun ending in a glottal stop, the glottal stop and the initial vowel of the case marker are deleted.[7] In (40), the noun *tikchi'* 'wife' plus the accusative case marker -*ano* combine to yield *tikchino*.

(40) *Illĭpa' ilaap-ill-aash   áapa-cha alla' hicha*
      food   self-alone-PREV eat:L-SS child and
      tĭkchi-no   ik-ipĭit-o-ttook.
      wife-AC2 N-feed:L-NEG-DPAST
      'He ate the food by himself and didn't feed his wife and children.'

(41) *Ópah tĭkchi' hicha alla-to   chonna-h-ookako̲*
      owl   wife   and   child-NM2 skinny-TNS-but:DS
      i̲-háttak-ato   niya-ttook.
      III-man-NM2 fat-DPAST
      'The owl's wife and children were skinny, but her husband was fat.'

These case markers most commonly appear on an NP which is being contrasted with some preceding NP. However, as (41) shows, -*ato* and -*ano* sometimes occur on both the contrastive NP and the NP with which it is contrasted. These examples also show that case markers follow the NP as a whole, and that the material preceding the case marker may consist of coordinated NPs, as in (40).

5.2.1.3. -*kia* 'too'

Though -*kia* 'too' is not a case marker, strictly speaking, it is nevertheless in complementary distribution with case marking. It occurs on NPs that are compared to a preceding NP. The suffix -*kia* is nearly always preceded by the oblique determiner -*ak*, discussed in the next section.

(42) *John-at tolobli-kma̲ an-ak-kia tolobli-h.*
      John-NM jump-IRR:DS I-OBL-too jump-TNS
      'John jumped and I did too.'

---

6. Nicklas (1974:97) and Davies (1981:24) call this the emphatic article and the emphatic nominal construction, respectively.

7. This phonological difference shows that these endings are not synchronically analyzable as the neutral nominative and accusative endings plus some element *o*, (Nicklas 1974:97; Davies 1981:24). However, given their similarity to the neutral case markers, and the existence of some independent evidence from the verb morphology for a morpheme *o*, it still seems likely that there is a diachronic connection.

Since -*kia* is in complementary distribution with case, it follows that NPs which have the -*kia* suffix may not be additionally marked nominative or accusative.

(43)   *John-at   tolobli-kma̱   hattak-ak-kia(*-at) tolobli-h*
       John-NM jump-IRR:DS man-OBL-too(-NM)   jump-TNS
       ('John jumped and the man did too.')

Since nominative case is otherwise obligatory for subjects, the fact that it does not occur here shows that the -*kia* suffix displaces the nominative.

The frequent occurrence of -*ak* before -*kia* suggests -*akkia* as a possible analysis. However, there is evidence against this analysis from relative clauses, where -*kia* may occur without a preceding -*ak*:

(44)   <. . . nan ʋlhtoka, ʋhleha fehna atuk kia yoshublicha hi oke.>
       . . . *na̱n-alhtóka-' alhiiha' fiihna-h   aa-tok-kia*
       thing-choose-NML group   very-TNS be-PT-too
       yoshoblich-ahii-okii.
       deceive-IRR-indeed
       'He will even deceive the very chosen.' (Matt. 24:24)

The suffix -*kia* on noun phrases also occurs following the indefinite wh-expressions *na̱na* and *ka̱na* (see chapter 7) to express the notion 'any X' and 'anyone' (or 'no X' and 'no one' when the verb is negative) as in the following examples:

(45)   <Ushi ya̱ hatak na̱na kia ik ithano ho̱>
       Oshi-ya̱ hattak na̱na-kia   ik-itháan-o-h-o̱
       son-AC   man   something-too N-know:L-NEG-TNS-PART:DS
       'no man knoweth the Son' (Matt. 11:27)

(46)   <Kʋna kia apehlichika isht anumpa ha̱ haklo cha . . .>
       Ka̱na-kia   apihlichúika' isht-anópah-a̱
       someone-too kingdom   INSTR-word-AC
       háaklo-cha . . .
       hear:L-SS
       'Anyone who hears the word of the kingdom . . .' (Matt. 13:19)

Following *achaffa* 'one', -*kia* means something like 'even':

(47)   *achʋfa kia ik hlakofecho ki tok*
       achaffa-kia ik-lhakoffíich-o-kii-tok
       one-too   3N-spare:L-NEG-NEG-PT
       'he did not spare even one' (Josh. 10:28)

The suffix *-kia* may also occur on verbs, with the meaning 'but' (see chapter 16).

The suffixes *-at*, *-a̱*, *-ato*, *-ano*, and *-kia* may be preceded by various determiners. After a determiner, the unmarked accusative is indicated by nasalizing the final vowel (*-V̱*) and the unmarked nominative by adding *-sh* if the preceding vowel is *o* and *-t* otherwise.

This allomorphy of the nominative case is not found in Chickasaw, which has *-t* after all preceding vowels. Some early Choctaw sources also have instances of *-t* nominative after *o*, as in the following example:

(48) <*Yʋmmak ash ot moyuma kʋt nan isht ahanta shilombish ai okcha̱ya pisa he im ai ʋlhpiesa ʋhelha . . . ?*>
      Yammak-aash-oot   móyyoma-kat   na̱n-isht-aha̱tta
      that-afore-PART:NM all:y-COMP:SS thing-INSTR-be:HN
      shilo̱bish aay-okcha̱yah pis-ahii-h   im-alhpiisa alhiiha . . . ?
      spirit   LOC-save   try-IRR-TNS III-correct group
      '[Are they not] all ministering spirits . . . ?' (Heb. 1:14)

Similar occurrences of *-oot* after the morpheme *-aash* are quite common in the New Testament (e.g., Acts 7:1, 2, 9). However, there are also occurrences of *-aash-oosh* (e.g., Acts 7:19). At this point, it is unclear what determines the form of the focus nominative after the previous-mention marker in these early texts.

As mentioned above, the initial vowel of *-ato* and *-ano* is deleted following a noun that ends in a glottal stop.

5.2.2. What conditions the appearance of accusative case marking?

There is a strong tendency in texts for only one overt accusative NP per clause, and speakers judge constructed examples with more than one accusative NP to be of doubtful grammaticality:

(49) *Bill-a̱   ofi' im-aa-li-tok.*
      Bill-AC dog III-give-1SI-PT
      'I gave Bill a dog.'

(50) **? Bill-a̱ ofi-ya̱   im-aa-li-tok.*
      Bill-AC   dog-AC III-give-1SI-PT
      ('I gave Bill a dog.')

There is at least one instance of a clause with two marked accusatives in the Choctaw Bible, but the idiomaticity of this example may be suspect.

(51) <Yohmi ma Lewi ʋt chuka ya̱ Tama ya̱ pit hoyo cha . . .>
      Yohmima Liiwi-yat chokka-ya̱ Tama-ya̱ pit   hóoyo-cha . . .
      and:then David-NM   house-AC   Tamar-AC away send:L-SS
      'Then David sent (word) home to Tamar . . .' (2 Sam. 13:7)

In Chickasaw, Munro (1984, 1987bc) reports a similar restriction on the accusative: only one NP per clause may be overtly marked accusative. In Chickasaw, if there is more than one object, the case-marked NP must precede any non-case-marked NP.[8] However, this does not seem to be true for Choctaw:

(52)   *Bill ofi-ya̲   im-aa-li-tok.*
        Bill dog-AC III-give-1SI-PT
        'I gave the dog to Bill.'

While sentences like the one just cited are accepted as grammatical, however, they are volunteered far less frequently than paraphrases with the accusative-marked NP in VP-initial position (as in (49) above). This may be due to the fact that Choctaw speakers tend to interpret NPs with overt accusative marking as topical. Thus (49) is most acceptable if the dog is under discussion for some reason. However, topical NPs independently tend to occur towards the left periphery of the phrase they appear in, and so it is natural that topical NP objects should be both VP-initial and overtly case-marked.

Most object NPs are not overtly marked accusative, and the conditions under which overt accusatives appear are not well understood. Munro (1984b) suggests that Chickasaw accusative marking occurs most frequently when a verb has two overt objects. Most volunteered instances of the accusative in Choctaw also appear in translations of English sentences with two objects. Therefore, it seems likely that the presence of two overt objects influences accusative marking in Choctaw as well.

Movement is another factor that influences the occurrence of case-marking. Noun phrases that have been extraposed to the right or the left must appear with overt case marking:

(53a)   *John-a̲   Pam-at pi̲sa-tok.*
        John-AC Pam-NM see:N-PT
        'Pam saw John.'

(53b)   **John Pam-at pi̲sa-tok.*
        John   Pam-NM see:N-PT

Examination of Choctaw texts reveals some additional factors that seem to influence the occurrence of the accusative.[9]

---

8. Apparent exceptions arise when an object is right-extraposed. However, it is still true that of two preverbal nonsubjects, only the first may be overtly case-marked.

9. It is my impression that the translation of the Choctaw Bible has an unusually high proportion of overtly marked accusatives compared to native texts. For this reason, the following remarks about the distribution of overt accusative marking excludes the Bible translation.

In the texts I have collected, around 80 to 90 percent of objects have no overt case marking. Some examples of unmarked accusatives follow:

(54) *Hitokoosh chókfi' oklah falaama-tok.*
      and:then   rabbit PLUR meet-PT
      'And then they met a rabbit.' (T3:3)

(55) "... *Kanı̨na   ish-yohmi-ka̲   ak-ikháan-o-h,"   tı̃kchi-it*
      why   2SI-do:so-COMP:DS 1SN-know:L-NEG-TNS wife-NM
      ópah   im-aachi-ttook.
      owl   III-say-dpast
      '"... I don't know why you acted like this," his wife said to the owl.'
      (T1:51)

Of the instances in which accusative is overtly marked, about two-thirds are NPs with determiners:

(56) *Chókfi-yaash-oosh   anǫkafókka'-mak-aash-o̲*
      rabbit-PREV-PART:NM underwear-that-PREV-FOC:AC
      shaa-cha bahli-ttook   miyah.
      take-SS   run:off-DPAST HSAY
      'Rabbit took the previously mentioned underwear and ran off, they say.' (T3:24)

(57) *Makaatokoosh ihası̲bis-ma̲ takaachi-ttook miyah.*
      and:then   tail-D:AC   hand-DPAST   HSAY
      'And then he hung it on his tail, they say.' (T3:25)

The remaining cases are made up of nouns borrowed from English, perhaps to bring these words into conformity with Choctaw phonology:

(58) *Courses-a̲ ayyowa-t   a̲ya-li-h.*
      courses-AC pick:up-PART go:along-1SI-TNS
      'I went along, picking up courses.' (T10:16)

(59) *Mako̲   school-a̲ twelfth grade aa-tahli-li-tok.*
      and:then school-AC twelfth grade LOC-finish-1SI-PT
      'And then I finished the twelfth grade at school.' (T10:5)

(Example 59 also shows accusative marking on the first of two objects.)

Thus it seems that factors in Choctaw that may influence overt accusative marking include presence of multiple objects, extra position of an object, occurrence with a determiner, and nonnative phonology. Factors such as definiteness and animacy, which influence accusative marking in other languages, do not seem to have an effect in Choctaw.

5.2.3. Determiner suffixes

The affixes that I call determiners are markers of various sorts of discourse and deictic functions. Unlike English, more than one determiner may appear in an NP. Possible cooccurrences of determiners are discussed at the end of this section. Recall that the unmarked accusative form of these determiners is indicated by nasalizing the final vowel (-*V̨*). The unmarked nominative is indicated by adding -*sh* if the preceding vowel is *o* and -*t* otherwise.

5.2.3.1. -*akoo* 'contrastive' and -*oo* 'focus'

The determiner -*akoo* is used in contrastive contexts, and is more emphatic than -*ato* and -*ano*. English translations of sentences with -*akoo* often involve clefts.

(60) *Fóni-yako̲   pi̲sa-li-tok.*
      bone-CON:AC see:N-1SI-PT
      'It was the bone that I saw (not the rock).'

The determiner -*oo* is used on focused phrases.

(61) *Ishki'   i̲-chokka-yo̲   ishi-t   ona-hma̲, ...*
      mother III-house-FOC:AC take-PART arrive-when:DS
      'When he took her to his mother's house ...'

The contexts in which these endings appear without following case markers are actually rather few. However, the following examples show them followed by -*kia*.

(62) *John-at   niya-kma̲,   hattak-ak-kia yohmi-h.*
      John-NM fat-IRR:DS man-OBL-too   do:so-TNS
      'John is fat, and that man is too.'

(63) *..., hattak-akoo-kia yohmi-h.*
            man-CON-too   do:so-TNS
      '..., and that man [contrastive] is too.'

(64) *..., hattak-oo-kia yohmi-h.*
            man-FOC-too do:so-TNS
      '..., and that man [focus] is too.'

It is also possible to use these determiners followed by neither a case marker nor -*kia*, although this rare. Thus the following sentences are possible, if somewhat unusual:

(65) *?Hattak-akoo pi̲sa-li-tok.*
      man-CON   see:N-1SI-PT
      'It was the man that I saw.'

(66) ?*Hattak-oo písa-li-tok.*
      man-FOC   see:N-1SI-PT
      'I saw the man.'

I differ with Davies (1981:25–28) and Nicklas (1974:97–98) in treating -*akoo* and -*oo* as distinct from each other. In their approaches, -*akoo* is segmented as follows:

(67) *hattak-a-k-oo-sh*
      man-det-?-FOC-NOM
      'man (contrastive)'

Davies suggests that the additional *k* is epenthetic in this environment, while Nicklas suggests that the articles have special combining forms which appear when another morpheme follows. Davies does not specifically say that the focus morpheme must be preceded by his determiner -*a*-, but all of his examples include it.

The problem for these approaches is that both contrastive and focus markers can appear on the same nouns:

(68a) *hattak-oosh*
      'the man (focus)'

(68b) *hattak-akoosh*
      'the man (contrastive)'

This suggests that it is mistaken to try to propose that these morphemes are the same.

Nicklas (1974:200) suggests that -*oo* is associated with indefinites, while -*akoo* is used with definites. This appears to be incorrect. A number of the sentences cited in this section (64, 66, 68) show the use of -*oo* with definites.

5.2.3.2. -*ma(k)* 'that' and -*pa(k)* 'this'

The determiners -*ma(k)* and -*pa(k)* are 'that' and 'this' respectively. When they occur without the case markers, the final *k* is absent:

(69) *Ofi'-ma   ish-písa-h-o?*
      dog-DEM   2sI-see:N-TNS-Q
      'Did you see that dog?'

These determiners reduce to -*m*- and -*p*- before the case markers:

(70) *Holisso'-p-a   sa-banna-h.*
      book-DEM-AC 1sII-want-TNS
      'I want this book.'

(71) *Hattak-m-at   iya-tok.*
      man-DEM-NM go-PT
      'That man left.'

The frequent combinations of determiner with case marker are glossed as portmanteaux elsewhere in the grammar.

In Mississippi Choctaw, the short forms of the determiners are also found before the previous-mention marker *-aash*:

(72)   <Hash kanimmah másh oklah hachi lhákaffáchih kiyoh.>
       Hash-kanimma-h-m-aash oklah hachi-lhaakaff-aachi-kiiyo-h.
       2PI-which-TNS-DEM-PREV   PLUR   2PII-be:saved-IRR-NEG-TNS
       'None of you will be saved.' (Amos 4:2 CBTC)

The Oklahoma Choctaws I consulted would use the long form of the demonstrative in an example like this; that is, *hashkanimmahmakaash* instead of *hashkanimmahmaash*.

When a consonant-initial suffix follows the determiner, the final *k* appears:

(73)   *Hattak-mak-ba-at aya-h-o*   *písa-li-tok.*
       man-DEM-only-NM go:along-TNS-PART:DS   see:N-1SI-PT
       'I saw only that man going along.'

Unlike English *that*, Choctaw *-ma(k)* is compatible with proper nouns, possessed nouns, and personal pronouns:

(74)   *John-mat   aaittanáaha' o-biniili-tok.*
       John-D:NM church   on-sit-PT
       'John was at the church.'

(75)   <ym alak usi mʋt anta cho? Antʋshke.>
       Am-aalakosi-mat   átta-cho? Átta-shkii.
       1sIII-brother:in:law-D:NM be:N-Q   be:N-EXHORT
       'Is my brother-in-law there? Yes, he is.' (Speller 117)

(76)   <Hʋsh ihimashke: yohmikmak osh hʋchishno mʋt hʋsh habihina hi oke . . .>
       Hash-ihíma-shkii: yohmi-km-akoosh hachishno-mat
       2PI-III:give:HN-EXHORT   do-IRR-CON:SS   y'all-D:NM
       hash-habihín-ahii-okii-h.
       2PI-receive:HN-IRR-indeed-TNS
       'Give and you shall receive.' (Luke 6:38)

There is presumably some meaning associated with these determiners that is not reflected in the English translation, but it is not clear what that meaning is. These uses do not seem like the somewhat dismissive or pejorative use of *that* in English in examples like *that brother of mine* or *that John*.

In Broadwell (1990a), I treated sequences like *-mak* as composed of the demonstrative *-m-* plus oblique *-ak-*, but this position is not tenable, due to examples like the following:

(77) *Hattak-mak-ba-ak pisa-li-tok.*
man-DEM-only-OBL see:N-1SI-PT
'I saw only that man.'

The alternate segmentation of -*mak*- as bimorphemic leads to a segmentation like the following, in which one is forced to say that the oblique -*ak*- appears twice.

(78) *Hattak-m-ak-ba-ak   pisa-li-tok.*
MAN-DEM-OBL-only-OBL see:N-1SI-PT
'I saw only that man.'

For this reason, it seems best to recognize -*mak*- and -*pak*- as allomorphs of the demonstrative determiners.

5.2.3.3. -*ak* 'oblique'

The suffix -*ak* is a rare nominal ending in Choctaw which use is not well understood. It occurs most frequently on locative and temporal expressions, and is more frequent on interrogative phrases than on regular NPs. The following are examples:

(79) *Book Chito community-ak   aay-alhpowa-li-tok.*
creek big   community-OBL LOC-born-1SI-PT
'I was born in the Bogue Chitto [lit., "Big Creek"] community.'

(80) *Lynn-at panaklo-tok, 'Katomm-ak-ako atta-li-h?'*
Lynn-NM ask-PT   where-OBL-CON:AC be-1SI-TNS
'Lynn asked, "Where do I live?"'

(81) *Katiim-ak oba-tok-chi.*
when-OBL rain-PT-wonder
'I wonder when it rained.'

(82) *Bonnie i-nákfi'   katimm-ak-akoosh chaaha-h?*
Bonnie III-brother which-OBL-CON:NM tall-TNS
'Which of Bonnie's brothers is tall?'

Another context in which -*ak* frequently occurs is on the predicate nominal in copular constructions:

(83) *John-ak   si-ya-h.*
John-OBL 1SII-be-TNS
'I am John.'

(84) *Chito-mak   si-ya-h.*
big-DEM:OBL 1SII-be-TNS
'I am the big one.'

(85) <Nanta hosh shukhai a okpuni? Nashoba ak oke.>
Nata-h-oosh   shókha-ya okpani-h? Nashoba-yak Ø-okii.
what-TNS-PART:SS hog-AC   hurt-TNS wolf-OBL   COP-indeed
'What is it that injured the hogs?' 'It was a wolf.' (Speller 119)

Haag (1995:96) calls *-ak* a "definite determiner." It is true that NPs marked with *-ak-* are generally definite, but by itself this description does not account for the facts just discussed.

The suffix *-ak* is a more frequent nominal ending in Chickasaw (Munro 1987a), but its use is not fully understood in Chickasaw either.[10]

5.2.3.4. *-akhii* 'pejorative'

The suffix *-akhii* is a pejorative, and is relatively infrequent:

(86) *John-akhi̱   himmakma pisa-h   sanna-kiiyo-h.*
      John-PEJOR:AC again   see-TNS I:want-NEG-TNS
      'I never want to see that darned John again.'

(87) *Hattak-m-akhi̱   himmakma̱ pisa-h   sanna-kiiyo-h.*
      man-DEM-PEJOR:AC again   see-TNS I:want-NEG-TNS
      'I never want to see that darned man again.'

(88) *A̱-hattak-(ak)hii-to*[11]   *háksi-na   kanah-ato*
      1sIII-man-PEJOR-NM2 drunk:L-DS someone-NM2
      ilokka' showi̱-t   i̱-tahli-toko̱
      clothes take:off-PART III-complete-PT:DS
      hochoowa-kat innoti-it   chalhaakachi-h.
      cold-COMP:SS teeth-NM chatter-TNS
      'My darned husband got drunk and someone took all his clothes and his teeth were chattering from the cold.'

The following example shows that *-akhii* follows *-ook* 'comparison':

(89) <. . . isht-ishko ampo aiena ka anu̱kaka yak o̱ ti̱kba ish kashofi ha yo̱, paknaka yokak heto kashofa mak inlashke.>
      Isht-íshko-'   ápo' ayna-ka   ano̱kaka-yako̱
      INSTR-drink-NML plate and-COMP inside-CON:AC
      ish-kashoffi-h-ayo̱, paknaka-yook-akhii-to
      2sI-clean-TNS-?   outside-COM-PEJOR-NM2
      kashoofa-m-aki̱li-shkii.
      be:clean-DEM-indeed-exhort
      'Clean the inside of the cup and plate first, so that the outside will be clean.' (Matt. 23:26)

5.2.3.5. *-ook* 'comparison'

The determiner *-ook* is poorly understood, and I tentatively gloss it as 'comparison'. Byington (1870) labels it the 'contradistinctive'.[12] It appears to single out a specific NP for comparison with some other NP

---

10. Broadwell (1987a) contains some discussion of morphemes in other Muskogean languages which may be cognate to *-ak*.

11. The form recorded apparently contained a haplology. Other consultants rejected *a̱hattakhiito*.

12. Nicklas (1974:97) lists an article *-óoka*, which he glosses as 'as such', though he does not give any examples of it. Perhaps this is the same as the determiner *-ook* described here.

in the discourse. Often it corresponds to 'but' plus focal stress in the English translation.

There may be a connection with the complementizer -*ookakoo* 'but', discussed in chapter 16.

(90) *N̲a̲na hoochokma-ka̲   isht   iya-l-aachi-k   kiiyo-h-ookakoosh*
thing good:PL-COMP:AC INSTR go-1SI-IRR-TNS NEG-TNS-but:SS
ofi-hook-ano isht   iya-l-aachi̲-h.
dog-COMPAR-AC2 INSTR go-1SI-IRR-TNS
'I'm not gonna take anything good, but the dogs I'll take.'

(91) <Chin chukɐpanta hatak a̲ ish i̲ hullo cha, chin tʊnʊp okʊno ish i̲ nukkillashke.>
Chi̲-chokk-apa̲ta' hattak-a̲ ish-i̲-hóllo-cha,
2sIII-house-near man-AC 2sI-III-love:L-SS
chi̲-tannap-ook-ano   ish-i̲-nokkill-ashkii.
2sIII-enemy-COMPAR-AC2 2sI-III-hate-exhort
'Thou shalt love thy neighbor but hate thy enemy.' (Matt. 5:43)

(92) <Amba himak okla aiasha ilʊppak okʊno nantak o̲ itapesa chi̲ cho?>
Amba himak oklah   aay-asha ilappak-ook-ano
but   this   people LOC-be   this-COMPAR-AC2
na̲t-ak-o̲   itt-apiis-aachi̲-cho?
what-OBL-FOC:AC RCP-measure-IRR-ques
'But whereunto shall I liken this generation?' (Matt. 11:16)

5.2.3.6. -*ba* 'only'

The suffix -*ba* is generally translated as 'only', as in the following example:

(93) *John-ba   pi̲sa-li-tok.*
John-only see:N-1SI-PT
'I saw only *John.*'

Mr. Henry Willis remarked that this is a rather sarcastic sentence. The implication seems to be that it is obvious that John is the only person the speaker saw. Since it is obviously true, the fact that the speaker is saying it seems to imply that the listener is stupid for not knowing it.

When case-markers follow this determiner, the forms are -*baat* (nominative) and -*ba̲* (accusative):

(94) *Hattak-mak-ba-at áya-h-o̲   pi̲sa-li-tok.*
man-DEM-only-NM go:along-TNS-PART:DS see-1SI-PT
'I saw only that man going along.'

(95) *John-ba̲   pi̲sa-li-tok.*
John-only:AC see:N-1SI-PT
'I saw only John.'

The determiner -ba was also used in Choctaw arithmetic, as recorded in Byington (1915), functioning as the equivalent of 'times' in multiplication.[13]

(96)   <Tuklo bvt tuchinakmvt hanali.>
       Toklo-ba-at tóchchiina-kmat hánnali-h.
       two-only-NM three-IRR:SS   six-TNS
       'Two times three is six.' Byington (1915:86)

Byington (1915:86) suggests that -ba is contracted from the quantifier suffix -baano 'only, each, really', discussed in chapter 14.

5.2.3.7. -*makoo* and -*óhmakoo* 'too'

The suffixes -*makoo* and -*óhmakoo*, apparently identical in meaning, are difficult to gloss. They are often used in sentences that involve introducing a new NP that is parallel to some previously mentioned NP. Translations include 'too', 'either', and 'even'. The case marked forms are -*makoosh*, -*óhmakoosh* (nominative), and -*mako*, -*óhmako* (accusative). Some speakers appear to use variant forms -*ókmakoo*- and -*áhmakoo* instead of -*óhmakoo*-.

(97)   *A̱-nákfi'   achaffa-makoosh Florida wiha-t   iya-tok.*
       1sIII-brother one-too:NM   Florida move-SS go-PT
       'My other brother moved to Florida.'

(98)   *Chokka-makoosh ik-sam-iksho-h.*
       house-too:NM   N-1sIII-not:exist-TNS
       'I don't even have a house.'[14]

(99)   *John-at niya-ttook, Bill-óhmakoo.*
       John-NM fat-DPAST   Bill-too
       'John was fat, and Bill was too.'

(100) *Mexico-óhmako̱ ona-li-kiiyo-h.*
       Mexico-too:AC   arrive-1sI-NEG-TNS
       'I haven't even been to Mexico.'

(101) *John-at   shiapha'   i̱-chapoli-kmat*
       John-NM   huckleberry III-like-IRR:SS
       biyo̱kko-óhmako̱ i̱-chapoli-h.
       strawberry-too   III-like-TNS
       'John likes huckleberries, and he like strawberries too.'

Although it looks as if -*makoo* and -*óhmakoo* might contain the determiner -*mak*-, this possibility is ruled out by forms like the following:

---

13. Relatively few Choctaw speakers do mathematics using Choctaw, so a pattern like that seen in this example is rare. It is also possible that such examples were always of questionable idiomaticity, and are somewhat artificial Choctaw constructed for the needs of missionaries and educators.

14. Literally, 'A house does not exist to me.' See section 3.1.3.2.

(102)   *Hattak-pak-makọ ak-ikhaan-o-h.*
        man-DEM-too:AC   1SN-know:N-NEG
        'I don't even know this man.'

Some of the uses of *-makoo* and *-óhmakoo* on nouns seem related to the use of a related morpheme on verbs in the concessive (see chapter 16).[15]

5.2.4. Against *-a-* as a determiner

Some authors, including Nicklas (1974:200) and Davies (1981:18), have analysed the nominative and accusative endings *-at* and *-ạ* as composed of two elements, a general determiner-*a*- and a case-marking portion *-t*, *-n*.

There are two problems for this segmentation. First, *-a-* is not an optional part of the case markers. It must be present with a consonant-final stem:

(103a) *hattak-at*
        man-NM

(103b) **hattak-t*
        man-NM

The second problem with this segmentation is identifying a meaning for *-a-*. Nicklas suggests that it is a marker of definiteness in situations like the following:

(104)   *Ofi(-yạ) písa-li-tok.*
        dog-acc   see:N-1sI-PT
        'I saw the/a dog.'

According to Nicklas, in careful speech, the form with *-yạ* is definite, while the form without it is indefinite.

However, as Davies (1981:71) points out, this difference is not found in colloquial speech. My own consultants freely accept both definite and indefinite interpretations of NPs like *ofi'* and *ofi-yạ*. Note also that any contribution that a supposed *-a-* morpheme makes to the interpretation of the sentence is obscured by the cooccurrence of the case marker.

As I noted, the conditions under which an overt accusative appears are not well understood, but they may be sensitive to discourse notions

---

15. These morphemes might be grouped with the clausal determiners below, and the final *oo* analysed as an instance of the participial *-oo*. However, there are two problems with this alternative. First, it would imply that these morphemes are *-mak* and *-óhmak*, but these forms are never found without following *oo*. Second, NP + *makoo* is attested in word-final position, but I know of no cases in which the participial *-oo* appears word-finally.

like topic. Since definiteness is also sensitive to these notions, the definiteness effect that Nicklas describes may be due to case-marking, rather than to his proposed -a- morpheme.

However, Davies (1981:72) cites one form which does seem to argue for this analysis:

(105)   *Hattak-mat alla-ya   i̱-katos hottopali-tok.*
        man-D:NM   child-DET III-cat hurt-PT
        'That man hurt the child's cat.'

In this example, *alla-ya* appears to end in a non-case-marked determiner, arguing strongly that it is a separable morpheme. I have not encountered such a form myself and suspect that it has been wrongly recorded.

5.2.5. Clausal determiners

In addition to the determiners just identified, there is also a set of determinerlike elements that are phonologically attached to the last element of the NP. I call such elements clausal determiners. Careful examination reveals evidence for a null copula which appears between a NP and a clausal determiner.

The syntax of these phrases is comparable to English sentences like *It must be John I saw* or *It is certainly John I saw*. In Choctaw, however, the elements corresponding to *it* and *be/is* are null, giving a situation in which elements with meanings like 'certainly' and 'must' appear cliticized to the noun phrase. That is, Choctaw NPs bearing clausal determiners seem to be best analysed as clefted NPs followed by a null copula. The clausal determiner acts like a suffix on the copula, although it is phonologically attached to the NP.

Consider, for example, the clausal determiner -polla- 'must'. It appears phonologically attached to nouns in examples like the following:

(106)   *An-ak-polla-k-akoosh yamma*
        I-OBL-must-?-CON:NM that
        michi-l-aachi̱-k-ako̱ am-anooli-tok.
        do-1sI-IRR-COMP-DS 1sIII-tell-PT
        'They told me that *I* had to be the one to do that.'

There are several advantages to treating -polla- as suffixed to a null copula, rather than suffixed directly to the noun. That is, (106) is better analysed with a null copula and cliticization of the material after the copula to the preceding noun, as in (107):

(107)   *An-ak-∅-polla-k-akoosh   yamma*
        I-OBL-COP-must-COMP-CON:NM that
        michi-l-aachi̱-k-ako̱ am-anooli-tok.
        do-1sI-IRR-COMP-DS 1sIII-tell-PT
        'They told me that *I* had to be the one to do that.'

First, the clausal determiners also appear as adverbial suffixes on verbs.[16] The element -*polla*-, for example, is found in examples like the following:

(108) *Oba-polla-tok.*
     rain-must-PT
     'It must have rained.'

An analysis in terms of affixation to a null copula explains why the same morphemes appear in both positions.

Second, the morphology that follows the clausal determiners is best analysed as verbal morphology, not nominal morphology. Consider again (106) above, and note that the clausal determiner -*polla*- is followed by a morpheme -*k*-. In the analysis suggested here, this is the complementizer -*ka* as in (107) above. It is unclear what nominal affix the *k* found in this form could be. The only nominal morpheme consistent with the phonology is -*ak*- 'oblique'. But the oblique appears before the clausal determiner, and so the best analysis one can provide without a null copula is following:

(109)   *An-ak-polla-k-akoosh*   *yamma* *michi-l-aachi-k-ako*
       I-OBL-must-OBL-CON:NM that   do-1SI-IRR-COMP-DS
       am-anooli-tok.
       1sIII-tell-PT
       'They told me that *I* had to be the one to do it.'

In the noncopular analysis, one is forced to say that the oblique -*ak* shows up twice in this NP and that -*ak* may be ordered either before or after -*polla*. No other nominal suffixes are known to appear twice on the same noun.

A third argument in favor of the analysis with a null copula is that in such an analysis the -*ak* sequence preceding many clausal determiners can be treated as the oblique -*ak*. As discussed in section 5.2.3.3, -*ak* is very common on the predicate nominal in a copular construction. On the null copula analysis, the noun preceding a clausal determiner is a predicate nominal, so this is explained.

Finally, there are a few cases in which an overt copula appears before the clausal determiners:

(110)   <huchi haknip okuto ai ashuchika yak atuk pulla kak o illi hoke>
       hachi-haknip-ook-ato   *aay-ashshachika-yak*
       2PII-body-COMPAR-NM2 LOC-sin-OBL
       aa-tok-polla-k-ako   *illi-h-okii.*
       be-PT-because-COMP-CON:AC die-TNS-INDEED
       'your body is dead because of sin' (Lit., 'It was because of sin your body died.') (Rom. 8:10)

---

16. As discussed below, this is not true for -*aash* 'previous-mention', which shares some properties with the clear instances of clausal determiners.

Since overt copulas may appear after the oblique suffix and preceding the clausal determiners, it is not surprising that null copulas may appear in the same position.

Since the clausal determiners form a phonological word with the preceding item, rules of the phonology apply just as if the unit were a single word. For example, the rules affecting word-final glottal stop continue to apply before these enclitic clausal determiners, and -ma(k) continues to take its short form -m- before a vowel:

(111)   ofi'-∅-aash → ofiyaash
        dog-COP-PREV
        'the previously mentioned dog'

(112)   opya-m-∅-akịli-h-ọ
        evening-DEM-COP-EMPH-TNS-PART:AC
        'that very evening'

The determinerlike elements that are probably best treated through a copular analysis include (at least) -polla 'must, because', -akịli 'emphatic', -fiihna 'very, precisely', and -baano 'only'. It is less clear whether -aash 'previous-mention' should be included in this group.

5.2.5.1. -polla 'because'

The element -polla is generally glossed 'because' or 'must' when it appears in a noun phrase.

(113)   Ofi'-∅-polla-k-akọ   chókfi' apa-li-tok.
        dog COP-because-COMP-CON:AC rabbit eat-1sI-PT
        'Because of the dogs, I had rabbits to eat.'

(114)   Hachishno'-∅-polla-k-akọ,   oklah nayoppa-t   áyyaasha-h.
        y'all-COP-because-COMP-CON:AC PLUR happy-PART   be:PL-TNS
        'Because of y'all, they're happy.'

(115)   An-ak-∅-polla-k-akoosh   yamma
        I-OBL-COP-must-COMP-CON:NM   that
        michi-l-aachị-k-akọ am-anooli-tok.
        do-1sI-IRR-COMP-DS 1sIII-tell-PT
        'They told me that I had to be the one to do that.'

The suffix polla is normally followed by the sequence -kakọ, which I have treated as the complementizer -ka plus the contrastive accusative -akọ. The forms -polla-kat and -polla-ka were also judged acceptable, if somewhat unusual, by Henry Willis. He suggested the following sentences in which they might be used:

(116)   Ofi'-∅-polla-k-at   toba-ttook-oosh,   okcháya-h.
        dog-COP-because-COMP-NM   make-DPAST-part:SS   live:N-TNS
        'As the dogs were made, so they live.'

(117) *Ofi'-Ø-polla-k-a̲*   *hattak-at i̲pa-t*   *okcháya-h.*
dog-COP-because-COMP-AC man-NM   eat-PART live:N-TNS
'Because of dogs, man eats and lives.'

Noun phrases containing *-polla* also occur with some frequency in the Choctaw Bible:

(118) <yohmi kak o̲ hᴜchishno pulla kak o̲ pim ilhfiopak isht pi nukshopa fehna hatuk osh>
Yohmikako̲ hachishno'-Ø-polla-k-ako̲
therefore   you:PL-COP-because-OBL-CON:AC
pim-ilhfiyopak isht   pi-nokshopa-fiihna-haatokoosh
1PIII-breath   INSTR   1PII-fear-very-because
'therefore we were sore afraid of our lives because of you.' (Josh. 9:24)

As discussed above, in general /-polla/ is best treated as a suffix on a null copula, but in a few cases, the copula is overt:

(119) hᴜchi haknip okᴜto ai ashᴜchika yak atuk pulla kak o̲ illi hoke
Hachi-haknip-ook-ato   aay-ashshachika-yak
2pII-body-COMPAR-NM2 LOC-sin-OBL
aa-tok-polla-k-ako̲   illi-h-okii.
be-PT-because-COMP-CON:AC die-TNS-indeed
'Your body is dead because of sin' (Rom 8:10)

The use of *-polla* in NP should be compared with its use as an adverbial, discussed in chapter 18.

5.2.5.2. *-akị̲li* 'emphatic'

The determiner *-akị̲li* has a variety of emphatic uses. It is generally followed by the tense marker *-h* and the participial *-oo*. In NPs with a possessor, it corresponds to English 'X's own':

(120) *Hattak-mat im-ofi-Ø-akị̲li-h   abi-tok.*
man-D:NM III-dog-COP-EMPH-TNS kill-PT
'That man killed his own dog.'

(121) <anonti ilap noshkobo pa̲shi akinli ho̲ ishit kasholinchi mᴜt>
ano̲ti ilaap noshkóbo' pá̲shi-Ø-yakị̲li-h-o̲   isht
and   self   head   hair-COP-EMPH-TNS-PART:AC INSTR
kasholị́chi-hmat
wipe:N-when:SS
'and she wiped them with her own hair' (Luke 7:38)

For other noun phrases, *-akị̲li* often corresponds to English focal stress, implying something like 'that one and no other'.

(122) *opya-m-Ø-akị̲li-h-o̲*
evening-DEM-COP-EMPH-TNS-PART:AC
'that very evening'

(123)   *Oklah hachishn-Ø-aki̱li-h-oosh itti' hash-ahoochi-ch-ahi̱la-h.*
        PLUR   y'all-COP-EMPH-PART:SS   tree 2PI-find-CAUS-POT-TNS
        'Y'all should find a tree for yourselves.'

The determiner *-aki̱li-* should be compared with the adverbial *-aki̱li-* 'indeed' (chapter 18).

5.2.5.3. *-fi̱hna* 'exactly'

The element *-fi̱hna* is generally translated as 'exactly' or 'very', as in the following examples:

(124)   *Hattak-mak-Ø-fi̱hna-h-oosh   ala-h.*
        man-DEM-COP-very-TNS-PART:NM   come-TNS
        'That very man came.'

(125)   *Ikkó̱la-Ø-fi̱hna-h   chináshshik-at nalhlhi-tok.*
        neck-COP-exactly-TNS   wasp-NM   sting-PT
        'The wasp bit him right on the neck.'

(126)   <Yohmi ka ku̱na hosh nana ilu̱ppak fehna ka Klaist a̱ isht im antia
        hoku̱no>
        Yohmika kanah-oosh   ná̱na-h   ilappak-Ø-fi̱hna-ka
        and   someone-FOC:NM something-TNS this-COP-exactly-COMP
        Christ-a̱ isht   im-a̱tiya-h-oo-kano
        Christ-AC INSTR   III-serve-TNS-LINK-COMP:AC
        'And he who serves Christ in [exactly] these things' (Rom. 14:18)

The suffix *-fi̱hna* is generally followed by the tense marker *-h* plus the participial *-oo*, but it is also possible to use the complementizer *-ka*:

(127)   *nittak yamma-Ø-fi̱hna-ka*
        day   that-COP-exactly-COMP
        'on that particular day'

The use of *-fi̱hna* in NPs should be compared to its use as an adverbial in clauses (chapter 18).

5.2.5.4. *-baano* 'only'

The suffix *-baano* is generally translated by English 'only' and *-ak* 'oblique' frequently precedes *-baano*:

(128)   *Chishn-ak-Ø-baano-h-o̱   chi-pí̱sa-li-tok.*
        you-OBL-COP-only-TNS-PART:DS2SII-see:N-1SI-PT
        'I only saw you; The only one I saw was you.'

(129)   <Hatak u̱t pu̱ska yak bano ho̱ ai okcha̱ya he keyu.>
        Hattak-atpaska-yak-Ø-baano-h-o̱   aay-okchá̱y-ahii-kiiyo-h.
        man-NM bread-OBL-COP-only-TNS-PART:DS LOC-live:N-IRR-NEG-TNS
        'Man does not live by bread alone.' (Matt. 4:4)

In combination with the nominal reflexive *ilaap*, *-baano* indicates 'alone' or 'by oneself':

(130)   *Ilaap-Ø-baano-h-oosh   i̱-chokka' iya-tok.*
        self-COP-only-TNS-PART:SSIII-house go-PT
        'He went home alone.'

5.2.5.5. *-aash* 'previous-mention'

It is less clear whether *-aash* 'previous-mention' should be included with the clausal determiners. This morpheme occurs on nouns that have been previously mentioned in the discourse. It is particularly frequent on relative clauses.

There is some reason to believe that the morphology following *-aash* is verbal, rather than nominal. An NP containing *-aash* cannot occur with the neutral nominative and accusative markers.

(131)   **Hattak-Ø-aash-at chaaha-h.*
        man-COP-PREV-NM tall-TNS
        ('The previously mentioned man is tall.')

A noun phrase with *-aash* need not be marked for case, but when it is marked, it is always in combination with the participial *-oo*:[17]

(132a) *Hattak-Ø-aash pi̱sa-li-tok.*
        man-COP-PREV see:N-1SI-PT
        'I saw the (previously mentioned) man.'

(132b) **Hattak-Ø-aash-a̱   pi̱sa-li-tok.*
        man-COP-PREV-AC   see:N-1SI-PT

(132c) *Hattak-Ø-aash-o̱   pi̱sa-li-tok.*
        man-COP-PREV-PART:AC   see:N-1SI-PT

The absence of neutral nominative and accusative marking would follow if *-aash* were affixed to a null copula.

On the other hand, *-aash* does not occur as an adverbial suffix on verbs, and in this respect it is unlike the clausal determiners. Nor is it followed by tense markers or complementizers, and so its classification is uncertain.

The usage of *-aash* varies from speaker to speaker, but some speakers and texts use it fairly regularly in a way analogous to the English definite article. The following brief passage illustrates this:

(133)   *Alla' himitta-at ohooyo' himitta-h ishi-tok miyah.*
        child young-NM woman young-TNS take-PT-HSAY
        Ishki' i̱-chokka' ona-hma̱,   alla'
        mother III-house arrive-when:DS child

17. The *-oo* which occurs in these forms should not be analyzed as the focus *-oo* because focus *-oo* alternates with ordinary case, while this *-oo* does not.

tiik-Ø-aash-oosh   *yaaya-tok miyah.   Hihmano*
female-COP-PREV-PART:NM   cry-PT-HSAY   and
alla' nakni-mak-Ø-aash-oosh,   "Náati-h-o̱
child   male-DEM-COP-PREV-PART:NM   why-TNS-PART:AC
ish-yaaya-h?" aa-tok . . .
2sI-cry-TNS   say-PT
'A young man and woman got married. When they arrived at his
mother's house, the girl began to cry. The boy said, "Why are you
crying?" . . . '

In this passage, 'young man' and 'young woman' are introduced as
characters. 'Young man' bears nominative case, and 'young woman' has
no case marking. In each subsequent mention, the name of these
characters is followed by *-aash+oo+sh*. This passage is particularly careful
about marking previously mentioned NPs. Such extensive use of *-aash* is
unusual.

The Choctaw Bible also uses *yammakaash* 'that (previously
mentioned) one' in many places where a simple pronoun appears in
English. This appears to be somewhat unidiomatic.

(134)   <Mihma Chisʋs ʋt ʋlla iskitini o̱ i̱ howa cha, yʋmmak ash intinlakla
        ya̱ hilechi tok.>[18]
        Mihma Jesus-at   alla' iskitiini-yo̱   i̱-hóowa-cha
        and   Jesus-NM child small-FOC:AC III-call:L-SS
        yammak-Ø-aash itt-i̱-takla-ya̱   hili-chi-ttook.
        that-COP-PREV   RECIP-III-middle-AC stand-CAUS-DPAST
        'And Jesus called a small child and put him in the middle of them.'
        (Matt. 18:2)

The suffix *-aash* attaches to NPs, and Choctaw NPs may end with words
that are verbal in character. In such cases, *-aash* must be preceded by the
tense marker *-k* 'embedded tense', discussed in chapter 11. For this
reason, *-k-aash* is found in relative clauses:[19]

(135)   *Na̱na=chapóli' Pam-at   nonaachi-k-Ø-aash apa-li-tok.*
        cake   Pam-NM cook-TNS-COP-PREV eat-1SI-PT
        'I ate the cake that Pam made.'

It is also found when the subject is a quantified noun or a bare quantifier:

(136)   <Yohmi ma nan-isht-ahullo okpula puta kash ot hatak ash a kocha
        wihʋt ia mʋt . . .>
        Yohmima na̱n=isht=ahóllo' okpólo'   potta-k-Ø-aash-oot
        and:then   spirit   bad-NML   all-TNS-COP-PREV-PART:NM

18. The Choctaw Bible has *intinlakla*, but this appears to be a misprint for
itintakla 'among'. *Intinlakla* is not recognizable and does not appear in the dictionary.
    19. See Gordon (1987) for a discussion of relative clauses with *-k-aash*. Gordon
(1987:78) suggests that the *-k* of this affix is to be identified as the complementizer *-ka*
rather than a tense affix *-k*. See chapter 11 for arguments that *-k* is better treated as
a tense marker.

hattak-aash aa-kochchawiiha-t iya-hmat . . .
man-PREV   LOC-move:out-PART go-when:DS
'And when all the demons left that man . . .' (Luke 8:33)

(137)   <. . . auahtuklo kash ot ai ʋlʋt . . .>
. . . awahtoklo-k-Ø-aash-oot   aayala-t . . .
twelve-TNS-COP-PREV-PART:NM   arrive:PL-PART
'Twelve of them arrived and . . .' Luke 9:12

Verbal elements like the indefinites also appear with -k-aash:

(138)   . . . nana kash ot ont aiahli nitak a onak mak a hi oke . . .
. . . nana-k-Ø-aash-oot   ot   aay-alhlhi nittak-a
thing-TNS-COP-PREV-PART:NM go& LOC-true   day-AC
ona-k   mak-ahii-okii . . .
arrive-TNS COP-IRR-indeed
'the things [that were previously mentioned] will truly come to pass
in their season' (Luke 1:20)

5.2.6. Cooccurrence of determiners

Certain types of determiners cooccur, as in the following examples:

(139)   Chokka' apáta-p-ako   áshwa-h.
house   next:to-DEM-CON:AC live:DU-TNS
'They [two] lived in the house next door.'

(140)   opya-m-Ø-akili-h-o
evening-DEM-COP-EMPH-TNS-PART:AC
'that very evening'

For NPs that do not include a clausal determiner, the ordering
possibilities seem to be as follows:

(141)   Noun + (demonstrative) + (other determiners) + (contrast/focus) + case

Only the determiners -ak 'oblique' and -ook 'comparison' seem good with
following contrast or focus markers. The determiners -ba 'only' and -akhii
'pejorative' may be optionally followed by a case marker, but not by other
determiners.

Noun phrases with a clausal determiner seem to have a structure
like the following:

(142)   [[Noun + (demonstrative/oblique)]_{NP1} + copula + clausal
determiner]_{NP2}

In this structure, NP$_1$ only allows a following demonstrative or the oblique
-ak. NP$_2$ is essentially like an ordinary noun phrase in its determiner
possibilities:

(143)   Hattak-mak-Ø-fiihn-akoosh sa-sso-tok.
man-DEM-COP-very-CON:NM 1sII-hit-PT
'That very man hit me.'

It is even possible for demonstratives to both follow and precede the
clausal determiner:

(144)   *Ohooyo-mak-Ø-fiihna-mat*   *a̲-nokoowa-tok.*
         woman-DEM-COP-very-DEM:NM 1sIII-angry-PT
         'That very woman chewed me out.'

6. Pronouns

6.1. Independent pronouns

The independent pronouns of Choctaw are shown in table 6.1.

Table 6.1. Independent pronouns

ano'	'I'	*pishno'*	'we (few)'
		hapishno'	'we (many)'
chishno'	'you'	*hachishno'*	'y'all'

There are no distinct third person pronouns. Sometimes speakers and texts use the demonstrative *yamma(k)* 'that one' or noun phrases like *hattak-ma* 'that person, that man', *ohooyo'-ma* 'that woman', or *alla'-ma* 'that child' in this context:

(1) <Mihma Paul ash ot, Iloh itibapishi ma! yʋmmak okʋt na holitompa
isht aṣha pehlichi ya̠, ak akostinincho ke tuk oke. . . achi tok.>
Mihma   Paul-aash-oot,   "Iloh-ittibapishi'-ma' yammak-ook-at
and:then Paul-PREV-FOC:NM 1MPI-brother-VOC   that-COMPAR-NM
na̠=holitọpa=isht=áṣha'   piihlichi-ya̠ ak-akostiních-o-kii-tok-okii
priests   leader-AC   1SN-know:N-NEG-NEG-PT-indeed
. . . *aachi-ttook.*
say-DPAST
'And then Paul said, "My brothers, I did not know that he (lit., "that one") was the high priest. . ."' (Acts 23:5)

Because pronouns are usually absent, when overt independent pronouns appear they occur primarily in positions of focus. For this reason they are often followed by the contrastive marker, as in the following example:

(2) *An-akoosh nípi' chọpa-li-tok.*
I-CON:NM meat   buy-1SI-PT
'*I* (not someone else) bought the meat'

In a more neutral context, the pronouns would ordinarily be omitted:

(3) *Nípi' chọpa-li-tok.*
meat buy-1SI-PT
'I bought the meat.'

The first person plural pronouns require some special discussion. Two forms, *pishno'* and *hapishno'*, are listed, but the difference between the two is somewhat difficult to determine. It is probably best called 'paucal' versus 'multiple', as Nicklas (1974:30) suggests. *Pishno'* and *hapishno'* trigger distinct II agreement: *pi-* and *hapi-* respectively. *Hapishno'* and the corresponding II prefix seem to be used primarily when speaking as a member of a large group, as in the following example:

(4)　　*Chahta' hapiy-a-h-okii!*
　　　　Choctaw 1MPII-be-TNS-indeed
　　　　'We are Choctaws!'

Since this example was addressed to the author, it clearly shows that *hapi-* is not a marker of inclusive first person, as Davies (1981:31) and Brinton (in Byington 1870:13, 23) suggest.[1]

Byington (1870:23) says that *pishno'* is the "definite or exclusive plural, and does not include all who are present, but only a fixed number," while *hapishno'* is the "distinctive or inclusive plural, and embraces the speaker and all who are present, but ignores all others."

There are class I agreement markers which seem to correspond to the difference between *pishno'* and *hapishno'*, namely *il-*, *ii-* and *iloh-*, *iiho-* respectively.[2] It initially seems that the agreement paradigm for first person plural is as in table 6.2.

Table 6.2. First person nonsingular agreement (initial hypothesis)

	I	II	III
PLURAL	il/ii-	pi-	pim-
MULTIPLE	iloh-/iiho-	hapi-	hapim-

However, I believe that a more accurate representation of the facts is that shown in table 6.3.

Table 6.3. First person nonsingular agreement (revised hypothesis)

	I	II	III
PLURAL	il/ii-	pi-	pim-
MULTIPLE	il/ii-	hapi-	hapim-

That is, Choctaw only distinguishes between first person plural and first

1. Brinton was the editor of Byington (1870) and makes some suggestions for revision in the footnotes.

2. In these forms, the first form cited is used before vowels, and the second before consonants.

person multiple in the II and III sets.

While both *pi-* and *hapi-* are still used with some regularity, *iloh-* and *iiho-* have all but disappeared from the language, and were judged archaic by all of my consultants. Two speakers said that they thought that *iloh-* and *iiho-* had something to do with talking to in-laws (see section 6.5 below). For this reason, it seems that *iloh-* and *iiho-* do not reflect the distinction between paucal and multiple found in the other agreement sets.

Perhaps on the analogy of the distinction between *pishno'* and *hapishno'*, one speaker also offered a pronoun *hashno'*, which he defined as 'y'all (few)' in opposition to *hachishno'*, which is 'y'all (many)'. I was not able to confirm this pronoun with other speakers of the language, suggesting that if it is genuinely in use by some speakers, this usage is not very widespread.

6.2. Possessive pronouns

Choctaw has a special set of possessive pronouns used in predicative contexts. The possessive pronouns are as shown in table 6.4.

Table 6.4. Predicative possessive pronouns

ámmi'	'mine'	*pímmi'*	'ours (few)'
		hapímmi'	'ours (many)'
chímmi'	'yours'	*hachímmi'*	'y'all's'
ímmi'	'his, hers, its, theirs'		

Sentences like the following seem to be accepted by all speakers of Oklahoma Choctaw:

(5)   *Ofi'-mat   ámmi'.*
      dog-D:NM mine
      'That dog is mine.'

However, only one of my consultants for Mississippi Choctaw accepted (5) as grammatical. All the Mississippi Choctaw speakers preferred the following alternative:

(6)   *Ofi'-mat   ano'.*
      dog-D:NM I
      'That dog is mine.'

That is, most speakers of Mississippi Choctaw use the independent pronouns in this context. My primary consultants for Oklahoma Choctaw (Josephine Wade, Henry Willis, and Edith Gem) all rejected (6).

Some speakers have a somewhat different form of the independent pronouns used as possessives. Two young speakers of Mississippi Choctaw volunteered the pronoun *sashno'* for 'mine', as in the following example:

(7)   *Ofi'-mat   sashno'.*
      dog-D:NM   mine
      'That dog is mine.'

Most older speakers I interviewed rejected *sashno'*, but several acknowledged that it is commonly used. *Sashno'* seems to be formed on analogy with the independent pronouns *chishno'* and *pishno'*, which appear to be the II agreement markers added to a pronominal base -*shno'*. Since *sa-* is the first person singular II agreement marker, *sashno'* is an expected analogical formation.

Perhaps since there is no independent third person pronoun, speakers sometimes use *ilaap* in this context:

(8)   *Ofi'-mat   ilaap.*
      dog-D:NM   self
      'That dog is his.'

Ilaap more generally is a reflexive pronoun meaning 'his own, her own, its own', so this sentence might be interpreted to mean something like 'That dog is his own'.

For the plural 'theirs', speakers frequently used the plural word *oklah* before *ilaap*. Sometimes the two words are phonologically combined:

(9)   *Ofi'-mat   okl-ilaap.*
      dog-D:NM   PLUR-self
      'That dog is theirs.'

These sentences are best analysed as involving a zero copula in the present tense. Nonpresent examples involve the copula *a*, as in the following:

(10a) *Ofi'-mat   ano' aa-tok.*
       dog-D:NM   mine be-PT
       'That dog was mine.'

(10b) *Ofi'-mat   ano'   ∅-aachi̱-h.*
       dog-D:NM   mine   COP-IRR-TNS
       'That dog will be mine.'

There may be some reason to suppose that the pronouns ending in -*mmi'* are more conservative. The Choctaw testament uses them in this context:

(11) <kiloh vbi na immi hatuk vt hvpimmi hashke>
      Kil-oh-áabi-na   ímmih-a-tok-at hapímmih-ashkii
      1PN-PL-kill:L-DS his-be-PT-NM   ours-EXHORT
      'Let us kill him, and what is his will be ours!'[3] (Mark 12:7)

(12) <achvfa kvt chishno ak o chimmi hokma, anonti achvfa kvt Moses ak
      o immi hokma, anonti achvfa kvt Elias ak o immi hashke>
      Achaffa-kat   chishno-ako̱ chímmih-okma, anóti'
      one-COMP:NM you-CON:AC yours-IRR   and
      achaffa-kat   Moses-ako̱   ímmih-okma,
      one-COMP:NM Moses-CON:AC his-IRR
      anóti achaffa-kat   Elias-ako̱   ímmih-ashkii.
      and   one-COMP:NM Elias-CON:AC his-EXHORT
      'One will be for thee, and one for Moses, and one for Elias.' (Matt.
      17:4)

(13) <ai vlhpiesa isht atobba hi okvt vmmi hoke>
      Aay-alhpíisa' isht-atobb-ahii-ook-at   ámmih-okii.
      LOC-correct   INSTR-pay-IRR2-COMPAR-NM mine-EXHORT
      'Vengeance is mine.' (Heb. 10:30)

However, Byington (1870:23–24) glosses both *ano'* and *ámmi'* as 'it
is mine', suggesting that both were in use when he wrote his
grammatical sketch. While I have not discovered any uses of *ilaap* as a
possessive predicate nominal in the Testament, Byington (1870:24)
includes 'it is his' as a gloss for *ilapah*, and the following example
appears in Byington's dictionary:

(14) <mi^nko ilap>
      mi̱ka'laap
      chiefhis
      'This is the chief's.' Byington (1915:182)

There is also some comparative evidence for the use of the *-mmi'*
series as more conservative. The following forms from Koasati (Kimball
1991:89) appear to show cognates to the possessive series:[4]

(15) *ámmo̱*   'to be mine'
      címmo̱   'to be yours [singular]'
      ímmo̱   'to be his/hers/its/theirs'
      kómmo̱   'to be ours'
      hacímmo̱   'to be yours [plural]'

---

3. A puzzling difference between the Choctaw recorded in the Bible passages cited
and in Byington (1870) is the presence of a *h* following these possessive pronouns. They
are definitely followed by glottal stop and not *h* in the speech of all the Choctaws I
consulted.
      4. Kimball treats these words as verbal in Koasati. However, the Choctaw
cognates are nominal.

6.3. Reflexives and reciprocals

In Choctaw, there are two anaphoric verbal prefixes, one reflexive and the other reciprocal. There is also a free-standing nominal anaphor that may be used with both reflexives and reciprocals.

The following examples show the reflexive and reciprocal prefixes:

(16) *Joan-at   ili-písa-tok.*
      Joan-NM RFL-see:N-PT
      'Joan saw herself.'

(17) *Hattak-at   itti-písa-tok.*
      man-NM   RCP-see:N-PT
      'The men saw each other.'

The free-standing nominal *ilaap* is shown in the following example:

(18) *Hattak-at   ilaap ili-písa-tok.*
      man-NM   self RFL-see:N-PT
      'The man saw himself.'

6.3.1. Reciprocals

Reciprocals are formed by a prefix *itti-*. The following examples contain reciprocals:

(19) *John Mary itt-atoklo-kat   itti-pisa-h.*
      John Mary RCP-two-COMP:SS RCP-see-TNS
      'John and Mary saw each other.'

When an applicative prefix is present, the reciprocal appears immediately before it:

(20) *Il-itt-ibaa-chaffa-h.*
      1PI-RCP-COMIT-one-TNS
      'We agree.' (Lit., 'We are one with each other.')

The reciprocal prefix *itti-* also appears on nouns that inherently involve relations:

(21) *ittikana'*
      'friends'

In some cases, the characterization of *itti-* as a reciprocal is problematic. In the following examples it seems to be more accurately translated as 'together':

(22) Yohmi ma hatak kanohmi kʋt hatak ʋt palsi ʋbi yǫ potʋlhpo ai it i̱
      sholit isht ʋla tok
      Yohmi-hma̱   hattak kanohmi-kat   hattak-at palsy abi-yǫ
      and-when:DS man   some-COMP:SS man-NM   palsy. disease-FOC:AC

patálhpo' aay-itt-i̱-shooli-t   isht   ala-ttook.
pallet   LOC-RCP-III-carry-PART INSTR arrive-DPAST
'And some men (together) brought in a man on a pallet who was
suffering from palsy.' (Luke 5:18)

(23)   <Mihma okla ai ʋla cha, peni ash it aieninchit okla atotoli>
       Mihma oklah áyyala-cha piini-yaash itt-ayinichi-t   oklah
       and   PLUR arrive:Y-SS boat-PREV RCP-do:too-PART PLUR
       atootoli-h
       fill-TNS
       'And they came and filled that ship (together) as well.' (Luke 5:7)

6.3.2. The verbal reflexive *ili-*

When two arguments of a verb are coreferent, the reflexive prefix *ili-* is
obligatory:

(24)   *John-at   pi̱sa-tok.*
       John-NM   see:N-PT
       'John$_i$ saw him$_j$/*himself$_j$.'

Conversely, if *ili-* is present, corefence with the subject is obligatory:

(25)   *John-at   ili-pi̱sa-tok.*
       John-NM   RFL-see:N-PT
       'John$_i$ saw himself$_i$/*him$_j$.'

When a reflexive occurs as the indirect object, or as an argument of one
of the oblique agreement markers, it appears before the applicative
prefix:

(26)   *John-at   holisso' il-i̱-cho̱pa-tok.*
       John-NM   book   RFL-III-buy-PT
       'John bought the book for himself.'

(27)   *Gus-at   il-o̱-fimmi-tok.*
       Gus-NM   RFL-on-splash-PT
       'Gus splashed it on himself.'

The prefix *ili-* generally does not appear on nouns:

(28)   *? *John-at   il-ishki   pi̱sa-tok.*
       John-NM   RFL-mother   see-PT
       'John saw his own mother.'

6.3.3. Cooccurrence of reciprocal and reflexive

A most unusual, and still unexplained, aspect of anaphora in Choctaw is
that for some speakers both a reciprocal and a reflexive may appear on
the same verb, apparently having the same referent:

(29)   *Itt-il-isso-h.*
       RCP-RFL-hit-TNS
       'They hit themselves.'

(30)   *John Mary itt-atoklo-kat   itt-il-ikhána-tokla-h.*
       John Mary RCP-two-COMP:SS RCP-RFL-know:N-DU-TNS
       'John and Mary know each other.'

If there is no reciprocal prefix, it is not possible for the extra reflexive
prefix to appear:

(31)   **John-at Mary il-ikhána-h.*
       John-NM Mary RFL-know:N-TNS
       'John knows Mary.'

Other speakers do not allow sentences like (29)–(30). This area merits
further study.

6.3.4. The nominal reflexive *ilaap*

In addition to the verbal affix *ili-*, there is also a free standing NP
reflexive *ilaap*. *Ilaap* plays a much less important role in Choctaw than
ili-, and it is probably best regarded as an optional emphatic element.

There are no sentences in which the use of *ilaap* is obligatory, and
even when *ilaap* is used, the verbal *ili-* is still obligatory:

(32)   *Aaron-at (ilaap) il-isso-h.*
       Aaron-NM (self)   RFL-hit TNS
       'Aaron hit himself.'

(33)   **Aaron-at ilaap isso-h.*
       Aaron-NM self   hit-TNS
       'Aaron hit himself.'

In contrast, *ili-* is obligatory for objects that are coreferent with the
subject, and its occurrence is not dependent on *ilaap*.

(34)   *John-at   písa-tok.*
       John-NM   see:N-PT
       'John$_i$ saw him$_j$/*himself$_i$.'

Ilaap may only be used with third person antecedents:

(35)   **Ilaap il-isso-lih.*
       self   RFL-hit-1SI
       'I hit myself.'

This restriction does not hold for the verbal affix *ili-*:

(36)   *John-at   il-isso-h.*
       John-NM RFL-hit-TNS
       'John hit himself.'

(37)   *Il-isso-li-h.*
       RFL-hit-1SI-TNS
       'I hit myself.'

Davies (1981:60) claims that there is no free-standing nominal reflexive. However, it seems that *ilaap* serves as the independent form of both the reflexive and the reciprocal:

(38)   *Ilaap itt-i̱-kahli-h   Bill-at im-ab-aachi̱-kma na̱na-ka̱.*
       self   RCP-III-bet-TNS Bill-NM III-kill-IRR-IRR   thing-COMP:DS
       'They bet each other about whether Bill would win.'[5]

Noun phrases in which the possessor is coreferent with another noun phrase in the sentence often appear with the clausal determiner *-aki̱li* 'indeed' (discussed in section 5.2.5.2):

(39)   *John-at im-ofi-yaki̱lih   abi-tok.*
       John-NM III-dog-indeed kill-PT
       'John killed his own dog.'

(40)   <Chisʊs ʊt ilap chu̱kash ak i̱li ka isht akostini̱chi mʊt . . .>
       Jesus-at   ilaap cho̱kash-aki̱li-ka   isht-akostini̱chi-hmat . . .
       Jesus-NM self   heart-indeed-COMP INSTR-find:out-when:SS
       'When Jesus perceived it in his (own) heart . . .' (Mark 2:8)

6.3.5. Possible antecedents for reflexives

The reflexive prefix *ili-* always takes a subject as its antecedent:

(41)   *Pam-at   Charles im-anooli-h   mat ili-tasi̱boh miyah i̱- maka-h.*
       Pam-NM Charles III-tell-SS   RFL-crazy   hearsay III-say-TNS
       'Pam$_i$ told Charles$_j$ that she/*he is crazy.'

The nominal *ilaap*, however, may take nonsubject antecedents:

(42)   *Katiimi-sh   ii-hokli-h   [ilaap im-annópa' il-ishi-h-oosh]*
       how-PART:SS 1PI-catch-TNS self   III-word   1PI-get-PART:SS
       'How can we catch him using his own words?'

6.3.6. Cooccurrence of the nominal and verbal reflexives

Contrast (42) with the following examples, repeated from above:

(43)   *Aaron-at   (ilaap) il-isso-h.*
       Aaron-NM (self) RFL-hit-TNS
       'Aaron hit himself.'

(44)   **Aaron-at   ilaap isso-h.*
       Aaron-NM self   hit-TNS
       'Aaron hit himself.'

---

5. *Imabih*, literally 'kill to s.o.', is an idiom meaning 'defeat them, win (over s.o.)'.

In (43) and (44) we see that verbal *ili-* must occur when *ilaap* is the direct object. However, in (42), *ilaap* occurs without *ili-*. What principle regulates the cooccurrence of the two reflexives?

For verbs, *ili-* is obligatory and *ilaap* is optional. For noun phrases, *ili-* is probably ungrammatical, while *ilaap* is possible as an emphatic element.

(45) *John-at   ilaap   im-ofi'   abi-h.*
      John-NM   self   III-dog   kill-TNS
      'John killed his own dog.'

(46) **? John-at   ilaap   il-im-ofi'   abi-h.*
      John-NM   self   RFL-III-dog   kill-TNS
      'John killed his own dog.'

(47) <Chisʋs ʋt ilap chu̲kash ak i̲li ka isht akostini̲chi mʋt . . .>
      Jesus-at   ilaap   cho̲kash-aki̲li-ka   isht-akostini̲chi-hmat . . .
      Jesus-NM   self   heart-indeed-COMP   INSTR-find:out-when:SS
      'When Jesus perceived it in his heart . . .' (Mark 2:8)

Ilaap also appears without the verbal prefix *ili-* in cases where it appears in subject position:

(48) *. . . hatak puta tahchi ma onachi hoka: yohmi kia ilap ak inli kʋto yʋmmak oka ibbak ushi achʋfona kia pit isht kanʋllicha hi a̲ okla ahni keyu. hoke.*
      . . . hattak   potta   tahchi-ma   onaachi-hooka,
             man   all   shoulder-DEM   place-but
      yohmi-kia   ilaap-aki̲li-k-ato   yammak-ooka
      do:so-but   self-indeed-TNS-NM2   that-COMPAR
      ibbakoshi'   achaffona-kia   pit   isht-kanallich-ahii-ya̲
      finger   even:one-but   away   INSTR-move-IRR-DS
      oklah   ahni-kiiyo-h-okii.
      PLUR   think-NEG-TNS-EMPH
      'They put it on the shoulders of all men, but they themselves will not move them with even one of their fingers.' (Matt. 23:4)

6.4. Long distance reflexives and reflexive movement

A surprising property of the Choctaw reflexive *ili-* is that it may sometimes appear in a higher clause than would generally be expected. For example, in the following sentence it is the embedded clause that is reflexive. Nevertheless, the reflexive prefix may also appear on the superordinate verb:

(49) *John-at   [ili-pisachokma-kat]   ikhá̲na-h.*
      John-NM   RFL-goodlooking-COMP:SS   know:N-TNS
      'John$_i$ knows that he$_i$ is goodlooking.' (Lit., 'John$_i$ knows that self$_i$ is goodlooking.')

(50)   *John-at*   [*pisachokma-kat*]   *il-ikhána-h.*
       John-NM goodlooking-COMP:SS RFL-know:N-TNS
       'John₁ knows that he₁ is goodlooking.' (Lit., 'John self-knows that he
       is goodlooking.')

It is also possible for the reflexive to appear in both places:

(51)   *John-at*   [*ili-pisachokma-kat*]   *il-ikhána-h.*
       John-NM RFL-goodlooking-COMP:SS RFL-know:N-TNS
       'John₁ knows that he₁ is goodlooking.' (Lit., 'John self-knows that self
       is goodlooking.')

In Broadwell (1988b, 1990a), I called this process "reflexive movement",
and gave a syntactic account of the phenomenon. Most Choctaw speakers
accept sentences like (49). The acceptability of (50) and (51) is less
general; speaker judgments are variable.

   I reported in Broadwell (1988b, 1990a) that Mrs. Josephine Wade
also accepted long-distance reflexive movement, so long as the
intermediate clause contained an auxiliary verb or a verb with a null
subject. The examples below show the optional appearance of the
reflexive *ili-* on the verb *nánah* 'to be the case that'.

(52)   *John-at ili-sipokni-kma nána-kat*   *ik-ikháan-o-h.*
       John-NM RFL-old-IRR:DS   be:the:case-COMP:SS N-know:L-NEG-TNS
       'John doesn't know whether he is old.'

(53)   *John-at sipokni-kma ili-nána-kat*   *ik-ikháan-o-h.*
       John-NM old-IRR:DS   RFL-be:the:case-COMP:SS N-know:L-NEG-TNS
       'John doesn't know whether he is old.'

(54)   *John-at sipokni-kma nána-kat*   *il- ik-ikháan-o-h.*
       John-NM old-IRR:DS   be:the:case-COMP:SS RFL-N-know:L-NEG-TNS
       'John doesn't know whether he is old.'

(55)   *John-at ili-sipokni-kma ili-nána-kat*
       John-NM RFL-old-IRR:DS   RFL-be:the:case-COMP:SS
       il- ik-ikháan-o-h.
       RFL-N-know:L-NEG-TNS
       'John doesn't know whether he is old.'

While sentences of this sort were acceptable to Mrs. Wade, other
Choctaws I consulted found long-distance reflexive movement either
unacceptable or less than fully grammatical. This suggests that my
earlier claims about these data should be approached with caution.

6.5. The pronouns of mother-in-law language

Byington (1870:28) describes what he calls the 'marriage pronouns',
which we may interpret as a special form of mother-in-law language.
Mother-in-law language was once used in talk between various classes
of in-laws, especially between a man and his mother-in-law.

The principal characteristic of mother-in-law language seems to be the use of *ho-* or *oh-* in place of ordinary verb agreement.[6] Byington says that this happens in the first, second, and third persons singular and in the second and third persons plural, but unfortunately he only gives the following examples:

(56) <Vmissuba ik hopeso?>
      Am-issóba' ik-ho-píis-o-h?
      1sIII-horse N-PL-see:L-NEG-TNS
      'Has he not seen my horse?' (Byington 1870:28)

(57) <Oh ia lih.>
      Oh-iya-li-h.
      PL-go-1SI-TNS
      'I went with him.' (Byington 1870:28)

(58) <Ho mintilih.>
      Ho-míti-li-h.
      PL-come-1SI-TNS
      'I come with him.' (Byington 1870:28)

(59) Oh ant ik sapeso ka hinlah?
      Oh-at   ik-sa-piis-ok-ahíla-h?
      PL-go:and N-1sII-see:L-NEG-POT-TNS
      'Will he not come to see me?' (Byington 1870:28)

These examples raise several questions. Why is the comitative *ibaa-* missing from (57) and (58)? How are we to explain *ik-ho* in (56)? Why does the *ho-* appear on the directional preverb in (59)?

Byington wrote that this form of speech was already becoming obsolete at the time that he wrote his grammar, the first draft of which was written in 1834. As mentioned above, two consultants thought that the class I prefixes *iloh-, iiho-* had something to do with talking to in-laws, but they were unable to give any details about their use. Apart from these forms of the class I prefixes, I am unaware of any traces of a special in-law language in modern Choctaw, so these questions may well be unanswerable.

While special verb agreement and pronouns for in-laws are no longer in use, there are deferential forms of address for particular relatives which are described in chapter 19.

6. The prefix *ho(o)-, o(o)h-* is a plural imperative marker in modern Choctaw, as discussed in section 12.3.5.

7. Interrogatives and indefinites

7.1. The morphology of interrogatives and indefinites

Interrogatives and indefinites are systematically related to each other in Choctaw, as in many other languages.[1] Choctaw interro-gatives are built on two bases: the stems *kát-* and *nát-* ~ *náat-*. The corresponding indefinites are built on the bases *kán-* and *nán-* ~ *náan-* respectively. Some examples are shown in table 7.1.

Table 7.1. Some interrogative and indefinite words

Interrogative		Indefinite	
kátah	'who'	*kánah*	'someone'
nátah	'what'	*nánah*	'something'
náatokah	'say what'	*náanokah*	say something'

    In comparison to English, there is a somewhat bewildering array of interrogatives and indefinites in Choctaw, and they occur with complex morphology. Choctaw interrogatives make some distinctions that are foreign to English (e.g., past and future 'when' are different), while failing to make other distinctions (e.g., the same word can be interpreted as either 'where' or 'which'). There is also a considerable amount of speaker and dialect variation in these forms.

7.1.1. Uses of the interrogatives and indefinites

The interrogatives are used in the same way as their English equivalents. The indefinites, however, correspond to several different English equivalents. They may correspond to English indefinites like 'someone', 'somewhere', 'something', 'sometimes', 'do something' and so on.

(1)   *Loksi-ato   kániichi-hmakoosh   fakit-ma̱*
     turtle-NM2 do:something-too:SS turkey-D:AC
     isht-il-awatta-kat   aatapa-ka̱   issa-ch-aachi̱-tok.
     INSTR-RFL-wide-COMP:SS too:much-COMP:DS stop-CAUS-IRR-PT

---

1. I have avoided referring to the words in this group as pronouns. Although they correspond to pronominals in English, they show many morphological properties of verbs in Choctaw, as discussed below.

'The turtle was wishing that he could do something that would make
the turkey stop boasting so much.' (T8:35–37)

(2)   *Kániimi-kma,   Charles-at   ittanáaha-' abooha'*
      sometimes-IRR:DS Charles-NM meet-NML house
      binii-t   nosi-h.
      sit-PART sleep-TNS
      'Sometimes Charles falls asleep in church.'

However, Choctaw indefinites are also used in embedded indirect
quotations where English would use interrogatives:

(3)   *Ik-itháan-o-h   kániimi-li-tokat.*
      N-know:L-NEG-TNS do:something-1SI-PT:COMP:SS
      'He doesn't know what I did.'

(4)   *Kániimi-h-o   ish-mihchi-toka   ak-itháan-o-h.*
      do:something-TNS-PART:DS 2SI-do-PT:COMP:DS 1SN-know:L-NEG-TNS
      'I don't know why you did that.'

Choctaw indefinites are used in the equivalent of the English free
relative construction.

(5)   *Bonnie-at   nána-h   nonaachi-kma, apa-l-aachi-h.*
      Bonnie-NM something-TNS cook-IRR:DS   eat-1SI-IRR-TNS
      'I'll eat what Bonnie cooks.'

Examples like (5) probably have the syntax of internally headed relative
clauses, which are discussed in more detail in chapter 16.
    The indefinites plus the determiner *-óhmakoo* (discussed in chapter
5) can have the senses 'everywhere', 'everyone', and so on:

(6)   *Bonnie-at   kánomma-h-óhmako   aa-nowa-h.*
      Bonnie-NM somewhere-TNS-too:AC LOC-walk-TNS
      'Bonnie walks everywhere.'

    Sentences of this type are translated with 'nowhere', 'no one', and
so on, when accompanied by sentence negation.

(7)   *Kana-h-óhmakoosh ishki'   im-ihaksi-kiiyo-h.*
      someone-TNS-too:NM mother III-forget-NEG-TNS
      'No one forgets their mother.'

When a quantified indefinite is the genitive within the noun phrase, the
determiner *-óhmakoo* follows the whole noun phrase:

(8)   *Kána-h   ishki-óhmakoosh im-ihaksi-kiiyo-h.*
      someone-TNS mother-too:NM III-forget-NEG-TNS
      'No one's mother forgets them.'

Indefinites with the determiner *-kia* 'too' are interpreted as 'anyone',
'anything', 'anywhere', and so on.

(9) *Nána-kia   am-anooli-h.*
something-too 1sIII-tell-TNS
'Tell me anything.'

(10) <Kʋna kia apehlichika isht anumpa ha haklo cha . . .>
Kána-kia   apihlichúika-'   isht-anópah-a   háklo-cha . . .
someone-too kingdom-NML INSTR-word-AC hear:L-SS
'Anyone who hears the word of the kingdom . . .' (Matt. 13:19)

(11) <Kanima kia ish ia chi ka? Kanima ia la chi keyu hoke.>
Kánimma-kia   ish-iy-aachi-ka? Kanimma-u
somewhere-too 2sI-go-IRR-Q   somewhere-TNS
iya-l-aachi-kiiyo-h-okii.
go-1SI-IRR-NEG-TNS-indeed
'Are you going away anywhere?' 'I'm not going anywhere.' (Speller
117)

The indefinite *nánah* may follow a noun to express the notion 'any
X' (or 'no X' when the verb is negative), as in the following example:

(12) <Ushi ya hatak nana kia ik ithano h-o, . . .>
Oshi-ya hattak nana-kia   ik-itháan-o-h-o, . . .
son-AC man   someone-too N-know:L-NEG-TNS-PART:DS
'no man knoweth the Son,' (Matt. 11:27)

The Choctaw phrases with an indefinite plus *-kia* 'too' correspond to the
"free choice" readings of 'anyone', 'anything', and so on in English.
    The suffix *-kia* is not used on ordinary indefinites in the scope of
negation:

(13) *Nána-h   ak-áay-o-tok.*
something-TNS 1sN-say:L-NEG-PT
'I didn't say anything.'

7.1.2. Interrogatives as verbs

All Choctaw interrogatives have the morphology of verbs. This is clearest
for the words *náatokah/nátokah/náatokaachih/nátokaachih* 'to say
what' and *kátiohmih/kátihmih/kátiimihchih* 'to do what'. The following
examples show that they can be inflected for subject, mood, tense, and
illocutionary force.

(14) *Ish-náatok-ahila-h?*
2SI-say:what-POT-TNS
'What would you say?'

(15) <Ish nan tuk achi ha? Ishi cha, a li kamo.>
Ish-nátokaachi-h-a? "Íishi-cha!" aa-li-k-aamo.
2SI-say:what-TNS-Q take:L-SS   say-1SI-TNS-EVID
'What did you say?' 'I said to take it' (Speller 119)

(16)   *Ish-kátiimihchi-h?*
       2sI-do:what-TNS
       'What are you doing?'

(17)   *Ii-kátiimi-km-akoosh   program ii-chokkow-aachi̱-h?*
       1PI-do:what-IRR-CON:SS program 1PI-enter-IRR-TNS
       'What can we do to get into the program?'

(18)   <Katiomi la chi̱ cho? Ak ikhaiyanoshke.>
       Kátiohmi-l-aachi̱-h-cho? Ak-ikháyyan-o-shkii.
       do:what-1sI-IRR-TNS-Q 1sN-know:Y-NEG-EXHORT
       'What shall I do?' 'I don't know' (Speller 117)

These interrogatives may have developed historically from noun-incorporation structures.[2]

Indefinite equivalents are translated as 'do something', 'say something'. They, too, have the full range of verbal morphology.

(19)   *Loksi-ato   kániichi-hmakoosh   fakit-ma̱*
       turtle-NM2 do:something-too:SS turkey-D:AC
       isht-il-awatta-kat   aatapa-ka̱   issa-ch-aachi̱-tok.
       INSTR-RFL-wide-COMP:SS too:much-COMP:DS stop-CAUS-IRR-PT
       'The turtle was wishing that he could do something that would make
       the turkey stop boasting so much.' (T8: 35–37)

(20)   *Ik- itháan-o-h   kániimi-li-tokat.*
       N-know:L-NEG-TNS do:something-1sI-PT:COMP:SS
       'He doesn't know what I did.'

Other interrogatives also have the morphology of verbs, as the following sections will demonstrate.

7.1.3. Adjunct questions

The Choctaw equivalents of 'why' and 'how' show the verbal morphology of subordinate clauses. The key to understanding this is the syntactic form of their answers. Both in English and Choctaw, questions with 'why' and 'how' generally imply answers with focussed reason and manner clauses.

While there is no overt reflection of this in English, in Choctaw the question words that imply clausal responses are themselves clausal in their morphosyntax. The word for 'why' is composed of the general interrogative stem *kátiimih* followed by one of the complementizing

---

2. *Kátiimihchih* seems to be composed of the generalized interrogative *katiimi* plus an identifiable proverb *mihchih* 'to do'. *Náatokaachih* is apparently composed of *náatah* 'what' and an archaic verb root *ka* or *oka* meaning 'to say', reconstructable on the basis of the cognate set 'say': Creek *kayc-ita*, Oklahoma Seminole *keyc-ita*; Hitciti *ka*, Mikasaki *ka-:c-*; Koasati *kaha*; Choctaw *aa-*, *aa-chi*, *aa-li*, Chickasaw *aa-chi*. (Munro et al. 1992)

suffixes appropriate for reason clauses, and 'how' is *kátiimih* plus the appropriate complementizing suffix for a manner clause.

'When' also falls into this category, since temporal expressions are almost invariably clausal in Choctaw.

7.1.3.1. 'Why'

As just mentioned, 'why' is expressed through the use of *kátiimih* with morphology appropriate for a reason clause. There are two ways of doing this in Choctaw:

(21a) *kátiimi* + *-h* 'default tense' + *-oo* 'participle' + different subject (DS)

(21b) *kátiimi* + *-na* 'different subject (DS) sequence'

Here are some examples of these two ways of saying 'why':

(22) *Kátiimi-h-o̱   kaniiy-aachi̱-h   miya-h?*
      INT-TNS-PART:DS go:away-IRR-TNS hearsay-TNS
      'Why is he going away?'

(23) *Katíimi-na kaniiy-aachi̱-h   miya-h?*
      INT-DS   go:away-IRR-TNS hearsay-TNS
      'Why is he going away?'

We can understand these sentences as approximately 'Someone did what and he is going away?'. The embedded verb is marked for different subject, perhaps reflecting an idea that when two events are causally linked, they typically have different agents. There is apparently no difference in meaning between *kátiimiho̱* and *katíimina*.[3]

Some speakers, primarily Mississippi Choctaws, use the form *náatiho̱* for 'why':[4]

(24) *Hílha-'-pa̱   náati-h-o̱ oklah   hilha-tok-chi*
      dance-NML-D:AC INT-TNS-PART:DS PLUR dance-PT-wonder
      'I wonder why they danced this dance?'

Another possibility for 'why' is *ná̱tah kátiohmih*, which combines *ná̱tah* 'what' and *kátiohmih* 'do what':

(25) <Suso hut nanta katiohmi ho̱ ish pi̱ yakohmichi>
      Sa-ssoh-at   ná̱ta-h   kátiohmi-h-o̱   ish-pi̱-yakohmichi-h?
      1sII-son-NM what-TNS do:what-TNS-PART:SS 2SI-1SP-do:this-TNS
      'My son, why have you treated us like this?' (Luke 2:48)

---

3. In general, the construction V_1-Participial V_2 indicates simultaneity of the events denoted by the two verbs, while V_1-*na* V_2 indicates that V_1 is prior to V_2. Perhaps for some speakers (or at some stage in the history of the language) there is or was a parallel distinction between prior causes and simultaneous causes.

4. Nicklas (1974:101) also gives *naatimi* for 'why' for some speakers of Oklahoma Choctaw.

Corresponding indefinites are *kániimiho̲, kániimina,* and *na̲nah kániohmih.* In complement clauses *kaniimika̲* is also found.

(26) *Kániimi-h-o̲*   *ish-mihchi-toka̲*   *ak-itháan-o-h.*
      INDEF-TNS-PART:DS   2SI-do-PT:COMP:DS   1SN-know:L-NEG-TNS
      'I don't know why you did that.'

(27) *Kániimi-ka̲*   *iya-toka̲*   *ak-ikháan-o-h.*
      INDEF-COMP:DS   go-PT:COMP:DS   1SN-know:L-NEG-TNS
      'I don't know why he left.'

7.1.3.2. 'How'

Unlike reason clauses, manner clauses generally give information about simultaneous actions carried out by the same subject as that of the matrix clause. For this reason, Choctaw equivalents of 'how' carry morphology appropriate for same-subject manner clauses. There are two main ways of doing this.

(28a) *kátiimi/kátiimihchi* + -*h* 'default tense' + -*oo* 'participle' + same subject (SS)

(28b) *kátiimi/kátih* + -*t* 'participial (PART)'

Consider the following example:

(29) *Kátih-t   al-aachi̲-h   miya-h?*
      INT-PART   arrive-IRR-TNS   hearsay-TNS
      'How is she going to get here?'

We can think of these sentences as having as syntax something like 'By doing what is she going to get here?', where the verbs 'do what' and 'get here' have the same subjects.

The difference between interrogatives formed with *kátiimih* and those formed with *kátiimihchih* is difficult to determine. *Kátiimih* seems to be neutral with respect to the type of action involved in the manner clause, while *kátiimihchih* appears to indicate a manner verb with a strongly active verb.

(30) *Kátiimihchi-h-oosh   pallaska'   ish-ikbi-hchaa-tok?*
      INT-TNS-PART:SS   bread   2SI-make-always-PT
      'How do you make bread?'

(31) *Kátiimi-h-oo-sh   al-aachi̲-h   miya-h?*
      INT-TNS-PART-SS   arrive-IRR-TNS   hearsay-TNS
      'How is she going to get here?'

The difference between these two sentences seems to be that making bread necessarily implies a highly active subject, while arriving in a particular location does not. (For example, one can arrive at a place by merely sitting in a car that someone else is driving.)

Kátiimih and *kátiimichih* appear in reduced forms lacking the syllable *-mi-* before some of these endings. The participial marker *-t* quite generally occurs with shortend versions of verbs (as discussed in section 13.4), and the ending *-h-oosh* alternates with *-sh*. This gives forms like *kátiht*, *kátiimish*, *kátihchish*, and *kátiimihchish*.

Finally, another possible version of 'how' is *kátiohmikakoosh*:

(32) <Hatak ʋt sipoknit taiyaha kʋt katiohmi kak osh ʋtta hinla ho̲?>
Hattak-at sipokni-t táyyaha-kat kátiohmi-k-akoosh
man-NM old-PART complete:Y-COMP:SS do:what-TNS-CON:SS
atta-hi̲la-h-o̲?
be:born-POT-TNS-Q
'How can a man be born when he is old?' (John 3:4)

Indefinites of manner include *kániohmit*, *kániimihoosh*, *kániht*, and *kániimish*:

(33) <Mihmʋt okla hak osh laua fehna hatuk o̲, kaniohmit pit isht chukowa hinla kʋt ik akostinincho . . .>
Mihmat oklah-akoosh laawa-fûhna-haatoko̲, kaniohmi-t
and:SS people-CON:NM many-very-because:DS do:something-PART
pit isht chokkow-ahi̲la-kat ik-akostiní̲ch-o . . .
away INSTR enter-POT-COMP:SS N-figure:out:L-NEG
'And because there were so many people, they couldn't figure out how to bring him in . . .' (Luke 5:19)

(34) . . . nana kaniohmi ho̲ yʋmmak oka potoli tuk, micha kaniohmit ashali̲ka hlakofi tuk aiena kʋt okla moma itikba ya̲ ai im anoli tok.
. . . *na̲na-h kaniohmi-h-o̲ yammak-ook*
something do:something-TNS-FOC:DS that-COMPAR
aa-potooli-tok micha kaniohmi-t ashali̲ka
LOC-touch-PT and do:something-PART immediately
lhakoffi-tok ayna-kat oklah mo̲ma-h itikba-ya̲
cure-PT and-COMP:SS people all-TNS front-AC
aay-im-anooli-ttook.
LOC-III-tell-DPAST
'She told him in front of all the people why she had touched him and how she was immediately healed.' (Luke 8:47)

(35) *Kaniimi-h-oosh ona-l-aachi̲-h-ba.*
do:something-TNS-PART:SS arrive-1SI-IRR-TNS-wonder
'I wonder how I'm going to get there.'

Example (34) conveniently shows how *kaniohmi* is interpreted as 'why' or 'how' depending on the morphology that follows. Some speakers also allow *kaniimichihoosh* and *kaniimichish* for indefinite 'how':

(36) *Shokháta-akoosh shawi' i-halíbis im-achokmahni-haatokoosh,*
possum-CON:NM   raccoon   III-tail   III-like-because:SS
kaniimihchi-h-oosh basoowa-chi-t pisa
do:how-TNS-PART:SS stripe-CAUS-SS see
achokmali-ka   i-ponaklo-h.
make:good-COMP:DS III-ask-TNS
'Because the possum liked the raccoon's tail, he asked him how he
made it striped and beautiful.' (T6:2–4)

Not all speakers recognize *kániimichihoosh* and *kániimichish,*
however.

7.1.3.3. 'When'

Equivalents of 'when' may be formed from the bases *nátah, kátiimih,*
and *kátiohmih.* 'When' is expressed differently in Choctaw depending
on whether the time being questioned is in the past or the future. For
example, *kátiimih* is interpreted as past 'when' if it is followed by the
tense marker *-k* and the previous-mention marker *-aash:*[5]

(37) *Kátiimi-k-aash ona-tok?*
INT-TNS-PREV   arrive-PT
'When did he get there?'

It is interpreted as future 'when' if followed by the irrealis
complementizing suffix *-kma:*

(38) *Kátiimi-kma on-aachi-h   miyah?*
INT-IRR:DS   arrive-IRR-TNS hearsay
'When do they say he's gonna get there?'

We can understand (38) to mean something like "What (time) will
it be when he gets there?".

Different-subject marking obligatorily appears on the end of
kátiimikma because *kátiimih* is a verb with an expletive subject ('it')
which is different from the subject of the following verb ('he'). It is
also possible to add different-subject switch-reference marking to past
tense 'when':

(39) *Kátiimi-k-aash-o   ala-h-a?*
INT-TNS-PREV-PART:DS arrive-TNS-Q
'When did he get here?'

Kátiimih 'when' may be used with the contrastive determiner
-akoo to form *kátiimikmako,* or with the adverbials *-fúhna* 'exactly'
and *-fokka* 'approximately' to form *kátiimifúhnakma* 'exactly when
(in the future)', *kátiimifúhnakaash* 'exactly when (in the past)',

---

5. Interrogatives involving the stem *kátiimi-* may reduce this to *káti-* before a
consonant-initial suffix. Thus, in addition to the form *kátiimikaasho* cited in the text,
some speakers also say *kátikaasho.*

katiimifokkakma 'approximately when (in the future)', and *katiimifokkakaash* 'approximately when (in the past)'.

A version of 'when' involving both -*fokka* 'approximately' and -*akoo* 'contrastive' is seen in the following excerpt from the Choctaw Bible:

(40) <Nan-ithʋnanchi ma katiohmi fokak mak ọ ilʋppa puta kʋt ai yʋmohma hi oh cho?>

Naṇ=ithanáchi-' ma' kátiohmi-fokka-km-akọ ilappa potta-kat
teacher-NML   VOC INT-about-IRR-CON:DS   this   all-COMP:NM
aa-yamohm-ahii-oh-cho?
LOC-happen-IRR-LINK-Q
'Master, when will all these teachings be fulfilled?' (Luke 21:7)

Another way of expressing future 'when' is to use the interrogative stem *nát-* with the irrealis and contrastive suffixes:

(41) *Naáta-km-akọ aaittanáaha-' illípa' isht   iya-l-aachịh?*
INT-IRR-CON:DS LOC-meet-NML food   INSTR go-1SI-IRR
'When am I going to take food to church?'

The expected past tense equivalent, *nátakaash*, does not seem to appear.

Some speakers use the form *kátiimak* for 'when'. This appears to be the interrogative root *kátiimih* plus the oblique -*ak*:

(42) *Kátiim-ak ọba-tok-chi.*
INT-OBL   rain-PT-wonder
'I wonder when it's gonna rain.'

Sometimes the English 'when' is also used in translations of Choctaw *kátiohmikmakoosh*:

(43) <Katiohmik mak osh Chihowa hạ e holitobli họ?>
Kátiohmi-km-akoo-sh Chihoowah-ạ ii-holitobli-h-ọ?
INT-IRR-CON-SS   God-AC   1PI-honor-TNS-Q
'When do we honor God?' (Catechism 31)

However, in this context 'when' is actually closer to 'how'. The sentence means something like 'We honor God when we perform what actions?'.

Indefinites of time are formed on the stems *kaniimih* and (more rarely) *kániohmih*:

(44) *Kániimi-kma, Charles-at ittanáaha-' abooha'*
INDEF-IRR:DS   Charles-NM meet-NML   house
binii-t   nosi-h.
sit-PART sleep-TNS
'Sometimes Charles falls asleep in church.'

(45) *Kániohmi-fûhna-toka*   *ak-itháan-o-h.*[6]
      sometimes-exactly-PT:COMP:DS 1SN-know:L-NEG-TNS
      'I don't know exactly when it was.' (Yale D:76)

Indefinite 'when, sometimes' is followed by the same affixes as interrogative 'when', giving forms like *kaniimikma* 'when (future)', *kániimifokkakma* 'approximately when (future)', *kániimifûhnakma* 'exactly when (future)', *kániimikaash* 'when (past)', and so on.

In complement clauses these indefinites sometimes show the complementizing suffix *-ka* rather than the expected *-kma* or *-kaash*:

(46) *Kániimi-ka*   *falaama-t   iy-aachi-ka*   *ak-ikháan-o-h.*
      INDEF-COMP:DS   return-PART go-IRR-COMP:DS 1SN-know:L-NEG-TNS
      'I don't know when she will leave.'

Kániimikat and *kániimika* also frequently appear with the meaning 'some, a part of':

(47) *Nípi' kániimi-ka*   *apa-li-tok.*
      meat INDEF-COMP:DS   eat-1SI-PT
      'I ate some of the meat.'

It is unclear how this sense of *kaniimikat/kaniimika* is connected to its temporal sense.

7.1.4. Quantificational and adjectival interrogatives and indefinites

7.1.4.1. 'How much, how many, what kind of'

Interrogatives that corresponding to 'how much', 'how many', and 'what kind of' are formed from the stem *katiohmih*. Unlike English, there does not seem to be a lexical distinction between 'how much, how many' and 'what kind of'; the context generally makes clear which is appropriate. *Katiohmih* is generally followed by the default tense *-h* and the participial *-oo*.

(48) *Ofi' kátiohmi-h-oosh*   *hattak-ma kopooli-h-a?*
      dog how:many-TNS-PART:SS man-D:AC   bite-TNS-Q
      'How many dogs bit that man?'
      'What kind of dog(s) bit that man?'

It may be followed by *-fokka* 'approximately' or *-fûhna* 'exactly' to give *kátiohmifokkaho* 'approximately how much, how many, what kind of' and *kátiohmifûhnaho* 'exactly how much, how many, what kind of'.

Like other quantifiers, *kátiohmih* may be inflected for subject:

---

6. This nineteenth-century example is unusual in showing the indefinite with the tense marker *-tok*. Speakers I consulted did not recognize this construction.

(49) *Hash-kátiohmi-h-oosh*   *hash-iy-aachị-h?*
      2PI-how:many-TNS-PART:SS 2PI-go-IRR-TNS
      'How many of you are going to go?'

In some older texts, *katiohmih* is followed by the tense marker *-tok,*
but this does not seem to be possible in modern Choctaw:

(50) *. . . wiiki   kátiohmi-fokka-tok   chi-yimmi-h?*
      heavy how:much-about-PT 2SII-believe-TNS
      'About how heavy do you believe it was?' (Yale A:25)

Indefinites are formed on the stem *kániohmih,* generally followed
by *-h* 'default tense' plus *-oo* 'participle'.

(51) *Illịpa' lawah kániohmi-h-ọ*   *nonaachi-tokạ*
      food   much   so:much-TNS-PART:DS cook-PT:COMP:DS
      ak-ikháan-o-h.
      1SN-know:L-NEG-TNS
      'I don't know how much food she cooked.'

(52) <Wak kaniohmi chimalachi[n]>
      Waak kániohmi-h   chim-aa-l-aachị-h.
      cow   some:kind-TNS 2SIII-give-1SI-IRR-TNS
      'I will give you a cow of some kind.' (Byington 1915:224)

(53) <Atuk osh nitak kániohmi họ yakohmi tok . . .>
      Aatokoosh   nittak kaniohmi-h-ọ   yakohmi-ttook . . .
      and:PT:SS day   some-TNS-PART:DS be:like:this-DPAST
      'And it came to pass on a certain day . . .' (Luke 8:22)

7.1.4.2. 'Which'

'Which' may be expressed in two ways. When comparing two
things, *kátiimạpoh, kátiimaapoh, kátoomạpoh* or *kátoomaapoh* is
used:

(54) <Pi haknip ak okma keyukmʋt pi shilombish ak okma katịmampo kak
      ʋsh Chihowa hạ holba fiehna họ?>
      Pi-haknip-ak-oo-kma   kiiyo-kmat
      1PI-flesh-OBL-LINK-IRR NEG-IRR:SS
      pi-shilọbish-ak-oo-kma kátiimạpo-k-akoosh
      1PI-spirit-OBL-LINK-IRR which-OBL-CN:NM
      Chihoowah-ạ holba-fịíhna-h-ọ?
      God-AC   resemble-very-TNS-Q
      'Which is most like to God, our body or our soul?' (Catechism 21–22)

(55) *Kátoomaap-oosh chaaha-h chaffa ị-shahli-h?*
      which-FOC:NM   tall-TNS one   III-exceed-TNS
      'Which one is taller?'

When the comparison is not explicitly between two things, *kátommah* or *kátimmah* is used, generally followed by *-akoo* 'contrastive'. The tense marker *-k* often appears between the two:

(57) *Aa-ittanáaha-' kátimma-k-ako̱   Pam-at   iya-tok?*
LOC-meet-NML which-TNS-CON:AC Pam-NM go-PT
'Which church did Pam go to?'

(58) *Bonnie i̱-nákfi'   kátimma-k-akoosh chaaha-h?*
Bonnie III-brother which-TNS-CON:NM tall-TNS
'Which of Bonnie's brothers is tall?'

(59) *Hattak kátomm-akoosh illi-tok?*
man   which-CON:NM die-PT
'Which man died?'

Kátommah and *kátimmah* may be inflected for subject in some cases:

(59) <Hʊsh katima kak osh hʊchim issuba haksobish falaia okmá, keyukmʊt wak toksʊli okmá, nana kʊt yakni chiluk hofobi o̱ pit itula ka, ashalika nitak hullo nitak a̱ halʊllit hʊch ik kohcho ka hinla cho?>
Hash-kátimma-k-akoosh hachim-issóba' haksobish falaaya-h
2PI-which-TNS-CON:NM   2PIII-horse   ear   long-TNS
oo-kma kiiyo-kmat waak to̱ksáli-'   oo-kma na̱na-kat
be-IRR NEG-IRR:SS cow   work-NML be-IRR be:the:case-COMP:SS
yakni' chilok hofóobi-y-o̱   pit   ittola-ka, ashshalika'
land   hole   deep-NML-FOC:AC toward   fall-COMP sin
nittak=hóllo' nittak-a̱ halalli-t hachik-kóhch-ok-ahi̱la-h-cho?
Sunday   day-AC pull-PART 2PN-take:out-L-NEG-POT-TNS-Q
'Which of you if your ass or ox falls into a pit will not pull him out on the Sabbath day?' (Luke 14:5)

There are also indefinite versions of these forms, *kánimmah*, generally translated into English as 'one of', 'any of', or 'none of', and *kániimapoh* 'either of', 'neither of'.

(60) *Hash-kánimma-k-ano hachishno' hapim-ahwa-tok.*
2PI-some-TNS-AC2   yours   1MPI-seem-PT
'It seemed to us that it belonged to one of you.'

(61) <Hash kanimmah másh oklah hachi lhákaffáchih kiyoh.>
Hash-kanimma-h-m-aash oklah hachi-lhaakáff-aachi̱-kiiyo-h.
2PI-some-TNS-DEM-PREV PLUR 2PII-be:saved-N-IRR-NEG-TNS
'None of you will be saved.' (Amos 4:2 CBTC)

(62) *Ii-kániimapo-m-ako̱   ik-pi-kháan-o-h.*
1PI-one:of:two-DEM-CON:AC N-1PII-know:L-NEG-TNS
'He doesn't know either of us two.'

Some speakers also use a longer form *kánimmáyyolih*. Speakers disagree on whether this is different in some way from *kánimmah*. One speaker said that *kánimmáyyolih* implies 'one out of a large group', but another speaker said that *kánimmáyyolih* is an older form of *kánimmah* and the two are synonymous. The following example shows *kánimmáyyoli*:

(63) *Hash-kánimmáyyoli-m-áko̱ ak-hachi-kháan-o-h.*
      2PI-some-DEM-CON:AC   1SN-2PII-know:L-NEG-TNS
      'I don't know any of you.'

7.1.5. Locative and nominal interrogatives and indefinites

7.1.5.1. 'Where'

Interrogatives for the locative are formed from the stems *kátimmah*, *kátommah*; the corresponding indefinites are formed from *kánimmah*, *kánommah*:

(64) *Kátomma-k-o̱   aay-atta-h?*
      where-TNS-PART:AC LOC-live-TNS
      'Where did he live?'

(65) *Kátimma-k-o̱   hoshi' híshi-ano   aay-ishi-tok-ba?*
      where-TNS-PART:AC bird   feather-AC2 LOC-get-PT-DOUBT
      'Where did she get the feathers?' (Yale A:11)

(66) *Kátomma-h iya-tok?*
      where-TNS go-PT
      'Where did he go?'

(67) *Ak-itháan-o-h   kánomma-k-o̱   Bill-at*
      1SN-know:L-NEG-TNS somewhere-TNS-PART:AC Bill-NM
      Pam aa-písa-toka̱.
      Pam LOC-see:N-PT:COMP:DS
      'I don't know where Bill saw Pam.'

(68) *Bonnie-at kánomma-h   iya-kma̱, iya-l-aachi̱-h.*
      Bonnie-NM somewhere-TNS go-IRR:DS go-1SI-IRR-TNS
      'I'll go where Bonnie goes.'

In nineteenth-century materials, apparent nominalized versions *katímma'* and *kanímma'* are found.[7]

(69) <Katima yo̱ hʋsh minti cho?>
      Katímma-yo̱   hash-mi̱ti-h-cho?
      where-FOC:AC 2PI-come-TNS-Q
      'Where do you come from?' (Josh. 9:8)

---

7. Recall that stem final glottal stop becomes *y* before a vowel-initial suffix (section 2.6), so *katímma'-o̱* → *katímmayo̱*. If these interrogatives and indefinites were verbal, as in modern Choctaw, we would expect *kátimmaho̱* and *kánimmaho̱* instead of the attested *katímmayo̱* and *kanímmayo̱*.

(70) <. . . yʊmmak o͟ api͟hʊt aboha kanima yo͟ pit chukowakma, hʊsh chukowashke.>

       yammak-o͟   *api͟ha-t*   *abooha'*   *aním̱ma-yo͟*
       that-FOC:AC   be:with-PART   house   somewhere-FOC:AC

   pit   *chokkowa-kma͟,*   *hash-chokkowa-shkii.*
   toward   enter-IRR:DS   2PI-enter-EXHORT

   'Enter whatever house he enters with him.' (Luke 22:10)

However, Mrs. Edith Gem did not recognize these forms, suggesting that such nominalizations are not present in at least some forms of modern Choctaw.

Kátommah may also be followed by the adverbials *-fíihna* and *-fokka* to yield *kátommafíihnaho͟* 'exactly where' and *kátommafokkaho͟* 'approximately where'.

7.1.5.2. 'Who' and 'what'

Kátah is 'who' and *náatah/nátah* is 'what'; the corresponding indefinites are *kánah* 'who, someone' and *náanah/na͟nah* 'what, something'. These words show a mix of verbal and nominal morphology.

The interrogative and indefinite words 'who, someone, anyone' and 'what, something, anything' are like verbs in that they are often followed by the *-h* or *-k* tense markers.

(71) *Káta-h-oosh*   *chi-pi͟sa-h-a͟?*
      who-TNS-PART:NM   2SII-see:N-TNS-Q
      'Who saw you?'

(72) *Kána-h-óhmakoosh*   *ishki'*   *im-ihaksi-kiiyo-h.*
      someone-TNS-too:NM   mother   III-forget-NEG-TNS
      'No one forgets their mother.'

(73) *Bonnie-at*   *na͟na-h*   *nonaachi-kma͟,*   *apa-l-aachi͟-h.*
      Bonnie-NM   something-TNS   cook-IRR:DS   eat-1SI-IRR-TNS
      'I'll eat what Bonnie cooks.'

(74) <nana kash ot ont aia͟hli nitak a͟ onak mak a hi oke>
      na͟na-k-aash-oot   *ot*   *aay-alhlhi nittak-a͟*
      something-TNS-PREV-PART:NM   go:and   LOC-true   day-AC
      ona-k   *mak-ahii-okii*
      arrive-TNS   COP-IRR-indeed
      'The things [that were previously mentioned] will truly come to pass in their season.' (Luke 1:20)

However, they are like nouns in that they are followed by case markers (as seen in the preceding examples) and the determiner *-kia* 'too'. In some of these cases, there is no tense marker present:

(75) *Nána-kia   am-anooli-h.*
      something-too 1sIII-tell-TNS
      'Tell me anything.'

(76) <Kʋna kia apehlichika isht anumpa ha haklo cha . . .>
      Kána-kia   apihlichúika' isht-anopah-a
      someone-too kingdom   INSTR-word-AC
      háklo-cha . . .
      hear:L-SS
      'Anyone who hears the word of the kingdom . . .' (Matt. 13:19)

(77) *Kána-at   a-chokka'   ala-h-a?*
      someone-NM 1sIII-house arrive-TNS-Q
      'Did anyone come to my house?'

Nátah 'what' may be used predicatively:

(78) <Enchil ʋt nanta ho?>
      Angel-at   nata-h-o?
      angel-NM what-TNS-Q
      'What are angels?' (Catechism 41)

The corresponding indefinite *nánah* is used in forming the equivalent of English 'whether':

(79) *Lynn-at   ik-ikháan-o-h   [iy-aachi-kma nána-kat].*
      Lynn-NM N-know:L-NEG-TNS go-IRR-IRR:DS be:the:case-COMP:SS
      'Lynn doesn't know if she will go.'[8]

Sentences of this type are discussed in more detail in chapter 16.

7.2. The syntax of interrogatives

7.2.1. General properties

In general, wh-questions may be formed by merely leaving an appropriate interrogative in situ. No special verbal morphology or word order is necessary:

(80) *John-at   káta-h-o   písa-tok?*
      John-NM who-TNS-PART:AC see:N-PT
      'Who did John see?'

(81) *Achokma-kat   náatahohmi-h?*
      good-COMP:SS how:much-TNS
      'How good is it?'

(82) *Hashshok is-sa-chali-kat   kátihmi-h*
      grass   2SI-1SIII-cut-COMP:SS how:much-TNS

---

8. Note that in this example the complement clause is extraposed to the right.

is-sam-apiis-ahiina-h?
2sI-1sIII-charge-POT-TNS
'How much will you charge me to cut the grass for me?'

(83) Kátihmi-li-km-akoosh   shiiki'   anopoli-h
      do:INT-1sI-IRR-CONTR:SS buzzard talk-TNS
      haklo-l-aana-cho?
      hear-1sI-IRR-Q
      'How can I hear the buzzards talking?' (Lit., If I do what will I hear
      the buzzards talking?)

Choctaw also has optional fronting of interrogatives in the syntax;
thus the following are acceptable:

(84) Káta-h-o   John-at   písa-tok?
      who-TNS-PART:AC John-NM see:N-PT
      'Who did John see?'

(85) Kátiimi-h-oosh   Charles-at okkissa' tiwwi-tok?
      how-TNS-PART:SS Charles-NM door   open-PT
      'How did Charles open the door?'

It is possible, though not obligatory, to move an interrogative outside
its clause:

(86) Pam-at [Charles-at tobi' honni-tok-o]   hokopa-tok.
      Pam-NM Charles-NM bean cook-PT-FOC:AC steal-PT
      'Pam stole the beans that Charles cooked.'

(87) Náta-h-o   Pam-at Charles-at honni-tok-o
      what-TNS-PART:AC Pam-NM Charles-NM cook-PT-FOC:AC
      hokopa-tok?
      steal-PT
      'What did Pam steal that Charles cooked?'

7.2.2. Restrictions on movement

There are some restrictions on what constituents may intervene
between an interrogative and the corresponding gap. However, wh-
movement fails to show the full range of island effects seen in
English.

Extraction from interrogative complement clauses is ungrammatical, as shown in the following examples:

(88) Ak-itháan-o-h   [CP kánomma-k-o   Bill-at   Pam
      1sN-know:L-NEG-TNS   where-TNS-PART:AC Bill-NM Pam
      aa-písa-toka].
      LOC-see:N-PT:COMP:DS
      'I don't know where Bill saw Pam.'

(89) *Kátahoosh ak-itháan-o-h   [cp kánomm-ako
who:NM   1sN-know:L-NEG-TNS   where-CN:AC
Pam aa-písa-toka]?
Pam LOC-see:N-PT:COMP:DS
(*'Who don't I know where saw Pam?')

(90) *Kátaho ak-itháan-o-h   [cp kánomm-ako
who:AC   1sN-know:L-NEG-TNS   where-CN:AC
Bill-at   aa-písa-toka]?
Bill-NM   LOC-see-PT:COMP:DS
(*'Who don't I know where Bill saw?')

(91) Ak-itháan-o-h   [cp John-at Mary ahpali-kma
1N-know-NEG-TNS   John-NM   Mary kiss-IRR
nána-toka].
whether-PT:COMP:DS
'I don't know whether John kissed Mary.'

(92) *Kátahoosh ak-itháan-o-h
who:NM   1N-know-NEG-TNS
[cp Mary ahpali-kma nána-toka].
Mary   kiss-IRR   whether-PT:COMP:DS
(*'Who don't I know whether kissed Mary?')

There are no Complex Noun Phrase Condition effects. This is due essentially to the fact that there are no complex noun phrases in the language. (See chapter 16 for discussion of relative clauses.)

Subject condition effects are also absent, and extraction of genitives is allowed. The clearest cases of this are seen in possessor raising, discussed in section 17.2.

7.2.3. Empty Category Principle effects

The Empty Category Principle (Chomsky 1981) imposes licensing conditions on the trace of wh-movement that have the effect of making movement from subject positions more restricted than movement from object positions, and movement from adjunct positions more restricted than movement from argument positions. There is little evidence for the standard Empty Category Principle effects in Choctaw, either of the subject-object or argument-adjunct variety. The lack of subject-object asymmetries may be due to a general scarcity of subject-object asymmetries in Choctaw, as in many head-final languages, and the lack of argument-adjunct asymmetries may be due to the unusual categorial status of adjunct interrogatives in Choctaw.

There seem to be no subject-object asymmetries for extraction in Choctaw. Example (93) contains an internally headed relative clause; (94) shows extraction from its subject position; and (95) shows an interrogative in situ in this position.

(93)   *Bill-at*   [$_{CP}$ *ofi-it ohooyo'-ma̱*   *kobli-tok-ma̱*]   *afaama-tok*
       Bill-NM   dog-NM   woman-NM   bite-PT-D:AC   meet-PT
       'Bill met the woman that the dog bit.'

(94)   *Nata-h-oosh*   *Bill-at* [$_{CP}$ *ohooyo'-ma̱ kobli-tok-ma̱]*   *afaama-tok?*
       what-TNS-PART:NM   Bill-NM   woman-D:ACbite-PT-D:AC   bite-PT
       'Bill met the woman that *what* bit?'
       (Lit., 'What did Bill meet the woman that __ bit?'')

(95)   *Bill-at* [$_{CP}$ *nata-h-oosh*   *ohooyo'-ma̱*   *kobli-tok-ma̱]*   *afaama-tok?*
       Bill-NM   what-TNS-PART:NM   woman-D:AC   bite-PT-D:AC   meet-PT
       'Bill met the woman that *what* bit?'

Superiority effects also fail to hold. In Choctaw, multiple wh-phrases are allowed, but there are no restrictions on their relative order:

(96)   *Kata-h-oosh*   *kátimmah ahi'*   *aa-honi-h?*
       who-TNS-PART:NM   where   potato   LOC-boil-TNS
       'Who boiled potatoes where?'

(97)   *Katimma-h kata-h-oosh*   *ahi'*   *aa-honi-h?*
       where-TNS   who-TNS-PART:NM   potato   LOC-boil-TNS
       'Who boiled potatoes where?'

7.2.4. Weak Crossover effects

The well-known Weak Crossover effect (Wasow 1979) fails to hold in Choctaw. Weak Crossover describes an ungrammatical configuration in which a pronoun and a trace are bound by the same operator, but neither c-commands the other, as in the following English example:

(98)   *Who$_i$ does his$_i$ mother love t$_i$?

The effect also holds for certain kinds of quantified phrases, which has been taken as evidence that quantifiers move at logical form (LF) leaving a trace which is subject to Weak Crossover.

(99)   *His$_i$ mother loves everyone$_i$.

Various explanations of these effects have been proposed (Chomsky 1975; Koopman and Sportiche 1982; Safir 1984; Georgopoulos 1991; Bresnan 1995).
     However, the analogous Choctaw examples are grammatical. Wh-movement is optional in Choctaw. Both sentences with moved interrogatives and interrogatives in situ show violations of Weak Crossover:

(100)   *Kata-h-o̱*   *ishki-it*   *i̱-hollo-h?*
       who-TNS-FOC:AC   mother-NM   III-love-TNS
       'Who$_i$ does her$_i$ mother love?'

(101) *Ishki-it*   *kata-h-o̱*   *i̱-hollo-h?*
mother-NM   who-TNSFOC:AC   III-love-TNS
'Who₁ does her₁ mother love?'

Sentences with quantifiers also show Weak Crossover violations. There are two common ways of saying 'everyone' in Choctaw. One involves the word *kánah* 'someone' plus the suffix *-ohmakoo-* 'too, just'. The other involves the phrase *oklah mo̱mah* 'all people'. As the following examples show, both behave the same with respect to Weak Crossover:

(102) *Ishki-it*   *kánah-ohmako̱ i̱-hollo-h.*
mother-NM   who-too:AC   III-love-TNS
'Her₁ mother loves everyone₁.'

(103) *Ishki-it*   *oklah   mo̱ma-h i̱-hollo-h.*
mother-NM   people   all-TNS   III-love-TNS
'Her₁ mother loves everyone₁.'

Speakers judged these sentences as potentially synonymous with the following:

(104) *Kánah ishki-yohmakoosh i̱-hollo-h.*
who   mother-too:NM   III-love-TNS
'Everyone₁'s mother loves her₁/them₁.'[9]

(105) *Oklah mo̱ma-h ishki-it   i̱-hollo-h.*
people all-TNS   mother-NM III-love-TNS
'Everyone₁'s mother loves them₁.'

These sentences could not be synonymous with the preceding sentences if there were Weak Crossover effects in the language.

---

9. My consultants preferred the more colloquial English translations with *them* as bound variable, and I have retained this in the translation.

8. Verbal derivational morphology

8.1. The transitive-intransitive alternation

Choctaw has no passive, but it does have a regular relationship between many pairs of transitive and intransitive verbs. This is the alternation that is often referred to as the causative-inchoative alternation crosslinguistically, and Choctaw shows the relationship known as "equipollent" (Haspelmath 1993), in which neither verb is derived from the other.[1]

8.1.1. Morphological relationships in the transitive-intransitive alternation

In the most common pattern, the intransitive ends in -a, and the transitive in -li, with assimilation of the l to a preceding b, f, lh, m, n, or w:[2]

(1a)	*tiw-a-h*	'to be open, to become open'
	tiw-wi-h	'to open [something]'
(1b)	*kobaaf-a-h'*	to be broken [of something long], to break [of something long]'
	kobaf-fi-h	'to break [something long]'
(1c)	*yoshoob-a-h*	'to be lost, to get lost'
	yoshob-bi-h	'to lose'[3]

When the root-final consonant is *t*, it completely assimilates to the following *l*:

(2)	*bichoot-a-h*	'to be bent, to bend'
	bichol-li-h	'to bend [something]'

When the root final consonant is *p*, it assimilates in voicing to the following *l*:

---

1. Because the suffixes -a/ and -li sometimes appear without the expected effect on the verb's valence, Ulrich (1986) and Munro and Willmond (1994) opt for a valence-neutral terminology and label the verb with the -a suffix the v1, and the verb with the -li suffix the v2.

2. For some speakers of Mississippi Choctaw, assimilation to a preceding b is optional, leading to alternations like *atoblih/atobbih* 'to pay'.

3. Many of the stative verbs in these examples show the effect of rhythmic lengthening, which lengthens the vowels of alternate open syllables. See chapter 2 for more discussion.

(3) tap-a-h   'to be cut off, to become cut off'
     tab-li-h (<tap-li-h)   'to cut [something] off'

Some intransitive verbs in this alternation have an infixed *l*. This *l* may be the only sign of the morphological relationship, or it may cooccur with the ordinary -*a* suffix:

(4a) a<l>wash-a-h   'to be fried, to get fried'
     awash-li-h   'to fry [something]'

(4b) ho<l>loh   'to be on [of shoes, stockings]'
     holo-h   'to put on [shoes, stockings]'

This *l* infix becomes *h* before *ch*, and *lh* before other following voiceless consonants:

(5a) ho<lh>tina-h   'to be counted'
     hotiina-h   'to count'

(5b) a<h>chifa-h   'to be washed'
     achiifa-h   'to wash'

Most verbs with the infix *l* have initial *a*- and *ho*-, suggesting that these initial syllables are diachronically segmentable.

The great majority of verbs that participate in the transitive-intransitive alternation have consonant-final roots, but Ulrich (1986) has shown that some alternating pairs suggest a vowel-final root. A root-final short vowel is deleted before the intransitive -*a* suffix:

(6a) bil-a-h (< bili-a-h)   'to melt [intransitive]'
     bilii-li-h (< bili-li-h)   'to melt [transitive]'

(6b) shil-a-h (< shili-a-h)   'to dry [intransitive]'
     shilii-li-h (< shili-li-h)   'to dry [transitive]'

When the verb root ends with a long vowel, an epenthetic glide appears. The glide is *w* after *oo* and *y* after *ii* or *aa*:

(7a) bóo-wa-h (< boo-a-h)   'to be hit'
     bóo-li-h   'to hit'

(7b) talaa-ya-h (< talaa-a-h)   'to sit [of a container or round object]'
     talaa-li-h   'to set down [a container or round object]'

In a small number of cases, the vowel changes between the two forms:

(8) wakaa-ya-h   'to rise, stand up'
     wakii-li-h   'to raise, lift up'

Ulrich notes that some speakers pronounce the second form here *wakeelih*, possibly suggesting *wakay-li-h* as an intermediate stage in the derivation.

8.1.2. The syntax of the transitive-intransitive alternation

In the regular pattern, the intransitive verb in such alternations can be used in either a stative or inchoative sense:

(9)   *Okhissa-yat tiw-a-h.*
      door-NM   open-INTR-TNS
      'The door is open.'
      'The door opened.'

Such verbs generally take subject agreement from the II class.[4]

(10) *Sa-bash-a-h.*
      1sII-cut-INTR-TNS
      'I have been cut.'
      'I got cut.'

In general, the transitive verb in such pairs takes class I agreement for subjects and II agreement for objects:

(11) *Chi-bash-li-li-tok-ǫ?*
      2sII-cut-TR-1sI-PT-Q
      'Did I cut you?'

Ulrich (1986:118) discusses a few pairs of verbs that do not conform to these generalizations. For the following pair, both the verb with the *-a* suffix and the verb with the *-li* suffix may be used intransitively:

(12) *lhakoof-a-h*   'to come off [e.g., of a scab]'
      lhakof-fi-h   'to heal [intransitive]'

However, *lhakoffih* also has a number of transitive senses including 'to miss [e.g., a target], 'to save [e.g., a life]', 'to heal [transitive]'.

There are also some pairs in which the verb with the *-a* suffix is an intransitive which has class I agreement for the subject rather than the expected II agreement:

(13a) *Wakaay-a-li-h.*
      rise-INTR-1sI-TNS
      'I stood up.'

(13b) *Sa-wakii-li-h.*
      1sII-raise-TR-TNS
      'She lifted me up.'[5]

These cases appear to be limited to verbs of position.

There are also some cases in which the absolute argument in the

4. Recall that I and II agreement are not distinguished for third person subjects. This means that for statives that only occur with inanimate subjects, there is in general no way to be sure which agreement class they occur with.

5. Ulrich (1986:118) lists this form v2 as *wakeelih*. See the discussion above for this phonological variation.

transitive-intransitive pair has III (dative) verbal agreement (Ulrich 1986:118):

(14) *Waak-at i̱-cho̱w-a-t   taha-h.*
     cow-NM   III-brand-INTR-PART   complete-TNS
     'The cattle are branded.'

(15) *Waak i̱-cho̱li-li-h.*
     cow   III-brand-TR-TNS
     'I branded the cattle.'

There is at least one pair in which the verb with the *-a* suffix is a transitive and the corresponding verb with *-li* is ditransitive:

(16) *bachaay-a-h*   'to lie across'
     bachaa-li-h   'to lay [something] across [something]'

8.1.3. The semantics of the transitive-intransitive alternation

The largest group of verbs participating in the transitive-intransitive alternation are change-of-state verbs. In this group, the stative means 'to be in or come to be in a particular state' and the active means 'to cause something to be in a particular state', as in the following examples:

(17a) *pataaf-a-h*   'to be split, to become split'
      pataf-fi-h   'to split [something]'

(17b) *lhitaaf-a-h*   'to be broken, get broken [of something like a thread]'
      lhitaf-fi-h   'to break [something like a thread]'

The Choctaw transitive-intransitive alternation applies to a different range of verbs than those which undergo the English causative alternation seen in sentences like the following:

(18a) The log split.
      I split the log.

(18b) The thread broke.
      I broke the thread.

As is well known, some English verbs fail to undergo this alternation (*I cut the meat/ *The meat cut*). The correct generalization for English seems to be that verbs which participate in the alternation are verbs in which an agent is not conceptually necessary (Levin 1993)—that is, verbs where it is possible to imagine the state arising without human intervention. But the following Choctaw verbs do participate in the transitive-intransitive alternation, despite the fact that their English translations do not undergo the causative alternation:

(19a) a<lh>tob-a-h   'to be paid'
      atob-li-h   'to pay [someone]'

(19b) *bash-a-h*   'to be cut, get cut'
      bash-li-h   'to cut [something]'

(19c) *tan-a-h*   'to be woven, to get woven'
      tan-ni-h   'to weave'

(19d) *lob-a-h*   'to be plucked, get plucked [e.g., of ears of corn]'

      lob-bi-h   'to pluck [e.g., ears of corn]'

The verbs participating in the transitive-intransitive alternation contrast with verbs like the following, which are always transitive:

(20)   Nonalternating transitives
      verbs of perception: *písah* 'to see', *hákloh* 'to hear'
      emotions: *ahnichih* 'to like, love', *anokpahlih* 'to desire'
      verbs of contact: *ahpalih* 'to kiss', *apaatah* 'to sit beside'
      verbs of consumption: *apah* 'to eat', *ishkoh* 'to drink'

8.2. The causative

8.2.1. Introduction

Choctaw has a productive morphological causative *-chi*, as shown in the following examples:

(21a) *Hattak-at taloowa-tok.*
      man-NM   sing-PT
      'The man sang.'

(21b) *Abanopoli-yat hattak taloowa-chi-tok.*
      preacher-NM   man   sing-CAUS-PT
      'The preacher made the man sing.'

The suffix *-chi* can be added to nearly every verb in the language. In the regular case, the addition of the causative increases the valence of the verb by one argument. Intransitive verbs become transitive and transitive verbs become ditransitive.

    As Ulrich (1986:138) notes, the causer always triggers class I agreement on the verb. If the subject of the noncausative verb normally takes I agreement, then the causee of the causative verb takes II agreement:

(22a) *Nowa-li-h.*
      walk-1SI-TNS
      'I walked.'

(22b) *Sa-nowa-chi-tok.*
1sII-walk-CAUS-PT
'He made me walk.'

Subjects that trigger other kinds of agreement retain the same agreement when converted to causees:

(23)   *Sa-nokhǎklo-h.*
1sII-sad-TNS
'I'm sad'

(24)   *Is-sa-nokhǎklo-chi-h.*
2sI-1sII-sad-CAUS-TNS
'You made me sad.'

(25)   *Am-ihaksi-h.*
1sIII-forget-TNS
'I forgot.'

(26)   *Is-sam-ihaksi-chi-h.*
1sI-1sIII-forget-CAUS-TNS
'You made me forget.'

When there are overt nominal arguments, the causer is in the nominative case, while the causee is in the accusative (marking of accusative case is optional, as usual):

(27)   *John-at   nowa-tok.*
John-NM   walk-PT
'John walked.'

(28)   *Bill-at   John(-a)   nowa-chi-tok.*
Bill-NM   John(-AC)   walk-CAUS-PT
'Bill made John walk.'

This is true, regardless of the type of agreement that the causee takes:

(29)   *Bill-at   John(-a)   im-ihaksi-chi-tok.*
Bill-NM   John(-AC)   III-forget-CAUS-PT
'Bill made John forget.'

Ulrich (1986) notes that there is a difficulty with causatives of transitive verbs which have II agreement for objects. If both the causee and the object are not third person, then by the description so far, we would expect II agreement for the causee and II agreement for the object, as in the following:

(30)   ??*Lynn-at   sa-chi-haabli-chi-tok.*
Lynn-NM   1sII-2sII-kick-CAUS-PT
'Lynn made me kick you.'

However, most Choctaw speakers are quite reluctant to accept this form, which seems to violate a general constraint against two instances of a II prefix on the same verb. Although Davies (1981) cites forms like this in his discussion of the causative, their grammaticality is problematic.

Speakers generally prefer biclausal paraphrases for sentences like (30). Ulrich reports one additional option, which is the use of a nonagreeing benefactive applicative in addition to the causee:

(31)   *Lynn-at   imị-chi-haabli-chi-li-h.*
       Lynn-NM BEN-2sII-kick-CAUS-1sI-TNS
       'Lynn made me kick you.' (Ulrich 1986:139)

8.2.2. *Li*-deletion and the causative

A peculiarity of the suffix *-chi* is that when a preceding verb ends with *-li*, *-li* optionally deletes. This deletion only occurs when the syllable preceding *-li* is open:

(32a) *baliili-h*
       run-TNS
       'to run'

(32b) *baliili-chi-h*
       run-CAUS-TNS
       'to cause to run'

(32c) *balii-chi-h*
       run-CAUS-TNS
       'to cause to run'

(33a) *bashli-h*
       cut-TNS
       'to cut'

(33b) *bashli-chi-h*
       cut-CAUS-TNS
       'to cause to cut'

(33c) *bash-chi-h

A similar deletion of *-li* is found before the participial suffix *-t*, discussed in chapter 13. Munro and Willmond (1994:xxxv) describe the operation of a comparable rule of *li*-deletion in Chickasaw.

8.2.3. *-chi* as a marker of affectedness

The suffix *-chi* sometimes does not behave as expected; when added to a verb stem, there is neither an increase in valence nor a change in grammatical relations. Consider the following examples:

(34)   *John-at   ashanni-tok.*
       John-NM twist-PT
       'John twisted it.'

(35) *John-at   ashanni-chi-tok.*
      John-NM twist-AFF-PT
      'John twisted it hard.'
      'John twisted it with difficulty.'
      'John twisted it and broke it.'

For ease of discussion, we may refer to the ordinary causative as *-chi*₁ and the morpheme shown in example (35) as *-chi*₂.

It is sometimes difficult for Choctaw speakers to explain the difference in meaning between sentences like (34) and (35) above. Consider the following four instances of *-chi*₂, which give a sample of the range of different English translations for such sentences:

(36a) *Shilosh aàyálhto' fokki-li-tok.*
       shoe   box   put:PL-1SI-PT
       'I put the shoes in the box.'

(36b) *Shilosh aayálhto' fokki-chi-li-h.*
       shoe   box   put:PL-AFF-1SI-TNS
       'I forced the shoes into the box.'

(37a) *Ak̲akoshi' hobi-tok.*
       egg   boil-PT
       'She boiled an egg.'

(37b) *Ak̲akoshi' hobi-chi-tok.*
       egg   boil-AFF-PT
       'She cooked an egg by boiling it.'

(38a) *Okhissa' ashanni-tok.*
       door   lock-PT
       'He locked the door.'

(38b) *Okhissa' ashanni-chi-tok.*
       door   lock-AFF-PT
       'He forced the door to lock.'

(39a) *Itti'   kobaffi-tok.*
       wood   break-PT
       'He broke the stick.'

(39b) *Itti   kobaffi-chi-tok.*
       wood   break-AFF-PT
       'He caused the stick to be broken [perhaps after some difficulty].'

Examining the range of English translation, two semantic regularities seem to account for the great majority of the data. Comparing verbs with and without *-chi*₂, one may state that in general, verbs with *-chi*₂ indicate either a more completely affected patient, or a greater effort on the part of the agent.

However, these two semantic effects are logically linked to each other. In general, the degree of effort on the part of the agent ought to correlate with the degree of affectedness of the patient. So it is possible to treat either of the two semantic effects as basic and derive the other by inference. Here I proceed on the assumption that $-chi_2$ is most perspicuously treated as marker of affectedness.

8.2.4. Homophony or polysemy?

I have argued in Broadwell (1996) that it is unsatisfying to claim that there are two homophonous morphemes $-chi_1$ 'causative' and $-chi_2$ 'affected'. Rather, we should view the reading 'affected' as derived from the causative in some way.

The reasoning is as follows. Nearly every Choctaw verb allows the suffix $-chi$. However, some verbs have only the causative reading for this suffix, while other verbs are ambiguous between the causative and affected readings. Let us call the verbs for which $-chi$ can mark either causation or affectedness "type A verbs," and those in which $-chi$ marks only causation "type B verbs." The two types of verbs show the following pattern:

(40) Type A verb
      Akakoshi' hobi-chi-tok.
      egg   boil-AFF-PT
      'She cooked an egg by boiling it.' (affected)
      'She made someone boil an egg.' (causative)

(41) Type B verb
      Ohooyo'-mat taloowa-chi-tok.
      woman-D:NM sing-CAUS-PT
      'That woman made someone sing.' (causative)
      (no other reading possible)

The following lists give a sample of the kinds of verbs that appear in each class.

(42) Type A verbs
      abohlih   'to be overgrown, get weedy, be
                            a thicket'
      acholih   'to sew'
      ashannih   'to twist, lock'
      awashlih   'to fry'
      fokkih   'to put [one object] in' (see also type C
                            verbs, below)
      hittopalih   'to hurt [someone]'
      hobih   'to boil [something like an egg]'
      honih   'to cook by boiling'
      kapassalih   'to cool [something]'
      kobaffih   'to break [something like a stick]'
      koolih   'to break [something like glass]'

polhommih	'to hem, fold over'
tablih	'to break [something] apart'
tiloffih	'to break off, knock off [so that a stump remains]'
tohnoh	'to hire, order'
bichiilih	'to pour out'
lhatablih	'to spill [something]'
alootalih	'to fill'
lhipiilih	'to spill'
kochchawihlih	'to take out'
kashoffih	'to clean'
kashoolih	'to wipe'
kihlih	'to wipe [oneself, after defecation], wipe out [some loose material from a tight area, e.g., ashes from under a grate]'
iskoonachih	'to gut, disembowel'
halallih	'to pull'
toblih	'to push'
hopiilah	'to distribute'
lohmih	'to hide'
fammih	'to whip, spank'
bahlih	'to gore'

(43) Type B verbs

imachokmah	'to feel well'
kanallih	'to move'
komootah	'to be fearful, jittery'
naayoppah	'to be happy'
nokshoopah	'to fear'
shataalih	'to swell'
shatammih	'to rise'
taloowah	'to sing'
wakiilih	'to raise'
shaalih	'to haul'
pilah	'to send, throw'
ishih	'to take'
isht alah	'to bring'
imah	'to give'
ikhanah	'to know, learn'
issoh	'to hit'
patoolih	'to touch'
ikbih	'to make'
hooyoh	'to search for'
apah	'to eat [something]'
ishkoh	'to drink'
itokfikoowah	'to hiccup'
hoksoh	'to fart'
okmochoklih	'to close the eyes, blink'

haksih	'to be drunk, duped, tricked, taken advantage of'

It also seems necessary to identify a group we can call type C, in which *-chi* yields an idiomatic reading. In some cases the regular causative reading is also available:

(44a)	*pisah*	'to see'
	pisaachih	'to breed [a female animal] with [a male animal]'
(44b)	*ahnih*	'to think, hope, wish'
	ahnichih	'to like, love, respect'
(44c)	*anih*	'to put [plural object or liquid] in'
	aniichih	'to blister'[6]
(44d)	*ʃokkih*	'to put [plural object] in'
	fokkichih	'to grease'[7]

The account that treats $-chi_1$ and $-chi_2$ as separate morphemes is unsatisfying because it is now necessary to mark every verb in the lexicon for whether it allows "affectedness *-chi*". But this treats the facts as if there were no generalizations about the semantics of type A and type B verbs, and this is surely false.

In Broadwell (1996), I suggest that two semantic properties, namely causation and telicity, account for the classification of most verbs. In general, verbs whose meaning includes a component of causation and which are bounded in their temporal semantics will fall into type A and show both causative and affected readings for *-chi*. For other verb types, *-chi* is unambiguously causative.

Applicative verb prefixes, which might also be thought of as valency-changing morphology, are discussed in section 9.2.

8.3. Verbal suppletion

Some verbs show partial or full suppletion for the number of one of their arguments. Typically the argument whose plurality is indicated is the subject of an intransitive verb or the object of an intransitive verb. In Broadwell (1988a), I argued that verbal suppletion generally indicates the number of the argument which bears the thematic role Theme. For a verb of motion, this is the moving argument; for a change of state verb, it is the argument that undergoes the change; for a verb of position, it is the argument whose position is specified.

Some verbs make a three-way distinction between singular, dual,

6. Perhaps this is appropriate because blisters fill up with liquid.

7. The semantic connection here seems to be that liquids and solids without definite shapes (such as flour, grease, or sand) are treated as plurals, and thus are related to the plural object sense of *fokkih*.

Some verbs make a three-way distinction between singular, dual, plural, while others only distinguish singular and plural stems:

(45a) *iyah*   'to go [singular]'
       ittiyaachih   'to go [dual]'
       ilhkolih   'to go [plural]'

(45b) *baliilih*   'to run [singular]'
       tilhaayah   'to run [dual]'
       yilhiipah   'to run [plural]'

(45c) *kobaffih*   'to break [one long object]'
       kobahlih   'to break [two or more long objects]'

There are some semantic subregularities in the suppletion patterns. For example, it seems to be the case that only verbs of motion and location have specifically dual forms.

Verbs stems that end in *f* also seem to form a semantic and morphological class. The great majority of verbs in this class refer to actions that alter the shape or form of an inanimate object. Some examples follow:

(46)   *bahaffih*   'to gore, jab'
       bakaffih   'to split up, away'
       bokaffih   'to break open, explode'
       boyaffih   'to rub the hair off'
       chakoffih   'to notch'
       chilhaffih   'to peel up [like the skin of a boiled potato]
       chokaffih   'to pull up'
       cholhaffih   'to split up'
       habiffih   'to dent'
       haboffih   'to subside, go down'
       hokoffih   'to cut off'
       hotoffih   'to unwind'
       kalaffih   'to scratch away'

Nearly all the verbs in this class supplete for the number of their theme in the following pattern:

(47)   *bakaffih*   'to split up [singular object]'
       bakahlichih   'to split up [plural object]'
       bakaafah   'to be split up [singular]'
       bakaahlih   'to be split up [plural]'

I suggested in Broadwell (1993) (following a suggestion by Kimball [1991] for Koasati) that *f* is a relic of a morpheme I labelled a stem-formative.

8.4. Archaic noun incorporation

There is no productive noun incorporation in Choctaw. There are some archaic instances of verbs that contain incorpated noun stems, however. Some of these are discussed by Haas (1941b) and by Heath (1980). The incorporated nouns include *ok-* 'water' or 'eyes'[8], *nok-* 'neck', *ibi-* or *ibak* 'nose' or 'face', and *yosh-* 'hair' or 'head'.

Only the first of these is transparently related to an independent noun, *oka* 'water'. The others are identifiable through comparison with their cognates in other Muskogean languages. In many cases, the verb is also unattested except in this form:

(48)	*okshalolih*	'to have sunken eyes'
	okmochoolih	'to close the eyes' (cf. *moshoolih* 'to go out [of lights]')
	okchabaahah	'to be thick [of a liquid], viscous'
	okloboshlih	'to sink'
(49)	*nokshilah*	'to be hoarse' (cf. *shilah* 'to be dry')
	noktakaalih	'to choke' (cf. *takaalih* 'to hang')
	noklhakacha	'to be startled'[9]
(50)	*ibakhatalih*	'to be sickly-looking' (cf. *hatah* 'to be pale')
	ibaktokolih	'to be blunt-nosed'
	ibiikowah	'to have a nosebleed'
(51)	*yoshbonoochih*	'to roll [hair]' (cf. *bonnih* 'to roll up')
	yoshmilaalih	'to be totally bald'

There also appear to be relics of incorporation with some interrogatives:

(52)	*náatokah*	'to say what'
	kátiimihchih	'to do what'

The first of these words seems to be composed of *náatah* 'what' plus an archaic verb root *ka* or *oka*, meaning 'to say'. The second seems to be a generalized interrogative *katiimi* plus the verb *mihchih* 'to do'.

---

8. There is a similar relation between the stems for 'eye' and 'spring' in Hebrew. Hebrew scholars have suggested this may be because the eyes are one place on the face that is constantly wet.

9. The Choctaw apparently once conceived of the neck as the seat of emotions, since many verbs with incorporated forms of 'neck' refer to emotions.

9. Verbal agreement and applicatives

The verbal prefixes convey information about the arguments of the verb—how many there are and their person and number features. The prefixes can be divided into three sorts: agreement markers, applicative markers, and anaphors (reflexives and reciprocals). These prefixes occur in the following order:

(1)   I agreement-Anaphor-Applicatives-II agreement-Verb Stem

The anaphoric prefixes were discussed in chapter 6. This chapter focusses on agreement and applicatives.

9.1. Agreement and person-marking clitics

9.1.1. The verbal agreement system

Choctaw has a complex system of verbal agreement that indexes the subject, object, dative, and certain oblique arguments. A partial display of the agreement morphology is shown in table 9.1, where the labelling of the sets follows Munro and Gordon (1982). I, II, and III are types of agreement that occur under conditions to be described below. N is an agreement set that occurs with negatives and hortatives, discussed in section 9.1.9 below. This system is extensively described in Ulrich (1986).

Table 9.1. Verbal agreement morphology[1]

	I	II	III	N
1S	-li	sa-	(s)am- /$\underline{a}$-	ak-
2S	ish-	chi-	chim-/ch$\underline{i}$-	chik-
1P PAUCAL	il-/ii-	pi-	pim-p$\underline{i}$-	kil-kii-
1P MULTIPLE	il-/ii	hapi-	hapim-/hap$\underline{i}$-	kil-/kii
2P	hash-	hachi-	hachim-/hach$\underline{i}$-	hachik-
unmarked*	Ø	Ø	im-/	ik-

*The "unmarked" form is used in the cases where the verb fails to agree: forms with third person subjects, imperatives, and equi-complements.

1. For the presence of the initial *s* in the first person singular III prefix, see section 9.1.6.

137

The affixes labeled unmarked are used for third person subjects, but also in imperatives and control complements, leading Ulrich (1986) to argue that they are unmarked for person. The agreement marker *hapi(m)-* indicates first person multiple plural, a somewhat infrequent category, discussed in more detail in chapter 6. The allomorphy of these affixes is discussed in section 9.1.6 below.

9.1.2. The morphological realization of the agreement markers

The first person singular I marker *-li* is the only suffix in the set, and immediately follows the verb.

(2) *Baliili-li-h.*
    run-1SI-TNS
    'I'm running.'

There is no regular distinction between singular and plural for the third person.[2]

(3) *Baliili-h.*
    run-TNS
    'He/she/it is running.'
    'They are running.'

The first person plural affix is *ii-* before a consonant and *il-* before a vowel.

(4) *Ii-taloowa-tok.*
    1PI-sing-PT
    'We sang.'

(5) *Il-ona-tok.*
    1PI-arrive-PT
    'We arrived.'

The second person I singular and plural affixes are *ish-* and *hash-* respectively. However, when they precede the first person singular II marker *sa-* or the first person singular II marker *(s)am-*, they have special forms *is-* and *has-*.

(6) *Ish-pi-pịsa-tok.*
    2SI-1PII-see:N-PT
    'You saw us.'

(7) *Is-sa-pịsa-tok.*
    2SI-1SII-see:N-PT
    'You saw me.'

---

2. As noted in chapter 8, some verbs have suppletive plurals. A plural animate subject may be optionally signalled by the preverb *oklah*, as discussed in chapter 3.

(8)   *Hash-pi-písa-tok.*
       2PI-1PII-see:N-PT
       'Y'all saw us.'

(9)   *Has-sa-písa-tok.*
       2PI-1SII-see:N-PT
       'Y'all saw me.'

The III set is based upon the dative applicative *im-*, discussed below in section 9.2.1. The first person singular III marker is *am-* when word-initial, but *sam-* otherwise. Given the morphological possibilities of the Choctaw verb, the only context where a III prefix is not word-initial is when it is preceded by a I or N prefix.[3]

(10)   *Am-anooli-tok.*
       1SIII-tell-PT
       "He/she/they told me.'

(11)   *Is-sam-anooli-tok.*
       2SI-1SIII-tell-PT
       'You told me.'

(12)   *Ik-sam-anóol-o-tok.*
       N-1SIII-tell:L-NEG-PT
       'He/she/they didn't tell me.'

9.1.3. Canonical transitive verbs

I, II, and III agreement are conditioned by various kinds of arguments. Transitive active verbs show the most predictable pattern. With a typical transitive active verb, the subject will take I agreement, the direct object will take II agreement, and the goal or source will take III agreement.

As the chart above shows, there is no person-number agreement for third person arguments. Consider the following paradigms:

(13)   *Písa-li-tok.*   'I saw him/her/it/them.'
       Ish-písa-tok.   'You saw him/her/it/them.'
       Písa-tok.   'She/he/it/they saw him/her/it/them.'
       Ii-písa-tok.   'We saw him/her/it/them.'
       Hash-písa-tok.   'Y'all saw him/her/it/them.'

(14)   *Sa-písa-tok.*   'She/he/it/they saw me.'
       Chi-písa-tok.   'She/he/it/they saw you.'
       Písa-tok.   'She/he/it/they saw him/her/it/them.'
       Pi-písa-tok.   'She/he/it/they saw us.'
       Hachi-písa-tok.   'She/he/it/they saw y'all.'

---

3. R.S. Williams (1995:56) notes that this morphological alternation no longer holds for younger speakers of Oklahoma Choctaw, who use *am-* after N prefixes.

(15)   *Am-anoli-tok.*   'She/he/it/they told me.'
       Chim-anoli-tok.   'She/he/it/they told you.'
       Im-anoli-tok.   'She/he/it/they told him/her/it/them.'
       Pim-anoli-tok.   'She/he/it/they told us.'
       Hachim-anoli-tok.   'She/he/it/they told y'all.'

Cases where transitive verbs are preceded by more than one prefix are discussed in section 9.1.11 below.

9.1.4. Split intransitivity

Choctaw intransitive verbs show more complicated patterns of agreement. For intransitive verbs, the subjects of active verbs typically trigger I agreement:

(16)   *Baliili-li-tok.*
       run-1SI-PT
       'I ran.'

(17)   *Akoshchonnoli-li-ttook.*
       nod-1SI-DPAST
       'I nodded.'

The subjects of stative verbs typically trigger II agreement:

(18)   *Sa-niya-h.*
       1SII-fat-TNS
       'I am fat.'

(19)   *Naah sa-yoppa-ttook.*
       thing 1SII-happy-DPAST
       'I was happy.'[4]

And the subjects of some psychological verbs show III agreement:

(20)   *A̱-ponna-h.*
       1SIII-skilled-TNS
       'I am skilled.'

(21)   *Am-achokma-h.*
       1SIII-be:well-TNS
       'I feel well.'

The following lists show some major semantic categories associated with each of the three types of intransitive verbs, along with some representative verbs.

(22)   Intransitives with I subjects:

       Verbs of directed motion and motion of body parts: *alah* 'to arrive (here)', *iyah* 'to go', *mi̱tih* 'to come', *onah* 'to arrive (there)', *baliilih*

---

4. *Naah yoppah* is an idiom meaning 'be happy'.

'to run', *hilhah* 'to dance', *chokwah* 'to enter', *hachokbilhkah* 'to kneel', *hachobilhiipah* 'to get down on your hands and knees', *hatollih* 'to jiggle, jump up and down', *hikah* 'to fly', *kochoofah* 'to bend over', *kochchah* 'to go outside', *lomah* 'to hide (oneself)', *nowah* 'to walk', *okchilaabih* 'to stick the tongue out', *okshinillih* 'to swim', *oyyah* 'to climb', *yoshchonoolih* 'to bow'

Verbs of washing: *ayihlih* 'to wash one's hair', *okaamih* 'to wash one's body'

Verbs of excretion: *howiitah* 'to vomit', *holaafah* 'to defecate', *hoshowah* 'to urinate', *okfiyah* 'to have diarrhea'

Quantifiers: *laawah* 'to be many', *momah* 'to be all', *tóchchiinah* 'to be three'

Verbs of position: *biniilih* 'to sit', *hikíyah* 'to stand', *takálih* 'to hang', *áttah* 'to exist'

Verbs of sound emission: *basaachih* 'to snap the fingers', *chalhaakachih* 'to rattle', *chamaakachih* 'to ring (like a bell)', *chisiimohah* 'to yawn', *hahah* 'to pant', *hiihiih* 'to sing "hiih! hiih!"' in a high voice, as Choctaw women do while the men are dancing', *hoksoh* 'to fart', *lhabakah* 'to snore', *lhikah* 'to blow one's nose; to make a rumbling noise', *saksobaachih* 'to be noisy', *taklholaalih* 'to holler', *taloowah* 'to sing'

Verbs of speech and thought: *anokfillih* 'to think', *aachih* 'to say', *holaabih* 'to tell a lie'

Others: *nosih* 'to sleep', *tabaashih* 'to mourn'

(23)   Intransitives with II subjects

Diseases and bodily states: *atiilhachih* 'to have a disease called *tilhali*' (possibly scrofula)', *ayokpolookah* 'to be disabled (mentally or physically)', *bikiilih* 'to have a condition characterized by tightness in the chest, difficulty breathing, and a feeling of faintness', *chaahah* 'to be tall', *chalakwah* 'to have measles', *chassalah* 'to be bent over backwards', *chokfollih* 'to be dizzy', *chokshonaalih* 'to have a crick in the neck', *chonookabih* 'to have pneumonia', *halahlih* 'to have a fit, spasm', *hoochafoh* 'to be hungry', *hottopah* 'to be hurt, wounded', *ibiikowah* 'to have a nosebleed', *ibiishanoh* 'to have a runny nose', *ilbashah* 'to be poor, pitiful', *illih* 'to die'[5], *itakbiloolih* 'to have droopy lips', *kayyah* 'to be pregnant, full', *kotah* 'to be weak', *kowaashah* 'to be short', *liyahpoh* 'to have leprosy', *masaalih* 'to heal', *niyah* 'to be fat', *nokbikiilih* 'to choke', *nokshilah* 'to be hoarse; have a sore throat', *wannichih* 'to shake (as with palsy)'

5. Cited by Davies (1986:37) as taking a I subject, but my consultants all inflect this verb with II agreement for the subject. Chickasaw (Munro and Willmond 1994) and nineteenth-century Choctaw documents (Byington 1915:186) also show II agreement for *illih*, suggesting this is the more conservative form.

Psychological states: *bashkah* 'to be friendly', *chokachih* 'to get mad', *haksih* 'to be drunk, crazy', *hoofahyah* 'to be embarrassed', *tasiboh* 'to be crazy, mentally deficient', *komootah* 'to be fearful', *kostiinih* 'to be sober, righteous, obedient', *nosiikah* 'to dream', *nokshopah* 'to be afraid', *nokhakloh* 'to be lonesome', *noklhakachah* 'to be startled', *okchah* 'to be awake', *shimoohah* 'to have a nightmare'

Verbs of scent emission: *balaamah* 'to smell good', *kalhaamah* 'to stink (like urine)', *kosoomah* 'to stink (like sweat)', *showah* 'to stink (like something dead)'

Statives: *chilosah* 'to be quiet', *choshoopah* 'to be sloppy-looking, unkempt', *achokmah* 'to be good', *lachchah* 'to be wet', *lashpah* 'to be hot', *litiihah* 'to be dirty', *salaahah* 'to be slow', *yoshbokoolih* 'to be grey-headed', *sipoknih* 'to be old'

Copula: *-a* 'to be'

Other: *famah* 'to be whipped', *hofatih* 'to grow', *ittolah* 'to fall', *lowah* 'to burn'

(24)   Intransitives with III subjects

Psychological states: *imachibbah* 'to be tired, bored', *ichiloosah* 'to be lonesome', *ihaboofah* 'to be exhausted', *imihaksih* 'to forget', *itakohbih* 'to be lazy'

Body states: *imachokmah* 'to feel well', *ikapassah* 'to feel cold', *imoklhiliikah* 'to faint', *isikiblih* 'to be sexually aroused', *ipalammih* 'to suffer

Others: *ikanihmih* 'to get better, recover', *itiballih* 'to make a mistake', *iponnah* 'to be skilled'

With the notable exception of the quantifiers, the semantic classes associated with I agreement are all clearly agentive and volitional. It is also clear that statives predominate among the verbs taking II agreement. The greatest difficulty is in understanding the difference between the sorts of psychological and body states associated with II marking and those associated with III marking.

Words for emotions show wide crosslinguistic variation and complex lexical semantics (Wierzbicka 1992). The English translations adopted for these Choctaw words, while the closest available, often seem to have different properties of volitionality and telicity than the originals. Similar problems apply to some of the words describing body states. It seems likely that a better understanding of the semantics of these words would make the distinction between verbs taking II subjects and those taking III subjects seem less arbitrary.

9.1.5. Types of transitives

Just as intransitives split into a number of types, there are also several subtypes of transitives. As discussed above, the canonical transitive verb has I agreement with its subject and II agreement with its object:

(25)   *Chi-ahpali-li-tok.*
        2sII-kiss-1sI-PT
        'I kissed you.'

(26)   *Ish-pi-háklo-h-o?*
        2sI-1pII-hear:N-TNS-Q
        'Do you hear us?'

However, we also find transitives with I agreement for the subject but III agreement for the object.

(27)   *I-ponaklo-l-aachi-h:*
        III-ask-1sI-IRR-TNS
        'I'm going to ask him.'

(28)   *Has-sa-hichaali-h.*
        2PI-1sII-hate-TNS
        'Y'all hate me.'

We can abbreviate these differing agreement properties by referring to transitives of the (I,II) or (I, III) class. Below are representative verbs from each class.

(29)   Transitives (I, II)

        Verbs of perception: *písah* 'to see', *hákloh* 'to hear', *hówah* 'to smell'

        Change of state verbs: *kobaffih* 'to break', *akammih* 'to close', *bakaffih* 'to split up (singlar object)', *hofatichih* 'to raise, rear', *honnih* 'to boil (something)', *hoppih* 'to bury'

        Verbs of emotion: *ahnichih* 'to like, love', *anokpahlih* 'to desire', *holiitoblih* 'to value (a thing, person)', *holloh* 'to love'

        Verbs of contact: *ahpalih* 'to kiss', *apaatah* 'to sit beside', *bachaayah* 'to lie across', *chikiichih* 'to poke', *chokcholih* 'to tickle', *halhlhih* 'to kick, step on (plural object)', *hammih* 'to rub'

        Verbs of consumption: *apah* 'to eat', *ishkoh* 'to drink', *shokah* 'to suck, smoke'

        Verbs of sound production: *bokkaachih* 'to beat (as with a plank)'

        Verbs of caused motion: *bohpollih* 'to throw', *lobaffih* 'to pull up out of the ground', *hanookichih* 'to swing, spin'

        Verbs of equation: *hochiifoh* 'to name', *hobaachih* 'to imitate', *wiikichih* 'to weigh'

Others: *awaayah* 'to marry', *bilhiblih* 'to point at', *habiinah* 'to receive', *haksichih* 'to trick, deceive; to get (someone) drunk', *holaabih* 'to lie about, tell falsehoods about', *hooloh* 'to put (shoes, socks) on (yourself)' *mihaachih* 'to make fun of, humiliate', *okhah* 'to take revenge on'

(30)   Transitives (I, III)

Verbs of emotion: *ihichaalih* 'to hate' *itakoobitahah* 'to be tired'

Verbs of contact: *imatiilichih* 'to massage', *ibilikah* 'to be close to', *itokoowah* 'to kiss', *iwishlichih* ' to milk'

Verbs of communication: *iponakloh* 'to ask', *imatohnoh* 'to challenge, urge on', *imaachih* 'to say (something) to (someone)', *imapiisah* 'to command (someone) to (do something)', *imasilhhah* 'to beg, beseech', *imanoolih* 'to tell'

As the list shows, the distinction between these two types of transitives is difficult to explain. It is probably easiest to think of (I, II) as the default type for transitives, since it covers a wide range of semantic categories.

Verbs of the (I, III) class are fewer and fall into just a few categories–contact, emotion, and communication. Verbs of communication are consistently found in the (I, III) class. But verbs of contact and emotion fall into both classes. The distinctions sometimes seem lexically arbitrary. For example, *ahpahlih* 'to kiss' is in the (I, II) group, but *tokoowah*, also meaning 'to kiss', is in the (I, III) group. There are also two verbs, *holloh* 'to love', *achaayah* 'to be attached to emotionally', which are variably (I, II) or (I, III) without any difference in meaning that I have been able to determine.

In other cases, however, it seems that there is a semantic effect of the agreement type. In some cases, verbs of the (I, III) class have an object that is less affected than in a canonical (I, II) transitive. Consider the following lexical entries.

(31a) *shokah*   'to suck' (I, II)
                         'to perform oral sex on'(I, III)
                         'to suck with a medicinal horn (as traditional Choctaw doctors do)' (I, III)

(31b) *tokaffih*   'to shoot' (I, II)
                         'to cause (someone else) to have an orgasm' (I, III)

(31c) *tiwwih*   'to open (I, II)'
                         'to break the hymen of (I, III)'

As these entries show, the (I, II) version of the verb typically refers to an event where all of the object is (potentially) affected. The (I, III) version, however, is used in a case where only some part of the object is affected.

A less clearcut distinction is that between two forms of the verb *ikhánah*. Used as a (I, II) transitive, it means 'know', while as a (I, III) transitive it means 'to understand, to be aware of'.

In addition to these two large classes of transitives, there a few transitives that require II or III agreement for their subject. Davies (1986) identifies three groups of such verbs: those with II agreement for both subject and object (II, II verbs), those with III agreement for the subject and II agreeement for the object (III, II verbs), and those with II agreement for the subject and III agreement for the object (II, III).

The set of (II, III) verbs is the largest of these three, and includes perhaps as many as ten verbs, including the following:

(32) Transitives (II, III)

noklhak*a*chah 'to be startled by', *nokoowah* 'to be angry at', *nokshoopah* 'to be afraid of', *noktalhah* 'to be jealous of'

For all of these verbs, the subject experiences an emotion which is caused by or directed at the object.

The groups of (II, II) and (III, II) transitives are very small – and some speakers have no verbs with these agreement patterns. Davies (1986:97) lists the following four verbs with (II, II) agreement:

(33) Transitives (II, II)

anoktokloh 'to doubt', *anokfohkah* 'to understand', *bannah* 'to want', *yimmih* 'to believe'

However, there appears to be considerable variation in speakers on this point. For Mrs. Edith Gem, *anokfohkah* 'to understand' and *yimmih* 'to believe' actually show (II, III) agreement rather than (II, II) agreement. For Mrs. Gem, *anoktokloh* is an intransitive verb meaning 'to be sad'. That leaves only one verb – *bannah* 'to want' – with (II, II) agreement.

Similar problems occurs with the (III, II) verbs. Davies (1986:97) lists the following members of the group:

(34) Transitive (III, II)

imahchibah 'to be tired of', *imihaksih* 'to forget', *itiballih* 'to miss (a target)', *ilhakoffih* 'to miss, to cure', *imachokmah* 'to like'

Mrs. Edith Gem and many other Choctaw speakers seem very reluctant to accept any verb in which a II agreement prefix precedes a III agreement prefix. The following example from (Davies 1986:97) is judged very odd or ungrammatical by many speakers:

(35) *? *Sa-chim-ahchiba-h-o?*
1sII-2sIII-tired-TNS-Q
Are you tired of me?'   (Davies 1986:97)

For many speakers, verbs of this group many be used with third person objects, but not with non-third person objects. When a non-third person object is required, then some verb with a different agreement pattern or some paraphrase must be used.

9.1.6. Is Choctaw a fluid-S language?

Choctaw has been cited as a "fluid-S" language (Dixon 1979), in which speakers may productively shift verbs from one subject class to another to signal differences in volitionality (Davies 1986, Nicklas 1974). Similar contrasts have been cited for Chickasaw by Munro and Gordon (1982). A typical example of the cited contrasts is the one below:

(36) *Sa-habisko-h.*
      1sII-sneeze-TNS
      'I sneezed [involuntarily].' (Davies 1986:36)

(37) *Habishko-li-h.*
      sneeze-1sI-TNS
      'I sneezed [voluntarily].' (Davies 1986:36)

Despite these reports, none of the speakers I have consulted reported a volitionality contrast of this sort. A very small group of verbs, including *habishkoh* 'to sneeze', *hotilhkoh* 'to cough', and *ittolah* 'to fall', alternates between I and II agreement, but for my consultants, the choice of verb agreement has no semantic effect at all. Volitionality can be signalled through the use of additional adverbial material, but not through choice of agreement affix.

Similarly, a small group of verbs alternates between II and III agreement. This group includes *tįkabih* 'to be tired' and *palaatah* 'to be lonesome'. For the speakers I consulted, there is no semantic effect associated with the choice of verb agreement.

9.1.7. Short verbs

There is a small group of verbs that show some irregularity in the agreement paradigm. Consider the following forms for the verb *apah* 'to eat (transitive)':

(38) *apa-li-tok*   'I ate'
      ish-pa-tok   'You ate'
      apa-tok   'He/she/it/they ate'
      ii-pa-tok   'We ate'
      hash-pa-tok   'Y'all ate'

These forms show that when there is an agreement prefix, the initial *a*- of the verb drops. The verbs that show this sort of agreement paradigm are all of the shape *aCV*: *abih* 'to kill', *alah* 'to arrive (here)', *abih* 'to kill', *amoh* 'to mow'. See Ulrich (1986) for more discussion.

9.1.8. The verb *bannah* 'want'

For many or most speakers of Mississippi Choctaw, the verb *bannah* 'want'. has an irregular paradigm. It may be characterized formally as the deletion of the initial CV of the verb *bannah* after a II prefix, as shown below:

(39)   *sa-nna-h*   'I want'
       chi-nna-h   'You want'
       banna-h   'She/he wants, they want'
       pi-nna-h   'We want
       hachi-nna-h   'Y'all want'

Speakers of Mississippi Choctaw generally also allow a regular paradigm for *bannah* (i.e., *sabannah, chibannah, bannah, pibannah, hachibannah*), but the irregular paradigm is more frequent.

    Speakers of Oklahoma Choctaw either do not recognize these forms or characterize them as "baby talk." In this regard, it is interesting that Mississippi Choctaw baby talk treats *-nna-h* 'I want' as a suffix that attaches to the preceding word. Consider the following examples:

(40a) Baby talk

       Oka-nna-h
       water-want-TNS
       'I want water'

(40b) Adult

       Oka' sa-nna-h.
       water 1sII-want-TNS
       'I want water'

9.1.9. Speaker variation in agreement morphology

R.S. Williams (1995:53) notes that there is some variation in the use of agreement morphology among younger speakers of Oklahoma Choctaw. The most prominent of these differences affect verbs with II subjects. The younger speakers in his study tended to show verb paradigms that mix agreement morphology from the I and II agreement sets. Consider the paradigms in table 9.2.

Table 9.2. Young speakers' agreement paradigms (after R.S. Williams 1995:53)

CONSERVATIVE SPEAKER	GLOSS	YOUNGER SPEAKERS AY	BY	CY
sa-nokowah	'I am angry'	sa-nokowah	sa-nokowah	sa-nokowah
chi-nokowah	'You are angry'	chi-nokowah	ish-nokowah	chi-nokowah
pi-nokowah	'We are angry'	ii-nokowah	pi-nokowah	pa-nokowah
hachi-nokowah	'Y'all are angry'	hash-nokowah	ish-nokowah	hash-nokowah

In general, the innovations in the paradigms used by the younger speakers can be characterized as the use of I prefixes in place of II prefixes. Williams found that this was near universal for the second person plural II person marker; none of his six younger speakers gave the conservative *hachi-* in this context.

9.1.10. N agreement and negative verbs

The set labelled N is used for negatives and hortatives:[6]

(41) *Ik-taloowa-h.*
N-dance-TNS
'Let him sing!'

(42) *Tamaaha' kil-iya-h.*
town 1PN-go-TNS
'Let's go to town!'

(43) *Ik-pĩis-o-tok.*
N-see:L-NEG-PT
'He didn't see it.'

(44) *Ak- itháan-o-h.*
1sN-know:L-NEG-TNS
'I don't know.'

The formation of negatives is particularly complex in Choctaw. There are two kinds of negation, which we might call internal and periphrastic. Internal negation is multiply marked, requiring that an agreement marker from the N set replace the ordinary I agreement, that the verb appear in the lengthened grade (see chapter 10), and that the suffix *-o(k)-*

---

6. That is, first and third person imperatives.

follow the verb, with deletion of the preceding final vowel. The optional suffix *-kii* may be added after *-o(k)-*. Consider the following examples:

(45a) *Ak-íiy-o-kii-ttook.*
       1SN-go:L-NEG-NEG-DPAST
       'I didn't go.'

(45b) *Ik-sa-púis-o-tok.*
       N-2sII-see:L-NEG-PT
       'She/he didn't see me.'

Compare these with their affirmative counterparts:

(46a) *Iya-li-ttook.*
       go-1SI-DPAST
       'I went.'

(46b) *Sa-písa-tok.*
       1sII-see:N-PT
       'She/he/it/they saw me.'

To make (46a) negative, the first person singular I suffix *-li* is replaced by the first person singular N prefix *ak-*; the verb root *iya* is lengthened to *íiya*; the suffix *-o* is added, the final vowel of *íiya* is deleted; and the suffix *-kii* is added. To make (47) negative, the unmarked N prefix *ik-* is added; the verb root changes from the n-grade *písa* to the l-grade *púisa*; the suffix *-o* is added; and the final vowel of *púisa* deleted.

There is an additional peculiarity if the verb requires II or III agreement with the subject. In this case, the verb continues to be marked with the appropriate II or III affix, but the N prefix *ik-* is added:

(47) *Ik-sa-núiy-o-h.*
      N-1sII-fat:L-NEG-TNS
      'I'm not fat.'

(48) *Ik-sa-pónn-o-h.*
      N-1sIII-clever:L-NEG-TNS
      'I'm not clever.'

As a result, the negatives of II and III intransitives look like negatives of a transitive verb with a third person subject, as in (45b) above.

Periphrastic negation is simpler. The affirmative form of the verb is unchanged, and only the negative adverbial *-kiiyo-* is added, as in the following examples:

(49) *Im-ikhana-li-fíihna-kiiyo-kiya . . .*
      III-understand-1SI-really-NEG-although
      'Although I didn't really understand her . . .'

(50) *naahollo'   anopa'   anopoli-l-ahii-kiiyo-ka.*
      white:people language speak-1SI-IRR-NEG-COMP:DS
      'that I didn't speak English'

(51)   *Sa-niiya-kiiyo-h.*
        1SII-fat-NEG-TNS
        'I'm not fat.'

The negative suffix -*o(k)* has two allomorphs, -*o* and -*ok*. The latter appears when a negated verb is followed by any vowel-initial suffix, as in the following examples:

(52)   *Mike-at   ik-íss-ok-ahii-h.*
        Mike-NM N-stop:L-NEG-IRR2-TNS
        'Mike won't shut up.'

(53)   *Ik-oklhilŭk-ok-įsha-h.*
        N-dark:L-NEG-yet-TNS
        'It wasn't dark yet.'

When not followed by a vowel initial suffix, the negative is -*o*:

(54)   *Ik-hŭilh-o-tok.*
        N-dance:L-NEG-PT
        'He didn't dance.'

Ulrich (1986:250) and Nicklas (1974:195) propose an alternate analysis of the suffix that occurs in the negative. In their analysis, there are two distinct negative suffixes -*o* and -*ki*. Thus they would analyze (50) as follows:

(55)   *Mike-at   ik-íss-o-ki-aahii-h.*
        Mike-NM N-stop:L-NEG-NEG-IRR2-TNS
        'Mike won't shut up.'

The *i* of the -*ki* suffix is then deleted before another vowel by the rule of Short Vowel Deletion. There is certainly a -*kii* negative suffix in Choctaw, but it is unclear whether Ulrich and Davies' morphological analysis for this example is the best one.

The suffix -*kii* is seen in examples like the following:

(56)   *Ak-pŭs-o-kii-tok.*
        1SN-see:L-NEG-NEG-PT
        'I didn't see.'

Nicklas's (1974:195) suggestion that -*kii* in such forms is a shortened form of the auxiliary *kiiyoh* seems quite plausible.

However, there is a difficulty positing a suffix -*kii* in the underlying representation of (55). Nicklas cites such examples with an underlying short vowel. All speakers I have consulted pronounced examples of this sort with a long-voweled suffix -*kii*. This might be thought to be the result of the rule of rhythmic lengthening, but the vowel is long even for speakers who do not apply rhythmic lengthening before -*tok*, as in the following examples:

(57) *Sa-nokowa-tok.* [sa-no:kowa-tok]
      1sII-mad-PT
      'I was mad.'

(58) *Ik-húlh-o-kii-tok.*
      N-dance:L-NEG-NEG-PT
      'He didn't dance.'

Both these examples are from the same speaker, and they show that the underlying form of this suffix must be *-kii,* not *-ki.* However, under Nicklas and Ulrich's account, this implies that the underlying representation for a form like *akpúsokaachih* is as follows:

(59) *ak-púis-o-kii-aachi-h > akpúisokaachih*
      1sN-see:L-NEG-NEG-IRR-TNS
      'I won't see it.'

The problem is that there is no phonological rule that regularly deletes a long vowel before another vowel. An underlying representation like that in (59) ought to surface as *akpúisokiiyaachih,* but that is not the form we want. So there are phonological difficulties with this account.

A second argument against their analysis comes from the distribution of the morpheme *-ki(i)* which they must posit in examples like (50). A negative verb followed by a vowel-initial suffix must always show a *k:*

(60a) *Ak-púis-ok-aachi-h.*
       1sN-see:L-NEG-IRR-TNS
       'I will not see it.'

(60b) **Ak-púis-o-aachih*

(60c) **ak-púis-aachih*

However, *-kii* is optional before a consonant-initial suffix:

(61a) *Ak-púis-o-tok.*
       1sN-see:L-NEG-PT
       'I didn't see it.'

(61b) *Ak-púis-o-kii-tok.*
       1sN-see:L-NEG-NEG-PT
       'I didn't see it.'

Under Nicklas and Ulrich's account, we have to say that we must insert an additional morpheme just in case a vowel-initial suffix follows a negative verb. But it is odd that the occurrence or nonoccurrence of an independent morpheme ought to be dependent on the phonological properties of the following morpheme.

Therefore the analysis proposed here is simpler and encounters fewer phonological difficulties than does the Nicklas-Ulrich analysis, and

I will continue to treat examples like the following as containing a single suffix -*o(k)*-:

(62)   *Ik-húlh-ok-aachị-h.*
        N-dance:L-NEG-IRR-TNS
        'He won't dance.'

Chickasaw regularly uses -*ki* before -*tok* (Munro and Willmond 1994):

(63)   *Kii-hali'l-o-ki-tok.*   Chickasaw
        1pN-touch-NEG-NEG-PT
        'We didn't touch it.'

9.1.11. The order of agreement prefixes

The ordering of agreement prefixes has certain complications, as Davies (1981, 1986) points out. When the subject takes a I class person-marker, the ordering is as follows:

(64)   I/N-III-II-Verb

Some examples follow:

(65)   *Is-sa-pịsa-tok.*
        2sI-1sII-see:N-PT
        'You saw me.'

(66)   *Ik-sa-pịis-o-tok.*
        N-2sII-see:L-NEG-PT
        'She/he didn't see me.'

(67)   *Ish-ị-pila-tok.*
        2sI-III-throw-PT
        'You threw it to him.'

(68)   *Ị-chi-tokcholi-tok.*
        III-2sII-tickle-PT
        'He tickled you for her.'

Transitive verbs whose subjects trigger I agreement are by far the largest group of transitives in the language.

There is also a smaller group of transitives whose subjects trigger II and III agreement. They show more complex morphosyntax. When the subject takes II or III agreement, the person marker for the subject appears immediately before the verb, and a person marker associated with an object precedes, as follows:

(69)   (Object agreement)-(II/III agreement)-Verb

Here are some examples:

(70)   *Chi-sa-banna-h.*
         2sII-1sII-want-TNS
         'I want you.'

(71)   *Sa-chim-ahchiba-h-ọ?*
         1sII-2sIII-tired-TNS-Q
         'Are you tired of me?' (Davies 1986:97)

(72)   *Chị-sa-nokshopa-h.*
         2sIII-1sII-afraid-TNS
         'I'm afraid of you.' (Davies 1986:111)

These examples show that no simple position-class analysis of the I, II, and III markers will correctly account for their ordering; their syntactic status must also be considered.

The III markers (dative applicatives) that result from possessor raising are also ordered differently from the III markers associated with subjects or ordinary datives. Consider the following examples:

(73)   *Ik-ị-makáach-o-h.*
         N-III-say:L-NEG-TNS
         'He didn't say it to him.'

(74)   *John-at   ofi-yat   im-ik-íll-o-h.*
         John-NM   dog-NM   III-N-die:L-NEG-TNS
         'John's dog didn't die.'

In (73), we see the normal order of N prefixes before III prefixes with an ordinary dative object. However, in (74) we see that the III prefix that results from possessor raising precedes the N prefix.

9.2. Applicatives

Choctaw applicatives occur with noun phrases that are dative, benefactive, comitative (corresponding to non-instrumental 'with'), superessive ('on'), locative, and ablative, as discussed by Ulrich (1986).[7] A somewhat more problematic case is the instrumental.

Applicatives are prefixed to the verb. We can distinguish two types of applicatives: simple and compound. The simple applicatives are *im-* 'dative', *ibaa-* 'comitative', *ọ-* 'superessive', and *aa-* 'locative'. A simple applicative appears with the appropriate II agreement marker when the associated noun phrase is pronominal.

The compound applicatives are *imaa-* 'ablative' and *imị-, imi-* 'benefactive'. Both appear to contain an initial III prefix. The compound applicatives show a different paradigm of agreement, discussed in more detail below.

---

7. Ulrich has shown that the oblique agreement markers have phonological properties consistent with an analysis of them as clitics.

9.2.1. *Im-*, *i̱-* 'dative'

The dative applicative markier *im-*, preceded by an agreement marker, constitutes the III set of agreement (following the terminology of Munro and Gordon 1982). It has a special role among the applicatives. All the other applicative prefixes add objects to the verb. However, for certain verbs, *im-* is obligatory and agrees with the subject. These are the verbs generally called III-subject or dative-subject.

The dative applicative/III agreement marker also shows an irregularity not found with other simple applicatives. The first person singular III marker is *(s)am-/(s)a̱-*, which would initially appear to be the result of adding the first person singular II marker *sa-* to the dative applicative *im-*. However, as previously noted, the initial *s* of this affix is omitted in word-initial position. The first person singular *sa-* does not lose its initial consonant in any other environment. This suggests that at least the first person singular dative applicative/III agreement marker is not synchronically segmentable.

Dative *im-* is used in a variety of functions. The most common are recipient and benefactive:

(75) *John im-aa-li-tok.*
    John III-give-1SI-PT
    'I gave it to John.'

(76) *Mary i̱-taloowa-tok.*
    Mary III-sing-PT
    'They sang for Mary.'

It is also used in the possessor raising and dative raising constructions discussed in chapter 17.

9.2.2. *Ibaa-* 'comitative'

The applicative comitative is formed by prefixing *ibaa-* to the verb.

(77) *Sa-baa-washooha-t hilha-t   taloowa-h!*
    1SII-COMIT-play-SS dance-SS sing-TNS
    'Sing, dance, and play with me!' (T2:7)

The applicative *ibaa-* indicates someone who performs the action, or participates in the event, jointly. For causative verbs, *ibaa-* is generally ambiguous between readings in which its object is a joint causer and readings in which its object is a joint causee.

(78) *Mary ibaa-taloowa-chi-h.*
    Mary COMIT-sing-CAUS-TNS
    'I made someone sing with Mary.' (two causees)
    'Mary and I made someone sing.' (two causers)

See section 9.2.5 below for some cases of co-objects with the locative *aa-*.

9.2.3. *Imaa-* 'ablative'

The ablative applicatives are seen in the following examples:

(79) *Ibishshano' chimaa-haliili-li-h.*
      cold   2SABL-touch-1SI-TNS
      'I caught a cold from you.' (Ulrich 1986:266)

(80) *Pimaa-habiina-h.*
      1PABL-receive-TNS
      'He received it from us.' (Ulrich 1986:266)

The ablative is rare relative to most other applicatives, and many speakers use the dative in its place. Ulrich (1986) suggests that the ablative is absent in Mississippi Choctaw.

A few potential examples of the ablative have been found in nineteenth-century materials:

(81) <Yohmi hokʋet hatak yʋmmak okʋt Chitokaka ya̲ nanasi kia im a habena hi a̲ ik im ahobo kashke.>
      Yohmi-hookat hattak yammak-ook-at Chitokaaka-ya̲ na̲nasi-kia
      do:so-for:SS   man   that-COM-NM   God-AC   anything-too
      imaa-habiin-ahii-ya̲ ik-im-ahóob-ok-ashkii.
      ABL-receive-IRR-DS N-III-seem-NEG-EXHORT
      'For let not that man think that he shall receive anything of the Lord.'
      (James 1:7)

9.2.4. *Imi̲-* 'benefactive'

Like the ablative, the benefactive is rather rare. Many speakers use the dative in its place. The following examples show the benefactive *imi̲-*.

(82) *Ami̲-baliili-h.*
      1SBEN-run-TNS
      'He ran for me.'

(83) *Ohooyo'-mat tamaaha' iya-hmat   sholosh nafókka'*
      woman-D:NM town   go-when:SS shoes   clothes
      yohmi-h-o̲   im-alla'   imi̲-cho̲pa-t iya-h-ookakoosh
      do-TNS-PART:DS III-CHILD BEN-buy-SS go-TNS-but:SS
      sholosh-akbaano-h-o̲   cho̲pa-tok.
      shoes-only-TNS-PART:DS buy-PT
      'That woman went to town to buy shoes and clothes for her kids, but she only bought shoes.'

Ulrich (1986:261) suggests that some subjects trigger benefactive agreement, citing examples like the following:

(84)   *Pam-at   imi̱-taklamma-h.*
       Pam-NM BEN-bother-TNS
       'Pam is bothered by it.'

(85)   *Ami̱-taklamma-h.*
       1SBEN-bother-TNS
       'I'm bothered by it.'

However, there is another possible analysis of these forms, as shown in
the following revisions of the above two examples:

(86)   *Pam-at   im-i̱taklamma-h.*
       Pam-NM III-bother-TNS
       'Pam is bothered by it.'

(87)   *Am-i̱taklamma-h.*
       1sIII-bother-TNS
       'I'm bothered by it.'

Under this analysis, the verb stem is *i̱taklammah* and it takes dative
subjects, rather than benefactive subjects. It appears that all the
benefactive subject verbs Ulrich cites may be reanalysed in this matter.

There is some advantage in adopting the dative subject analysis,
since it reduces the number of verb classes. Both the verbs listed by
Ulrich in the benefactive subjective class—*taklammah* 'to be bothered
(by)' and *kalloh* 'to be in difficulty (because of)'—conform to the
semantics of the III-subject verbs.

9.2.5. Aa- 'locative'

The locative applicative is formed by adding *aa-* to the verb. Before a
vowel, an epenthetic *y* appears, yielding *aay-*.

(88)   *Illi̱pa' kaniimi-ka̱   lowak apákna'*
       food   some-COMP:DS fire   top
       aa-nonáachi-cha . . .
       LOC-cook:L-SS
       'She cooked some food on the fire and . . .' (T1:26)

(89)   *Oklahoma aay-oktosha-h.*
       Oklahoma LOC-snow-TNS
       'It's snowing in Oklahoma.'

For most verbs, *aa-* adds a static location where the event takes place.
For some verbs of motion and transfer, however, *aa-* indicates the source
or starting point of the motion:

(90)   *Aaíshko'-ma̱ am-aa-pota-tok.*
       cup-D:AC   1sIII-LOC-borrow-PT
       'He borrowed the cup from me.'

(91)   *Oklahoma aa-miti-tok.*
       Oklahoma LOC-come-PT
       'He came from Oklahoma.'

Perhaps in the following example 'Nellie' should also be interpreted as
a source:

(92)   *Si-oshi'   tiik-ma̱   Nellie-ya̱*
       1sII-child female-D:AC Nellie-AC
       aa-hochiifo-li-tok.
       LOC-name-1sI-PT
       'I named my daughter after Nellie.'

Some combinations of *aa-* with a verb have idiomatic or metaphoric
locative meanings:

(93)   *Hattak-m-akhii-t   si-aa-holaabi-tok-achiini-tok.*
       man-DEM-PEJOR-NM 1sII-LOC-lie-PT-EVID-PT
       'That damned man told lies about me.'

(94)   *Alla'-mat   underclothes aa-banna-h.*
       child-D:NM underclothes LOC-want-TNS
       'That child needs underclothes.'

In Chickasaw, partitive interpretations of *aa-* are found with verbs that
might be loosely termed verbs of consumption (e.g., 'eat', 'drink', 'kill',
'pour') (Munro and Willmond 1994). There are some examples of this
partitive interpretation in the Choctaw Bible, but the speakers I
consulted did not recognize them:

(95)   <. . . iti osapushi anu̱ka aiashaka̱ ʋni ya il ai ʋpa hinla hoke.>
       itti' osáaposhi' ano̱ka' aay-aasha-ka̱   ani-ya̱
       tree garden   in   LOC-be-COMP:DS fruit-AC
       il-aay-ap-ahi̱la-h-okii.
       1PI-LOC-eat-POT-TNS-indeed
       'We may eat of the fruit of the trees of the garden.' (Gen. 3:2)

Ulrich notes that "locative arguments of weather verbs that
otherwise have no subjects may be optionally promoted to subject"
(1986:263), and cites the following examples:

(96a) *Oklahomma-no aay-oktosha-h.*
       Oklahoma-AC2 LOC-snow-TNS
       'It's snowing in Oklahoma.'

(96b) *Oklahomma-to aay-oktosha-h.*
       Oklahoma-NM2 LOC-snow-TNS
       'It's snowing in Oklahoma.'

An unusual case of *aa-* is seen in the following example:

(97)   <Ak̠akushi yo̱ shuka nipi a̱ aiaʋʋshlichih.>
       Ak̠ákoshi-yo̱ shókha' nipi-ya̱   aay-awashli-chi-h.
       egg-FOC:AC   pig   meat-AC   LOC-fry-CAUS-TNS
       'She fries eggs with pork.' (Byington 1870:36)

This is unusual because *awashlih* 'to fry' has an extra causative affix *-chi*, and because the semantic role of the locative is unclear. It seems as if the combination of *aa-* and *-chi* is being used to indicate a co-object. Other examples that show this peculiar syntax are the following:

(98)   <. . . onush ash haiyu̱kpulo yo̱ ant a hokchichi cha, kʋnia tok.>
       onoosh-aash hayyo̱kpolo-yo̱ a̱t   aa-hokchi-chi-cha
       wheat-PREV   weed-FOC:AC   COME:AND LOC-plant-CAUS-SS
       kaniiya-tok.
       go:away-PT
       'He came and sowed weeds among the wheat.' (Matt. 13:25)

(99)   <Sa noshkobo pa̱shi tʋnna untuklo ka ponola ʋpi ish a tʋnʋchi
       hokmʋno . . .>
       Sa-noshkóbo' pá̱shi' tánna' á̱toklo-ka   ponool-api'
       1sII-head   hair   plait   seven-COMP   cotton-stalk
       ish-aa-tana-chi-h-oo-kmano . . .
       2sI-LOC-weave-CAUS-TNS-LINK-IRR:DS2
       'If you weave seven plaits of my hair with cotton . . .' (Judg. 16:13)

Byington writes that *-chi* is "a suffix to verbs, which take the locatives *a* or *ai*; others make a new form of verbs, where one thing is made to act on or with another"(1915:102). Speakers I consulted did not recognize this construction.

9.2.6. *On-* 'superessive'

The superessive *on-* indicates that the action takes place on top of something:

(100) *Oklah si-o̱-hilha-tok.*
       PLUR   1sII-on-dance-PT
       'They danced on top of me.'

As with the other oblique markers, there are some idiomatic combinations:

(101) *Am-ofi'   ish-haabli-kma̱, chi-o̱-chiliita-l-aachi̱-h.*
       1sIII-dog 2sI-kick-IRR:DS 2sII-on-mad-1sI-IRR-TNS
       'If you kick my dog, I'll get mad at you.'

9.2.7. *Isht* or *isht-* 'instrumental'

Instrumentals are somewhat more complex than the other applicatives just discussed. The best analysis seems to be that they are formed with a preverb *isht* which is phonologically cliticized to the beginning of the verb. Historically, *isht* derives from a reduced form of the verb *ishih* 'to take' with the participial ending *-t*.[8]

(102) *Itti'   iskífa'   isht-chaya-tok.*
      wood axe   INSTR-chop-PT
      'He chopped the wood with an axe.'

Isht is usually phonologically incorporated to the following verb, and has sometimes been treated as an applicative prefix, like the others considered in this section.[9] However, this analysis misses some important differences between *isht* and the applicative prefixes. For example, when a verb takes a II or III prefix, this will normally occur between *isht* and the verb:

(103) *Isht   si-ona-tok.*
      INSTR 1sII-arrive-PT
      'They took me.'

In this respect, *isht* is different from other uncontroversial applicative prefixes:

(104) *Si-aa-chakaapa-tok.*
      1sII-LOC-gossip-PT
      'They gossiped about me.'

Isht may also precede directional particles such as *pit* and *iit*, as in the following example:

(105) *Chifak-ma úishi-cha pállaska' ishit iit   am-aa-tok.*
      fork-D:AC take:L-SS bread   INSTR toward 1sIII-give-PT
      'He passed me the bread with a fork.' (Lit., 'He took a fork and passed me the bread with it.')

See chapter 15 for arguments that the directional particles must be treated as separate words.

The ordinary applicative prefixes never precede the directionals:

(106a) *Iit   pim-aa-tok.*
       toward 1pIII-give-PT
       'They gave them to us.'

(106b) **Pim-iit   aa-tok.*
       1sIII-toward give-PT

8. The unreduced form *ishit* is also found, though less frequently.

9. In this book, I write *isht* together with the following verb when such phonological cliticization has taken place.

From these facts, it seems that most speakers treat *isht* as an applicative preverb, rather than an applicative prefix.

Some combinations of the instrumental and a root are idiomatic. For example, *isht-iyah* is literally 'to go by means of', but is an idiom meaning 'to begin.' *Isht* is also used to indicate causes of emotions, illnesses, or death.

(107) *Chiliswa' isht-illi-ttook.*
      measles   INSTR-die-DPAST
      'He died of the measles.'

Isht is used in the formation of ordinal numerals:

(108) *Alla   nakni   ot   isht-pókkooli-akoosh   chokka'   ala-h.*
      child male   DIR INSTR-ten-CON:NM   house   arrive
      'The tenth boy came home.'

Isht is used with a few verbs of motion to form transitives:

(109) *onah*   'to arrive (there)'
      isht-onah   'to take'

(110) *mitih*   'to come'
      isht-mitih 'to bring'

As mentioned in chapter 4, many instrumental nouns include *isht*:

(111) *isht-ípa-'*
      INSTR-eat-NML
      'spoon'

(112) *isht-tíwa-'*
      INSTR-open-NML
      'key'

10. Aspectual grades

Choctaw verb stems undergo various segmental and accentual modifications to indicate their aspect. These stem variants are traditionally referred to as "grades" in the Muskogeanist literature. Ulrich (1986) discusses the semantics and morphology of the grades, and identifies seven distinct grades: n-grade, hn-grade, l-grade, h-grade, g-grade, y-grade, and zero grade (the unmodified form of the verb stem). Most of the following examples are from this work.[1]

Choctaw grades differ in their degree of productivity. The most productive grades are the l-grade and the hn-grade, available for nearly every verb in the language. The g-grade and y-grade are intermediate in productivity, and the n-grade and h-grade are the least productive. These restrictions are partially lexical in nature, but they also result from the interaction of the semantics of each grade and the lexical aspect (or *aktionsart*) of particular verbs. Some of these interactions are noted below, but this area of Choctaw grammar is not well understood, and needs more careful examination.

The grades involve a change in pitch accent as well as the infixation of consonants and vowel lengthening. These changes must be defined with respect to the verb stem. Section 10.7 below discusses which affixes are considered within the scope of the verb stem.

10.1. The n-grade

The n-grade is formed by nasalizing and accenting the penultimate vowel of the verb stem. Nicklas (1974) refers to this as the incompletive. It is associated with the semantics of duration:

(1a) *Bashli-h.*
      cut-TNS
      'He cut it.' (Ulrich 1986:169)

(1b) *Báshli-h.*
      cut:N-TNS
      'He keeps cutting it.' (Ulrich 1986:169)

---

1. The number of distinct grades is somewhat controversial, depending on what counts as a grade. Munro (1985) argues that the Chickasaw stem pattern cognate to the l-grade is a type of stem-modification distinct from the grades. Nicklas (1974) combines the g-grade and the y-grade. The grade that I refer to as the l-grade is called the glottal grade by Ulrich (1986).

Ulrich notes that when the penultimate vowel is followed by geminate *bb* or *ll*, there is degemination of the consonant, and a homorganic nasal consonant occurs:

(2a)   *Atobbi-h.*
pay:N-TNS
'She paid.'

(2b)   *Atómbi-h.*
pay:N-TNS
'She's still paying.'

As these examples show, for punctual verbs, the n-grade typically shows an extended, continuous action. For certain statives (typically those expressing temporary states), the n-grade shows an extended state:

(3)   *John-at   háksi-moma-h.*
John-NM   drunk:N-still-TNS
'John is still drunk.'

Ulrich (1986:170) notes a related use of the n-grade in examples like the following:

(4)   *Ii-washóha-kma   ip-aachi-h.*
1PI-play:N-IRR:DS   eat-IRR-TNS
'They're going to eat while we play.'

In this example, the use of the n-grade on the subordinate verb focuses on the the fact that the duration of the first clause extends into that of the second.

For other semantic classes of verbs, the n-grade may have somewhat different semantics. Verbs of location typically appear in the n-grade, and there is no special implication of duration:

(5)   *Isht=holissóchi-yat aaipa'   ittóla-h.*
pencil-NM   table   lie:N-TNS
'The pencil is lying on the table.'

(6)   *Kafi'   aayíshko-yat taláya-h.*
coffee cup-NM   sit:N-TNS
'The coffee cup is sitting [there].'

Verbs of perception are also normally in the n-grade:

(7)   *Chi-písa-l-aachi-h.*
2SII-see:N-1SI-IRR-TNS
'I'll see you.'

(8)   *Háklo-l-ahila-h.*
hear:N-1SI-POT-TNS
'I can hear him.'

Ulrich (1986:171) notes that for some verbs that indicate a change of state (or change of clothes) the n-grade indicates the state resulting from that action. For example:

(9a) *Si-okcha-h.*
      1sII-awake-TNS
      'I woke up.'

(9b) *Si-ǫkcha-h.*
      1sII-awake:N-TNS
      'I'm awake.'

Munro and Willmond (1994) note that the n-grade in Chickasaw is regularly used with some stative verbs to form a standardless comparative:

(10a) *chofata*
       clean
       'to be clean'

(10b) *chofata*
       clean:N
       'to be cleaner'

Nicklas (1974:74) reports similar uses in Choctaw:

(11a) *chito-h*
       big-TNS
       'to be big'

(11b) *chįto-h*
       big:N-TNS
       'to be largish, larger than usual, larger than expected'

There are also nineteenth-century uses of the n-grade as a comparative, as shown in the following example:

(12)   <Na chiyimmi kʋt chintoshke.>
       Naa   chi-yimmi-kat   chįto-shkii.
       thing 2sII-believe-COMP:NM big:N-EXHORT
       'Thy path (lit., "what you believe") is greater.' (Byington 1915:107)

However, it seems that such uses are lexicalized in Choctaw. While Mr. Henry Willis accepts forms like *chįtoh* 'quite large', many other adjectival predicates are not acceptable in the n-grade:

(13)   *Ofi-mat   losa-h.*
       dog-D:NM black-TNS
       'That dog is black.'

(14)   *?Ofi-mat lǫsa-h.*
       dog-D:NM black:N-TNS[2]

2. Mr. Willis said this might possibly be interpreted as 'The dog is becoming black'.

10.2. The hn-grade

The hn-grade is formed by inserting $h\underline{V}$ after the penultimate vowel of the verb stem, where $\underline{V}$ is a nasalized copy of the vowel in the preceding syllable, and accenting the inserted vowel. With punctual verbs, the hn-grade generally indicates iteration:

(15a) *Habishko-h.*
     sneeze-TNS
     'He sneezed.'

(15b) *Habihíshko-h.*
     sneeze:HN-TNS
     'He sneezed repeatedly.'

The implication in (15b) is that there are several individual events of sneezing which are joined together.

For nonpunctual verbs, however, the hn-grade generally indicates extension in time with no necessary implication of separate startings and endings:

(16a) *Oba-tok.*
     rain-PT
     'It rained.'

(16b) *Ohóba-na   nittak   pókkoli   oshta-ttook.*
     rain:HN-DS   day   ten   four-DPAST
     'It kept on raining for forty days.'

(17)   <Tama ʋt . . . i nakfi Absalom in chuka ahanta tok.>
     Tamar-at . . . i-nákfi'   Absalom i-chokka' ahátta-ttook.
     Tamar-NM   III-brother Absalom III-house be:HN-DPAST
     'Tamar remained in the house of her brother Absalom.' (2 Sam. 13:20)

In the examples, there is no implication that the rain started and stopped for forty days or that Tamar repeatedly took up residence in the house; rather, the idea is that the action was prolonged through time.

10.3. The l-grade

The l-grade is formed by accenting the penultimate vowel and lengthening it if it is in an open syllable. The l-grade occurs before the negative suffix -*o(k)* and before the complementizers -*cha* and -*na*. In this respect the l-grade is somewhat different from the other grades, since it makes no independent contribution to the semantics, but is merely an automatic accompaniment of certain morphemes. As a result it is the most frequent and productive of the grades.

(18)   *Naksika'   ish-íiya-cha ish-átt-aachi-h.*
     somewhere:else 2SI-go:L-SS   2SI-be:N-IRR- TNS
     'You will go and live somewhere else.'

(19)   *Ópah-at ik-n̠anokáay-o-h-oosh   hikíya-ttook.*
        owl-NM   N-respond:L-NEG-TNS-PART:SS stand:N-DPAST
        'The owl stood there, saying nothing.'

Nicklas (1974:74) suggests that the l-grade is used in forming what
he calls the nomic tense. Ulrich (1986:180–81) shows that his
examples are better analysed as nominalizations, and not true
examples of the l-grade.

10.4. The h-grade

The h-grade is formed by inserting *h* before the penultimate vowel of
the stem and accenting the penultimate vowel. Verbs in the h-grade
indicate a sudden inception of the event, and are typically translated
'just V-ed' or 'V-ed quickly':

(20a)   *Nosi-h.*
        sleep-TNS
        'He slept.'

(20b)   *Nóhsi-h.*
        sleep:H-TNS
        'He took a quick nap.' (Ulrich 1986:168)

A distinct use of the h-grade is shown in the following example:

(21)   *Anokfilli-li-kano   chíhto-h.*
        think-1sI-COMP:DS2 big:H-TNS
        'He's bigger than I thought.'

In this example the h-grade is used in the formation of a sort of
comparative, and the object of the comparison is contained in an
"according to" clause. Nicklas (1974:76) also mentions this use of the
h-grade.

    This use of the h-grade in Choctaw is of historical interest
because the h-grade is regularly used in the formation of
comparatives in Alabama and Koasati (Kimball 1985; Hardy and
Montler 1986; Cline 1987).

10.5. The g-grade

The g-grade is formed by "lengthening the penultimate vowel of the
stem if it is followed by a single consonant and geminating the
preceding consonant" (Ulrich 1986:173).[3] The vowel preceding the
geminate consonant receives the accent. Verbs in the g-grade indicate
that there is a delayed inception for the event, and are generally
translated 'finally V-ed' in English.

---

3. Ulrich argues that this is accomplished by an empty consonant slot before the
penultimate vowel and a glottal stop after it. The glottal stop is deleted before a
consonant, with compensatory lengthening of the preceding vowel.

(22a) *Taloowa-h.*
       sing-TNS
       'He is singing.'

(22b) *Tálloowa-h.*
       sing:G-TNS
       'He finally sang.'

Textual examples of the verbs in g-grade seem to occur when the action they describe takes place after a pause in the action flow of the narrative.

10.6. The y-grade

The y-grade is formed by inserting *Vyy* before the penultimate vowel of the verb stem (where *V* is a copy of the penultimate vowel) and accenting the inserted vowel. The semantics of the y-grade seem to be the same as those of the g-grade.

(23a) *Basha-h.*
       be:cut-TNS
       'He got cut.'

(23b) *Báyyasha-h.*
       be:cut:Y-TNS
       'He finally got cut.'

Another common form of the y-grade is lengthening of the penult plus falling tone:

(24)   *Báàsha-h.*
       cut:Y-TNS
       'He finally got cut.'

There has been some controversy about whether the g-grade and y-grade are distinct from each other or whether they are allomorphs of the same grade. Nicklas (1974:93) suggests that they are allomorphs of a single intensive grade, where the choice between the two is determined by the phonology of the verb stem. According to Nicklas, when the penultimate vowel of the stem is preceded by a consonant cluster or when the verb stem is only two syllables long, then the intensive shows the pattern labelled the y-grade. In other cases, the verb appears in the g-grade. However, Ulrich (1986:175) shows that many verbs can occur in both the g-grade and the y-grade, albeit with no semantic difference:

(25a) *Habishko-h.*
       sneeze-TNS
       'He sneezed.'

(25b)   *Habíyyishko-h.*
        sneeze:Y-TNS
        'He finally sneezed.'

(25c)   *Hábbishko-h.*
        sneeze:G-TNS
        'He finally sneezed.' Ulrich (1986:175)

Ulrich (1994) gives an account that unifies the two grades.

10.7. The definition of verb stem

All the grades described above affect the penult or antepenult of the verb stem. The verb stem always includes the *-a* and *-li* of the transitive-intransitive alternation (section 8.1.1). Consider the following example, which includes the *-li* suffix (assimilated to the preceding consonant). The verb stem has been bracketed.

(26a)   *[Kobaffi]-h*
        break:TR-TNS
        'He broke it.'

(26b)   *[Kobaháffi]-h.*
        break:TR:HN-TNS
        'He kept on breaking it.'

(26c)   *[Kohóbaf]-fi-h.*
        break:HN-TR-TNS

The hn-grade nasalizes and accents the penult of the verb stem; it is never possible for it to appear on the penult of the verb root instead, as in (26c).

In the general case, the causative *-chi* is also within the verb stem. Consider the following examples, where (27b) shows the hn-grade of a non-causative verb, and (27d) shows the hn-grade of the corresponding causative.

(27a)   *Hattak-at [taloowa]-tok.*
        man-NM   sing-PT
        'The man sang.'

(27b)   *Hattak-at [talohówa]-tok.*
        man-NM   sing:HN-PT
        'The man kept on singing.'

(27c)   *Abanopoli-yat hattak [taloowa-chi]-tok.*
        preacher-NM   man   sing-CAUS-PT
        'The preacher made the man sing.'

(27d)   *Abanopoli-yat hattak [taloowaháchi]-tok.*
        preacher-NM   man   sing:CAUS:HN-PT
        'The preacher kept on making the man sing.'

The hn-grade affects the penult of the verb stem. Since the addition of the causative -*chi* makes the verb stem one syllable longer, the penult changes and the effects of the hn-grade show up in different syllables of the causative and non-causative verbs.

However there is some variability in whether the causative is included in the verb stem. Some speakers also accept the following variant of (27d):

(28)   *Abanǫpoli-yat   hattak   [talohǫwa]-chi-tok.*
        preacher-NM   man   sing:HN-CAUS-PT
        'The preacher kept on making the man sing.'

This example is unusual because the vowel that receives the accent and nasalization is the penult of the verb, excluding its causative suffix. Ulrich (1986:228) reports similar variations from his consultant.

One might expect that there could be a semantic contrast between (27d) and (28), depending on whether the aspectual semantics applies to the causation or the caused event. Thus (27d) might mean 'The preacher kept on making the man sing', while (28) would mean 'The preacher made the man keep on singing'. While judgments were a bit uncertain, speakers I consulted preferred to interpret both examples as 'The preacher kept on making the man sing.' That is, the aspectual semantics seem to apply to the act of causation, whether the causative -*chi* is included in the verb stem or not.

11. Tense and modality

Markers of tense and modality occupy the following position within the verb's inflectional complex:

(1)   Verb stem + (Modal) + (Tense) + (Evidential/Illocutionary Force)

Evidentials and markers of illocutionary force are discussed in chapter 12. Adverbial elements can intervene at various points in this string. They are discussed in more detail in chapter 18.

Derivational suffixes like -*li* 'active', -*a* 'stative', and -*chi* 'causative' are part of the verb stem, and hence precede all these affixes. Immediately following the verb stem and preceding modal, tense, and evidential or illocutionary suffixes are the first person singular class I suffix -*li* and the negative -*o(k)*, which have been described in preceding chapters.

11.1. Modality

Choctaw modals provide information about the status of the event as real or unreal. There are four members of this set. The first two, -*aachi̲* and -*ahii*, are primarily markers of simple irrealis. When these modals are followed by the tense marker -*h*, they are both generally translated by the English future tense. However, -*aachi̲* is more frequent in affirmative main clauses. The modal -*ahii* appears more frequently in sentences with negation.[1]

(2)   *O̲b-aachi̲-h.*
       rain-IRR-TNS
       'It's going to rain.'

(3)   *Mike-at   ik-iss-ok-ahii-h.*
       Mike-NM   N-stop-NEG-IRR2-TNS
       'Mike won't shut up.'

The interpretation of the irrealis markers in an embedded clause without overt tense marking is the same:

(4)   *Lynn-at   ik-ikháan-o-h   [iy-aachi̲-kat].*
       Lynn-NM   N-know:L-NEG-TNS   go-IRR-COMP:SS
       'Lynn doesn't know that she will go.'

---

1. Munro and Willmond label the Chickasaw cognate -*a'hi*, the 'convictional', and say that it is used in "statements reflecting the speaker's firm belief rather than sure knowledge, generally about the future" (1994:xlvi).

169

When -*ahii* or -*aachi̱* is followed by -*tok*, the modal is interpreted as 'was supposed to' or 'was going to'.

(5)   *I̱p-aachi̱-tok.*
        eat-IRR-PT
        'He was going to eat.'

(6)   *Ish-nos-ahii-kiiyo-tok.*
        2SI-sleep-IRR2-NEG-PT
        'You weren't supposed to fall asleep.'

The irrealis -*aachi̱*, but not -*ahii*, may appear in questions:

(7a)   *Pam-at   taloow-aachi̱-h-o̱?*
        Pam-NM   sing-IRR-TNS-Q
        'Is Pam going to sing?'

(7b)   **Pam-at   taloow-ahii-h o̱?*
        Pam-NM   sing-IRR2-TNS-Q
        ('Is Pam going to sing?')

I have sometimes recorded verbs with -*ahii* that appear to end in glottal stop, rather than the expected *h*.[2]

The other members of the set of modals are -*aana* and -*ahila*.[3] Speakers disagree over whether there is any difference in meaning between them. When followed by the default tense -*h*, they are generally translated 'can, could, might'.

(8)   *Chi-pi̱sa-l-ahila-h.*
        2SII-see:N-1SI-POT-TNS
        'I can see you.'

The interpretation of the potential in an embedded clause without overt tense marking is the same:

(9)   *Ná̱na-h   nonaachi-l-aana-kat   ik-sam-iksho-h.*
        thing-TNS   cook-1SI-POT-COMP:SS   N-1SIII-not:exist-TNS
        'I don't have anything that I can cook.'

---

2. Nicklas (1974:140) also notes that -*ahii* (his <āhi>) is not followed by -*h*. The correct analysis is uncertain, but it is probably best to say that some speakers have an underlying form of the morpheme which is -*ahii'*. Since otherwise all modals are followed by some tense marker, the unexpected lack of -*ahii'-h* is probably phonologically motivated.

3. The modal -*ahila* has dialectal or idiolectal variants -*ahiina* and -*ayna*. Some speakers also have a reduced form -*a̱*, which only occurs after -*li*, the first person singular class I agreement affix:

    Chi-pi̱sa-l-a̱.
    2SII-see-1SI-IRR
    'I can see you.'

When followed by the past marker -*tok*, the modals are translated as 'would have, could have':

(10)   *Piláashaash ik-ób-o-tokma,*
       yesterday   N-rain:L-NEG-PT:IRR:DS
       chi̲-chokka' ii-l-aana-tok.
       2sIII-house 1PI-arrive-POT-PT
       'If it hadn't rained yesterday, we would have come to your house.'

The modal -*ahi̲la* can also be used to describe potential situations in the future. In the following sentences it is used in the consequent to the conditional clause, and is translated 'would be':

(11)   <sa hokchi hokma, sa kotʋt, hatak inla kak inli chohmi la hinla hoke>
       sa-hokchi-ho-kma, sa-kota-t,   hattak i̲la-k-aki̲li-h
       1sII-tie-link-IRR   1sII-weak-PART   man   other-COMP-indeed-TNS
       chohmi-l-ahi̲la-h-okii
       be:like-1sI-POT-TNS-indeed
       'If they were to tie me up, I would be weak and like other men.'
       (Judg. 16:7)

(12)   *Okchálhlha-at oklah to̲shpa-kma̲, achokm-aana-h.*
       blackbird-NM   PLUR   hurry-IRR:DS good-POT-TNS
       'If the blackbirds hurried, it would be good.'

Clauses which are realis have no suffix in the modal position. The distinction between tense and modal suffixes in Choctaw has not always been recognized. See section 11.3 below for a discussion of some differences between them.

11.2. Tense

The second suffix position contains markers of tense. There are three clear members of this set: -*ttook* 'distant past', -*tok* 'past, perfect', and -*h* 'unspecified'. There is also perhaps a fourth member of this group, -*k*.

11.2.1. -*ttook* 'distant past'

The suffix -*ttook* marks distant past, and may be used for events approximately a year or more in the past, although usage varies considerably.

(13)   *Im-okla-yat   illi̲pa' oklah ik-im-iksho-ttook.*
       III-people-NM food   PLUR   N-III-not-DPAST
       'His people didn't have any food (long ago).'

In older Choctaw materials, the distant past tense marker is generally written <tok> (-*ttook*), contrasting with the ordinary past marker <tuk> (-*tok*).

11.2.2. -tok 'past'

The suffix -*tok* is used in contexts that correspond to those of the English past tense plus certain uses of the present perfect. It may mark simple past tense, as in the following example:

(14)   *John-at   Mary písa-tok.*
       John-NM Mary see:N-PT
       'John saw Mary.'

It is also used for certain events that begin in the past and continue up to the present.

(15)   *Káfi-yo̲   ishko-li-biika-tok.*
       coffee-FOC:AC drink-1SI-extent-PT
       'I have usually drunk coffee.'

(16)   *Ik-sa̲-chókm-o-tok   palaata-hma̲*
       N-1SIII-be:well:L-NEG-PT lonesome-when:DS
       'I've been unhappy because I'm lonesome.' (R.S. Williams 1995:62)

Use of the morpheme -*hchaa* 'usually, always' forces the past tense -*tok* to appear:

(17)   *Hihi̲lha-li-hchaa-tok.*
       dance:HN-1SI-generic-PT
       'I always dance.'

It is important to note that there is no necessary association between -*tok* and realis. The following example shows that -*tok* is perfectly compatible with the irrealis:

(18)   *Piláashaash ik-ó̲b-o-tokma̲,   chi̲-chokka'*
       yesterday   N-rain:L-NEG-PT:IRR:DS 2SII-house
       ii-l-aana-tok.
       1PI-arrive-POT-PT
       'If it hadn't rained yesterday, we would have come to your house.'[4]

Nor is -*tok* a marker of the perfective, since uncompleted events can appear with -*tok*:

(19)   *I̲-chokka' falaama-t ona-li-hma̲,   ipa-sh biniili-mo̲ma-tok.*
       III-house return-PART arrive-1SI-when:DS eat-PART:SS bit-still-PT
       'When I got back to his house, he was still (sitting there) eating.'

11.2.3. -h 'default tense'

11.2.3.1. -h on nonpast events

The suffix -*h* is the unmarked or default tense. It occurs on all nonpast

---

4. When -*tok* is followed by a *k*-initial suffix, only one *k* appears. Thus we have -*tokma̲* instead of -*tok-kma̲*.

events, whether present or future:

(20) *Iya-l-aachi̱-h.*
      go-1sI-IRR-TNS
      'I will go.'

(21) *Ta̱chi' apa-h*
      corn   eat-TNS
      'He's eating corn.'

All verbal elements in Choctaw must have some tense marker, including ones that do not refer to events (e.g., adjectives and quantifiers); -*h* is the tense standardly found on such elements.

(22) *Hattak chaaha-h pi̱sa-li-tok.*
      man   tall-TNS   see:N-1sI-PT
      'I saw the tall man.'

(23) *Hattak-at chaaha-h.*
      man-NM   tall-TNS
      'The man is tall.'

11.2.3.2. -*h* on past events

Use of -*h* for events that occurred in the past is more restricted. The suffix -*h* often corresponds to the resultative use of the English present perfect, describing a past event whose result still holds and is relevant to the current situation:

(24) Q: *John-ato katómma-h?*
          John-NM2 where-TNS
          'Where is John?'

      A: *Chókkosi' iya-h.*
          bathroom go-TNS
          'He's gone to the bathroom.'

Use of -*h* in the answer to this question implies that John is still in the bathroom and that this is relevant to the current situation.

There are a few sentence elements that seem to be significant in licensing past tense interpretations of -*h*. They include the completive auxiliary *tahah/tahlih* and the adverbial *hímo'/hómo'* 'just now':

(25) *Pola̱ka apa-t   tahli-h.*
      finally eat-PART complete-TNS
      'He finally ate it up.'

(26) *Homo' haklo-h-a*
      just   hear-TNS-GUESS
      'Apparently, they have just now heard it.'

It seems that -*h* is used more freely with past events when the completive auxiliary or the adverbial 'just now' is present. When neither of these licensing elements is present, -*h* on past events implies that the event described resulted in a state with current relevance. But sentences with the completive or adverbial 'just now' may appear with -*h* even when there seems to be no state that is a result of the event.

Clauses linked by the complementizers -*cha* and -*na* (see chapter 16) necessarily imply actions in the past, and -*h* is often used on the final verb in these cases:

(27)   *Talóowa-cha   hilha-h.*
         sing:L-SS   dance-TNS
         'He sang and danced.'

The default -*h* may not be used when an explicit past time adverbial is present:[5]

(28)   *Piláashaash   tamaaha'   iya-tok/*iya-h).*
         yesterday   town   go-PT/*go-TNS)
         'Yesterday he went to town.'

However, adverbials referring to an earlier time on the same day are allowed:

(29)   *Onnahíli-pano   ak-háklo-h.*
         morning-D:AC2 1SN-hear:L-TNS
         'This morning I didn't hear it.'

11.2.3.3. Alleged absence of -*h*

In claiming that -*h* follows the irrealis *aachi̲,* I differ with Munro (1987a) and Ulrich (1986). When this -*h* appears in word-final position, it is largely inaudible, though it is clearly present when any suffix follows. I suggest that it is optionally deleted by the following rule (discussed in chapter 2):

(30)   *h* →∅ / __# *(optional)*

Given that *h* is difficult to hear when it appears at the end of a verb, it is perhaps not surprising that there has been some disagreement over whether there is a suffix -*h* that occurs in this position.

Davies says of -*h* in general:

> however prevalent this marker was historically, many speakers no longer use it, and are, in fact, aware that they do not. My consultants generally use the suffix only when predicates and nominals might be confused due to word order, full or partial homophony, or some other reasons. [1981:13]

---

5. Note that there is a similar restriction on the present perfect in English: **Yesterday he has gone to the market.* See Brugger (1997) and references therein for discussion.

For this reason Davies does not include final *-h* for most of his examples.

I believe that a rule optionally deleting final *h* is responsible for Davies' conclusion that the suffix is absent or only sporadically present in the speech of his consultants. Other examples show that *-h* is present when non-final:

(31)   *Chi-kapassa-h-o̲?*
        2sII-cold-TNS-Q
        'Are you cold?' (Davies 1981:35)

Davies treats *-ho̲* as a single morpheme, but this analysis cannot be maintained, since the past tense form is as follows:

(32)   *Chi-kapassa-tok-o̲?*
        2sII-cold-PT-Q
        'Were you cold?'

There is no possibility of a rule deleting *h* in this environment, given nouns like *shokha'* 'pig'.

Davies (1986), without discussion, includes final *h* in the places it is absent in Davies (1981).

11.2.3.4. Alternative analyses of *-h*

Nicklas (1974) and Haag (1995) favor an analysis of *-h* in which it marks predication rather than tense. A difficulty of these analyses is that *-h* is in complementary distribution with the past and distant past tense markers *-tok* and *-ttook*. It seems necessary either to posit some phonological reason that sentences with these tenses are not marked for predication or to simply stipulate that sentences are only marked for predication when there is no overt tense marker.

A second difficulty is that certain phrases that might well be regarded as predicates nevertheless fail to show the *-h* suffix (Haag 1995:9):

(33)   *Chi̲-nakfi'-at   laaya'(*-h).*
        2sIII-brother-NM   lawyer(-TNS)
        'Your brother is a lawyer.'

(34)   *John-at topa' apáknaka'(*-h) átta-h.*
        dog-NM bed   top(-TNS)   be:N-TNS
        'John is on top of the bed.'

On most theories of predication, 'lawyer' is predicated of 'your brother' and 'on top of the bed' is predicated of 'John'.[6] Nevertheless no *-h* appears. In Haag's view, this is because marking for predication is restricted to categories such as "verbs, adjectives, degree specifiers, and others" (1995:8) that are inherently predicated of other things. While

6. See, for example, Napoli (1989:34–46).

such a view may be workable, it suggests that the necessary definition of predication is somewhat complex. It is not obvious that this alternative is simpler or more explanatory than the treatment of *-h* as a tense marker.

Ulrich says that *-h* "occurs on verbs in the absence of certain other suffixes, such as the aspect marker *-tok* and the nominalizing *-'*" (1986:78). This is somewhat close to my view on the matter, but Ulrich assigns no meaning to *-h*. Given the fact that it occurs in the same position as tense markers, it seems best to regard it as one of the tense markers.

11.2.4. *-k* 'embedded tense'

A fourth possible tense marker is *-k*. Unlike the other tense markers, *-k* does not appear on verbs of main clauses:

(35)   **John-at ch*o*pa-k.*
        John-NM buy-TNS
        ('John buys/bought it.')

The suffix *-k* only appears in more complex syntactic environments. One of the environments for *-k* is in relative clauses followed by the previous-mention marker *-aash* (introduced in chapter 5):

(36)   *N*a*na=chap*ó*li'Pam-at   nonaachi-k-aash apa-li-tok.*
        cake   Pam-NM   cook-TNS-PREV   eat-1SI-PT
        'I ate the cake that Pam made.'

The only tense marker allowed in this context is *-k*; *-tok* and *-h* are ungrammatical:[7]

(37)   **N*a*na=chap*ó*li' Pam-at   nonaachi-tok-aash/nonaachi-h-aash*
        cake   Pam-NM   cook-PT-PREV/cook-TNS-PREV
        apa-li-tok.
        eat-1SI-PT
        ('I ate the cake that Pam made/is making.')

Alternations like these, where *-k* excludes other tense markers, are the strongest evidence that *-k* ought to be regarded as one of the tense markers.

In chapter 5, I suggested that *-aash* on noun phrases may belong to the group of clausal determiners—adverbial elements which appear after a null copula. That implies that relative clauses ending in *-k-aash* have a structure like the following:

---

7. Gordon (1987) and Haag (1995) report the same result. Gordon seems to imply that modals like *-aachi* are also disallowed in this position, but see below for evidence that this is incorrect.

(38) *Nana=chapóli' Pam-at nonaachi-k-∅-aash   apa-li-tok.*
      cake   Pam-NM cook-TNS-COP-PREV eat-1SI-PT
      'I ate the cake that Pam made.'

The occurrence of the tense marker -*k* in this structure may then be due to some restrictions that copular structures place on their complements. Occurrence in copular structures may be the conditioning factor for some other instances of -*k* as well. Consider the following examples:

(39) *Mike-at   issa-k   mak-ahii-tok.*
      Mike-NM stop-TNS COP-IRR-PT
      'I wish Mike would shut up.'

(40) <Mihmʋt ịki ak osh nana họ hohchifa hi a̱ ahnik mak a chị ka, okla pit abʋchi tok.>
      Mihmat   ịki-yakoosh   ná̱na-h-ọ   hohchif-ahii-ya̱
      and:then:SS father-CON:NM what-TNS-AC be:named-IRR-AC
      ahni-k   mak-aachị-ka oklah pit   aabachi-ttook.
      think-TNS COP-IRR-COMP PLUR away show-DPAST
      'And then they made signs to his father [to find out] what he wanted him to be named.' (Luke 1:62)

It is far from clear how sentences like these should be analyzed. However, *mak-* shows copular properties in other sentences, like the following:

(41) . . . Chan a̱ yʋmmak osh Klaist mak okmá keyukmá, nanta họ chishba?
      John-a̱   yammak-oosh Klaist mak-okmá kiiy-okmá na̱tah-ọ
      John-AC that-FOC:NM   Christ be-or   not-or   be:what-Q
      chishba?
      DON'T.KNOW
      'Was John the Christ or not?' (Luke 3:15)

If we treat *mak-* as a copular element, then the occurrence of the tense -*k* before it is like the occurrence of -*k* before the null copula.

The diachronic origin of -*tok* may provide some insight into the appearance of -*k* in certain contexts. Booker (1980) has suggested that Choctaw sequences of verb plus -*tok* derived historically from reanalysis of sequences like the following:

(42) Verb-t   *oo-k*
      verb-PART COP-TNS

Booker reconstructs *oo* as a copula in Proto-Muskogean, and there are still clear contexts in which it appears as a copula in Chickasaw.

At an earlier stage in the development of Choctaw, perhaps there were alternations like the following:

(43a) Verb-*t*   copula-*k*   (main clause)
      verb-PART copula-TNS

(43b) Verb-*k*   copula   (embedded clause)
       verb-TNS copula

That is, main clauses were required to appear with a copula after the verb and tense marking followed the copula. But when verbs were embedded beneath a copula, tense appeared directly on the verb. This would explain why -*k* only seems to show up in embedded environments.[8]

A few other environments may also sometimes allow -*k*. The complement of *miyah*, indicating hearsay information, is sometimes suffixed with -*k*:

(44) *Bonnie-at   maka-kat   chi̱-chokka' kana-sh*
       Bonnie-NM say-COMP:SS 2sII-house someone-FOC:NM
       ona-k   miyah.
       arrive-TNS say
       'Bonnie says someone's at your house.'

However, some speakers do not accept -*k* in this context, and use -*h* instead.

When verbs in the irrealis are followed by the negative *kiiyo*, the expected default tense -*h* is replaced by -*k*, and the nasalization in -*aachi̱* is lost:

(45) *Sa-nayopp-aachi-k kiiyo-h.*
       1sII-happy-IRR-TNS NEG-TNS
       'I won't be happy.'

It is not completely clear whether this ought to be regarded as use of a different tense ending or whether -*h* has undergone some sort of phonological assimilation.

Byington also recognizes /-k/ as one of the tense markers in the following entry:

> **k**, sign of the past tense, as *chumpak*, which may be a contraction from *chumpa tuk*, he bought; he did buy; here *k* limits the act of buying. It is thus like *don't* in English. *k* is a contracted form of the adv. *kʋmo*, as in *ialek*, I went (for *iali kʋmo*.) . . . [1915:219]

Byington seems to be presenting two different hypotheses about -*k* in this entry, however. In one view, it is contracted from -*tok*, and in the other from -*kaamo*.

Haag identifies -*k* as a morpheme, but labels it "a marker of local predication . . . [used] in subjunctive mood" (1995:8). Haag does not specify what the contexts for the subjunctive are, so it is difficult to say whether this definition correctly predicts the distribution of -*k*. It is not obvious that the contexts for -*k* just described correspond to subjunctives.

---

8. This is not a tenable synchronic account, however, since -*tok* now appears freely in embedded clauses, and the contexts where -*k* appears are essentially fossilized copular constructions.

11.2.5. Other proposed tenses

11.2.5.1. Nomic tense

Nicklas also mentions "nomic tenses" which he said were not well understood, but frequently "tell what the general rule about something is" (Nicklas 1974:74). This tense is characterised by a glottal stop in place of the tense marker and accent on the penult of the verb stem. A question and answer pair is shown below:

(46) Q: *okof   ish-pay-o?*
          persimmon 2sI-eat:NM-Q
          'Do you eat persimmons?'

      A: *A,   apá-li-'.*
          yes eat-1sI-NM
          'Yes, I eat them.'

Ulrich (1986:180–81) argues that Nicklas's examples appear to be instances of nominalizations rather than another tense. (And thus the question above might be paraphrased 'Are you a persimmon eater?') Note that the final glottal stop and penult accent are also found in nominalizations (section 4.1). If Ulrich is correct, what is somewhat unusual about these nominalizations is that they include agreement morphology.

11.2.5.2. *-hatok* and *-hookat*

In Broadwell (1990a) I listed two other unusual verbal suffixes, *-hatok* and *-hookat*, as possible instances of tense, but I no longer believe this to be correct.[9]

The orthographic sequence <ha tok> is found after some verbs in nineteenth-century Choctaw texts, and Byington cites this suffix as 'remote past tense'. I now believe that this is better analyzed as *-attook*, which is the copula followed by the distant past tense marker. This appears after a verb with the default tense marker *-h* and forms a cleft sentence, as in the following example:

(47) <hopoyuksa ʋhleha ak o hoyot aya li ha tok keyu>
      hopooyoksa alhiih-ako   hoyo-t   aya-li-h   a-ttook
      righteous   group-CON:AC call-PART go-1sI-TNS COP-DPAST
      kiiyo-h
      not-TNS
      'I did not come to call the righteous.' (Lit., 'It was not that I came to call the righteous.') (Matt. 9:13)

---

9. In Broadwell (1990a) I also listed the first vowel of *-hookat* as short: *-hokat*. After listening to this ending more times, I now believe that the first vowel is long.

This construction is very frequently used in translating the Biblical formula "For it is written." In Choctaw, this is translated with an initial "according to" clause and a final verb of saying, followed by *a-ttook*:

(48) <Holihiso kʋt, Chekob ano i hullo li tok: amba Esau yokʋno ak i hullo ki tok, ahanchi hatok oka.>
Holihísso-kat,   Jacob-ano i-hollo-li-tok;   amba
write:HN-COMP:SS Jacob-AC2 III-love-1sI-PT but
Esau-yook-ano   ak-i-hóllo-kii-tok,
Esau-COMPAR-AC2 1sN-III-love:L-NEG-PT
aháchi-h   a-ttook-ooka.
say:HN-TNS COP-DPAST-for
'For it is written, I love Jacob, but hate Esau.' (Rom. 9:13)

The following example also shows an initial subordinate clause ('as God willed') which influences the interpretation of the following main clauses with *attook*:

(49) <Chihowa ak osh ahni hosh, chukʋsh a kʋllochi na Islael a ant itiba chi hatok; yʋmohmi ho ʋbit tahlit ʋmohmicha chi hatok.>
Chihoowa-akoosh ahni-h-oosh,   chokash-a
God-CON:NM   will-TNS-PART:SS heart-AC
kallóochi-na Islael-a   at   ittib-aachi-h a-ttook;
harden:L-DS Israel-AC come:and fight-IRR-TNS COP-DPAST
yamohmi-h-o   abi-t   amohmich-aachi-h a-ttook.
do:thus-TNS-DS kill-PART utterly-IRR-TNS   COP-DPAST
'As God$_i$ willed, it was the case that he$_i$ would harden their hearts so that they$_j$ would go to fight Israel$_k$, and having done that, it was the case that they$_k$ would kill them$_j$ utterly.' (Josh. 11:20)

Although there are still some questions about the use of this construction, there seems to be little reason to regard *-hatok* as a tense marker.

The sequence *-hookat* occasionally appears following a verb in a main clause, and I also labelled it a tense marker in Broadwell (1990a). A more careful examination of the contexts in which this ending is used shows that in general a sentence with *-hookat* is an objection to something in the preceding discourse. It is usually possible to felicitously add the word 'but' to the English translation.

I now think that these sentences are better analysed as elliptical. The usual complementizer for 'but' is *-ookakoo*, and *-ookat* appears to be a variant form of 'but'.

(50) *Lashpa-h-o   ish-aachi-h-ookat.*
hot-TNS-PART:DS 2SI-say-TNS-but
'But you said it was hot.'

(51)   <. . . nana kʋt ai ʋlhpesa keyu, kashofa keyu hokʋno himmona kia,
       ʋpa li chatuk keyu hokʋt achi tok.
       n̲a̲na-k-at   aay-alhpı́isa' kiiyo-h,   kashóofa'
       thing-TNS-NM LOC-right   NEG-TNS clean
       kiiyo-h-ook-ano   himmona-kia apa-li-hchaa-tok
       NEG-TNS-COMPAR-AC2   now-too   eat-1sI-generic-PT
       kiiyo-h-ookat,   aachi-ttook.
       not-TNS-but   say-DPAST-TNS
       '"Until now, I have never eaten anything common or unclean," he
       said.' (Acts 10:14)

As with a-ttook, there are still questions about -ookat, but it does not
seem necessary to treat it as a tense marker.

11.3. Tense versus modality

In the previous discussion, I have distinguished between the modals
-aachi̲ and -ahii and the tenses -tok, -ttook, -h, -k. This distinction is not
surprising from a crosslinguistic perspective. In English, for example,
future events are signaled with the modal *will*, which shows the same
distribution as other modals like *can*. Neither *can* nor *will* has a
distribution like the present and past tense markers of English.

Nevertheless, the distinction between tense and modal positions in
Choctaw has not always been made. Nicklas (1974:139–40), for example,
lists -tok, -ttook, -aachi̲h as the past, distant past, and future tense
markers.[10] In this section, I discuss some of the differences between
modals and tenses that justifies this distinction.

First, there are some syntactic contexts where tense is suppressed,
but modals are not. Clauses in -cha and -na, for example, do not allow
the verb to which they are suffixed to be marked for tense:

(52a) *John-at   talóowa-na Bill-at   hilha-tok.*
       John-NM sing:L-DS   Bill-NM dance-PT
       'John sang and Bill danced.'

(52b) **John-at talóowa-tok-na Bill-at   hilha-tok.*
       John-NM sing-PT-DS   Bill-NM dance-PT
       ('John sang and Bill danced.')

However, -na may be preceded by the modals:[11]

(53)   A̲-kaah   apoksi-ahi̲la-na i̲-hili-chi-sh   iya-li-tok.
       1sIII-car fix-POT-DS   III-stand-CAUS-PART:SS go-1sI-PT
       'He was able to fix the car, so I left it there for him and went on.'

---

10. Nicklas writes that the suffix /-h/ "marks the word as being part of the
predicate or mode" (1974:140). In this respect his view is similar to that of Haag
(1995). See arguments above against this point of view.

11. The fact that -aachi̲ may precede -na while -tok may not was first noted by
Linker (1987:104). Since Linker treated both -tok and -aachi̲ as tense-aspect markers,
however, this difference needed to be stipulated in her account.

(54)   *John-at   yopp-aachi̲-na   Mary-at   nokoow-aachi̲-h.*
    John-NM   laugh-IRR-DS   Mary-NM   angry-IRR-TNS
    'John is going to laugh and Mary is going to get angry.'[12]

Clauses with *-na* show that the irrealis *-aachi̲* groups with the potential *-ahi̲la* and not with the tense marker *-tok*. It is thus a modal and not a tense.

    A very similar argument is available from relative clauses. As mentioned above, relative clauses ending in *-aash* only allow the tense marker *-k*; *-tok* is ungrammatical in this context:

(55)   *Ná̲na=cha̲póli'   Pam-at   nonaachi-k-Ø-aash   apa-li-tok.*
    cake   Pam-NM   cook-TNS-COP-PREV   eat-1SI-PT
    'I ate the cake that Pam made.'

(56)   **Ná̲na=cha̲póli'   Pam-at   nonaachi-tok-Ø-aash   apa-li-tok.*
    cake   Pam-NM   cook-PT-COP-PREV   eat-1SI-PT
    ('I ate the cake that Pam made.')

However, modals may precede *-k-aash*:

(57)   *An-ato   ak-ikháan-o-h   nakni'-ma̲   John-at   ot*
    I-NM2   1SN-know:L-NEG-TNS   male-D:NM   John-NM   go:and
    pis-aana-k-Ø-aash.
    see-POT-TNS-COP-PREV
    'I don't know the man that John was supposed to go see.'

(58)   *An-ato   ak-ikháan-o-h   nakni'-ma̲   John-at   ot*
    I-NM2   1SN-know:L-NEG-TNS   male-D:NM   John-NM   go:and
    pis-aachi̲-k-Ø-aash.
    see-IRR-TNS-COP-PREV
    'I don't know the man that John was supposed to go see.'

If *-aachi̲* is a tense marker it should be prohibited from these environments (like *-tok*). Instead, it behaves like one of the modals.

    Finally, the modals may directly precede tense markers:

(59)   *I̲p-ahii-tok.*
    eat-IRR2-PT
    'He was supposed to eat.'

(60)   *I̲p-aachi̲-tok.*
    eat-IRR-PT
    'He was going to eat.'

---

12. This sentence is grammatical, but somewhat unusual. If Mary's anger is conditioned on John's laughter, a more common way to express this would use the conditional:

    John-at   yoppa-kma̲   Mary-at   nokoow-aachi̲-h.
    John-NM   laugh-IRR:DS   Mary-NM   angry-IRR-TNS
    'If John laughs, Mary is going to get angry.'

(61)   *Ip-ahila-tok.*
       eat-POT-PT
       'He could eat.'

Nicklas (1974:140) discusses "compound tenses" and cites the following form, which appears to show that modals may also follow the tense markers:

(62)   *Malahta-tok-aachi-h.*
       lightning-PT-IRR-TNS
       'There will have been lightening.'

However, there is an alternate analysis of such forms:

(63)   *Malahta-tok ∅-aachi-h.*
       lightning-PT COP-IRR-TNS
       'It will be the case that there was lightening.'

One of the forms of the copula is *a*, and the suffix *-aachi* deletes a preceding vowel, yielding a form like that shown above. This analysis of the "compound tenses" seems preferable to Nicklas's account, given the existence of forms like the following:

(64)   *Malahta-tok aa-tok.*
       lightning-PT COP-PT
       'It was the case that it rained.'

Since *aa* appears in these forms, there is no alternative to the copular analysis. Given that copular constructions of this sort are allowed, it is more consistent to analyse (62) in the same way.

12. Evidentiality and illocutionary force

The third position in the verb suffix complex is occupied by markers of evidentiality and illocutionary force. The two sorts of suffix are in complementary distribution, and so can reasonably be considered together.

The class of evidentials includes -a 'guess', -aamo 'certainty', -chi 'wonder', -chiichi 'guess', -chichook 'doubt', -chihba 'doubt', -hli 'certainty', -ká' 'certainty', -kasha 'guess', -kia 'emphatic' and -ta 'warning'.

12.1. Evidential suffixes

The evidential suffixes are exemplified in the following sections. Some of these suffixes are rare and the glosses are correspondingly uncertain.

As a first approximation, Choctaw sentences containing an evidential are interpreted as if the evidential were an upper clause whose subject was first person, and this is reflected in the English translations given:

(1) Oba-tok-chi.
     rain-PT-wonder
     'I wonder if it rained.'

However, the Choctaw contains no first person morpheme. Rather, evidentials are interpreted from the point of view of some person, and that person is generally the speaker.

12.1.1. -aamo 'certainty'

The ending -aamo is archaic and found in only a few examples. Consultants aged around seventy identify it as a way the "old-timers" used to talk. In my data it is generally preceded by the tense affix -k. It is tentatively glossed 'certainty', based on Byington (1915:222), whose entry for kaamo says, in part, "immediate past tense . . . it implies that the speaker has knowledge of what he speaks and not the hearer."

(2) Mashkooki' yakni' iya-li-k-aamo.
     Creek   land   go-1sI-TNS-CERT
     'I went to Creek land.'

(3) Piláashaash ittanáaha' iya-li-k-aamo.
     yesterday   church   go-1SI-TNS-CERT
     'Yesterday I went to church.'

(4) <. . . chi písa li kamo im achi tok.>

184

... *chi-pisa-li-k-aamo   im-aachi-tok*
    2SII-see:N-1SI-TNS-CERT   III-say-PT
'"I saw you," he said to him.' (John 1:48)

In a few cases, *-aamo* appears to be preceded by an element *-hch-*. This looks like *-hchaa* 'always':

(5)   *Iya-li-hch-aamo.*
    go-1SI-GENERIC-CERT
    'I went (long ago).'

(6)   <Yau ish ona mʋhli chamo.>
    Yaw, ish-ona-malhlhi-hch-aamo.
    yes   2SI-arrive-truly-GENERIC-CERT
    'Yes, you came.' (Byington 1827:118)

However, the analysis here is far from clear. Generally *-hchaa* must be followed by *-tok*, so if it appears here, this is unusual. It is also unclear what about this verb shows that the event occurred in the distant past. Perhaps there is some other unidentified *-hch-* morpheme at work.

12.1.2. -a 'guess'

The suffix *-a* 'guess, probably', occurs in examples like the following:

(7)   *Iya-l-aana-kmat am-achokma-h-a.*
    go-1SI-IRR-IRR:SS 1sIII-good-TNS-GUESS
    'I guess it would be good for me if I could go.'

(8)   *Iya-l-aachi-h-a.*
    go-1SI-IRR1-TNS-GUESS
    'I guess I'm going too.'

(9)   *Ob-aachi-h-a.*
    rain-IRR-TNS-GUESS
    'It's probably going to rain.'

12.1.3. -ba 'no expectation'

The suffix *-ba* is relatively rare in modern Choctaw. Speakers have somewhat different intuitions about its meaning. One speaker said that *-ba* "means you really don't know the answer," while another suggested that *-ba* indicates skepticism about the truth of the statement:

(10)   *Apa-tok-ba.*
    eat-PT-DOUBT
    'Oh sure, he ate it.'

(11)   *Katimm-ak-o̲ hoshi' híshi-yano aay-ishi-h-oosh*
         where-OBL-AC bird   feather-AC2 LOC-get-TNS-PART:SS
         ibaa-kahli-tok-ba?
         COM-pile-PT-DOUBT
         'Where did she get the feathers and pile them up?'

(12)   *Ishtti̲wa-yo̲ ishi-h-oosh   abooha-yano tiwwi-kma̲*
         key-FOC:AC take-TNS-PART:SS house-AC2   open-IRR:DS
         na̲ta-tok-ba?
         whether-PT-DOUBT
         'Did she get the key and open the house?'

Although -*ba* often appears on sentences that are translated as questions, -*ba* is not a true question particle. It is likely that -*ba* means something like 'I wonder' or 'I really don't know'. Sentences with -*ba* have the syntax of declaratives, but may be pragmatically interpreted as requests, in a manner similar to English sentences like "I wonder what time it is."[1]

12.1.4. -*chi*, -*chichook* 'unsure'

These suffixes indicate speaker uncertainty and are often translated with 'I wonder if' or by translating the sentence as a question.

(13)   *Pam-at   tamaaha' iya-tok-chi.*
         Pam-NM town   go-PT-WONDER
         'I wonder if Pam went to town.'

(14)   *Chik-píis-o-tok-chi.*
         2SN-see:L-NEG-PT-WONDER
         'You didn't see it, did you?'

(15)   *Itt-afaam-ahii-tok-chichook.*
         RCP-meet-IRR-PT-WONDER
         'I guess they met, but I don't know for sure.'

12.1.5. -*chiit* 'presumed false'

This suffix seems to show that the speaker believes the proposition should be false. It is often translated into English as a negative sentence with a tag. Speakers say that this particle gives the sentence a somewhat hostile tone. Perhaps -*chiit* is related to the morpheme -*chi* 'unsure'.

---

1. Byington (1915:82) has the following entry for /-ba/:

ba, adv., nothing; merely; certainly; surely; *ia li ba*, I merely go; I just go; I will just go, and meaning that nothing shall prevent; a word used chiefly by children.

This seems roughly compatible with the suggestions above.

(16) *Nosi-h-chiit.*
sleep-TNS-UNTRUE
'He's not sleeping, is he?'

(17) *Maka-tok-chiit.*
say-PT-UNTRUE
'He better not have said it.'

12.1.6. *-chiichi, -chiichik* 'suppose'

These suffixes indicate a speaker's lack of commitment to the truth of a proposition and are usually translated 'I suppose'.

(18) *Bailey-ako̱   immi-h-oh-chiichik.*
Bailey-CON:AC his-TNS-LINK-SUPPOSE
'I suppose it was Bailey's.' (Yale B:32)

(19) *O̱ba-h-chiichi.*
rain-TNS-SUPPOSE
'I suppose it's raining.'

12.1.7. *-chihba, -chishba* 'no knowledge'

These suffixes show that the speaker does not know whether the proposition is true, and they are often translated as 'I don't know if'.

(20) *Issi pi̱sa-l-aachi̱-kma̱   na̱n-aachi̱-h-chihba.*
deer see:N-1sI-IRR-IRR:DS whether-IRR-TNS-DON'T:KNOW
'I don't know if I'm going to see a deer or not.'

(21) <. . . Chan a̱ yɒmmak osh Klaist mak okmá keyukmá, nanta ho̱ chishba?>
John-a̱   yammak-oosh Klaist   mak-okmá   kiiy-okmá   na̱tah-o̱
John-AC   that-FOC:NM   Christ   be-or   NEG-or   be:what-Q
chishba?
DON'T:KNOW
'Was John the Christ or not?'[2] (Luke 3:15)

12.1.8. *-hli, -hlik, -hnik* 'first-hand evidence, certainty'

These suffixes indicate that the speaker has first-hand evidence for the truth of the proposition. In the following two sentences, use of *-hli* implies that the speaker saw it raining, while *-tok* is silent about the sort of evidence for the statement.

---

2. If the glossing is correct, *na̱taho̱ chishba* seems to present a problem for the analysis of *-chishba* as an evidential. The problem is that *-o̱* is either the question particle or the same-subject switch-reference marker. Both of these morphemes appear in the complementizer-illocutionary force position in the verb suffix complex, and so they ought to be in complementary distribution with an evidential suffix.

(22) Ǫba-tok.
      rain-PT
      'It rained.' (evidence not stated)

(23) Ǫba-hli.
      rain-CERTAIN
      'It rained.' (the speaker saw it)

It appears that -hli is used in Oklahoma Choctaw, -hnik in the Conehatta community of Mississippi Choctaw, and -hlik in other Mississippi Choctaw communities.

This evidential -hli necessarily implies a past tense semantics, and sentences with -hli have no overt tense marker. The initial h of this suffix probably should not be identified with the default tense marker -h since other tense markers cannot appear in this position (*ǫba-tok-li).

R. S. Williams (1995) notes that some younger speakers of Oklahoma Choctaw use the suffix -hli in translating sentences in the immediate past, even when the event has not been witnessed; for example:

(24) Alla' nakni-mat fama-hli.
      child male-D:NM whipped-CERTAIN
      'Those boys were just whipped.' (Williams 1995:45)

This is a surprising example. For the speakers of Mississippi Choctaw and the older speakers of Oklahoma Choctaw that I have consulted, this sentence would imply that the speaker witnessed the action described. Examples like these may show a shift in the meaning of -hli for some speakers.

12.1.9. -kasha 'guess'

The evidential -kasha corresponds approximately to English 'I guess', as in the following examples:

(25) Ǫba-tok-kasha.
      rain-PT-GUESS
      'I guess it rained.'

(26) John-at taloow-aana-kasha.
      John-NM sing-POT-GUESS
      'I guess John can sing.'

12.1.10. -ká' 'affirmative'

The evidential -ká' is an affirmative which seems to appear in the same discourse context as the English phrase 'I'm telling you', especially when affirming a statement that has just been denied.[3]

---

3. There are precedents for morphemes with this meaning in other languages, especially Japanese (Kuno 1973). I believe that this morpheme may be derived from a Proto-Muskogean root *ka 'say' (see Broadwell 1987a for more discussion).

(27) *Lashpa-ká'!*
      hot-AFFIRM
      'I'm telling you, it's hot!'

The forms *-kat* and *-kato* appear to be variants of the same affix:

(28) *Chokka' chito-kat!*
      house   big-AFFIRM
      'The house is big!'

(29) *Geri pisachokma-kat!*
      Geri goodlooking-AFFIRM
      'Geri is good looking!'

(30) *Alikchi'-mat ohooyo-kato!*
      doctor-D:NM   woman-AFFIRM
      'That doctor is a woman!'

As in insults, there is frequent omission of the nominative case in exclamations that have one of these suffixes (see chapter 5).

12.1.11. *-kia* 'emphatic'

The suffix *-kia* is sometimes translated 'sure enough' or 'surely' by my consultants. It occurs in examples like the following:

(31) *Lashpa-h-kia!*
      hot-TNS-EMPH
      'It sure is hot!'

(32) *Aa-li-h-kia!*
      say-1SI-TNS-EMPH
      'I'll say!'

12.1.12. *-ta* 'warning'

The suffix *-ta* seems to mark exclamations that are warnings of some sort. For example, the following sentence might be said to someone who is about to touch a hot burner:

(33) *Lashpa-ta!*
      hot-WARN
      '(Watch out,) it's hot!'

The Chickasaw cognate to this suffix is *-ta*, which is the ordinary marker of yes-no questions in that language. It takes the form *-tam* in the past tense.

Byington gives the following entry for a particle *ta*, which appears to be related:

ta, adv. of time, doubt, and surprise, as *ish lat ta?* have you been here some time, and I did not know it (recent past tense)? [1915:336]

Byington says that the remote past tense form of this affix is *tah*. His description sounds surprisingly more like modern Chickasaw than Choctaw.

12.1.13. *-okii* 'emphatic'

The evidental *-okii* is a frequent final suffix, often translated as 'indeed'. This suffix is especially common in the affirmative answer to a question, as in (34):

(34) *Chahta' hapiy-a-h-okii!*
      Choctaw 1MII-be-TNS-INDEED
      'We are Choctaws!'

(35) <Miko ʋt ia cho? Ia tuk oke.>
      Mikko'-atiya-cho?   Iya-tok-okii.
      chief-NM go-Q   go-PT-INDEED
      'Has the chief gone? He has gone.' (Byington 1827:117)

Because of the rule lowering word-final *ii*, this morpheme is generally pronounced [okee], and it is written <oke> in the traditional orthography.

12.1.14. *-ashkii* 'exhortation'

The suffix *-ashkii* appears on various kinds of commands, exhortations, and admonitions.

(36) <chiso i nafohka yokmá, keyukmá nanakmá himak a ish ithʋnashke>
      chi-sso' i-nafokka'   yoo-kma   kiiyo-kma   nana-kma
      2sII-son III-clothing COP?-IRR:DS NEG-IRR:DS whether-IRR
      himmaka ish-ithána-shkii.
      now   2sI-know:N-EXHORT
      'Know now whether it be thy son's coat or no.' (Gen. 37:32)

(37) <Yʋmohmi hoka himak a pilla kʋno nan it im apesʋt kil ahanto kashke.>
      Yamohmih-ooka himmaka pilla-kano   nán
      PROV-for   now   from-COMP:DS thing
      itt-im-apiisa-t   kil-ahátt-ok-ashkii.
      RECIP-III-judge-PART 1PN-be:HN-NEG-EXHORT
      'Therefore, let us not judge each other from now on.' (Rom. 14:13)

-ashkii is generally pronounced with a final [e], and is written <-(a)shke> in the traditional orthography.

12.2. Markers of illocutionary force

12.2.1. Question particles -o and -a

Yes-no questions in Choctaw are formed by suffixing either of the question particles -o or -a to the verb. The question particle -o is the more common of the two and is seen in the following examples:

(38)   *John ish-písa-h-o?*
       John 2SI-see:N-TNS-Q
       'Do you see John?'

(39)   *John ish-písa-tok-o?*
       John 2SI-see:N-PT-Q
       'Did you see John?'

(40)   *John ish-pís-aachi-h-o?*
       John 2SI-see:N-IRR-TNS-Q
       'Will you see John?'

As the examples show, the question particle always follows the tense marker. Yes-no questions obligatorily occur with particle -o. For my consultants, wh-questions occur without a question particle:

(41)   *John-at   kátah-o   písa-tok?*
       John-NM   who-FOC:AC   see:N-PT
       'Who did John see?'

(42)   **?John-at   kátah-o   písa-tok-o?*
       John-NM   who-FOC:AC   see:N-PT-Q
       ('Who did John see?')[4]

However, some wh-questions with final question particles do appear in nineteenth-century texts:

(43)   <Hatak ʋt sipoknit taiyaha kʋt katiohmi kak osh ʋtta hinla ho?>
       Hattak-at sipokni-t táyyaha-kat   kátiohmi-k-akoosh
       man-NM   old-PART   complete:Y-COMP:SS   do:what-TNS-CON:SS
       atta-hila-h-o?
       be:born-POT-TNS-Q
       'How can a man be born when he is old?' (John 3:4)

4. This sentence is acceptable in an elliptical reading where the final -o is interpreted as the different-subject participial ending. In that case the sentence has the approximate translation 'What was John seeing when . . . ?'

The discrepancy between my consultants' judgements and the texts is difficult to explain. The likeliest possibilities seem to be either historical change in the use of the suffix or less than fully idiomatic translations in the relevant texts.

The question particle -a̱ is much more restricted in its distribution. It seems to appear only after the tense marker -h:

(44a) *Ish-pa-h-a̱?*
       2sI-eat-TNS-Q
       'Did you eat it?'

(44b) **Ish-pa-tok-a̱?*
       2sI-eat-PT-Q

The question particle -a̱ is only compatible with verbs in the realis mode, and is not compatible with verbs containing a potential or irrealis modal:

(45) *?Pam-at taloow-ayna-h-a̱?*
      Pam-NM   sing-POT-TNS-Q
      ('Can Pam sing?')

(46) *?Pam-at taloow-aachi̱-h-a̱?*
      Pam-NM   sing-IRR-TNS-Q
      ('Will Pam sing?')

The difference between -a̱ and -o̱ is difficult to determine. Speakers sometimes, but not always, translate the difference into one of tense:

(47a) *Apa-h-o̱?*
       eat-TNS-Q
       'Is he eating it?'

(47b) *Apa-h-a̱?*
       eat-TNS-Q
       'Did he eat it?'

The English translations of questions with -a̱ often have focal stress on the predicate; for example, 'Did he eát it?' Some speakers have suggested that questions with -a̱ are used in a context where the speaker did not expect the statement to be true.

Since the corresponding affirmative is ambiguous between present and past tense readings, the translations of the questions are somewhat surprising:

(48) *Apa-h.*
      eat-TNS
      'He is eating it; he ate it.'

Nicklas (1974:139–43) suggests that -a̱ shows the immediate past tense, which is marked only in questions (as discussed in section 11.3.5.2).

However, it is grammatical to use the -*a* question particle in sentences with adverbials that seem to require a present tense:

(49)   *Himmonasi' apa-h-a?*
        right:now   eat-TNS-Q
        'Is he eating right now?'

This seems incompatible with the idea that -*a* is a marker of immediate past tense. While the analysis is unclear, it seems possible that the difference between -*a* and -*o* is one of presupposition. More investigation is necessary.

12.2.2. Question particle -*ka*'

The suffix -*ka*' is used in some Choctaw questions. It seems more frequent in Mississippi Choctaw than in Oklahoma Choctaw:

(50)   *Ofi'-mat   losa-h-ka'?*
        dog-D:NM   black-TNS-Q
        'That dog's black, isn't it?'

This morpheme also shows up in some nineteenth-century texts.

(51)   <Kanima kia ish ia chi ka? Kanima ia la chi keyu hoke.>
        Kanimma-kia   ish-iy-aachi-h-ka'? Kanimma-h
        somewhere-too 2SI-go-IRR-TNS-Q   somewhere-TNS
        iya-l-aachi-kiiyo-h-okii.
        go-1SI-IRR-NEG-TNS-indeed
        'Are you going away anywhere? I'm not going anywhere.' (Byington
        1827:117)

Byington says that -*ka*' is "spoken by way of inquiry. The interrogative tone makes it adverbial" (1915:219).

12.2.3. -*mat* and -*cha* 'insult'

Insults seem to have a special syntax in Choctaw. There are special suffixes -*mat* and -*cha* which may appear on insult phrases:

(52)   *Ishkish   showa-mat!*
        buttocks stink-INSULT
        'Stinking ass!'

(53)   *Hasibish faláaya-cha!*
        tail   long:L-INSULT
        'Long tail!'[5]

The lack of nominative case in these insults is mentioned in section 5.2.1.

---

5. 'Long tail' is an idiomatic insult in Choctaw whose semantics are obscure.

There must be a synchronic or diachronic relationship between the insult marker -*cha* and morpheme -*cha* (section 16.2.3), which is a same subject switch-reference marker, since both morphemes idiosyncratically trigger the l-grade on a preceding verb. However, the same subject marker -*cha* does not occur on main clauses, and the semantic relationship between the switch-reference marker and the insult marker is unclear.

12.2.4. -*kat* and -*kato* 'exclamation'

The suffixes -*kat* and -*kato* appear on some exclamations:

(54)   *Chokka' chito-kat!*
       house   big-EXCLAM
       'The house is big!'

As with insults, exclamations show the lack of nominative case where it would normally be expected (section 5.2.1).

12.2.5. Imperative and prohibitive

There are two optional markers of imperative: -*cha* and -*oo*, both of which are optional. Negative imperative is obligatorily marked by -*nna* 'prohibitive'.

Both the imperative -*cha* and the -*cha* used on insults must be related to the subordinator -*cha* (chapter 16), since all three have the idieosyncratic morphological property of requiring a preceding verb to appear in the l-grade.

(55)   *Ot   ahpáali-cha!*
       go:and kiss:L-IMP
       'Go and kiss her!'

(56)   *Looma-h-oosh   sa-sso-h-oo!*
       light-TNS-PART:SS 1sII-hit-TNS-IMP
       'Hit me lightly!'

As these examples show, Choctaw imperatives show no subject agreement with their understood second person singular subject. Nor is any special imperative suffix required:

(57)   *Ot   ahpali-h!*
       go:and kiss-TNS
       'Go and kiss her!'

When the understood subject is second person plural, there is a special prefix *ho(o)-*. For many speakers, this prefix appears as *o(o)h-* before vowels.[6]

(58) *Hoo-hilha-h!*
      PLUR-dance-TNS
      'Y'all dance!'

(59) *Ooh-ipa-h!*
      PLUR-eat-TNS
      'Y'all eat!'

However, some speakers use *ho(o)-* regardless of the following segment. For these speakers the preceding example would be *hoipah!* or *hooipah!*

The suffix *-nná* is specifically a negative imperative, and occurs with overt second person (singular or plural) subject agreement.

(60) *Ish-kopooli-nná!*
      2SI-bite-PROHIB
      'Don't bite it!'

(61) *Hash-kopooli-nná!*
      2PI-bite-PROHIB
      'Y'all don't bite it!'

Note that the negative imperatives do not appear with agreement markers from the N paradigm (section 9.1.10), nor do they appear in the l-grade.

12.2.6. Question marker *-fo*

A question marker *-fo* shows up in some nineteenth-century examples:

(62) <Katima ia fo? Osapai a ia tuk oka.>
      Katimma-h iya-fo? Osaapa-ya iya-tok-ooka.
      where-TNS go-Q   field-AC   go-PT-for
      'Where has he gone? He's gone to the field.' (Byington 1827:118)

Speakers I consulted did not recognize this morpheme.

12.2.7. Question marker *-cho*

Another suffix that sometimes occurs on questionlike sentences is *-cho*. This suffix is more common in nineteenth-century texts than it is in modern Choctaw:

6. The variation in the length of the vowel is idiolectal.

(63)   <Miko ʋt ia cho? Ia tuk oke.>
       Mikko'-at iya-cho? Iya-tok-okii.
       chief-NM go-Q   go-PT-indeed
       'Has the chief gone? He has gone.' (Byington 1827:117)

(64)   <Katimak o ish ia cho? Yvmmak o ia li hoke.>
       Katimma-k-o ish-iya-cho? Yammak-o   iya-li-h-okii.
       where-TNS-AC 2SI-go-Q   there-FOC:AC go-1SI-TNS-indeed
       'Where are you going? I'm going there.' (Byington 1827:117)

As these examples, show, -*cho* appears in both yes-no and wh-questions.
Byington describes this suffix in the following way:

> **cho**, ha; sign of a question and having an adverbial meaning
> also, like eh! in English . . . **cho** implies ignorance in those who
> inquire. It implies a question and demand for an answer.
> [1915:108]

12.3. The syntax of evidentials

12.3.1. The distribution of evidentials

The distribution of evidentials displays several syntactic constraints.
First, evidentials may only occur in root (i.e., unembedded) clauses.
Consider the following examples:

(65)   *Oba-tok-chi.*
       rain-PT-wonder
       'I wonder if it rained.'

(66)   **Mary-at [oba-tok-chi-ka]*   *anokfilli-h.*
       Mary-NM _rain-PT-wonder-COMP:DS think-TNS
       ('Mary thought that I wondered if it rained.')

(67)   **Mary-at [oba-tok-chi-kat]*   *im-ihaksi-h.*
       Mary-NM _rain-PT-wonder-COMP:SS III-forget-TNS
       ('Mary forgot that she wondered if it rained.')

Direct quotes in Choctaw (and other languages as well) have the status
of root clauses. Consequently, evidentials may also appear in direct
quotes:

(68)   *"Katina mato   niya-h-chi,"*   *ópah tikchi-it ahni-ttook.*
       why   that:NM2 fat-TNS-wonder owl   wife-NM think-DPAST
       '"I wonder why that one is fat?," the owl's wife thought.'

However, they may not appear in indirect quotes:[7]

---

7. See chapter 16 for discussion of complements to verbs of speech and thought.

(69)   *Mary-at maka-hmat o̱ba-tok-chi   miya-h-oosh/-o̱
       Mary-NM say-SS   rain-PT-WONDER say-TNS-PART:SS/-PART:DS
       maka-tok.
       say-PT
       ('Mary said that she/I wondered if it rained.')

A second important characteristic of evidentials is that only one may appear per sentence. Thus the following examples are ungrammatical:

(70)   *O̱ba-tok-chi-ka̱sha.
       rain-PT-WONDER-GUESS
       ('I guess I wonder if it rained.')

(71)   *O̱ba-tok-ka̱sha-chi.
       rain-PT-GUESS-WONDER
       ('I wonder if I guess it rained.')

(72)   *O̱ba-h-chisba-hli.
       rain-TNS-DOUBT-CERTAIN
       ('I'm certain I doubt it rained.')

(73)   *O̱ba-h-hli-chisba.
       rain-TNS-CERTAIN-DOUBT
       ('I doubt that I'm certain it rained.')

Evidentials are also incompatible with markers of illocutionary force:

(74)   *O̱ba-tok-chi-o̱?
       rain-PT-WONDER-Q
       ('Do I wonder if it rained?')

(75)   *O̱ba-tok-o̱-chi.
       rain-PT-Q-WONDER
       ('I wonder if it rained.')

(76)   *O̱ba-hli-oo!
       rain-CERTAIN-IMP
       ('Be certain it's raining!')

(77)   *Ish-mi̱t-aachi̱-h-chisba-nna!
       2SI-come-IRR-TNS-DOUBT-PROHIB
       ('Don't doubt that he'll come!')

Note that evidentials are not incompatible with questions per se. Wh-questions do not require a final question particle, and they are compatible with evidentials:

(78)   "Kati̱na-h mato   niya-h-chi,"   ópah tíkchi-it ahni-ttook.
       why-TNS that:NM2 fat-TNS-WONDER owl wife-NM think-DPAST
       '"I wonder why that one is fat?," the owl's wife thought.'

Rather, it seems that the evidential and the question particle may not cooccur.

This is an important point, since one might expect that the factors governing the distribution of evidentials are largely semantic in motivation. However, the contrast between wh-questions and yes-no questions suggests that the motivation is instead morphological or syntactic in origin.

A third restriction on the distribution of evidentials is that they may not be followed by negation:

(79)   *Oba-tok-chi-kiiyo-h.
       rain-PT-WONDER-NEG-TNS
       ('It's not the case that I wonder if it rained.')

(80)   *Mit-aachi-h-chisba-kiiyo-h.
       come-IRR-TNS-DOUBT-NEG-TNS
       ('It's not the case that I doubt he will come.')

However, negation may occur within the scope of the evidential.

(81)   Ik-ób-o-tok-kasha.
       N-rain:L-PT-NEG-GUESS
       'I guess it didn't rain.'

(82)   Hattak-mat chahta'   kiiyo-hli.
       man-D:NM   Choctaw   NEG-CERTAIN
       'I'm certain that man's not Choctaw.'

12.3.2. Default interpretations of evidentials

As mentioned above, in the absence of syntactic context to the contrary, evidentials are interpreted from the point of view of the speaker, as in the following examples.

(83)   Pam-at   tamaaha' iya-tok-chi.
       Pam-NM   town   go-PT-wonder
       'I wonder if Pam went to town.'

(84)   John-at   taloow-aana-kasha.
       John-NM   sing-POT-guess
       'I guess John can sing.'

These evidentials cannot be interpreted from the viewpoint of a third person subject (except in a construction to be discussed in section 12.3.3 below). Therefore, all the following sentences are ungrammatical.

(85)   *Bill-at Pam-at   tamaaha' iya-tok-chi.
       Bill-NM Pam-NM   town   go-PT-WONDER
       ('Bill wonders if Pam went to town.')

(86)   *Bill-at John-at   taloow-aana-ka̱sha.
         Bill-NM John-NM sing-POT-GUESS
         ('Bill guesses that John can sing.')

To express the English glosses of (85) and (86), it is necessary to use direct quotation with the verb *ahnih* 'to think', as in the following example:

(87)   *"Pam-at tamaaha' iya-tok-chi"*   Bill-at   ahni-h.
         Pam-NM town   go-PT-wonder Bill-NM think-TNS
         'Bill thinks "I wonder if Pam went to town."'

12.3.3. The "according to" construction

There is one construction, however, in which evidentials are interpreted from the point of view of someone other than the speaker. This is in the "according to" construction, discussed in chapter 16.

In this construction, an assertion is preceded by a subordinate clause which gives the evidential basis for making the assertion. It is frequently capable of being paraphrased 'according to . . .' or 'based on the evidence from . . .' in English. Two examples are given below.

(88)   [*Joyce-a̱ pisa-ka̱*]   nokoowa-h ahooba-h.
         Joyce-AC see-COMP:DS angry-TNS seem-TNS
         'Joyce looks angry.' (More literally, 'Based on seeing Joyce, she seems to be angry.')

(89)   *J.P.-at [ashshowa-ka̱]* okhata'
         J.P.-NM smell-COMP:DS ocean
         alhlhi' ot   *atta-tok ahooba-h.*
         edge   go:and be-PT   seem-TNS
         'J.P. smells like he's been to the beach' (More literally, 'Based on smelling him, J.P. seems to have been to the beach.')

In (88) the "according to" clause precedes the entire asserted clause, and in (89) it precedes the verb phrase of the asserted clause.

When a verb of thinking occurs in the "according to" clause, it licenses a shift in the point of view from which evidentials are interpreted.[8]

(90)   [*John-at anokfilli-ka̱*]   katiimih-o̱ niya-h-chi.
         John-NM think-COMP:DS why-AC   fat-TNS-wonder
         'John_i wondered why he_j was fat.' ('John thought, "I wonder why he's fat."')

---

8. The translations of these sentences must be approximate, since we do not have English sentences with structures parallel to those in Choctaw.

(91)   [*John-at anokfilli-ka*]   *oba-tok-kasha.*
       John-NM think-COMP:SS rain-PT-guess
       'John guessed it rained.' ('John thought, "I guess it rained."')

However, the shift in point of view does not allow personal pronouns to be interpreted from the point of view of *John* in these examples. Personal pronouns continue to be interpreted from the point of view of the speaker.

(92)   [*John-at anokfilli-ka*],   *sa-haksi-h.*
       John-NM think-COMP:DS 1sII-drunk-TNS
       'John thinks that I'm drunk.' ('According to John, I'm drunk.')
       *'John$_i$ thinks that he$_i$ is drunk.'

(93)   [*John-at anokfilli-ka*]   *sa-tasibo-h.*
       John-NM think-COMP:DS 1sII-crazy-TNS
       'John thinks that I'm crazy.' ('According to John, I'm crazy.')
       *'John$_i$ thinks that he$_i$ is crazy.'

These facts are discussed in more detail in Broadwell (1991a).

13. Auxiliaries, semiauxiliaries, and participles

13.1. What is an auxiliary?

Choctaw has a distinguishable set of auxiliary verbs with special syntactic behavior. They are distinct on the one hand from main verbs, and on the other hand from verbal suffixes. Syntactically, auxiliaries behave like verbs that take VP complements. To distinguish auxiliaries from main verbs, I will rely on several criteria: word order, placement of person markers, occurrence of overt sub-ordinators, placement of tense and modal morphemes, and auxiliary selection.

13.1.1. Word order

While main verbs may occur either before or after their complements, auxiliaries must occur immediately after their complements. Contrast the following examples:

(1a) *John-at apa-t   tahli-h.*
      John-NM eat-PART complete-TNS
      'John ate it up.'

(1b) **John-at tahli-h apa-t.*

(2a) *John-at iya-tokat   anooli-h.*
      John-NM go-PT:COMP:SS tell-TNS
      'John said that he went.'

(2b) *John-at anooli-h iya-tokat.*
      John-NM tell-TNS go-PT:COMP:SS

We can explain these facts if we assume that there is a rule which optionally extraposes clausal complements to the right of the main verb. Since the complements to auxiliary verbs are verb phrases, not clauses, the extraposition rule does not apply to them.

13.1.2. Placement of person markers

Word order alone is not sufficient to identify auxiliaries in some cases. Several of the adverbial suffixes in the verb are similar to auxiliaries. Consider the suffix -*mǫma* 'still, again':

(3)   *Hikíya-moma-tok.*
        stand:N-still-PT
        'He was still standing.'

Since the adverbial suffixes have a fixed order with respect to the main verb, like the auxiliaries, we might ask what evidence shows that examples like (3) are in fact one complex word, rather than two words. One difference is that while an auxiliary may serve as host to a pronominal clitic, as in example (4), this is impossible for the adverbial suffixes, as shown in example (5b).

(4)   *Yolhlhi-t   hapi-tahli-tok.*
        run:off-PART 1MPII-complete-PT
        'He ran us all off.'

(5a)   *Chi-ahpali-moma-h.*
        2SII-kiss-still-TNS
        'He's still kissing you.'

(5b)   **Ahpali-chi-moma-h.*
        kiss-2SII-still-TNS

13.1.3. Occurrence of subordinators

Auxiliaries can also sometimes be distinguished from verbal suffixes by the presence of an overt subordinating morpheme on the main verb. The majority of auxiliary verbs in Choctaw require the preceding main verb to have the suffix *-kat* (the same-subject form of the general complementizer, discussed in chapter 16) or the suffix *-t* (discussed in more detail below).

Some auxiliaries do not require any subordinator on the preceding verb, so this is not a foolproof test for auxiliaries. However, whenever an overt subordinator is present, we know that the following morpheme is not a verbal suffix but an independent main or auxiliary verb. On this criterion, *moma* in (6) is potentially a suffix (and indeed clearly is one on other grounds), wheras *tahli* in (7) is clearly not a suffix.

(6)   *Hikíya-moma-tok.*
        stand:N-still-PT
        'He was still standing.'

(7)   *John-at apa-t   tahli-h.*
        John-NM eat-PART complete-TNS
        'John ate it up.'

13.1.4. Placement of tense and modal morphemes

When a verb appears with an auxiliary, any tense or modal morphemes will generally appear on the auxiliary verb, not on the main verb:

(8) *Yolhlhi-t   hapi-tahli-tok.*
     make:run-PART 1PII-complete-PT
     'They ran us all off.'

(9) *Yolhlhi-t   hapi-tahl-aachi-h.*
     make:run-PART 1PII-complete-IRR-TNS
     'They will run us all off.'

In this respect, the combination of main verb plus auxiliary is unlike the combination of complement clause plus main verb, since complement clauses may in general have their own tense marking.

13.1.5. Auxiliary selection

Many of the auxiliaries come in pairs, where the choice of auxiliary depends on semantic or morphological features of the main verb. This is unlike any relationship between an ordinary matrix verb and its complement.

For example, the choice of *tahah* or *tahlih* for the meaning 'complete' is dependent on the agreement class of the subject of the main verb. In general, verbs that take I subjects select the auxiliary *tahlih* and verbs that take II or III subjects select *tahah*.

(10) *Bashli-t tahli-li-tok.*
      cut-PART complete-1sI-PT
      'I cut it up completely; I finished cutting it.'

(11) *Kobaafa-t   taha-h.*
      broken-PART complete-TNS
      'It's completely broken.'

(12) *A-palammi-t   taha-h.*
      1sIII-suffer-PART complete-TNS
      'I've suffered a lot.'

The variation in the form of the auxiliary is linked to semantic properties of the main verb, and in this respect it resembles more well-known auxiliary alternations in languages such as Italian, French, and German. This sort of alternation is a clear diagnostic of auxiliary behavior in Choctaw.

13.2. Types of auxiliaries

The auxiliaries fall into three semantic categories: aspectual, positional, and evidential. I also distinguish a group of semi-auxiliaries, which show more freedom of word order with respect to their complements, but a greater degree of selectional restriction than is found in ordinary main verb-complement relationships.

13.2.1. Aspectual auxiliaries

13.2.1.1. *Tahah, tahlih* 'completive'

Tahlih and *tahah* are auxiliary verbs that usually select a participial complement marked with the suffix *-t*[1]. *Tahah/tahlih* may be used to indicate both a completed action and an action completely affecting the patient. In general, the latter use of the auxiliary is translated into English by pluralizing some argument of the verb, as is shown in the following examples:

(13)   *Kobaffi-t   tahli-li-h.*
       break-PART complete-1SI-TNS
       'I finished breaking it/them; I broke them all.'

(14)   *Taloowa-t tahli-li-h.*
       sing-PART complete-1SI-TNS
       'I finished singing.'

(15)   *Kobaafa-t   taha-h.*
       broken-PART complete-TNS
       'It is completely broken; they are all broken.'

As mentioned above, *tahlih* generally appears with verbs that take I subjects, while *tahah* appears with verbs that take II or III subjects. However, with verbs of motion and position (including those that take class I subjects), *tahah* occurs to show a completely affected theme:

(16)   *Iya-t   ii-taha-h.*
       go-PART 1PI-complete-TNS
       'We all went.'

(17)   *Nowa-t   taha-h.*
       walk-PART complete-TNS
       'They all walked.'

With verbs of perception, *tahah* may also occur immediately after the verb stem with the meaning 'finally'. In this case, we may interpret it as referring to the completion of some preliminary period prior to the beginning of the event. For example, the following sentence might be appropriately said by a person who has just had an operation that restores his or her sight.

---

1. Occasionally *tahah/tahlih* occurs after a main verb with no explicit participial suffix, as in the following example:

Oklhika-h   taha-h.
get:dark-TNS complete-TNS
'It got completely dark.'

It is unclear to me whether there are any morphosyntactic consequences of the lack of participial suffix here.

(18) *Pisa-taha-li-h.*
      see-finally-1SI-TNS
      'I finally see.'

All of the agreement and tense morphemes which would logically show up on the main verb show up on *tahah/tahlih* instead. In the following examples, (19a)–(20b) show that I marking and N marking appear on the auxiliary rather than the main verb. Example (21) shows a II marker associated with the object of the main verb on *tahlih*. These examples also show that the tense marker *-tok* follows the auxiliary, rather than the main verb. Example (22) shows the irrealis *-aachi* after *tahlih*. Examples (23) and (24) show that the III marker associated with object possessor raising may appear on the auxiliary. Example (25) shows negation on the auxiliary.

(19a) *Apa-t   tahli-li-tok.*
       eat-PART complete-1SI-PT
       'I ate it up.'

(19b) **Apa-li-t   tahli-tok.*[2]
       eat-1SI-PART complete-PT

(20a) *Apa-t   ak-táhl-o-h.*
       eat-PART 1SN-complete:L-NEG-TNS
       'I didn't eat it up.'

(20b) **Ak-p-o-t   tahli-tok.*
       1SN-eat-NEG-PART complete-PT

(21)   *Yolhlhi-h   hapi-tahli-tok.*
       make:run-TNS 1PII-complete-PT
       'They ran us off.'

(22)   <Chihowa ʋt Moses a im achi tok mak o i nukhaklo keyu hosh, amba okpʋnit tahla chi hatok.>
       Chihoowah-at Moses-a   im-aachi-tok-mako
       God-NM   Moses-AC III-say-PT-?:DS
       i-nokhaklo-kiiyo-h-oosh   amba okpani-t   tahl-aachi-h
       III-pity-NEG-TNS-PART:SS but   destroy-PART complete-IRR-TNS
       a-ttook.
       COP-DPAST
       'God commanded Moses that he show no mercy and kill them all.'
       (Josh. 11:20)

(23)   *Tạchi' apa-t   ạ-tahli-h.*
       corn   eat-PART 1SIII-complete-TNS
       'They ate up all my corn.'

---

2. Nicklas (1974:187) gives as an example *Kobaffi-li-t tahli-li-h* 'I finished breaking it', but my consultants judge this to be ungrammatical.

(24) *Sink-at   lapa-t   a̱-taha   hi-tok-achiini-h.*
      sink-NM stopped:up-PART 1sIII-complete PROV-PT-EVID-TNS
      '[It seems that] my sink is all stopped up.'

(25) <. . . Ai okla ha mominchit ʋbit ik tahlo hokʋto, ik isso tok oka.>
      Ai oklah-a̱   momi̱chi-t abi-t   ik-tahl-o-h-ookato
      Ai people-AC all-PART kill-PART N-complete:L-NEG-TNS-until?
      ik-iss-o-tok-ooka.
      3N-quit-NEG-PT-for
      'For he did not quit until he had killed all the people of Ai.' (Josh.
      8:26)

There is a contrast between II prefixes that mark object and those
that mark subject. Object II prefixes consistently appear on the auxiliary,
as in (21). As examples (26a) and (27a) show, all speakers accept subject
II prefixes on the main verb instead of the auxiliary. Some speakers
allow the subject II prefixes to be placed on the auxiliary as well, as
shown in (26b) and (27b).

(26a) *Si-abiika-h   taha-h.*
       1sII-sick-TNS complete-TNS
       'I'm completely sick.'

(26b) *%Abiika-h sa-taha-h.*

(27a) *Sa-tikabi-t   taha-h.*
       1sII-exhausted-PART complete-TNS
       'I'm completely exhausted.'

(27b) *%Tikabi-t sa-taha-h.*

Parallel to this subject-object asymmetry for II affixes, there is a
similar tendency to avoid placing III subject clitics on the auxiliary:

(28a) *A̱-palammi-t   taha-h.*
       1sIII-suffer-PART complete-TNS
       'I've suffered a lot.'

(28b) **Palammi-t a̱-taha-h.*
       suffer-SS   1sIII-complete-TNS

For more discussion of these data see Broadwell and Martin (1993).

13.2.1.2. *Ámmohmih, ámmohmichih* 'do completely'

Another auxiliary that may be termed aspectual is *ámmohmih,*
ámmohmichih, which means something like 'to do completely,
entirely'.

It may be used as a main verb in sentences like the following:

(29)   *Ish-ámmohmichi-h-o?*
       2SI-complete-TNS-Q
       'Did you complete them all?'

It may also be subordinated to another verb with either the *-hoo* or
the *-t* suffix, as in the following examples:

(30)   *Ámmohmichi-h-oosh   im-aabi-tok.*
       complete-TNS-PART:SS III-kill-PT
       'He completely beat everybody.'

(31)   *. . . ʊmohminchit nana im asha moma ka okpʊnit ish tahlashke.*
       ámmohmichi-t   nana-h   im-asha-h moma-ka
       complete:N-PART thing-TNS III-be-TNS all-COMP
       okpani-t   ish-tahl-ashkii.
       destroy-PART 2SI-complete-exhort
       'Utterly destroy all that they have!' (1 Sam. 15:3)

   In addition to its use as a main verb, *ámmohmih/ámmohmichih*
also appears as an auxiliary taking a *-t* verb complement:

(32)   *Im-aabi-t   ámmohmich-aachi-h.*
       III-kill-PART complete-IRR-TNS
       'He's going to completely beat them all.'

(33)   *Holisso' hokmi-t   ámmohmichi-li-tok.*
       paper   burn-PART complete-1SI-PT
       'I completely burned all of the papers.'

(34)   <Choshua ʊt Ai ya ishi cha, okpʊnit ʊmohmichi tuk>
       Choshua-at Ai-ya úshi-cha   okpani-t   ámmohmichi-tok.
       Joshua-NM Ai-AC take:L-PART destroy-PART completely-PT
       'Joshua took Ai and destroyed it utterly.' (Josh. 10:1)

As these examples show, the auxiliary can bear the subject
agreement, tense, and modal morphemes.
   Selection of *ámmohmih/ámmohmichih* operates on similar
principles to those for *tahah/tahlih*: *ámmohmih* appears with verbs
that require a II or III subject, while *ámmohmichih* appears with
verbs taking a I subject.
   Recall that Choctaw verbs often come in pairs differing in valency
(chapter 8). In these cases, the intransitive member of the pair
generally occurs with *ámmohmih*, while the transitive occurs with
ámmohmichih:

(35)   *Sa-basha-t   ámmohmi-tok.*
       1SII-be:cut-PART completely-PT
       'I was all cut up.'

(36)   *Sa-bashli-t   ámmohmichi-h.*
       1sII-cut-PART completely-TNS
       'He cut me up badly.'

(37)   *Į-ponna-t   ámmohmi-h.*
       1sIII-skilled-PART completely-TNS
       'He's completely expert at it.'

The judgments above are the usual ones, but rules for the selection
of *ámmohmih/ámmohmichih* are a bit more variable than selection
of *tahah/tahlih* appears to be. Mr. H. Willis accepted both of the
following as grammatical:

(38a) *Fammi-t   pi-ámmohmichi-tok.*
       whip-PART 1PII-completely-PT
       'They whipped up badly.'

(38b) *Fama-t   pi-ámmohmichi-tok.*
       whipped-PART 1PII-completely-PT
       'They whipped us badly.'

In the cases where an intransitive main verb occurs with the
transitive auxiliary, the translation shows that the phrase is being
interpreted as transitive. Perhaps in these cases the *-t* verb is being
interpreted adverbially, along the lines of 'As for being whipped, they
did it completely to us'.

     In the negative this auxiliary expresses the sense of the English
'at all'.

(39)   <kil isso kʋmohma chi hoke>
       kil-iss-ok   ámohm-aachi̠-h-okii.
       1PN-stop-NEG entirely-IRR-TNS-indeed
       'We won't stop at all.' (Acts 6:4)

(40)   <Anumpa kʋllo chik ile onocho kʋmohmashke.>
       Annópa' kallo' chik-ili-onóoch-ok   ámohm-ashkii.
       word   hard   2SN-RFL-place:on-NEG entirely-EXHORT
       'Swear not at all.' (Matt. 5:34)

The examples below seem to show variant forms of the same morpheme:

(41)   *Báshpo'-mat haloppa-h amomi-h.*
       knife-D:NM   sharp-TNS really-TNS
       'That knife is really sharp.'

(42)   *Chi-nakshobi-h amomi-h   kaniiya-h.*
       2sII-stink-TNS really-TNS really-TNS
       'You smell really bad.'

     Chickasaw shows a related word, *ammohmi*. According to Munro
and Willmond (1994), this word always follows a negative verb

followed by *k*, and is usually pronounced as a single word with the preceding. *Ammohmi* is reduced to *ammoh* before a CV sequence. They give the following example:

(43) *Ik-ayy-ok   ammoh-tok.*   (Chickasaw)
      N-go-NEG never-PT
      'He never did go.'

13.2.1.3. *Kaniiyah, ka̲chih* 'really, extremely'

Kaniiyah and *ka̲chih* occur as main verbs meaning 'go away' and 'cause to go away; sell' in examples like the following:

(44) *Ká̲tiimina   wiha-t   kaniiy-aachi̲-h   miyah?*
      why   move-PART   go:away-IRR-TNS   HSAY
      'Why is he moving away?'

They are also used as auxiliaries, meaning something like 'really, extremely.'

(45) *A̲-taah-at   bokaafa-t   kaniiya-h.*
      1sIII-tire-NM busted-PART   really-TNS
      'My tire is [really] busted.'

(46) *Hattak-ma kaah-at aa-nowa-naaha-na   wannichi-h kaniiya-h.*
      man-DEM   car-NM   LOC-walk-almost-DS shake-TNS   really-TNS
      'A car nearly ran over that man, and he was really shaking.'

(47) *I̲-taloowa-t   ka̲chi-li-tok.*
      III-sing-PART really-1sI
      'I *really* sang it for them.'

(48) <. . . Choshua ʋt ishi cha bushpo falaia halupa isht issot kanchi
      cha . . .>
      Joshua-at   ii̲shi-cha bá̲shpo' faláaya' haloppa' isht   isso-t
      Joshua-NM take:L-SS knife   long   sharp   INSTR hit-PART
      ka̲chi-cha . . .
      really:L-SS
      'Joshua took them and (really) smote them with the edge of the sword
      and . . .' (Josh. 11:12)

13.2.2. Positional auxiliaries

The positional verbs mentioned in section 3.1.3.2 and described in section 19.2.3 may also function as auxiliaries. Positional auxiliaries seem to signal two things: the uncompleted nature of the action and the posture of the subject during the action.

(49) *Ot̲   chokkowa-li-hma̲ taloowa-h-oosh   hiki̲ya-tok.*
      come:and   enter-1sI-when:DS sing-TNS-PART:SS stand:N-PT
      'He was already (standing and) singing when I came in.'

(50) *Pam-at taloowa-sh   ittǫla-h.*
Pam-NM sing-PART:SS lie:N-TNS
'Pam is lying down and singing.'

Attah, ashwah, and *mayah* (singular, dual, and plural, respectively) are neutral with respect to the posture of the subject.

(51) *John-akhi-it   isht   aatapa-t   atta-tok-oosh,*
John-PEJOR-NM INSTR too:much-SS be-PT-PART:SS
  at   ittola-t hottóopa-na, "Makhalih," il-aa-hlik.
come:and fall-SS hurt:L-DS   good:enough 1PI-say-EVID
'That darn John was showing off and fell down and got hurt, and we said, "Good enough for you!"'

(52) *Ohooyo'-mat akni'   ayyina-sh   atta-h miya-h.*
woman-D:NM elder:sibling cuckold-PART:SS be-TNS HSAY-TNS
'That woman is carrying on with her older sister's husband, they say.'

Since an atelic verb with the default tense suffix -*h* can also be interpreted as continuous without the positional auxiliary, it is sometimes difficult to differentiate the meanings of sentences with and without a positional auxiliary. However, use of the positional does seem to emphasize that the action is located in a specific place.

(53a) *Bob-at akǎka' nipi' apa-h.*
Bob-NM chicken meat eat-TNS
'Bob is eating chicken.'

(53b) *Bob-at akǎka' nipi' apa-sh   ǎtta-h.*
Bob-NM chicken meat eat-PART:SS be:N-TNS
'Bob is eating chicken [in a specific place].'

It is generally ungrammatical to use stative verbs with a positional auxiliary. Consider the following examples:

(54a) *J.P.-at Pam hólba-h.*
J.P.-NM Pam resemble
'J.P. resembles Pam.'

(54b) **J.P.-at Pam hólba-sh   ǎtta-h.*
J.P.-NM Pam resemble-PART:SS be:N-TNS
('J.P. is resembling Pam in a specific place.')

The Choctaw construction of verb plus positional auxiliary is reminiscent of the English progressive *be V-ing,* and similarly seems restricted to nonstatives.

Inanimate subjects occur with positional auxiliaries in accordance with a classification scheme described in chapter 19.

(55) *Itti'=kobáhli-yat toshbi-h-oo-sh   kahm<u>a</u>ya-h.*
      stick-NM   rot-TNS-PART-SS lie:PL-TNS
      'The sticks are rotting.'

The positional auxiliaries often take quantifiers as complements. In this usage, it is difficult to interpret the positional auxiliary as indicating the progressive.

(56) *Mary-at alla-at   hánnaali-sh <u>i</u>-m<u>a</u>ya-h.*
      Mary-NM child-NM six-PART:SS III-be:PL-TNS
      'Mary has six children.'

(57) *Tákkon=chíto'-mat itti'-m<u>a</u>   laawa-h-oosh   takohm<u>a</u>ya-h.*
      apple-D:NM   tree-D:AC many-TNS-PART:SS hang:PL-TNS
      'There are a lot of apples hanging on that tree.'

Some combinations of main verb plus auxiliary seem to be idiomatic. *Alhtaklah* 'to be widowed, orphaned, bereaved' may take the auxiliary *hikiiyah* 'to stand':

(58) <Yohmi kʋt ʋlhtaklʋt hikia tuk . . .>
      Yohmi-kat   alhtakla-t   hikiiya-tok . . .
      do:so-COMP:SS bereaved-PART stand-PT
      'And she was a widow . . .' (Luke 2:37)

Meterological verbs like *<u>o</u>bah* 'to rain', *mahlih* 'for the wind to blow', *oktoshah* 'to snow', and *oktobiichih* 'to be foggy' sometimes also occur with the auxiliary *hikiiyah* 'to stand'.

(59) *<u>O</u>ba-sh   hik<u>í</u>ya-h.*
      rain-PART:SS stand:N-TNS
      'It's pouring down rain.'

(60) *Mahli-t   hik<u>í</u>ya-h.*
      blow-PART stand:N-TNS
      'The wind is blowing.'

13.2.3. Evidential auxiliaries

This group of auxiliaries only partly conforms to the properties of the auxiliaries described above. There are two morphemes in this uncertain group: *aachiinih* 'deduced from evidence'[3] and *miyah* 'hearsay'. These auxiliaries share semantic features with the evidential affixes discussed in chapter 12, but their syntactic and morphological properties are different. While the evidential suffixes occur in the complementizer position of a main clause and are never

---

3. Nicklas (1974:141) lists this as a particle *tokaachiinih*. However, the *tok* at the beginning of this must be the familiar past tense suffix *-tok*, rather than the beginning of the auxiliary.

followed by other suffixes, these evidential auxiliaries act more like verbs and may appear in embedded clauses.

(61) *John-at chaaha-h miya-h-o̱ ish-maka-h.*
John-NM tall-TNS HSAY-TNS-DS 2SI-say-TNS
'You said that John is tall.'

(62) *Hi-tok-ako̱ akka pisa-hma̱ loksi'*
PROV-PT-CN:AC down see-when:DS turtle
aa-tok aachiini-na i̱-yokpa-h.
be-PT EVID-DS III-laugh-TNS
'But when he looked down it was the turtle, and he laughed at him.'
(T8:19)

(63) *Hikmat hiili-t ittanowa-makoosh hilooha' ahwa-tok*
and:SS fly-PART go-when?:SS thunder seem-PT
aachiini-h-oosh a̱t oklah hayaaka-h.
EVID-TNS-PART:SS come:and PLUR appear-TNS
'And when they flew it was like thunder, and they appeared.'

Unlike the uncontroversial auxiliaries, *miyah* and *aachiinih* never host pronominals:

(64a) *Chokka' ish-cho̱pa-tok miya-h-o̱ há̱klo-li-tok.*
house 2SI-buy-PT hearsay-TNS-PART:DS hear:N-1SI-PT
'I heard that you bought a house.'

(64b) **Chokka' cho̱pa-t ish-miya-h-o̱ há̱klo-li-tok.*
house 2SI-buy-PART 2SI-hearsay-TNS-PART:DS hear:N-1SI-PT

(65a) *Chi-holiitopa-tok aachiini-h.*
2SI-rich-PT EVID-TNS
'It seems like you're rich.'

(65b) **Holiitopa-tok chi-achiini-h.*
rich-PT 2SI-EVID-TNS

If *miyah* and *aachiinih* are correctly labelled auxiliaries, then they are also unusual in occurring with main verbs that are not marked with any overt subordinator. Instead, the verb preceding *miyah* or *aachinih* is marked for tense like a nonsubordinated verb.

13.3. Semiauxiliaries

In addition to the clear cases of auxiliaries identified above, there is also a class that I label "semiauxiliary." Semiauxiliaries are like main verbs in that their complements need not be adjacent and may occur with switch-reference marking. Consider the following example:

(66) *Hattak-mat chaaha-kat   ohooyo' i̱-shahli-ka.*
      man-D:NM   tall-COMP:SS woman III-exceed-AFFIRM
      'I'm telling you, that man is taller than the woman.'

In this example, the complement of the semiauxiliary *i̱shahlih* 'to exceed' is the subordinate verb *chaaha-kat* 'to be tall', yet the two are not adjacent and a switch-reference marker appears on the subordinate verb.

However, several of the semiauxiliaries seem like auxiliaries in that they show the selectional properties characteristic of auxiliary verbs. For example, the semiauxiliary 'to exceed' has two forms, *i-shahlih* and *i-shahlichih*, where the choice is dependent on the agreement class and/or semantics of the subordinate verb.

13.3.1. *I̱shahlih, i̱shahlichih* 'to exceed'; *aatapah, aatablih* 'to be too much'

I̱shahlih/i̱shahlichih 'to exceed' and *aatapah/aatablih* 'to be too much' function as both main verbs and auxiliary verbs. The follow-ing examples show them as main verbs used without clausal complements:

(67) <. . . iluppa i shahli fehna ka im otunincha hi oke.>
      . . . *ilappa i̱-shahli-fíhna-ka   im-otani̱ch-ahii-okii.*
      this   III-great-very-COMP III-show:N-IRR-indeed
      'He will show him greater works than these.' (John 5:20)

(68) <. . . boshulli atapa-t asha ka kishi alota auah-tuklo ho okla ishi tok.>
      . . . *bosholli' aatapa-t   asha-ka kishi' alóota'*
      piece   excess-PART be-COMP basket full
      awahtoklo-h-o̱   oklah ishi-ttook.
      twelve-TNS-PART:DS PLUR take-DPAST
      'They took up twelve baskets of extra pieces.' (John 14:20)

(69) *John-akhi-it   isht   aatapa-t   atta-tok-oosh,*
      John-PEJOR-NM INSTR too:much-PART be-PT-PART:SS
      at   ittola-t   hottóopa-na, "Makhalih," il-aa-hlik.
      come:and fall-PART hurt:L-DS   good:enough 1PI-say-EVID
      'That darn John was showing off and fell down and got hurt, and we said, "Good enough for you!"'

The verb *i-shahlih/i-shahlichih* is used as a semiauxiliary in the formation of comparatives in Choctaw. It takes as its complement the verb (active or stative) that is being compared. In Stassen's (1985) typology of comparatives, *i̱shahlih/i̱shahlichih* forms a comparative of the type he labels the 'exceed comparative'.[4]

4. Stassen (1985:44) finds that the only languages in his sample with an exceed comparative have the word order SVO. However, the Choctaw data show that such a construction is also possible in SOV languages.

Similarly, *aatapah/aatablih* can be used with complements to express that some activity or state is considered excessive.

For both the verbs *i̱-shahlih/i̱-shahlichih* and *aatapah/aatablih*, the first form is generally used when the complement verb takes a class II or III subject, and the second when the complement verb takes a class I subject. Both verbs usually take clausal complements marked with the complementizer *-ka,* though sometimes complements with participial *-t* or no overt complementizer also appear:

(70) *Hattak-mat chaaha-kat ohooyo' i̱-shahli-ka.*
man-D:NM   tall-COMP:SS woman III-exceed-AFFIRM
'I'm telling you, that man is taller than the woman.'

(71) *Tamaaha' iya-kat   Nellie i̱-shahlichi-li-h.*
town   go-COMP:SS Nellie III-exceed-1SI-TNS
'1 go to town more than Nellie does.'

(72) *Aloota-kat   aatapa-ka   kanimma-h*
full-COMP:SS too:much-COMP somewhere-TNS
aa-binohl-ahii-t   iksho-h.
LOC-sit:PL-IRR-NM not:exist-TNS
'It was too full and there was no place to sit.'

Note that in (71) the semiauxiliary *i̱-shahlichih* is inflected for the subject of the comparative clause 'go to town'.

In addition to *aatapah/aatablih* 'to exceed', some texts also show a form *aatablichih*, generally in the n-grade:[5]

(73) <. . . micha chi apaknvchi atambliche lashke, im achi tok.>
"*. . . micha chi-apakna-chi-h   aatábli-chi-l-ashkii,*"
and:SS   2SII-increase-CAUS-TNS too:much:N-CAUS-ISI-EXHORT
im-aachi-ttook.
III-say-DPAST
'He said, ". . . and I will multiply thee exceedingly."' (Gen. 17:2)

(74) <Yakeh, yukpali lishke, wayvchit apaknvchi kvt atamblichi la chi̱ hoke!>
Yakkiih, yokpali-li-shkii,   wayya-chi-t   apaknachi-kat
behold   bless-1SI-EXHORT grow-CAUS-PART multiply-COMP:SS
aatáblichi-l-aachi̱-h-okii!
too:much:N-1SI-IRR-indeed
'Behold, I have blessed him, and will make him fruitful, and will multiply him exceedingly.' (Gen. 17:20)

(75) <. . . chisht aiunchololi ka apaknvchit atamblichi la hi oke.>
. . . ch-isht=aayo̱chol óoli-ka   apaknachi-t
2SII-descendants-COMP:DS   multiply-PART

5. The position of the n-grade for this verb is surprising, since the final *-chi* is not included in the verb stem. See section 10.8 for more discussion.

aatáblichi-l-ahii-okii.
too:much:N-1SI-IRR-indeed
'I will multiply thy seed exceedingly.' (Gen. 16:10)

However, auxiliary selection is sometimes more complex than stated above. The following examples show exceptions to the general rule for auxiliary selection:

(76)   *Hattak-mat taloowa-kat   i-ponna-kat   ohooyo'*
       man-D:NM   sing-COMP:SS III-skill-COMP:SS woman
       i-shahlichi-ka.
       III-exceed-AFFIRM
       'I'm telling you, that man is more skilled at singing than the woman.'

(77)   *Anopoli-h ish-aatapa-h   yohmikako chi-taklah*
       talk-TNS   2SI-too:much-TNS and:so:DS   2SII-with
       nowa-h   sa-nna-kiiyo-h.
       walk-TNS   1SII-want-NEG-TNS
       'You talk too much, and so I don't want to walk with you.'

In (76) the auxiliary verb *ishahlichih* is used with the complement *taloowakat iponnah*, 'skilled at singing'. Although the verb *iponnah* 'be skilled at' takes a III subject, *ishahlichih* is used, which is generally appropriate for class I subjects. This is presumably because its complement, *taloowakat* 'sing', takes a I subject.

It is unclear to me what accounts for the use of *aatapah* in (77). *Aatapah* is normally used with stative verbs, but *anopolih* 'to talk' seems active. Possibly it is relevant that *anopolih* is not marked with the normal complementizer *-ka* here.

Other problems for the distribution of these forms arise when there is a perceived mismatch between the semantics of a verb and its agreement class, as is the case for stative verbs with class I subjects. In this case there is some speaker variability in auxiliary use; for example:

(78)   *Mary achokmahni-li-kat John i-shahli-h/i-shahlichi-h.*
       Mary love-1SI-COMP:SS   John III-exceed-TNS/III-exceed-TNS
       'I love Mary more than John does.'

Mrs. Josephine Wade judged both auxiliaries to be grammatical in this context.

13.3.2. *(Isht) onah, onaachih* 'to do enough'

Another possible semiauxiliary is *(isht) onah*. This is normally a main verb with the meaning 'to reach, to arrive (there)'. When it is used in the negative, it means 'not to have enough', as in the following examples:

(79) *Apaata' ona-l-ahila-h.*
      plate   reach-1sI-POT-TNS
      'I can reach the plate.'

(80) *Iskali' ik-sam-óon-o-h.*
      money N-1sIII-reach:L-NEG
      'I don't have enough money.'

In the negative, this verb participates in the dative raising construction (discussed in chapter 17):

(81) *John-akoosh   iskáli' ik-im-óon-o-h.*
      John-CON:NM money N-III-reach:L-NEG-TNS
      'John doesn't have enough money.'

The same verb may also be used in the negative as a semiauxiliary meaning 'not (do something) enough', as in the following examples:

(82) *Ipa-kat   chik-óon-o-h.*
      eat-COMP:SS 2sN-reach:L-NEG-TNS
      'You don't eat enough.'

(83) *Sa-piita-kat   ish-onaachi-kiiyo-h.*
      1sII-feed-COMP:SS 2sI-reach:CAUS-NEG-TNS
      'You don't feed me enough.'

These examples show that either internal or periphrastic negation may be used. The choice of *onah/onaachih* is determined by some unidentified property of the main verb, possibly related to agentivity or causality. The selection rule for this semiauxiliary could not be based on the agreement class, since both the verbs *ipah* 'to eat' and *ipiitah* 'to feed' have class I agreement with their subjects.

13.3.3. *Alhlhih* 'truly'

Perhaps *alhlhih* 'truly' should also be grouped with the semiauxiliaries. Like them, it takes a clausal complement with the -*ka* complementizer. However, it does not appear to show auxiliary selection properties like the other semiauxiliaries.

(84) <Ish shitilemʋt ʋmohmi ahni li kʋt ahli tuk.>
      Ish-shittiliima-t   ámmohmi-h   ahni-li-kat   alhlhi-tok
      2sI-despise-PART completely-TNS think-1sI   truly-PT
      'I truly thought that you completely hated her.' (Judg. 15:2)

13.3.4. *Biliiyah* 'forever'

This is another puzzling morpheme. It normally appears as a temporal verb in the duration clause construction (see chapter 16).

(85)   <. . . sa tikba a nohọwa na bilia hi oke.>
       . . . sa-tikba' aa-nohǫwa-na   bílliy-ahii-okii.
       1sII-front   LOC-walk:HN-DS   forever-IRR-EMPH
       '. . . (they) should walk before me forever.' (1 Sam. 2:30)

This verb very frequently appears in the g-grade as bílliyah.

However, in other cases it seems to behave somewhat like an auxiliary. It may occur preceded by a verb with no complementizer (86), the complementizer -oo (87), or the complementizer -ka (88). In all cases, it receives the tense marking of the main-verb-plus-auxiliary complex.

(86)   Pisa si-achokma-h   bílliy-aachị-h.
       see   1sII-good-TNS   forever-IRR-TNS
       'I'll always be good looking.'

(87)   <. . . chin chuka achʋfa yạ hatak sipokni ʋt iksho họ bilia hi oke.>
       . . . chị-chokka' achaffa-yạ   hattak   sipókni-yat   iksho-h-ọ
       2sIII-house one-AC   man   old:NML-NM   not:exist-TNS-PART:DS
       bílliy-ahii-okii.
       forever-IRR-EMPH
       '. . . there shall not be an old man in your house forever'.[6] (1 Sam. 2:32)

(88)   <Hatak ʋt ʋba pit anumpohonli kʋt bilia cha . . .>
       Hattak-at aba'   pit   anọpohǫli-kat   bílliya-cha . . .
       man-NM   up   away   talk:HN-COMP:SS forever-SS
       'Men should always pray and . . .' (Luke 18:1)

13.4. Participial phrases

Participial phrases are formed with the suffix -t. Following the analysis of Munro (1983, 1984a), I will treat -t as a relic of the same-subject switch-reference marker that no longer contrasts with a different-subject marker. While the subject of the verb marked with -t is the same as the verb that follows it in the great majority of cases, there are some cases where this is not true. Consider the following examples:

(89)   A-nokoowa-tok-ooka,   ik-att-o-t   ahni-li-h.
       1sIII-mad-PT-because   N-be-NEG-PART   think-1sI-TNS
       'Because he was mad at me, I hope he's not there.'

---

6. The Choctaw text has chokka' achaffa', which literally means 'one house', but idiomatically means 'family'. The English translation uses the word 'house', but in the context of this verse, 'house' refers to the family lineage (e.g., 'the house of Jacob').

(90)   *Hash-momichi-t   hachi-nowa-li-tok.*
        2PI-do:all-PART   2PIII-walk-1SI-PT
        'I visited all of you.'

In both these examples, verbs ending in the *-t* suffix are followed by verbs that have different subjects, due to the selectional properties of the verbs in these sentences.[7] Therefore, it is not possible to treat *-t* as a same-subject marker, even though it usually appears in same-subject contexts and is diachronically related to the same-subject switch-reference marker.

The following examples show some more typical examples of the use of *-t*:

(91)   *Bashli-t   kinaffi-li-tok.*
        cut-PART   fell-1SI-PT
        'I cut it down; I felled it by cutting.'

(92)   *Hihmah   loksi'-ma-k-aash-o*   *aa-halhlhi-t*
        and   turtle-DEM-TNS-PREV-FOC:AC   LOC-stomp-PART
        pichiffi-t   kachi-hmat   *iya-ttook.*
        squash-PART throw:away-when:SS   go-DPAST
        'And he stomped, squashed, and threw away that turtle, and then he left.'

As these examples show, the verbs marked with *-t* show no other inflection. Example (92) is typical of the style of much of Choctaw discourse. It consists of several verbs marked with *-t* followed by a fully inflected verb. Note that the verbs in these reduced clauses must be interpreted as sharing the inflectional categories of the final verb.[8]

13.4.1. The structure of *-t* phrases

An object of the *-t* verb must precede it, unless it can also be construed as an object of the main verb. Contrast the following two examples:

(93a)   *Bill-at   itti'   bashli-t   kinaffi-tok.*
        Bill-NM   tree   cut-PART   fell-PT
        'Bill cut the tree down.'

(93b)   *Bill-at   bashli-t   itti'   kinaffi-tok.*
        Bill-NM   cut-PART   tree   fell-PT
        'Bill cut the tree down.'

---

7. In (89), the *-t* suffix appears because the main verb *ahnih* 'to think' may take a complement marked with *-t* regardless of its subject. The *-t* in (90) is due to the quantifier *momichih* 'to do to all', which is discussed in section 14.3.1.

8. The Choctaw construction bears a striking similarity to the clause chaining phenomena in several Papuan languages (Haiman 1983, Foley 1986).

(94a) *Bill-at   itti'   cha̱-t   a̱ya-h.*
    Bill-NM tree chop-PART go:along-TNS
    'Bill went along chopping (down) trees.'

(94b) **Bill-at cha̱-t   itti'   a̱ya-h.*
    Bill-NM chop-PART tree go:along-TNS

In the first pair of examples, 'tree' is an object of both 'cut' and 'fell';
while in the second pair, 'tree' is only the object of 'chop'. These
examples seem to show that -*t* phrases are like VPs, and not like
compound verbs.

13.4.2. Irregular participles

Many participles show some sort of phonological reduction of the verb
stem. The most frequent change is the loss of the affix -*li*, the marker
of transitive verb stems, before participial -*t* (Nicklas 1974:258; Ulrich
1986: 270–76). The affix -*li* is discussed in more detail in chapter 8.
Table 13.1 shows some examples.

Table 13.1. Deletion of -*li* in participles

PARTICIPLE FORM	VERB	GLOSS
baliit[9]	*baliilih*	'to run'
basht	*bashlih*	'to chop, cut'[10]
tapt	*tablih*	'to cut (in two)'
bini̱t	*bini̱lih*	'to sit'
cha̱t	*cha̱lih*	'to chop'

Deletion of -*li* applies only to unassimilated -*li*, and -*li* in its
unassimilated form appears after vowels and the consonants *b, k, s,
sh, h.* It appears that this sort of contraction is always optional, so in
addition to short forms like *baliit*, it is also possible to say *baliilit.*

---

9. For some speakers, this is pronounced *balit.*

10. Nicklas suggests that *basht* is contracted from *bashat* rather than *bashlit.*
Bashlih as an independent verb means 'to cut', while *bashah* means 'to be cut'. They
are related by the transitive-intransitive alternation discussed in chapter 8. Since the
most regular form of the contracted participles shows deletion of final -*li*, the account
given here seems preferable.

Table 13.2. Other irregular participles

PARTICIPLE FORM	GLOSS	VERB	GLOSS
pist	'seeing'	*pisah*	'to see'
hikiit	'starting from'	*hikiiyah*	'to stand'
wakaat	'starting from'	*wakaayah*	'to rise'
·*ot*	'towards there'	*onah?*	'to arrive there'
pit	'towards there'	*pilah?*	'to send, throw'
iit	'towards here'	*?*	
at	'towards here'	*ayah?*	'to go along'[11]
isht	'with (instrumental)'	*ishih*	'to take, get'
hoot	'looking for'	*hoyoh*	'to seek'
awat	'with (accompaniment)'	*?*	

As table 13.2 shows, some of the contracted participles do not have clear parallels in uninflected verbs. Speakers disagree, for example, about the etymologies of the directional particles *iit, pit, at,* and *ot,* and it seems safe to say that they are synchronically underived.

11. Nicklas suggests that *at* comes from the verb *alah* 'to arrive (here)', while Ulrich suggests that it is from *ayah* 'to go along'. As Ulrich notes, a derivation from *alah* is closer to the semantics of the participle, but a derivation from *ayah* is closer to the phonology.

14. Adjectives and quantifiers

14.1. Are adjectives and quantifiers distinct parts of speech?

One might claim that adjectives and quantifiers are not categories distinct from verbs in Choctaw, but instead they are a subclass of verbs. As evidence for this claim, consider the following examples, in which adjectives display a full range of verbal morphology:

(1) *Litiiha-h.*
     dirty-TNS
     'He is dirty.'

(2) *Litiiha-hlik.*
     dirty-CERTAIN
     'He was dirty (first-hand knowledge).'

(3) *Sa-litiiha-h.*
     1sII-dirty-TNS
     'I'm dirty.'

(4) *Sa-litiiha-tok.*
     1sII-dirty-PT
     'I was dirty.'

Quantifiers also occur with verbal morphology, as in the following examples:

(5) *Hapishn-ato oklah ii-lawa-haatokoosh*
     we-NM2   PLUR 1PI-many-because:SS
     itti-it   hapim-oon-ahii-kiiyo-h.
     tree-NM 1PIII-arrive-IRR-NEG-TNS
     'Since there are many of us, there won't be enough trees for us.' [1]

However, there are some subtle ways in which the behavior of adjectives and quantifiers differs from that of verbs. These may justify treating them as identifiable subclasses of verbs whose properties depart in some ways from what might be expected by the category label "Verb."

The most reliable difference between adjectives and verbs lies in the interpretations that they receive in the grades, as noted by Haag (1995, 1997). In some grades, the semantics of verbs and adjectives diverge considerably.

---

1. There is dative raising (chapter 17) in the second clause, which is responsible for the same-subject marking in this example.

Verbs in the h-grade are typically translated 'just V-ed' or 'V-ed quickly', emphasizing the sudden inception of the event.

(6)   *Nokshóhpa-h.*
       afraid:H-TNS
       'He suddenly got scared.' (Ulrich 1986:168)

Adjectives have two distinct interpretations. The first, which is similar to the verbal interpretation, is 'just became Adj' or 'suddenly became Adj':

(7)   *Níhya-h.*
       fat:H-TNS
       'He just got fat.' (Ulrich 1986:169)

However, adjectives also appear in the h-grade when they are interpreted as a sort of comparative (as first noted by Nicklas 1974:76):

(8)   *Anokfilli-li-ka̲   chíhto-h.*
       think-1SI-COMP:DS big:H-TNS
       'It's bigger than I thought.'

(9)   *Aa-ípa-'   chíhto-h   nota'   pisa-li-h.*
       LOC-eat-NML big:H-TNS under   see-1SI-TNS
       'I looked under the bigger table.'

This second interpretation of the h-grade is pecular to adjectives, and distinguishes them from verbs.

The g-grade and y-grade typically express delayed inception for verbs, but are intensifiers for adjectives:[2]

(10)   *láyyakna-h*
       yellow:Y-TNS
       'completely, extremely yellow' (Nicklas 1974:77)
       (*lakna-h* 'yellow')

(11)   *Hina'-mat fállaaya-tok.*
       road-D:NM long:G-PT
       'That road was extremely long.'

The n-grade typically expresses duration for a verb, but (for some speakers) is a standardless comparison for adjectives (Nicklas 1974:74; Haag 1995, 1997):

(12)   *písa-h*
       see:N-TNS
       'to look at, see'
       (*pisa-h* 'to see')

2. Ulrich (1986:177) notes that his consultant prefered 'too' as a translation for the y-grade on adjectives.

(13) *chito-h*
      large:N-TNS
      'larger (than usual, expected, normal)'
      (*chito-h* 'large')

The hn-grade (iterative) is almost never used with adjectives, except when they are interpreted as inchoatives; for example, *lahákna-h* 'becoming yellow over and over again'.

A second distinctive property of adjectives is the occurrence of "nominalization morphology." When adjectives are postnominal, they optionally show penultimate pitch accent and final glottal stop:

(14) *Hattak cháaha-' písa-li-tok.*
      man   tall-NML see:N-1SI-PT
      'I saw a tall man.'

When followed by a vowel-initial suffix, this glottal stop surfaces as *y*, as discussed in chapter 2.

I have some reservations about the appropriateness of the label "nominalization" in this context. The penultimate pitch accent and final glottal stop clearly have such a function when they occur on verbs (as discussed in chapter 4):

(15a) *hilha-h*
       dance-TNS
       'to dance'

(15b) *hílha-'*
       dance-NML
       'dancer'

Such nominalized interpretations are also possible for adjectives:

(16a) *chaaha-h*
       tall-TNS
       'to be tall'

(16b) *cháaha-'*
       tall-NML
       'the tall one'

However, when this morphological process applies to postnominal adjectives, it is difficult to find any morphological or syntactic process that makes them seem more nominal than comparable adjectives that do not show nominalization morphology. It is also difficult to find any interpretive or syntactic difference between the nominalized and nonnominalized adjectives. This suggests to me that "nom-inalization" may be a misnomer in this context. Although the combination of final glottal stop and penultimate pitch accent clearly indicates nominalization in other contexts, it is not clear that this is the correct treatment in the case of postnominal adjectives. In the interest of discussing the two forms of the adjective in a way that does not bias the analysis, I will refer to the form of the adjective that shows final glottal stop and penultimate accent as the "marked" form of the adjective.

Some adjectives preferentially appear in either the marked or the usual form, for reasons that are not clear. All color adjectives seem to require the marked form:

(17a) *Shapo' hómma-' chopa-li-tok.*
      hat   red-NML   buy-1SI-PT
      'I bought a red hat.'

(17b) *Shapo' hómma-y-o   chopa-li-tok.*
      hat   red-NML-FOC:AC buy 1SI-PT

(17c) **Shapo' hómma-h-o   chopa-li-tok.*
      hat   red-TNS-FOC:AC buy-1SI-PT

In the speech of Mrs. Edith Gem, the adjective *chitoh* 'big' never appears in the marked form in the postnominal position:

(18a) *Ofi' chito-h písa-li-tok.*
      dog big-TNS   see:N-1SI-PT
      'I saw a big dog.'

(18b) *Ofi' chito-h-o   písa-li-tok.*
      dog big-TNS-FOC:AC   see:N-1SI-PT

(18c) **Ofi' chíto-y-o   písa-li-tok.*
      dog   big-NML-FOC:AC   see:N-1SI-PT

However, Choctaw speakers must vary on this point, given examples like the following:

(19) <Kówi chito yat nan apa ik ahóchoh másh kilíháhinah choh?>
      Koowi' chíto-y-at   nan-ápa-'   ik-ahóoch-o-h-m-aash
      bobcat big-NML-NM thing-eat-NML N-find:L-NEG-TNS-DEM-PREV
      kiliih-ahina-h-cho?
      roar-POT-TNS-Q
      'Will a lion roar (in the forest) if he hath no prey?' (Amos 3:4 CBTC)

In this example, *chítoyat* is the nominative form of *chíto'*, the marked form of the adjective.

However, most adjectives can appear in either the marked or the ordinary form:

(20a) *Ofi' achokma-h-o̜   cho̜pa-li-tok.*
       dog good-TNS-FOC:AC buy-1SI-PT
       'I bought a good dog.'

(20b) *Ofi' achókma-' cho̜pa-li-tok.*
       dog good-NML buy-1SI-PT

(20c) *Ofi' achókma-y-o̜   cho̜pa-li-tok.*
       dog good-NML-FOC:AC buy-1SI-PT

The analysis of adjectives and quantifiers as verbs has implications for the structure that we assign to examples like the following:

(21) *Hattak chaaha-'-mat Chahta' kiiyo-h.*
      man   tall-NML-D:NM Choctaw NEG-TNS
      'That tall man is not Choctaw.'

If we analyze the adjective 'tall' as a verb, then it is unclear what label the constituent 'tall man' bears. One possibility is that such sentences contain relative clauses, of the sort 'The man who is tall is not Choctaw.'

However, there is reason to believe this conclusion is incorrect. An important difference between adjectival modification and true relative clauses is the failure of a modifying adjective to assign nominative case. Thus, the following example is ungrammatical:

(22) **Hattak-at chaaha-'-mat Chahta' kiiyo-h.*
      man-NM   tall-NML-D:NM Choctaw NEG-TNS
      ('That tall man is not Choctaw.')

Compare this to a relative clause with an intransitive verb:

(23) *Hattak-at hilha-tok-mat Chahta' kiiyo-h.*
      man-NM   dance-PT-D:NM Choctaw NEG-TNS
      'The man who danced is not Choctaw.'

While noun-plus-adjective combinations need to be distinguished from relative clauses, these phrases have the distribution of NPs.

14.2. Quantifiers

Quantificational elements in Choctaw show strikingly different properties from their English counterparts. First, they are not determiners, but verbs. This is clear from their morphology. Second, there is an important contrast between nominal and verbal quantification that is unlike that found in English.[3]

3. My analysis of Choctaw quantifiers was strongly influenced by the work of Evans (1995) on the Australian language Mayali.

14.2.1. Verbal properties of quantifiers

Quantifiers appear in verb grades, and are followed by subordinating verb suffixes like -t and -oo 'participle' and -ka 'complementizer'. Some of them may also be inflected for subject, where the subject is the quantified noun phrase. These properties are illustrated for *momah* 'all'. We see the y-grade of the verb in (24), subject agreement in (25), same-subject marking in (24) and (25), and different-subject marking in (26). A different quantifier, *tóchchiinah* 'three', serving as a main verb is shown in (27).

(24) *Alla' nakni' móyyoma-kat oklah aa-ittanáaha-'*
      child male   all:Y-COMP:SS PLUR LOC-meet-NML
      itt-afaama-tok.
      RCP-meet-PT
      'All the boys met at church.'

(25) *Hash-moma-kat hash-iya-k mak-aachi-h.*
      2PI-all-COMP:SS 2PI-go-TNS be-IRR-TNS
      'You must all go.'

(26) *Hattak moma-ka   yoppali-chi-h.*
      man   all-COMP:DS happy-CAUS-TNS
      'He made all the people happy.'

(27) *Ii-tóchchiina-h.*
      1PI-three-TNS
      'We are three; there are three of us.'

14.2.2. Adnominal and coverbal quantification

Many English sentences containing quantifiers can be translated into Choctaw in two ways. Consider the following examples:

(28) *Shókha' moma-ka   abi-tok.*
      hog   all-COMP:DS kill-PT
      'He killed all the hogs.'

(29) *Shókha' momichi-t abi-tok.*
      hog   do:all-PART kill-PT
      'He killed all the hogs.'

In (28), we see an example of adnominal quantification, while in (29) we see verbal quantification. Adnominal quantification is the sort most comparable to English. *Shokha'* 'hog' and *momaka* 'all' form a noun phrase, as we can see from examples like the following where noun and quantifier are fronted as a unit:

(30) *Shókha' moma-kano, John-at abi-tok.*
      hog   all-AC2   John-NM kill-TNS
      'John killed all the hogs.'

In (29), however, *momichit* is a coverbal element meaning something like 'to do it to all of them'. A more literal translation of (29) might be 'He killed hogs, doing it to all of them'. It is not possible to front the combination of NP and *momichit*, as the following example shows:

(31) **Shóka momichi-t John-at abi-tok.*
      hog   do:all-PART John-NM kill-TNS
      ('John killed all the hogs.')

From the impossibility of (31), we can conclude that the combination of a NP and coverbal quantifier does not form a noun phrase.

Most nonnumerical quantifiers come in related adnominal and coverbal pairs, as shown in table 14.1.

Table 14.1. Paired adnominal and coverbal quanitifiers

ENGLISH GLOSS	ADNOMINAL	COVERBAL
'all'	*momah*	*momit, momichih*
'half'	*iklannah*	*iklannachih*
'most of; a lot of'	*lawah*	*lawaat, lawaachih*
'all of them, one by one'	*áyyokah*	*áyyokaalih, áyyokaachih*
'only'	*illah*	*illachih*
'additional'	*aynah*	*aynachih*

14.3. A survey of Choctaw quantifiers

14.3.1. *Momah, momichih* 'all'

Momah is the adnominal form of the quantifier. There are few syntactic restrictions on its occurrence; it appears with both subjects and objects, and is generally followed by the complementizer *-ka*:

(32) *Hattak moma-ka   yoppali-chi-h.*
      man   all-COMP:DS happy-CAUS-TNS
      'He made all the people happy.'

The subject of *momah* is shown with a class I marker:

(33) *Hash-moma-kat hash-iya-k mak-aachi-h.*
      2PI-all-COMP:SS 2PI-go-TNS be-IRR-TNS
      'You must all go.'

Momah also appears in the y-grade as *móyyomah*, which seems to mean something like 'completely all' or 'every single one':

(34) *A-skali'   móyyoma-ka am-alla' alhiiha' im-aa-li-tok.*
      1sIII-money   all:Y-COMP:DS 1sII-child group   III-give-1sI-PT
      'I gave every bit of my money to my children.'

Momit and *momichih* are the coverbal quantifiers. They only take scope over an object. Consider the following contrast:

(35) *Ii-moma-t   il-ip-aachi-h.*
      1PI-all-PART 1PI-eat-IRR-TNS
      'We will all eat.'

(36) **?Ii-momichi-t il-ip-aachi-h.*
      1PI-do:all-PART 1PI-eat-IRR-TNS
      ('We will all eat.')

Example (36) is ungrammatical because *momichih* should indicate that all of an object is affected.

Momichih appears as a main verb in examples like the following:

(37) *Himmak nittak i-nowa-kat   momichi-li-tok.*
      now   day   III-walk-COMP:SS do:all-1sI-PT
      'I visited all of them today.'[4]

(38) *Ish-okpani-kat   ish-momichi-h.*
      2sI-break-COMP:SS 2sI-do:all
      'You broke them all.'

As these two examples show, both *momichih* and the other verb may be marked for the subject, or subject marking may omitted on the embedded verb.

Momichih may also appear as the subordinate verb, with the suffixes *-oos*, *-sh*, or *-t*:

(39) *Momichi-li-sh   i-nowa-li-tok.*
      do:all-1sI:SS   III-walk-1sI-PT
      'I visited them all.'

(40) *Momichi-t ik-polhómm-o-tok.*
      do:all-PART N-fold:L-NEG-PT
      'He didn't fold all of it.'

(41) *Hattak momichi-t aba'   isht   iya-tok.*
      man   do:all-PART heaven INSTR go-PT
      'He took all the men to heaven.'

---

4. *I-nowah*, literally 'walk to him/her', is an idiom meaning 'visit'.

Momichih shares with other quantifiers the unexpected property of taking class I person markers, even when an object is being quantified over:

(42) *Hash-momichi-t hachi-nowa-li-tok.*
      2PI-do:all-PART   2PIII-walk-1SI-PT
      'I visited all of you.'

Momichi-t frequently has a reduced form *momit*. I am not aware of any syntactic or semantic differences between *momichi-t* and *momit*. See chapter 13 for discussion of reduced participial verbs.

14.3.2. *Lawah, lawaachih* 'many, much, a lot of'

The adnominal *lawah* may be used alone, or followed by *-t, -oo* or *-ka*:

(43) *Ílhpak lawa-h   ima-h   ik-fiihn-o-kiya,*
      food   much-TNS   give-TNS   N-very-NEG-although
      chi-chokash-ako   lawaa-t   ipiita-tok.
      2SII-heart-CON:DS   much-PART   feed-PT
      'Although he didn't give you much food, he fed your heart greatly.'

(44) *Tákkon lawa-ka   apa-li-tok.*
      peach   many-COMP:DS   eat-1SI-PT
      'I ate a lot of peaches.'

(45) *Tákkon lawa-h-o   áapa-li-sh   si-abiika-h.*
      peach   many-TNS-PART:DS   eat:L-1SI-SS   1SII-sick-TNS
      'I ate so many peaches that I got sick.'

The coverbal *lawaachih* means 'to do to many.' *Lawaachih* is generally subordinated to another verb. The most common subordinating suffix is *-t*, but *-oo* and *-ka* are also possible.

(46) *Tákkon=chíto' lawaachi-t   apa-t   tahli-li-h.*
      apple   do:many-PART   eat-PART   complete-1SI-TNS
      'I ate many apples.'

There may also be a form of this quantifier that includes the transitive *-li*, though the evidence is not entirely clear. In some sentences the word *lawaat* appears, and the length of the vowel in the final syllable would not be expected if this were the participial form of *lawah*:

(47) *Tákkon lawaa-t   apa-li-tok.*
      peach   do:many-PART   eat-1SI-PT
      'I ate many peaches.'

Lawaat appears to be a contracted form of a verb like **lawaalih*. As mentioned in chapter 13, verbs ending in *-li* frequently delete it before the participial suffix *-t*. Mr. Henry Willis did not recognize the verb *lawaalih*, at least in this form. However, he was familiar with the verbs *láwwaalih* and *láwwaalichih*, which appear to be the g-grade and causative g-grade of this verb:

(48) *Láwwaalichi-t   shaali-t   aya-tok.*
      do:many:G-PART haul-PART go:along-PT
      'He was hauling a whole bunch of stuff.'

(49) *Láwwaali-kiiyo-h-oosh   isht   ala-h.*
      do:many-NEG-TNS-PART:SS INSTR arrive-TNS
      'He didn't bring very many!'

Mr. Willis thought that these words sounded somewhat old-fashioned and unusual, which may explain the unavailability of the zero-grade.

14.3.3. *Iklannah, iklannachih* 'half'

Iklannah is the adnominal form of the quantifier. It is followed by *-h* or *-ka*:

(50) *Oka' isht-íshko-'   iklanna-ka   ishko-li-tok.*
      water INSTR-drink-NML half-COMP:DS drink-1SI-PT
      'I drank half of the cup of water.'

(51) *Oka' taláya-k-aash iklanna-h ishko-li-tok.*
      water lie:N-TNS-PREV half-TNS   drink-1SI-PT
      'I drank half the water that was placed there.'

The coverbal form is *iklannachih*:

(52) *Iklannachi-t a-chokka'   isht   iya-li-tok.*
      half-PART   1SIII-house INSTR go-1SI-PT
      'I took half of it home.'

(53) *Iklannachi-t polhommi-tok.*
      half-PART   fold-PT
      'He folded half of it.'

14.3.4. *Áyyokah, áyyokaalih, áyyokaachih* 'all of them, one by one'

This quantifier differs from *momah* and *momichih* 'all' in implying that the whole group was distributed over different events. The English translations often include words like 'one by one'. The adnominal form is *áyyokah*, followed either by *-h*, *-oo*, or both:

(54) *Ohooyo' áyyoka-h-oosh   oklah tamaaha' ilhkoli-tok.*
      woman   all:DISTR-TNS-PART:SS PLUR town   go:PL-PT
      'All the women went to town (in different groups).'

Some sources on Choctaw translate *áyyokah* as 'every' or 'each'.
There are some similarities between the two glosses, since English *every*
and *each* are distributed and the distribution can be over events.
However, Choctaw *áyyokah* lacks certain other properties of English
every and *each*. *Every* and *each* take singular verb agree-ment, but
Choctaw *áyyokah* occurs with a plural verb (for those verbs that have a
distinct plural form). This can be seen in example (54), where the plural
verb *ilhkolih* occurs with *áyyokah*.

The coverbal forms are *áyyokaalih* and *áyyokaachih*; but the
speakers I consulted were unsure what the difference was between the
two.

(55) *Hattak áyyokaali-h   písa-li-h.*
      man   all:DISTR-TNS see:N-1SI-TNS
      'I saw each person.'

(56) *At   ima-hmat   ilaap áyyokaachi-h ima-tok.*
      come:and give-when:SS self all:DISTR-TNS give-PT
      'When he came to give them out, he handed them out separately to
      each individual.'

In combination with a numeral like *achaffah* 'one' or *tokloh* 'two',
áyyokachih indicates that the action was carried out in groups of that
size.

(57) *Achaffa-h áyyokachi-h-oosh   oklah itt-afaama-tok.*
      one-TNS   all:DISTR-TNS-PART:SS PLUR RCP-gather-PT
      'They gathered one by one.'

14.3.5. *Íllah, íllachih* 'only'

The adnominal *illah*, followed by *-h*, *-oo*, or *-ka*, is more common than its
coverbal counterpart *illachih*.[5] *Íllah* is often preceded by *-mak* 'that',
-pak 'this', or *-ak* 'oblique'.

(58) *Tákkon illa-ka   apa-li-tok.*
      peach only-COMP:DS eat-1SI-PT
      'I only ate the peaches.'

(59) *Tákkon illa-h   apa-li-tok.*
      peach only-TNS eat-1SI-PT
      'I only ate the peaches.'

5. Some speakers have variant forms *állah* and *állachih*.

(60)   *Akáka' nípi'-mak   álla-h-o*   *apa-li-tok.*
       chicken meat-DEM   only-TNS-PART:DS eat-1SI-PT
       'I ate only that chicken.'

(61)   *Akáka' nípi'-pak   álla-h-o*   *apa-li-tok.*
       chicken meat-DEM   only-TNS-PART:DS eat-1SI-PT
       'I ate only this chicken.'

(62)   *An-ak ílla-kat   ak-íiy-o-tok.*
       I-OBL only-COMP:SS   1SN-go:L-NEG-PT
       'I was the only one who didn't go.'[6]

(63)   *Ilaap ílla-h   chaffichi-tok.*
       him   only-TNS   run:off-PT
       'He ran him off by himself.'

Íllah may also appear as the main predicate of the sentence, in which case its object generally has the oblique suffix *-ak*, a pattern often found in copular sentences:

(64)   *An-ak ílla-tok.*
       I-OBL only-PT
       'It was only me.'

The coverbal form is *íllachih*. It is somewhat unusual, perhaps because the postverbal suffix *-makálla*, discussed below in section 14.6.1, is used in its place.

(65)   *Ilaap íllachi-t   iya-chi-tok.*
       him   do:only-PART go-CAUS-PT
       'I only made him go.'

14.3.6. *Aynah, aynachih* 'in addition, too'

Aynah is the adnominal form, and freely shows up after any noun phrase, generally followed by an appropriate form of the complementizer *-ka*:

(66)   *Barbara ii-tatoklo-kat   ipa-t   il-iy-aachi-h;   Matthew*
       Barbara 1PI-and-COMP:SS   eat-PART   1PI-go-IRR-TNS   Matthew
       ayna-kat   pi-awat iy-aachi-h.
       too-COMP:SS   1PII-with go-IRR-TNS
       'Barbara and I are going out to eat and Matthew is also coming with us.'

---

6. Note that the English translation of this sentence requires a clefted form of the word *one*, which induces third person agreement on the verb *go*. The Choctaw example, however, shows ordinary first person negative agreement on the verb *iyah* 'go'.

(67) *Ahi'   cho̱pa-li-h;   ta̱chi' ayna-ka̱.*
     potato buy-1SI-TNS corn   too-COMP:DS
     'I bought potatoes, and corn too.'

The coverbal form is generally *aynachih* or *áyyinachih* for current
speakers. In older texts forms like *ayini̱chih* and *ayinah* also occur:

(68) *Ta̱chi' isht   ala-li-h   ahi'   aynachi-t   isht*
     corn   INSTR arrive-1SI-TNS potato do:too-PART INSTR
     ala-li-h.
     arrive-1SI-TNS
     'I brought the corn, and I brought the potatoes too.'

(69) <Mihma okla ai υla cha, peni ash it aieninchit okla atotoli>
     Mihma oklah áyyala-cha piini-yaash itt-ayini̱chi-t
     and   PLUR arrive:Y-SS boat-PREV   RCP-do:too-PART
     oklah atootoli-h
     PLUR   fill-TNS
     'And they came and filled that ship as well.' (Luke 5:7)

(70) <. . . tυmaha Nain hohchifo ho̱ ia tok; mihma nan im ai ithυna laua,
     micha okla laua aienυt apehυt ilhkoli tok.>
     . . . tamaaha' Nain hóhchifo-h-o̱   iya-ttook; mihma
     town   Nain be:named-TNS-PART:DS go-DPAST and:then
     na̱n=imaayithá̱na' lawa-h   micha oklah lawa-h
     disciple   many-TNS and   people many-TNS
     ayina-t   apiiha-t   ilhkoli-ttook.
     do:too-PART be:with-PART go:PL-DPAST
     'He went to a town called Nain and many disciples went with him,
     and many people too.' (Luke 7:11)

14.3.7. Unpaired quantifiers

A few Choctaw quantifiers do not appear in the characteristic paired
adnominal and coverbal forms.

14.3.7.1. *Bi̱kah* 'both'

Bi̱kah 'both' occurs only as an adnominal; a related form appears as a
verbal suffix, and is discussed in section 14.6.2 below. In some cases such
as (72), it seems to be an independent verb meaning 'be like'.

(71) *Chokka' bi̱ka-h   áyyaasha-h.*
     house   both-TNS live:PL-TNS
     'They live in both houses.'

(72) *Sipókni-' sa-bika-sh*   *átta-h.*
old-NML 1sII-be:like-PART:SS be-TNS
'He's an old man, like me.'

(73) *Chokka' bika-kat*   *homma-h.*
house both-COMP:NM red-TNS
'Both houses are red.'

Bikah may also appear with the reciprocal *itti-*:

(74) *Konih itti-bika-h-oosh*   *ittibi-h.*
skunk RCP-both-TNS-PART:SS fight-TNS
'Both of the skunks are fighting against each other.'

14.3.7.2. *Ittatokloh* 'both; and; together'

The verb *ittatokloh* appears to be composed of the reciprocal prefix /itti-/ 'together; each other' plus a form of the numeral *tokloh* 'two'. It frequently occurs in translating English coordination:

(75) *John Mary ittatoklo-kat*   *tamaaha'*   *ittiyaachi-tok.*
John Mary and-COMP:SS town   go:DU-PT
'John and Mary went to town.'

Subject agreement may also appear on *ittatokloh* when one of its arguments is pronominal:

(76) *Hash-tatoklo-h hachi-písa-li-tok.*
2PI-and:N-TNS 2PII-see:N-1SI-PT
'I saw the two of you.'[7]

14.3.7.3. *Kanohmih* 'a few, some'

Kanohmih corresponds to English 'several, a few, some kind of'.

(77) *Am-aafo-yat*   *ohooyo' kanohmi-h ittihaalalli a-ttook.*
1sIII-grandfather-NM woman several-TNS marry be-DPAST
'My grandfather was married to several women.'

(78) *Mak-o*   *oklah at*   *ib-áyyasha-na hashi' kanohmi-h.*
there-FOC:AC PLUR come:and COMIT-live:Y-DS month several-TNS
'They came and lived there for a few months.'

(79) *Kaniimi-ka*   *isht iya-li-h.*
some-COMP:DS INSTR go-1SI-TNS
'I took some of them.'

---

7. In this example, *ittatokloh* has undergone initial *i*-deletion, followed by cluster simplification.

(80) \<Yohmi ma hatak kanohmi kʋt hatak ʋt palsi ʋbi yo̱ potʋlhpo ai it i̱
      sholit isht ʋla tok.\>
      Yohmi-hma̱   hattak   kanohmi-kat   hattak-at palsy
      and-when:DS man   some-COMP:SS   man-NM   palsy
      abi-yo̱   patálhpo' aay-itt-i̱-shooli-t   isht
      disease-FOC:AC pallet   LOC-RCP-III-carry-PART INSTR
      ala-ttook.
      arrive-DPAST
      'And some men brought in a man on a pallet who was suffering from
      palsy.'[8] (Luke 5:18)

It is possible that at some point *kanohmih* served as an adnominal
quantifier, while *kanohmichih* was the corresponding coverbal form. Mrs.
Edith Gem thought that she had heard the form *kanohmichih*, but was
unable to say how it might be used.

14.4. Numerals

14.4.1. Cardinal numerals

Numerals in Choctaw behave morphologically and syntactically like
verbs. When they appear with a noun, they must be suffixed with a
complementizer, tense marker, or participial ending. The following
examples show adnominal numerals:

(81) *Ofi' tóchchiina-kat ik-sam-iksho-h.*
      dog three-COMP:SS N-1sIII-not:exist-TNS
      'I don't have three dogs.'

(82) *John-at aa-i̱pa-'   toklo-h-oosh   i̱-hiili-h.*
      John-NM LOC-eat-NML two-TNS-PART:SS III-stand:DU-TNS
      'John has two tables.'

For the lower numerals 'two' through 'four', there are also related
coverbal forms:

(83) \<. . . achʋfalichit ai i̱ hotofa hi a̱ ʋlhpesa ha tok.\>
      . . . *achaffalichi-t aay-i̱-hotof-ahii-ya̱   alhpiisa-h a-ttook.*
      do:one-PART   LOC-III-release-IRR-DS correct-TNS be-DPAST
      'It was necessary for him to release one of them . . .' (Luke 23:17)

(84) *John-at   shókha' toklo̱chi-t   abi-tok*
      John-NM hog   do:two-PART kill-PT
      'John killed two hogs.'

---

8. It is unclear to me why the verb *shoolih* 'carry' has a reciprocal prefix in this
example. Perhaps it should be interpreted as 'carried together'.

(85) <Hatak nana kia i̱ shahli ha̱ tuklochit holitobla he keyu.>
Hattak na̱na-kia i̱-shahlih-a̱   toklochi-t   holiitobl-ahii-kiiyo-h.
man   some-too III-master-AC do:two-PART honor-IRR-NEG-TNS
'No man can serve two masters.' (Matt. 6:24)

(86) *Tokloli-h-oosh   iya-h.*
do:two-TNS-PART:SS go-TNS
'They went by twos.'

(87) *Toklo̱li-t   ittiyaachi-h.*
do:two:N-PART go:DU-TNS
'They went, two together.'

(88) *Nittak achaffa-ka̱   oshtali-sh   ipa-h.*
day   one-COMP:DS do:four:times-PART:SS eat-TNS
'He eats four times a day.'

Choctaw cardinal numerals are listed below:

(89) *achaffah/chaffah*   'one'
      tokloh   'two'
      tóchchiinah   'three'
      oshtah   'four'
      tálhlhaapih   'five'
      hánnaalih   'six'
      o̱tokloh   'seven'
      o̱tóchchiinah   'eight'
      chákkaalih   'nine'
      pókkoolih   'ten'
      awahchaffah   'eleven'
      awahtokloh   'twelve'
      awahtóchciinah   'thirteen'
      awahoshtah   'fourteen'
      awahtálhlhaapih   'fifteen'
      awahhánnaalih   'sixteen'
      awaho̱tokloh   'seventeen'
      awaho̱tóchchiinah   'eighteen'
      abihchákkaalih,   'nineteen'
      awahchákkalih
      pókkooli tokloh   'twenty'
      pókkooli tóchchiinah   'thirty'
      talhiipah achaffah   'one hundred'
      talhiipah sipóknih   'one thousand'

14.4.2. Analysis of the numerals

Some of the numerals listed above are composed of more than one
morpheme; 'seven' and 'eight' each contain a prefix o̱- 'superessive', so

that 'seven' is literally 'two on top (of five)' and 'eight' is 'three on top (of five)'.

The numbers from 'eleven' to 'nineteen' contain a prefix *awah-* which seems to mean something like 'with'. This prefix may be related to the verb *awaayah* 'to marry' or the postposition *aw<u>a</u>t* 'with', as in the following examples:

(90) *Ohooyo'-m<u>a</u> awaaya-l-aachi̲-h.*
      woman-D:AC marry-1sI-IRR-TNS
      'I'm going to marry that woman.'

(91) *Im-ohooyo' aw<u>a</u>t <u>a</u>ya-tok.*
      III-woman with ̲go:along-PT
      'He went with his wife.'

Byington (1915:68) notes that 'eleven' may be expressed as <pokoli auahchafa> (*pókkooli awahchaffah*) 'ten with one', but that <pokoli> (*pókkoolih*) is generally omitted. It is interesting that in Koasati the numerals between ten and twenty still retain the word for 'ten'. Thus 'eleven' is *pokkó:l awáh caffá:kan* in Koasati (Kimball 1991:355).

The prefix *abih-* that appears in the word for 'nineteen' is mysterious. The word *abih* means 'to kill', but it is unclear why this should appear in a word for 'nineteen'.

The word for 'thousand' is composed of the words *talhiipah* 'hundred' and *sipóknih* 'old'.

The numerals for 'three', 'five', 'six', 'nine', and 'ten' all share the pattern CV́CCVVCV, leading Nicklas (1974:215) to suggest that they are in the g-grade. However, if this is correct, the corresponding zero grade forms are unavailable (**tochinah*, **talhapih*, etc.).

14.4.3. Variant forms of the numerals

Some of the numerals have variants. 'One' is *chaffah* for some speakers and *achaffah* for others. Speakers sometimes attribute these differences to regional dialects, but both varieties seem to be widely distributed, and the form used seems to depend on factors like personal idiosyncracy and degree of formality.

'Three' is listed by Byington (1870:51) as <tukchina> (*tókchiinah*), a form I have not recorded from modern speakers.

'Nineteen' appears as both *abichakali* and *ahbichakali* in Byington (1915:5,15). I have not recorded the second variant from a modern speaker.

14.4.4. Ordinal numerals

The Choctaw ordinal numerals are as follows:

(92) *tikbah, ámmonah*   'first'
      atóklah/atoklah   'second'
      atóchchiinah   'third'
      ayóshtah   'fourth'
      (isht) tálhlhaapih   'fifth'
      (isht) hánnaalih   'sixth'
      isht áyyoopih   'last'

As can be seen, the numerals from 'two' to 'four' add a prefix *a-* to form their ordinals. Higher ordinals are generally identical to the cardinals and are differentiated through optional use of *isht* 'instrumental' or through context.

The following example shows an ordinal numeral:

(93) *Ohooyo' atókla-m-akoosh   tálloowa-h.*
      woman   second-DEM-CON:NM sing:G-TNS
      'The second woman is (finally) singing.'

14.4.5. Multiplicative numerals

Multiplicatives correspond to our terms 'once', 'twice', etc.

(94a) *Nittak himmona-h ipa-h.*
      day   once-TNS   eat-TNS
      'He eats once a day.'

(94b) *Nittak hitókla-h ipa-h.*
      day   twice-TNS eat-TNS
      'He eats twice a day.'

(94c) *Nittak hitóchchiina-h ipa-h.*
      day   thrice-TNS   eat-TNS
      'He eats three times a day.'

(94d) *Nittak ayóshta-h   ipa-h.*
      day   four:times-TNS eat-TNS
      'He eats four times a day.'

The lower multiplicatives are derived from the ordinals by adding a prefix *hi-* for the numerals 'one' through 'three'. Some speakers also allow the *hi-* prefix for the numeral 'four', hence *hiyoshtah*. Higher multiplicatives are identical to the ordinals.

14.5. The preverb *oklah*

Oklah indicates the plurality of an animate subject.[9] The final *h* or *ah* may be dropped in some cases, and the remainder cliticized to the verb.

(95) *Tamaaha' oklah iya-tok.*
      town   PLUR go-PT
      'They went to town.'

(96) *Oklhiili-kma̠ okl-ii-taloow-aachi̠-h.*
      dark-IRR:DS   PLUR-1PI-sing-IRR-TNS
      'When it gets dark, we'll sing.'

The positioning of *oklah* is of some importance in arguments for constituency in Choctaw. The most frequent position is immediately before the verb, following any objects:

(97) *Hitokoosh   chokfi' oklah falaama-tok.*
      and:then:SS rabbit PLUR meet-PT
      'And then they met a rabbit.' (T3:3)

However, it is also possible for *oklah* to appear before the direct object:

(98) *Oklah Amazing Grace o̠t   taloow-aachi̠-h.*
      PLUR   Amazing Grace go:and sing-IRR-TNS
      'They're gonna go sing Amazing Grace.'

(99) *Hattak-at oklah ta̠chi' apa-tok.*
      man-NM   PLUR corn   eat-PT
      'The men ate all the corn.'

Oklah may not appear before the subject:

(100) **Oklah hattak-at ta̠chi' apa-tok.*
      PLUR   man-NM   corn   eat-PT
      ('The men ate the corn.')

For some speakers, it is also marginally possible for *oklah* to appear between the directional particle and the verb. All three of the following sentences are possible, though the second and third are more natural than the first.

---

9. *Oklah* is also a noun meaning 'people'. However, its use as a preverb is distinct. We can see this from the fact that the preverb may be used with plural nonhuman subjects:

Ofi-it   oklah homma-h.
dog-NM PLUR red-TNS
'The dogs are red.'

(101a) *?Hattak-at*   *tạchi' ạt*   oklah *apa-tok.*
       man-NM   corn   come:and PLUR eat-PT
       'The men came and ate corn.'

(101b) *Hattak-at*   *oklah tạchi' ạt*   *apa-tok.*
       man-NM   PLUR   corn   come:and eat-PT

(101c) *Hattak-at*   *tạchi' oklah ạt*   *apa-tok.*
       man-NM   corn   PLUR   come:and eat-PT

Oklah may also appear between instrumental preverb *isht* and the verb, though as with the directionals, this is the least natural position:

(102a) *Oklah*   *bashpo-yọ*   *ishit*   *bashli-h.*
       PLUR   knife-FOC:AC INSTR cut-TNS
       'They cut it with a knife.'

(102b) *Bashpo-yọ*   *oklah ishit*   *bashli-h.*
       knife-FOC:AC   PLUR   INSTR cut-TNS

(102c) *?Bashpo-yọ*   *ishit*   *oklah bashli-h.*
       knife-FOC:AC   INSTR PLUR   cut-TNS

We can account for this distribution if we assume a syntactic structure as in figure 14.1, and the following distributional statement for *oklah*:

(103) *Oklah* must be adjoined to the left of some projection of the verb.
Figure 14.1.

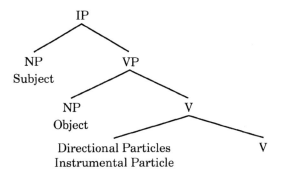

Figure 14.1.

14.6. Quantifier suffixes

14.6.1. -makálla 'only'

The suffix -makálla corresponds to English 'only', as in the following example.

(104) *Cake-ma̱ ak-p-o-h,*   *piih ashshowa-li-makálla-tok.*
       cake-D:NM 1SN-eat-NEG-TNS only smell-1SI-only-PT
       'I didn't eat the cake, I only smelled it.'

If a modal is present, -makálla must occur before the modal; the other order is ungrammatical:

(105a) *Chi̱-cake-ma̱*   *ashshowa-li-makáll-aachi̱-h.*
        2SII-cake-D:AC   smell-1SI-only-IRR-TNS
        'I'm only going to smell your cake.'

(105b) **Chi̱-cake-ma̱*   *ashshowa-l-aachi̱-makálla-h.*
        2SII-cake-D:AC   smell-1SI-IRR-only-TNS

A related morpheme, *íllah* or *állah*, occurs within noun phrases, as discussed above.

The similarity between the verbal -makálla and the independent word *íllah* or *állah* is puzzling. If we attempt to make them morphologically related, then we would divide verbal -makálla into -mak + állah. But this segmentation is problematic. Neither -akálla nor -pakálla is allowed following a verb, so it is difficult to treat the initial -mak as an instance of the demonstrative 'that'. But there is no other clear candidate for the identity of this -mak.

Perhaps the best solution to this problem is a diachronic one. Verbs followed by -makálla may have originated as clefted nominalizations like follows:

(106) [*Cake-ma̱ ashshowa*]ₙₚ-*mak álla-tok.*
       cake-D:AC smell-DEM   only-PT
       'It was only that smelling of the cake.'

Compare the following example, repeated from above, which shows a similar synchronic syntax:

(107) *An-ak ílla-tok.*
       I-OBL only-PT
       'It was only me.'

In verbal structures, this has been reanalysed as a single morpheme -makálla, while in noun phrases there are still two discernable morphemes involved.

14.6.2. -bịka 'both'

This adverbial suffix is a marker of duality, and requires that some dual argument (usually the subject) be present in the sentence.[10] It may occur after any predicate, but is most common on numeric predicates:

(108) *Hattak toklo-mat shapo' chọpa-bịka-tok.*
       man   two-D:NM hat   buy-both-PT
       'Those two men both bought a hat.'

(109) *Hattak toklo-mat shapo' tóchchiina-bịka-h-ọ   chọpa-tok.*
       man   two-D:NM hat   three-both-TNS-PART:DS buy- PT
       'Those two men bought three hats apiece.'

The suffix -*bịka* can refer to both dual subjects and objects.

(110) *Ii-hilha-bịka-tok.*
       1PI-dance-both-PT
       'We (two) danced.'

(111) *Ittatoklo-ka   achokmahni-li-bịka-h.*
       two-COMP1:DS like-1SI-both-TNS
       'I like both of them.'

(112) *Taloowa-bịka-h-oosh   mọmịchi-t   tahli-h.*
       sing-both-TNS-PART:SS do:all-PART complete-TNS
       'They both sang them all.'

It occurs in pre-tense position:

(113) *Taloowa-bịka-tok.*
       sing-both-PT
       'They both sang.'

(114) *Taloow-aachị-bịka-h.*
       sing-IRR-both-TNS
       'They will both sing.'

The suffix -*bịka* 'both' is related to an independent verb *bịkah* 'to be like', discussed in section 14.3.7.1 above. It is also phonologically similar to -*biika* 'distribution' (discussed immediately below), but the two must be carefully distinguished, since they have different meanings.

14.6.3. -biika 'distribution'

This suffix is used with verbs that describe actions which are distributed. The distribution must be over some plural entity, such as an individual

---

10. For some speakers, this restriction may be loosening. One speaker initially volunteered sentences using -*bịka* with non-dual subjects. However, she later reconsidered and rejected the same sentences as unacceptable.

or a place. The distribution may also be over times, and in this interpretation the reading is something like a habitual. However, *-biika* is not precisely a habitual, since there is no necessary implication that the action was continued at times other than that described. See, for instance, example (115) below, where the action of calling occurs several times, but would not be described as a habitual action. The suffix *-biika* differs from *-bika* in not requiring a dual subject. It appears only in pre-modal position.

The following examples show distribution over events.

(115) *Kanohmi   pit   ii-hoyo-kia,   ik-l-o-biika-h.*
      several:times away 1PI-call-but N-come-NEG-DISTR-TNS
      'Although we called several times, he didn't come.'

(116) *Sa-litiiha-biika-tok.*
      1SII-dirty-DISTR-PT
      'I used to be dirty.'

(117) *Tiih-ano ishko-li-biika-tok.*
      tea-AC2   drink-1SI-DISTR-PT
      'I usually drink tea.'

The following examples show distribution over individuals and places:

(118) <. . . okchayʊt ik mạyo ka chị ka, im ʊllosi ạ isht kampila beka tok.>
      . . . *okchạya-t ik-mạy-ok-aachị-ka,   im-allosi-yạ*
      live-PART   N-be:PL-NEG-IRR-COMP   III-baby-AC
      isht-kampila-biika-ttook.
      INSTR-throw:away-DISTR-DPAST
      'They threw their children away so that they wouldn't (have to) live.'
      (Acts 7:19)

(119) <Mihmʊt yakni yʊmma hatak ont iba fohka tok; atuk ọ yʊmmak osh shukha laua ipeta beka chị kaim osapa puta ka pit chʊffichi tok.>
      Mihmat yakni' yamma hattak ọt   ibaa-fokka-ttook; aatokọ
      and:SS land   that   man   go:and COMIT-join-DPAST and-DS
      yammak-oosh shókha' lawa ipiita-biik-aachị-ka   im-osaapa'
      that-FOC:NM hog   many feed-DISTR-IRR-COMP III-field
      potta-ka pit   chaffichi-ttook.
      all-COMP away send-DPAST
      'And he went and joined with a man of that land, and (that man) sent him out to feed the many hogs in all his fields.' (Luke 15:15)

(120) *Abanópa'=isht=anọpóli-yat tamaaha' piih móyyoma-ka*
      preacher-NM   town   just all:Y-COMP:DS
      iya-biika-tok.
      go-DISTR-PT
      'The preacher went to every town.'

14.6.4. -*tokla* 'dual'

This suffix marks a dual subject. It is sometimes used with the singular forms of suppletive verbs. The similarity of -*tokla* to the number *tokloh* 'two' should be noted.

(121)   *Tamaaha' iya-tokla-tok.*
       town   go:SG-DU-PT
       'They (two) went to town.'

(122)   *John, Mary ittatoklo-kat nittak=hóllo' aa-ittanáaha-'*
       John Mary and-NM   Sunday   LOC-meet-NML
       aa-taloowa-tokla-h.
       LOC-sing-DU-TNS
       'John and Mary sang at church on Sunday.'

Some speakers of Choctaw do not use the suffix -*tokla*.

14.6.5. -*baano* 'only, each, really'

The suffix -*baano* may modifiy either the verb itself or one of the arguments of the verb. When it modifies the verb, it is usually translated as 'really';[11] when it appears inside the NP or is interpreted as modifying some NP, it is usually translated 'each' or 'only'.

(123)   *Pam-at taloow-ahii-baano-h.*
       Pam-NM sing-IRR2-really-TNS
       'Pam really can sing.'

(124)   *John-at akáka' abi-baano-h; akáka'=cháaha-no kiiyo-h.*
       John-NM chicken kill-only-TNS turkey-AC2   NEG-TNS
       'John only killed chickens, not turkeys.'

This suffix is best in pre-tense position. It is marginally acceptable for -*baano* to appear in pre-modal and post-tense positions.

(125a) John-at   *akáka' ab-aachi-baano-h.*
       John-NM   chicken kill-IRR-really-TNS
       'John is really going to kill that chicken.'

(125b) ?*John-at*   *akáka' abi-baan-aachi-h.*
       John-NM   chicken kill-really-IRR-TNS

(126)   ?*John-at nípi' apa-tok-baano.*
       John-NM meat eat-PT-only
       'John really ate the meat.'

---

11. Note that the English 'really' has two senses: something like 'in reality' and 'very much'. Choctaw -*baano* only corresponds to the first of these two senses. The second, intensive, sense corresponds to Choctaw -*fíihna*.

Mrs. Gem said that (126) sounded like "old-time" talk. She strongly preferred (127).

(127) *John-at nípi' apa-baano-tok.*
John-NM meat eat-really-PT
'John really ate the meat.'

If the sentence contains a plural subject, -*baano* seems best translated as 'each', and it causes the sentence it is attached to have a distributed interpretation:

(128) *Ohooyo-ot tóchchiina-sh shapo' toklo-h chopa-h.*
woman-NM three-PART:SS hat   two-TNS buy-TNS
'Three women bought two hats (together).'
(total number of hats = 2)

(129) *Ohooyo-ot tóchchiina-sh shapo' toklo-baano-h-o   chopa-h.*
woman-NM three-PART:SS hat   two-each-TNS-PART:DS buy-TNS
'Three women bought two hats (each).'
(total number of hats = 6)

(130) *Ohooyo-ot tóchchiina-sh oshi' toklo-baano-sh   im-ashwa-h.*
woman-NM three-PART:SS son   two-each-PART:SS III-exist:DU-TNS
'Those three women have two sons each.'

When the subject of the sentence is singular, -*baano* is generally interpreted as 'only'.

(131) *Shokha' tóchchiina-baano-h-o   chopa-h.*
pig   three-only-TNS-PART:AC buy-TNS
'He bought only three pigs.'

We can understand the connection between the two readings in the following way: -*baano* seems to signal that each subject has a particular number of objects associated with it. When there is a group subject, every member of the group is associated with that number of objects; this is naturally translated as 'each' or 'apiece' in English. When there is a singular subject, the sentence with -*baano* on the object stresses that this number of objects (and no other) is associated with the subject. This is most naturally translated into English as 'only'.

15. Adpositions and their equivalents

Choctaw uses a variety of syntactic and morphological means to express the range of concepts expressed by adpositions in many other languages. This chapter discusses the semantics and categorial status of adpositions and their equivalents.

15.1. Semantic fields

15.1.1. Sources and goals

Choctaw does not have adpositions corresponding to the familiar *to* and *from* of English. Instead, verbs of motion in the language can be divided into those that have a goal object and those that have a source object. The verb *iyah* 'to go', for example, has as its object a goal:

(1) *John-at   tamaaha' iya-tok.*
     John-NM town   go-PT
     'John went to town.'

The verb *ifalammih* 'to leave', however, has as its object a source:

(2) *Oklahoma i-falammi-t   California ala-li-ttook.*
     Oklahoma III-leave-PART California arrive-1SI-DPAST
     'I left Oklahoma and came to California (long ago).'

We might say that in such cases the adposition is part of the lexical semantics of the verb. Thus *iyah* 'to go' and *ifalammih* 'to leave' might have lexical representations like the following:

(3a) GO [x, [$_{PATH}$TOWARD (y)]]   *iyah*

(3b) GO [x, [$_{PATH}$FROM (y)]]   *ifalammih*

Verbs like *iyah* 'to go', which include the goal in their lexical semantics, are considerably more common than verbs that include the source. In general, sources need to be licensed by some additional grammatical element.

For some verbs, a source is indicated by the locative prefix *aa-*:

(4a) *South Carolina aa-miti-li-h.*
     South Carolina LOC-come-1SI-TNS
     'I came from South Carolina.'

(4b) *South Carolina miti-li-h.*
     South Carolina come-1SI-TNS
     'I came to South Carolina.'

246

For other verbs, a source is indicated with the word *hikiit*, a reduced participle form of the verb *hikiiyah* 'to stand':

(5) *Moore   hikii-t   Norman ona-li-tok.*
    Moore   stand-PART Norman   arrive-1SI-PT
    'I went from Moore to Norman.'

Hikiit to indicate source must be an idiomatic use of *hikiiyah* 'to stand', since *hikit* it is used in situations where there is no literal standing involved:

(6) *Qbah-at m-akọ   aa-hikii-t   iya-h.*
    rain-NM   there-CON:AC LOC-stand-PART go-TNS
    'The rain started off over there.'

The most basic verbs of motion in Choctaw are also distinguished according to whether the motion reaches its destination. *Iyah* 'go' and *miṭih* 'come' do not presuppose that the subject reaches the destination, while the verbs *onah* 'arrive (there), reach (there)' and *alah* 'arrive (here), reach (here)' do presuppose that the subject arrives at his or her intended destination. Thus the following sentences are possible:

(7) *Aaron-at Moore miṭi-h-kiya, ik-l-o-kii-tok.*
    Aaron-NM Moore come-TNS-but N-arrive-NEG-NEG-PT
    'Although Aaron started off for Moore, he didn't get there.' (Lit., 'Although Aaron came to Moore, he didn't get there.')

(8) *Marcia-at tamaaha' iya-h-kiya, ik-óon-o-kii-tok.*
    Marcia-NM town   go-TNS-but N-arrive:L-NEG-NEG-PT
    'Although Marcia left for town, she didn't get there.'

Sentences that involve manner of motion verbs generally indicate the goal of the motion through combination with one of the basic motion verbs just mentioned. Consider the following example:

(9) <Mihma Pita yʊt wakaya cha, malelit sepʊlka yạ onʊt . . .>
    Mihma Piita-yat wakáaya-cha maliili-t   scpulchre-yạ ona-t . . .
    and   Peter-NM get:up:L-SS   run-PART sepulchre-AC arrive-PART
    'And Peter arose and ran to the sepulchre .. .' (Luke 24:12)

In this example, the goal of the verb 'run' is shown by combining it with the verb *onah* 'arrive'.

The objects of verbs of motion may receive accusative case, just like other objects:

(10) <tʋmaha ha ont hʋsh chukowakma>
      tamaaha-ya[1] *ot*   *hash-chokkowa-kma*
      town-AC   come:and   2PI-enter-IRR:DS
      'when you enter the town' (Luke 22:10)

15.1.2. Location

Sentences with static locations may indicate location in two ways: through use of the applicative prefixes or through the use of postpositionlike elements.

15.1.2.1. Applicative prefixes

Sentences with prepositional phrases headed by 'at' and 'in' in English often correspond to sentences containing a verb with the locative applicative prefix *aa-* in Choctaw, as in the following example:

(11) *Chokka' chito-ma   aa-hilha-tok.*
      house   big-that:AC LOC-dance-PT
      'They danced in that big house.'

The prefix *on-* corresponds to English 'on':

(12) *Aaípa' o-hilha-tok.*
      table   on-dance-PT
      'He danced on the table.'

See chapter 9 for more discussion of both these applicative prefixes.

15.1.2.2. Postpositionlike words

Choctaw has a set of apparent postpositions that indicate location, as shown below:

(13) *Ofi-it [chokka' notaka'] ittóla-h.*
      dog-NM house   under   lie:N-TNS
      'The dog is lying under the house.'

(14) *Hashshok isht-chali-it [chokka' asháka'] hikíya-h.*
      grass   INSTR-cut-NM house   behind   stand:N-TNS
      'The lawnmower is behind the house.'

However, it is not entirely clear whether such words constitute a distinct category or whether they should be considered a subclass of

---

1. The Choctaw text suggests *tamaahaha*, the accusative case of a noun *tamaahah* 'town'. However, all speakers I consulted have instead *tamaaha* 'town', with a final glottal stop, and the accusative form should be *tamaahaya*. Either the Choctaw text reflects an unusual dialect or it is in error at this point.

verbs or nouns. See section 15.2 for discussion.

The postpositionlike words include the following:

(15) *mishsha'*   'on the other side of'
      pakna'/paknaka'   'on top of'
      anoka'/anokaka'   'inside'
      ashaka'   'behind'
      nota'/notaaka'   'under'
      itakla'   'between, in the middle of'
      tanap   'across from'

As the preceding list shows, many postpositionlike words have two forms: one with the suffix *-ka'* and another without.

Speakers sometimes say that they feel there is a difference between the two forms, but it is difficult to determine any consistent semantic difference between the two. Broadwell (1987a) suggests that *-ka'* may be related to nominalization morphology.

15.1.3. Accompaniment

Accompaniment is indicated by either an applicative prefix or the use of a verb of accompaniment.

15.1.3.1. The applicative prefix *ibaa-*

Comitatives are generally formed with the prefix *ibaa-*:

(16) *Sa-baa-taloowa-h!*
      1SII-COMIT-play-TNS
      'Play with me!'

This is the most common way of indicating accompaniment. However, with verbs of motion, use of the morphemes *awat* and *apiihat*, discussed in the next section, is also very common.

15.1.3.2. *Awat* and *apiihat*

A second way of indicating accompaniment is through the use of the words *awat* and *apiihat*, which seem to be reduced participial forms of verbs. They function in a way similar to postpositions in Choctaw, as the following examples show:

(17) *Awat ish-iy-aachi-h-o?*
      with 2SI-go-IRR-TNS-Q
      'Are you going with him?'

These words are clearly not nominal. They cannot be case-marked.

(18)   *Aw<u>a</u>t-<u>a</u> ish-iy-aachi̱-h-<u>o</u>?
       with-AC   2SI-go-IRR-TNS-Q
       ('Are you going with him?')

The phonological shape of aw<u>a</u>t suggests that the final t of this word is the participial -t, since there are no monomorphemic words of the shape (V)CV̱C in Choctaw. However, there is no corresponding independent verb with quite the same meaning. There may be a relationship to the verb awaayah 'to marry', or to the prefix awah- 'with' (which occurs in the numeral system on the teens), though in either case there has clearly been some semantic shift.

Apiihat, however, is more clearly related to a verb meaning 'go with, be with, accompany, join', as in the following example:

(19)   Pi-apiiha-tok.
       1PII-join-PT
       'They joined us.'

(20)   <. . . okla pisa mʋt itapeha chi̱ka it i̱ kana pokoli tuchina ho̱ okla isht ʋla tok.>
       Oklah pisa-hmat,   itt-apiih-aachi̱-ka   itt-i̱-kánah
       PLUR   see-when:SS   RCP-be:with-IRR-COMP   RCP-III-friend
       pókkoli tóchchiina-h-<u>o</u>   oklah isht-ala-ttook.
       ten   three-TNS-PART:DS   PLUR   INSTR-come-DPAST
       'When they saw him, they brought thirty friends to be with him.'
       (Judg. 14:11)

Syntactically, aw<u>a</u>t and apiihat behave like participles, and show the morphology associated with such verbs. When the object of the aw<u>a</u>t is pronominal, it appears as a II object clitic:

(21)   <. . . hʋchi awant ia lashke.>
       Hachi-aw<u>a</u>t iya-l-ashkii.
       2PII-with   go-1SI-EXHORT
       'I will go with you.' (1 Sam. 23:23)

Pronominal third person is represented by zero, as is normal in the II paradigm:

(22)   <Simeon ʋt awant ia tok.>
       Simeon-at   aw<u>a</u>t iya-ttook.
       Simeon-NM   with   go-DPAST
       'Simeon went with him.' (Judg. 1:3)

Aw<u>a</u>t may assign accusative case to its object:

(23)   <. . . Balak a awant Ketesh a ona tok.>
       Balak-<u>a</u>   aw<u>a</u>t Ketesh-<u>a</u>   ona-ttook.

Barak-AC with Kedesh-AC arrive-DPAST
'She went with Barak to Kedesh.' (Judg. 4:9)

Apiihat seems similar to *awat*, but carries an additional element of plurality, generally plurality of its object:

(24) *Apiihat aaittanáaha' ilhkoli-tok.*
      with   church   go:PL-PT
      'They went to church with them.'

(25) <Chebusait ʋhleha hʋt Benchamin im ʋlla ʋhleha ha̱ apehʋt
      Chelusalem ai asha tok . . .>
      Chebusait alhiihah-at Benchamin im-alla'
      Jebusite   group-NM   Benjamin   III-child
      alhiihah-a̱ apiihat Chelusalem aay-aasha-ttook.
      group-AC   with   Jersualem LOC-be:PL-DPAST
      'The Jebusites dwell with the children of Benjamin in Jersualem.'
      (Judg. 1:21)

Awat and *apiihat* are the words normally used to show accompaniment for verbs of motion or position like 'come', 'go', 'sit', 'stay', and 'live'. The comitative *ibaa-* seems infrequent in this context, though constructed examples of this sort were judged grammatical:

(26) *Mary ibaa-iya-li-tok.*
      Mary COM-go-1SI-PT
      'I went with Mary.'

15.1.3.3. *Ta̱klah, ata̱klah* 'to be with, within'

It is also possible to express the notion of accompaniment with the verb *ta̱klah* or *ata̱klah*, which is frequently followed by the participial suffix *-t*. Consider the following examples:

(27) *Si-ata̱kla-t   áya-h.*
      1SII-with-PART go:along-TNS
      'He's coming along with me.'

(28) <. . . pi̱ ta̱kla ish antashke, achit okla tok. Mihma ta̱kla anta chi̱ hosh
      ont chukowa tok.>
      . . . pi̱-ta̱kla-h   ish-átta-shkii,   achi-tokla-ttook. Mihma
      1PIII-with-TNS 2SI-be:N-EXHORT say-DU-DPAST   and
      ta̱kla-h   átt-aachi̱-h-oosh   o̱t   chokkoowa-ttook
      with-TNS be-IRR-TNS-PART:SS go:and be:in-DPAST
      'Abide with us, they said. And he went in to tarry with them.' (Luke 24:29)

15.1.4. Instrument

Instruments are indicated through the applicative preverb or prefix *isht,*
isht- which is a reduced participial form of the verb *ishih* 'to take'.

(29)   *Mary-at   báshpo'   isht-bashli-tok.*
       Mary-NM knife   INSTR-cut-PT
       'Mary cut it with a knife.'

Applicative *isht-* is discussed in more detail in chapter 9.

15.1.5. Benefactive

Benefactives are typically indicated through the use of the dative
applicative *im-*, as in the following example:

(30)   *John-at   i-taloowa-h.*
       John-NM III-sing-TNS
       'John is singing for him.'

Occasionally, the benefactive applicative *imi-* is used instead:

(31)   *John-at   imi-taloowa-h.*
       John-NM BEN-sing-TNS
       'John is singing for him.'

Speakers say there is little if any difference between these two sentences.
    The applicatives *im-* 'dative' and *imi-* 'benefactive' are discussed
further in chapter 9.

15.2. The categorial status of postpositions

It is unclear whether the postpositionlike elements discussed above
should be regarded as a separate part of speech. They show certain
properties that are like verbs and others that are like nouns. The
strongest evidence that the items just mentioned have verbal properties
is their occurrence in various grade forms; and example is shown in table
15.1.

Table 15.1. Grade forms of a postposition

zero grade	*notaaka'*	'under, beneath'
n-grade	*notaka'*	'partially under'
y-grade	*notáyyaka'*	'under (something like a shelter)'[2]
h-grade	*notáhka'*	'just under'
hn-grade	*notahaka'*	'repeatedly under'

Here are some examples of these forms in sentences:

(32a) *Nohóta-t   aya-h.*
    under:HN-PART go:about-TNS
    'He keeps going under things.'

(32b) *Notáyyaka' ittóla-h.*
    under:Y   lie:N-TNS
    'He's lying under it [something like a shelter].'

Example (32a) also shows that postpositions may be followed by the participial suffix *-t*, which is otherwise found only on verbs and quantifiers.

Another property of postpositions that is more like verbs is their ability to take reciprocal prefixes:

(33) *Holisso-yat pi-tt-itákla'   ittóla-h.*
    book-NM   1PII-RCP-between lie:N-TNS
    'The book is between us.'

Verbs generally allow reciprocal prefixes, but very few nouns do.

We might imagine that the postpositions should have glosses like 'to be/go under NP', where NP is the overt object of the postposition. The subject of the postposition would then be the Theme of the sentence: that argument whose location or change of location is specified. A sentence like the following:

(34) *Ofi-it   [chokka' notáka'] ittóla-h.*
    dog-NM house   under   lie:N-TNS
    'The dog is lying under the house.'

might thus be more literally translated as 'The dog is lying (down), being under the house.'

One might wonder why these verblike postpositions do not show agreement with their presumed subjects. That is, why is (36) not an acceptable variant of (35)?

2. It is unclear to me why the y-grade, typically glossed 'finally', should have this meaning in this particular word.

(35) *Chokka' notáka' ittóla-li-h.*
      house   under   lie-1sI-TNS
      'I am lying under the house.'

(36) **Chokka' notáka-li   ittóla-li-h.*
      house   under-1sI lie-1sI-TNS
      'I am lying under the house.'

Two options seem to be possible, both of which have some plausibility.

One possibility is to treat the construal of the theme with the postposition as an example of secondary predication. This would make it analogous to an English example like *John lay on the beach naked,* where *naked* is predicated of *John,* but *John* is not the syntactic subject of *naked.* If only true syntactic subjects trigger agreement, then the lack of subject agreement on the postposition is explained.

Another possibility is that subject agreement depends on the presence of some functional category (perhaps Infl or Agr), and that the phrase headed by a postposition does not contain the appropriate functional head necessary for agreement.

While I have just presented some evidence for the verbal properties of apparent postpositions, other researchers (Nicklas 1974:207; Munro 1989) have suggested that the apparent postpositions in these constructions may be more accurately described as nouns which express relation or orientation.

Some evidence for this position is the fact that these phrases may be case-marked like uncontroversial nouns, as the following example shows:

(37) *Aaípa' paknaka-yat homma-h.*
      table   top-NM   red-TNS
      'The top of the table is red.'

Also consistent with the nominal analysis of postpositions is their failure to take tense morphology, and the fact that they do not require participial or subordinating morphology.

(38) **Ofi-it aaípa' notáka-h   taláya-h.*
      dog-NM table   under-TNS lie:N-TNS
      ('The dog is lying under the table.')

However, if postpositionlike words are considered to be nominal, it is unclear whether the noun phrases that accompany them are to be considered object complements of the nouns or (inalienable) possessors of the nouns (Nicklas 1974:207). That is, for an example like the following, should *John* be considered the possessor of the noun *asháka '* 'behind' or its complement?

(39) *Ofi-yat* [*John ashaka'*] *ittolah.*
      dog-NM John behind lie:N
      'The dog is lying behind John.'

The ambiguity arises because of the lack of morphology on *ashaka'*. If it
were an ordinary alienable noun, it would show a III agreement marker:

(40) *am-ofi'*   'my dog'
      chim-ofi'   'your dog'
      John im-ofi'   'John's dog'

However, an inalienably possessed noun shows no agreement with a
third person possessor:

(41) *sa-noshkobo'*   'my head'
      chi-noshkobo'   'your head'
      John noshkobo'   'John's head'

Compare the paradigm for a postposition:

(42) *sa-notaka'*   'under me'
      chi-notaka'   'under you'
      John notaka'   'under John'

There are nouns that show II agreement with their complements, but
III agreement with their possessors. Consider the case of *holbatoba'*
'picture, photograph, likeness', shown with possessors in (43a) and with
complements in (43b):

(43a) *a-holbatoba'*   'my picture [which I own]'
       chi-holbatoba'   'your picture [which you own]'
       John i-holbatoba'   'John's picture [which he owns]'

(43b) *sa-holbatoba'*   'the picture of me'
       chi-holbatoba'   'the picture of you'
       John holbatoba'   'the picture of John'

Is a phrase like *John ashaka'* 'behind John' comparable in its syntax to
John noshkobo 'John's head' or to *John holbatoba* 'the picture of John'?
    In this case, there is evidence for the latter structure, in which *John*
is the complement of *ashaka'*, rather than its possessor. Several of the
postpositionlike words also function as ordinary NPs, often referring to
body parts. *Ashaka'*, for example, also refers to the back and buttocks,
like the English word *behind*. When it is used as a body part, it takes III
possession (44a), but when it is used as a postposition, it takes no overt
possessive marker (44b):

(44a) *John im-ashaka'*   'John's behind'

(44b) *John ashaka'*   'behind John'

When there is no overt NP possessor, however, *im-ashaka'* is ambiguously 'behind him' or 'his behind'. This suggests that noun complements may optionally become noun possessors in some cases, in a manner comparable to the English phrase *my picture*, which is ambiguously 'the picture that I own' or 'the picture of me'. This ambiguity of III marking persists in non-third-person examples:

(45a)　*am-ashaka'*　　　　　'behind me; my behind'

(45b)　*si-ashaka'*　　　　　'behind me'

The data just presented, however, are also compatible with an analysis that treats words like *notaka'* and *ashaka'* as verbal or postpositional. Recall that verbs also show II agreement with their objects:

(46)　*Sa-pisa-h.*　　　　　'She/he sees me.'
　　　Chi-pisa-h.　　　　　'She/he sees you.'
　　　John pisa-h.　　　　　'She/he sees John.'

There is at least one other way in which the postpositionlike words behave like the verbs in relative clauses. In relative clauses, quantifiers and demonstratives associated with the head of the relative clause tend to appear to the right of the verb, while the head remains in situ:

(47)　[*Mary-at paska' chapoli' ikbi-tok*]-*ma*　　　*chopa-li-tok.*
　　　Mary-NM bread sweet　made-PT-DEM:AC buy-1SI-PT
　　　'I bought that cake that Mary made.'

(48)　[*Mary-at paska' chapoli' ikbi-tok*]-*a*　　*moma-ka*　　*chopa-li-tok.*
　　　Mary-NM bread sweet　made-PT-AC all-COMP:AC buy-1SI-PT
　　　'I bought all the cakes that Mary made.'

In postpositional phrases, demonstratives and quantifiers tend to occur to the right of the postposition, even when they are interpreted as modifying its object:

(49)　[*Aaipa'nota'*-]*ma*　　John-at　*ofi'*　aa-pisa-tok.
　　　table　under-D:AC John-NM dog　LOC-see-PT
　　　'John saw a dog under that table.'

(50)　[*Aaipa'nota'*]　*moma-ka*　　*pisa-li-h.*
　　　table　under all-COMP:DS see-1SI-TNS
　　　'I looked under all the tables.'

In (49), the demonstrative -*ma* 'that' follows the postposition, but it is interpreted as if it modifies the object of the postposition. Similarly, in (50) the quantifier *momah* 'all' follows the postposition, but is interpreted as quantifying over the object of the postposition.

15.3. The directionals

When a verb has a motion component, either as a part of its inherent lexical semantics or as an additional element, Choctaw tends to express the orientation of this motion with respect to the speaker by means of a set of directionals. These words are used much more frequently than any equivalent in English, and often do not translate well.

The directional particles are shown below:

(51a) Group A directional particles
  pit   'motion away from (a reference point)'
  iit   'motion towards (a reference point)'
  [*awiit*   'motion towards [a reference point]']'³

(51b) Group B directional particles
  ot   'motion away from [a reference point]'
  at   'motion towards [a reference point]'

These directional particles are never used alone, but always before some other verb or verb phrase.

There are several interesting questions about these directional particles. First, what is the syntactic status of the directional particle? Second, what is the difference between the directionals of group A and those of group B? Third, what sorts of predicates involve motion?

15.3.1. The syntax of the directional particles

15.3.1.1. Directionals are syntactically independent words

A directional particle always follows any overt object and precedes the verb:

(52a) *Hattak-at tachi' at   apa-tok.*
  man-NM   corn   come:and eat-PT
  'The men came and ate the corn.'

(52b) **Hattak-at at   tachi' apa-tok.*
  man-NM   come:and corn   eat-PT

Only one directional may be used in a clause, even when the combination of a group A and a group B directional might seem coherent, as we can see from the following example:

---

3. For modern speakers, *iit* and *awiit* are essentially synonymous. Speakers of Choctaw I consulted considered *awiit* a somewhat archaic variant of *iit*.

However, Byington (1915:70) suggests that in nineteenth-century Choctaw, *awiit* and *iit* contrasted with each other. *Awiit* was used to indicate an endpoint of motion closer to the speaker than the endpoint for *iit*. Despite this, the Choctaw Bible almost always uses *awiit* and very rarely uses *iit*.

(53)   *Chokka' ila-h*   (*ot*)   *pit   kanalli-tok.*
       house   other-TNS   (go:and)   away   move-PT
       'They (*went and) moved to a different house.'

There is some disagreement about whether the directionals are actually separate words or whether they are prefixes.[4] Ulrich (1986) shows that the directionals share phonological properties with other morphemes that he labels clitics.

Despite their phonological relationship with the following verb, they should be treated as having the syntactic status of independent words. We can see this through their interaction with the word *oklah* (discussed in chapter 14) and the instrumental *isht*.

15.3.1.2. Interaction of directionals and *isht*

As discussed in chapter 9, *isht* is an instrumental preverb. When both a directional and *isht* appear in the same sentence, either may precede the other:

(54a) *Chifak-ma ṻshi-cha pállaska' ishit   iit   am-aa-tok.*
       fork-D:AC   take:L-SS   bread   INSTR   toward   1sIII-give-PT
       'He passed me the bread with the fork.' (Lit., 'He took the fork and passed me the bread with it.')

(54b) *Chifak-ma ṻshi-cha pállaska' iit   ishit   am-aa-tok.*
       fork-D:AC   take:L-SS   bread   toward   INSTR   1sIII-give-PT

This shows that both items must be regarded as separate words, given their free ordering with respect to each other and their ordering with respect to *oklah* (chapter 14).

15.3.2. The semantics of the directional particles

15.3.2.1. Previous discussion

There has been little discussion of the meaning of directional particles in previous literature on Choctaw. Nicklas merely glosses *pit* 'thither' and *iit* 'hither' and says that they "state the direction of the action relative to the position of the speaker" (1974:209).

Ulrich (1986) is the only author to address the difference between group A and group B directionals. He writes, "The dynamic directional particles [*at-* and *ot-*] are used to indicate motion of the subject . . . *Iit-* and *pit-* are like *at-* and *ot-* in indicating actions directed toward (*iit-*) or away from (*pit-*) the speaker. However, the static directional clitics are used when the subject is not itself moving, but merely sending

---

4. In Chickasaw, for example, the comparable particles are written as part of the same word as the following verb by Munro and Willmond (1994).

something else, physical or otherwise" (1986:276–77).

However, Ulrich himself notes that there are problems with this generalization. Textual data show clearly that *pit* and *iit* occur in cases where the subject is in motion, as in the following examples:

(55)   <. . . ʋba pit anumpula chi̱ hosh ilap illʋt nʋnih chaha yo̱ pit oiya tok.>
       . . . *aba pit   anopol-aachi̱-h-oosh   ilaap illa-t*
       up   away talk-1SI-IRR-TNS-PART:SS self   only-PART
       nanih cháaha-yo̱   pit   oyya-ttook.
       hill   high-FOC:AC away go:up-DPAST
       '. . . he went up into a mountain apart to pray.' (Matt. 14:23; Mark
       6:46)

(56)   <Mihma lumʋt peni pit ʋlhto cha, a haiaka ka pit ilhkoli tok.>
       Mihma lohma-t   piini' pit   álhto-cha   aahayaakaka'
       and   secret-PART boat   away enter:L-SS wilderness
       pit   ilhkoli-ttook.
       away go-DPAST
       'And they departed into a desert place by ship privately.' (Lit., 'They
       secretly entered a boat and went away to the wilderness.') (Mark 6:32)

15.3.2.2. One event versus two events

The difference between group A and group B directionals can be described as follows: The group A directionals (*pit* and *iit*) are used when the motion is conceived of as forming a single event with the following predicate. Group B directionals (*ot* and *at*) are used when the motion is conceived of as an event distinct from the following predicate.

Group B directionals correspond most closely to English phrases like 'go and' and 'come and'.

15.3.2.3. Simple cases

In the great majority of cases, the distinction between single events and distinct events explains the interpretations of sentences with group A and group B directionals. Consider the following contrasting examples:

(57)   *Im-Ø-aachi̱-h-o̱*   *ot*   *im-anooli-li-tok.*
       III-give-IRR-TNS-PART:DS go:and III-tell-1SI-PT
       'I went and told them to give it to him.'

(58)   *Im-Ø-aachi̱-h-o̱*   *pit*   *im-anooli-li-tok.*
       III-give-IRR-TNS-PART:DS away III-tell-1SI-PT
       'I told them to give it to him.'

In example (57), use of the group B directional *ot* implies that there was a distinct event of motion prior to the action of telling. In contrast, the use of the group A directional *pit* in (58) does not imply any such motion prior to the telling. Instead, *pit* shows that telling is an event in which the motion is directed away from the speaker.

However, there are a few special cases, discussed in the following sections.

15.3.2.4. Directionals and inchoatives

With certain verbs, the two-event directionals are used in the formation of inchoatives as in (59b and (60b):[5]

(59a) *Itt__ola-tok.*   (stative)
        lie:N-PT
        'It lay there.'

(59b) *A__t   ittola-tok.*   (inchoative)
        come:and lie-PT
        'It fell.' (Lit. 'It came and lay; it came to lie.')

(60a) *Sholosh-at taha-h.*   (stative)
        shoe-NM   completed-TNS
        'The shoes are worn out.'

(60b) *Sholosh n__owa-t   hopaaki-sh*   (inchoative)
        shoe   walk:N-PART long:time-PART:SS
        a__t   i__-taha-h.
        come:and III-completed-TNS
        'He walked in the shoes for a long time and they wore out on him.'

Such use of directional with inchoatives seem particularly common with verbs of position.

15.3.2.5. Idiomatic uses

There are also some idiomatic uses of the group B particles. For example, *o__t iyah* means 'pass by' (literally 'go and go').

(61) <. . . okhvta paknaka y__a a noh__owvt, a__yvt im ona, yohmi kvt ont ia hi a__ aiahni tok.>
        okhata' paknaka-ya__ aa-noh__owa-t   a__ya-t   im-ona-h,
        ocean   top-AC   LOC-walk:HN-PART go:by-PART III-reach-TNS
        yohmi-kat   o__t   iy-ahii-ya__ aay-ahni-ttook.
        do:so-COMP:SS go:and go-IRR-AC LOC-think-DPAST
        '. . . he was walking on the water, coming towards them, as if he would pass them by.' (Mark 6:48)

With the positional verbs, *o__t* and *a__t* are sometimes interpreted as 'over there' and 'over here', respectively. In (62), *o__t m__aya-tok* is literally 'went

---

5. An additional difference between the stative and inchoative senses is that the stative usually occurs in the n-grade (durative). Inchoative senses usually appear in other grades.

and were' but is interpreted as 'were there'.

(62) <Micha anonti ohoyo il ai itapeha tuk a̱ a kanimi kʋt onnahinli fehna
      sepʋlka ya̱ ont ma̱ya tuk ʋt . . . okla pi nukhlakʋshli tuk oke.>
      Micha   ano̱ti' ohooyo' il-aay-itt-apiiha-tok-a̱
      and   and   woman 1PI-LOC-RCP-be:with-PT-AC
      aa-kaniimi-kat   onnahi̱li' fi̱hna sepulka-ya̱   o̱t
      LOC-some-COMP:SS morning very   sepulcher-AC go:and
      ma̱ya-tok-at . . . oklah pi-noklhakashli-tok-okii.
      be:PL-PT-NM   PLUR   1PII-astonish-PT-indeed
      'And some of the women who were with us and who were there at the
      sepulcher early in the morning astonished us.' (Luke 24:22–23)

(63) *O̱t   is-sam-a̱tt-aachi-h-o̱?*
      go:and 2SI-1SIII-be-IRR-TNS-Q
      'Are you going to stay there with me?'

(64) <ho takchi cha isht iʋt kocha aioklhililika ya̱ ont hʋsh kanchashke>
      hoo-tákchi-cha isht   iya-t   kochcha aay-oklhiliika-ya̱ o̱t
      PL-tie:L-SS   INSTR   go-PART   out   LOC-dark-AC   go:and
      hash-kanch-ashkii
      2PI-throw-EXHORT
      'Tie him take him and cast him(there) into the outer darkness.' (Matt,
      22:13)

The classes of verbs that are compatible with the single-event
directionals are discussed in more detail in chapter 19.

15.4. Path modifiers: *píllah* and *pilah*

Pilah and *píllah* are often used in sentences where some locative,
temporal, or directional relationship is expressed. However, *pilah* and
píllah are not themselves postpositions or directionals, but serve to
modify information about paths that is either included in the lexical
representation of a verb or provided by some other element in the
sentence.

   Píllah indicates that there is a path of motion or orientation in the
sentence which is very long or longer than expected. In example (65),
píllah is appropriate because there is a visual path from the subject to
the sky, and this is a (very) long path. Similarly, in (66) there is a long
path between the son and his father.

(65) <pit aiokchifelit shutik pilla ka pit hopo̱koyot hieli ma>
      pit   aay-okchifiili-t shotik pílla-ka   pit
      away LOC-stare-PART sky   long:path-LOC away
      hopo̱koyo-t   hi̱ili-hma
      look:at-PART stand:Y-when
      'While they looked steadily towards heaven' (Acts 1:10)

(66)   <. . . atuk osh auet hopaki pilla minti kak inli ho̱, i̱ki ash osh pit pisa
       mʋt . . .>
       . . . aatokoosh awiit   hopaaki-h pílla-h
       but:SS   toward far-TNS   long:path-TNS
       mi̱ti-k-aki̱li-h-o̱   i̱ki-yaash-oosh   pit   pisa-hmat. . .
       come-?-indeed-TNS-PART:DS   father-PREV-FOC:SS away see-when:SS
       'But while he (the prodigal son) was still coming from far off, his
       father saw him and . . .' (Luke 15:20)

In example (67), the sentence implies that the subject did not intend to
go as far as Las Vegas and that the path was longer than expected as a
result.

(67)   Las Vegas pílla-h   iya-tok.
       Las Vegas long:path-TNS go-PT
       'He went all the way to Las Vegas.'

Pilah indicates that the path of motion or orientation does not reach its
goal. In English translations this is often translated as 'to around' or
'from around'. 'Not quite' also frequently captures the sense of Choctaw
pilah.

(68)   Las Vegas pila-h   iya-tok.
       Las Vegas not:quite-TNS go-PST
       'He went to somewhere around Las Vegas.'

(69)   Las Vegas pila-h   mi̱ti-tok.
       Las Vegas not:quite-TNS come-PT
       'He came from the general vicinity of Las Vegas.'

In these examples, Las Vegas is a location that serves to fix the
general orientation of the subject's motion, though there is no
implication that the subject is ever in Las Vegas.
       With temporal expressions, *pilah* seems to serve as an
approximative:

(70)   <himmak pila ha̱, nitak kanohmi keyukma>
       himmak pila-h-a̱   nittak kanohmi kiiyo-kma
       now   not:quite-TNS-AC day   some   NEG-IRR
       'not many days hence' (Acts 1:5)

Both *pilah* and *píllah* are probably related to the verb *pilah* 'to send,
throw'. *Pilah* is homophonous and *píllah* appears to be the g-grade of the
same verb. However, in their uses as path modifiers they should be
regarded as distinct lexical items, probably best grouped with the
directionals.

16. Switch-reference and embedded clauses

Choctaw has an extensive system of switch-reference that signals whether a subordinate clause has the same subject as a superordinate clause.

For the majority of complementizing suffixes, same-subject marking is signalled by -*sh* after the vowel *o*, and -*t* elsewhere. Different-subject marking is signalled by -*n* or vowel nasalization. The only exceptions are the complementizing suffixes -*cha* and -*na*, discussed in section 16.2 below.

It is significant that the ordinary switch-reference markers for clauses (-*t* and -*sh* 'same subject', -*n* or vowel nasalization 'different subject') correspond to nominative (-*t* or -*sh*) and accusative marking (-*n* or vowel nasalization) for noun phrases. A likely historical scenario is that switch-reference markers developed diachronically from case markers.

Switch-reference marking shows up on complement clauses, adverbial clauses, and relative clauses.

16.1. General properties of switch-reference

16.1.1. Introduction

Choctaw switch-reference markers only appear in embedded clauses, and they show coreference or lack of coreference between the subject of the embedded clause and the subject of the higher clause.

(1)   *Kaah sa-nna-haatokoosh,   iskali' ittahobli-li-tok.*
      car   1SI-want-because:SS money   save-1SI-PT
      'Because I wanted a car, I saved money.'

(2)   *Kaah banna-haatoko̲,   iskali' ittahobli-li-tok.*
      car   want-because:DS money   save-1SI-PT
      'Because he wanted a car, I saved money.'

In (1), same-subject marking is appropriate because both clauses have the same subject ('I'), while in (2), the clauses have different subjects.

In examples like those above, it is apparent from the differing subject agreement that the subjects of the two clauses must be different. However, switch-reference marking may also distinguish sentences with third person arguments that would otherwise be ambiguous:

(3)   *Pisachokma-kat*   *ikhą́na-h*
       handsome-COMP:SS   know:N-TNS
       'He$_i$ knows that he$_i$ is handsome.'

(4)   *Pisachokma-ka̱*   *ikhą́na-h*
       handsome-COMP:DS   know:N-TNS
       'He$_i$ knows that he$_j$ is handsome.'

Nearly every subordinate clause in Choctaw ends in a switch-reference marker, which is suffixed to the complementizing suffix of the clause. Table 16.1 shows the same-subject and different-subject forms of some common complementizing suffixes.

Table 16.1. Switch-reference forms of common complementizing suffixes

GLOSS	SAME-SUBJECT FORM	DIFFERENT-SUBJECT FORM
'that'/'when'/COMP	-kat	-ka̱
'that'/'for'/PART	-oosh	-o̱
'because'	-haatokoosh	-haatoko̱
'when'	-hmat	-hma̱
'if'	-kmat	-kma̱
'although'	-ohmakoosh	-ohmako̱
'but'	-ookakoosh	-ookako̱
'and then'	-cha	-na

The following are some examples of switch-reference markers from texts. As they show, the clause bearing a switch-reference marker may either follow or precede the main clause.

(5)   . . . *am-ikhą́na-aḵili-ttook*   *naahollo'*
       1sIII-know:N-indeed-DPAST   white:people
       ano̱pa'   *ano̱poli-li-ahii-kiiyo-ka̱*
       language   speak-1sI-IRR-NEG-COMP:DS
       '. . . they knew that I didn't speak English.'

(6)   *Wakáaya-cha chi-hohchifo' makaachi-h*
       rise:L-SS   2sII-name   say-TNS
       'Stand up and say your name!'

16.1.2. Identity and inclusion

Choctaw generally requires strict identity for same-subject marking. In the available data, Choctaw uses different-subject marking if the subject of one clause is a part or subset of the other subject.

In the following examples, different-subject marking appears when the subject of one clause is a part of the subject of the other.

(7)   <chi nishkin ʋt chi ibetʋblichi hokma, kohchit ish kanchashke>
      chi-nishkin-at   chi-biitablichi-h-oo-kma̱,   kohchi-t
      1sII-eye-NM   2sII-offend-TNS-LINK-IRR:DS   take:out-PART
      ish-ka̱ch-ashkii
      2sI-go:out-EXHORT
      'If thine eye offend thee, pluck it out.' (Matt. 18:9)

(8)   *Itti'   cha̱li-t   issa-li-kma̱   sa-bbak   sa-ttopa-h.*
      wood   chop-PART   stop-1sI-IRR:DS   1sII-arm   1sI-hurt-TNS
      'After I stopped chopping wood, my arm ached.'

In the next group of examples, one subject is included in the set
denoted by the second subject. Different-subject marking is used in the
available data.

(9)   <Chitokaka ya̱ ibafoyuka kʋllot hʋsh hielikma, himak a̱ pi okcha̱ya
      mak okʋt.>
      Chitokaaka-ya̱ ibaafoyyoka-h kallo-t   hash-hiili-kma̱
      Lord-AC   be:inside-TNS   hard-PART   2PI-stand:DU-IRR:DS
      himak-a̱ pi-okchaya-mak-ookat.
      now-AC   1PII-live-DEM?-for
      'For now we live, if ye stand fast in the Lord.' (1 Thess. 3:8)

(10) *Hi-tok-oosh   1930-ako̱   Tucker pit   okl-ii-wiha-ttook.*
      do-PT-PART:SS   1930-CON:AC   Tucker away   PLUR-1PI-move-DPAST
      Makaa-tok-oosh   1936-ako̱   Pearl River wiha-t
      do:so-PT-PART:SS 1936-CON:AC   Pearl River   move-PART
      il-ala-ttook-o̱   aha̱tta-li-sh   ohmi-h.
      1PI-arrive-DPAST-PART:DS   exist:HN-1sI-PART:SS   do-TNS
      'And in 1930, we moved to Tucker. In 1936, we moved to Pearl River,
      and I live (there) now.'

(11) *Aka̱ka' nipi' isht   ala-li-tok-o̱,   oklah il-i̱pa-tok.*
      chicken meat INSTR arrive-1sI-PT-PART:DS   PLUR   1PI-eat-PT
      'I brought chicken and we ate.'

(12) *Il-ittihaalalli-hma̱, ohooyo' i̱la-h   apistikiili-t*
      1PI-marry-WHEN:DS   woman   other-TNS   pester-PART
      ish-no̱yyoowa-h.[1]
      2sI-walk:Y-TNS
      'We got married, but you flirt with other women.'

Payne (1979) discusses switch-reference and inclusion in Chickasaw and
notes that the use of same-subject or different-subject marking is affected
by the person of the subjects of the two clauses, and also by the
interrogative or indicative mood of the clause. This suggests that the
Choctaw data may be more complex than what is described here.

---

1. *Apistikiili-t nowah*, literally 'go around pestering, teasing' is an idiom meaning
'to flirt with, to cheat with'.

16.1.3. Switch-reference and weather verbs

Choctaw shows some variability in the use of switch-reference markers when connecting clauses containing weather verbs, though same-subject marking seems more common.

(13)   Oba-t   íssa-cha   mashii-t   taha-h.
       rain-PART stop:L-SS clear:up-PART complete-TNS
       'It stopped raining and cleared up.'

(14a) Óba-na   oktosha-h.
       rain:-L-DS snow-TNS
       'It rained and snowed.'

(14b) Óba-cha   oktosha-h.
       rain:-L-SS snow-TNS
       'It rained and snowed.'

Payne (1979) notes that same-subject marking is typically used in this environment in Chickasaw.

16.1.4. Switch-reference in discourse

The switch-reference markers that appear on the verbs of subordinate clauses can almost all be accounted for strictly in terms of the grammatical relation "subject." It is generally the case that the Choctaw switch-reference markers signal changes in subject, not changes in agent, topic, or some other notion.

However, there are some cases where switch-reference seems to function in a less strictly syntactic way. Such cases are found with the sentence-initial pro-verbs.

In most spontaneous texts, the majority of sentences begin with one of the pro-verbs hi-, mi-, or a-. These pro-verbs are typically translated 'and then' or 'so' in English, but they are more syntactically and semantically complicated in Choctaw. The basis for choosing one pro-verb over another is not well understood, but it is clear that these pro-verbs are followed by switch-reference markers, as in the following example:

(15)   A-hma   holisso pisáachi-yat atókla-t   si-hohchifo'
       be-when:DS   teacher-NM   again:N-PART   1sII-name
       aachi-ttook. Hi-cha biniili-l-aachi-h-o   maka-ttook.
       say-DPAST   do-SS   sit-1sI-IRR-TNS-PART:DS   say-DPAST
       '[I said my name timidly and softly] and then the teacher said my name. And then she told me to sit down.'

   If we assume that the understood subject of a pro-verb is identical to that of the preceding sentence, then the switch-reference markers on pro-verbs can be interpreted as markers of same-subject or different-subject. The different-subject pro-verb ahma is used because the subject of the preceding sentence is 'I' and the subject of the following sentence is 'the teacher.' Similarly, the same-subject pro-verb *hicha* is appropriate because 'the teacher' is subject of both the preceding and following clauses.

However, there are some examples where this analysis will not work. Consider the following:

(16) *Alla' alhiiha ila-kat   hohchifo' ima-ka*
      child group   other-COMP:SS name   give-COMP:DS
      háklo-li-ttook.   Aa-tok-o   an-akkia nokshópah
      hear:N-1SI-DPAST be-PT-PART:DS I-also   afraid:N
      chóyyohmi-h-oosh   si-hohchifo' lohma-t
      sort:of:Y-TNS-PART:SS 1SII-name   quiet:N-PART
      anooli-li-ttook
      tell-1SI-DPAST
      'I heard the other kids give their names. So I also said my name, timidly and softly.'

In this example, the different-subject pro-verb *aatoko* is used, even though 'I' is the subject of both the preceding and following clauses.

Changes in topic may be important to understanding the switch-reference marking in passages like this. While the grammatical subject of the first sentence is 'I', the topic of the sentence seems to be 'the other kids'. The topic of the second sentence is 'I', and it is apparently the change of topic that is responsible for the use of the different-subject marker.

The following example also shows switch-reference marking in discourse which is not explicable on a simple analysis in terms of preceding and following clauses:

(17) <... akni hʊt nakfish a, Yakeh, pilashash okhlili ma aki ya iba tʊshki
      li tuk oke: himak ninak ak kia oka paki il ipetashke; mikma ish iba
      chukowa cha, ish iba tʊshkashke, yʊmohmi hosh piki im ishtatiaka ya
      il apoanchashke, im achi tok.>
      Aknih-at   nakfish-a,   (i) "Yakkii, piláashaah oklhiili-hma,
      oldest-NM younger:sibling-AC look:here yesterday   dark-when:DS
      a-ki-ya   ibaa-tashki-li-tok-okii. (ii) Himak ninak-akkia
      1SIII-father-AC COM-sleep-1SI-PT-indeed   now   night-too
      oka' pákki' il-apiita-shkii. (iii) Mikma ish-ibaa-chokkóowa-cha
      water grape 1PI-feed-exhort   and:DS 2SI-COMIT-enter:L-SS
      ish-ibaa-tashk-ashkii. (iv) Yamohmi-h-oosh
      2SI-COMIT-sleep-EXHORT   and:so-TNS-PART:SS
      pi-ki' im-ishtaatiaka-ya   il-apowach-ashkii," im-aachi-ttook.
      1PII-father III-descendants-AC 1pI-preserve-EXHORT III-say-PAST
      'The oldest [daughter] said to her younger sister, "Look here, last evening, I slept with my father. Tonight also we will give him wine to drink. Then you enter and sleep with him. And so we will preserve our father's lineage."' (Gen. 19:34)

In this example, the quoted material contains four clauses. It is the pro-verb *yamohmihoosh* at the beginning of clause (iv) which is of interest here. It is marked same-subject, although the subject of the previous clause is 'you' (the younger sister) and the subject of the following clause is 'we' (both sisters). It appears that *yamohmihoosh* is marked same-subject because of clause (ii), which also has 'we' as its subject.

Very little is now known about the organization of sentences into paragraphs or other larger discourse units in Choctaw. It seems likely, however, that switch-reference in the sort of examples discussed here is sensitive to such notions, and that a complete understanding of the switch-reference system requires a better understanding of the discourse structure than is now available.

The problematic instances of switch-reference seem to be confined to the sentence-initial pro-verbs. Sentence-internal switch-reference markers far more reliably depend on strictly syntactic notions of subject. Still, the interplay between switch-reference marking and topic continuity needs more careful study. Payne (1979) discusses similar problems in the use of switch-reference markers in Chickasaw.

16.2. Complement clauses

Complement clauses are those which serve as arguments to main verbs. The following sections discuss ordinary complement clauses, interrogative complement clauses, and equi complements.

16.2.1. Complement clauses with *-ka*

16.2.1.1. Noninterrogative complements

The most neutral complementizing suffix in Choctaw is *-ka*. It appears on the complement clauses to the following verbs, among others:

(18) *yimmih*   'to believe'
      ikhánah   'to know'
      anokfillih   'to think'
      imikalloh   'to be difficult'
      ipalammichih   'to be difficult'
      holaabih   'to tell a lie'
      hopaayih   'to foretell'
      makah   'to say'
      panakloh   'to ask'
      achokmah   'to be good'
      hákloh   'to hear'
      issah   'to let'
      imihaksih   'to forget'
      apiisah   'to charge, measure'

Its switch-reference marked forms are -kat ' same subject' and -ka 'different subject'. The combination of complementizing suffix and switch-reference marker is glossed as a portmanteau, as in the following examples:

(19) John-at   anokfilli-h [pisachokma-kat]
      John-NM think-TNS   goodlooking-COMP:SS
      'John_i thinks that he_i is goodlooking.'

(20) John-at   anokfilli-h [pisachokma-ka]
      John-NM think-TNS   goodlooking-COMP:DS
      'John_i thinks that he_j/she is goodlooking.'

(21) [Hashok is-sa-chali-kat]   kátihmi-h
      grass   2SI-1SIII-cut-COMP:SS how much-TNS
      is-sam-apiis-ahiina-h?
      2SI-1SIII-charge-POT-TNS
      'How much will you charge me to cut the grass for me?'

A morphological peculiarity of -ka is that when the complementizing suffix follows the tense marker -tok, only one k surfaces:

(22) A-palammichi-h   [a-hattak-a   toksáli'
      1sIII-difficult-TNS 1sIII-man-AC   work
      issa-chi-toka].
      quit-CAUS-PT:COMP:DS
      'It's hard on me that they laid my husband off from work.'

There are also alternate forms of these complementizing suffixes, -kato 'same subject' and -kano 'different subject', which are found in some examples. These forms seem especially frequent in the Choctaw Bible, but are less common for modern speakers. It is not clear how the usage of these alternative forms may differ from that of the ordinary complementizing suffixes (-kat, -ka). However, it seems clear that the two forms of this complementizing suffix must be related to the two forms of the nominative and accusative case endings (discussed in chapter 5).

(23) Alhiipa'   chíto-ot timiikachi-kano háklo-li-tok.
      instrument big-NM   beat-COMP:DS2   hear:N-1SI-PT
      'I heard the drum beating.'[2]

(24) <E chiyuhmi hosh e laua kia, Klaist il ibai achʋfa kʋto haknip achʋfa
      pia . . .>
      Ii-chóyyohmi-h-oosh,   ii-lawa-kia; Christ
      1pI-be:alike:Y-TNS-PART:SS 1PI-many-but Christ
      ibaay-achaffa-kato,   haknip achaffa' pi-ya-h.
      COMIT-one-COMP:SS2 body one   1PII-COP-TNS
      'We, being alike, are many; but being one with Christ, we are one
      body.' (Rom. 12:3)

      2. Alhiipa' chíto', literally 'big instrument', is an idiom that means 'drum'.

Some less usual examples of the complementizing suffix -*ka* occur when certain adverbial and adjectival verbs take other verbs as their complements:

(25) *Chopa-toka achiiba-t taha-h.*
buy-PT:COMP:DS while-PART complete-TNS
'He bought it a while back.'

(26) *Pihlichi-kat achokma-h.*
lead-COMP:SS good-TNS
'He leads well.'

(27) *Illi-kat alhlhi-tok.*
die:COMP:SS true-PT
'She really did die.'

(28) *Chahta' anopa' anopoli-li-kat*
Choctaw language speak-1sI-COMP:SS
alhpisaali-l-akili-h-o?
do:correctly-1sI-indeed-TNS-Q
'Am I speaking Choctaw correctly?'

16.2.1.2. Interrogative complements

The complementizing suffix -*ka* also occurs on interrogative complement clauses. For embedded wh-questions, an indefinite is used, but the syntax is otherwise the same.

(29) *Kániimi-ka iya-toka ak-ikháan-o-h.*
WH-COMP:DS go-PT:COMP:DS 1sN-know:L-NEG-TNS
'I don't know why he left.'

(30) *Illípa' lawah kániohmi-h-o nonaachi-toka*
food much how:much-TNS-PART:DS cook-PT:COMP:DS
ak-ikháan-o-h.
1sN-know:L-NEG-TNS
'I don't know how much food she cooked.'

(31) *Ak-ikháan-o-h kániimi-h-o John-at*
1sN-know:L-NEG-TNS why-TNS-PART:DS John-NM
kaniiya-toka.
go:away-PT:COMP:DS
'I don't know why John left.'

However, the syntax of interrogative yes-no complements is rather more complex than that of the noninterrogative complements just discussed.

An interrogative yes-no complement is distinguished from a noninterrogative complement by the use of a special auxiliary verb *nánah*, which may be glossed 'to be the case that':

(32) *Lynn-at   ik-ikháan-o-h*   [*iy-aachi̲-kma̲   na̲na-kat*].
      Lynn-NM N-know:L-NEG-TNS   go-IRR-IRR:DS   be:the:case-COMP:SS
      'Lynn doesn't know if she will go.'[3]

Contrast this example with a non-interrogative complement of the same matrix verb:

(33) *Lynn-at   ik-ikháan-o-h*   [*iy-aachi̲-kat*].
      Lynn-NM N-know:L-NEG-TNS   go-IRR-COMP:SS
      'Lynn doesn't know that she will go.'

The auxiliary verb *na̲nah* invariably takes a complement with the irrealis different subject complementizing suffix *-kma̲*. We can understand this if we imagine that *na̲nah* has an expletive subject which is judged to be different from the subject of its complement. Thus a more careful translation of the sentence above might be as follows:

(34) *Lynn-at   ik-ikháan-o-h*   [CP *pro* [CP *iy-aachi̲-kma̲*]
      Lynn-NM N-know:L-NEG-TNS   go-IRR-IRR:DS
      na̲na-kat].
      be:the:case-COMP:SS
      'Lynn doesn't know [CP if it is the case [CP that she will go.]]'

Proposing a null expletive subject for *na̲nah* solves the switch-reference problem for different-subject *-kma̲*, since the expletive subject of the middle clause ('it') is different from the subject of the lowest clause ('she').

However, there is still a problem with the same-subject switch-reference marker *-kat* in the middle clause. It seems that the middle subject ('it') should also count as different from the highest subject ('Lynn'). Nevertheless, a same-subject marker is used.

This example illustrates a general property of Choctaw switch-reference, which can be stated as follows:

(35) Expletive transparency

      In the following structure:

      $[_{XP}...NP_1...[_{YP}...NP_2...[_{ZP}...NP_3...]]]$

      (where NP_1, NP_2, and NP_3 are the subjects of XP, YP, and ZP respectively),

      if NP_2 is an expletive, then any switch-reference marker on YP signals coreference (or lack of coreference) between NP_1 and NP_3.

In Broadwell (1988b, 1990a) I suggested that this general property of Choctaw switch-reference could be captured formally by a rule that moves or copies the subject agreement features (as well as certain tense and mood features) from ZP into YP when the subject of YP is an

3. Note that in this example the complement clause is extraposed to the right.

expletive. Expletive transparency will also play a role in understanding the switch-reference marking in duration clauses, which are discussed in section 16.3.1.3 of this chapter.

It is also possible to omit switch-reference marking on interrogative yes-no complements, as in the following example:

(36) <. . . Chihowa i̱ nana ʋlhpisa puta ... haponaklokmá, nana chi̱ ka imomaka pisa chi̱ hatok.>

    Chihoowa' i̱-na̱nalhpísa'   *pootta-h . . . haponaklo-kma̱*
    God   III-commandment all-TNS   hear-IRR
    ná̱n-aachi̱-ka   *i̱-mo̱ma-ka pis-aachi̱-h a-ttook.*
    be:the:case-IRR-COMP III-all-COMP see-IRR-TNS COP-DPAST
    '. . . they were to test [Israel] to know whether they would hearken to the commandments of the Lord.' (Judg. 3:4)

Interrogative yes-no complements with *ná̱nah* also have the unusual property that the tense or aspect marking appropriate to the embedded verb may show up on *ná̱nah* as well:

(37) *John-at   sipokn-aachi̱-kma̱ ná̱na-kat*
    John-NM old-IRR-IRR:DS   be:the:case-COMP:SS
    ik-ikháan-o-h.
    N-know:L-NEG-TNS
    'John doesn' t know whether he will be old.'

(38) *John-at   sipokni-kma̱ ná̱n-aachi̱-kat*
    John-NM old-IRR:DS   be:the:case-IRR-COMP:SS
    ik-ikháan-o-h.
    N-know:L-NEG-TNS
    'John doesn't know whether he will be old.'

(39) *John-at   sipokn-aachi̱-kma̱*
    John-NM old-IRR-IRR:DS
    ná̱n-aachi̱-kat   *ik-ikháan-o-h.*
    be:the:case-IRR-COMP:SS N-know:L-NEG-TNS
    'John doesn't know whether he will be old.'

16.2.2. Complement clauses with *-oo*

The following verbs take complement clauses with the complementizing suffix *-oo*. These complementizing suffixes only occur on verbs in with the default tense.

(40)   *makah*   'say, order'
      hopaayih   'foretell'
      panakloh   'ask'
      tohnoh   'hire'

Some examples follow:

(41)   *Iya-l-aachị-h-ọ*   *a-maka-tok.*
       go-1sI-IRR-TNS-PART:DS   1sIII-say-PT
       'She ordered me to go.'

(42)   *Lynn-at   panaklo-tok   [kátimma-h   aa-hilh-aachị-h-ọ].*
       Lynn-NM   ask-PT   where-TNS   LOC-dance-IRR-TNS-PART:DS
       'Lynn asked where to dance.'[4]

When these verbs occur with a past tense complement, the complementizing suffix *-ka* occurs instead of *-oo*:

(43)   *Pam ị-ponaklo-li-tok   [kániimi-h-ọ   katos-at illi-tokạ].*
       Pam III-ask-1sI-PT   why-TNS-PART:DS cat-NM   die-PT:COMP:DS
       'I asked Pam why the cat died.'

The alternative with *-oo* is ungrammatical:

(44)   **Pam ị-ponaklo-li-tok   [kániimi-h-ọ   katos-at*
       Pam III-ask-1sI-PT   why-TNS-PART:DS cat-NM
       illi-tok-ọ].
       die-PT-PART:DS
       'I asked Pam why the cat died.'

The suffix *-oo* is also common in the complements to the positional auxiliaries (see chapter 13):

(45)   *Nosi-kiiyo-h-oosh   ittọ́la-tok.*
       sleep-NEG-TNS-PART:SS   lie:N-PT
       'She lay there not sleeping.' (T1:17)

(46)   *Ópah-at ik-nạnokáay-o-h-oosh   hikị́ya-ttook.*
       owl-NM   N-respond:L-NEG-TNS-PART:SS stand:N-DPAST
       'The owl stood there saying nothing.' (T1:53)

(47)   *Chonna-t   taha-h-oosh   máya-ttook.*
       skinny-PART complete-TNS-PART:SS   be:PL:N-DPAST
       'They were getting skinny.' (T1:2)

(48)   *Alla-at   kochcha' washooha-h-oosh máya-ttook.*
       child-NM   outside   play-TNS-PART:SS be:PL:N-DPAST
       'The children were playing outside.'

16.2.3. Complement clauses with *-cha* and *-na*

Some verbs, usually psychological verbs, may select for the complementizing suffixes *-cha* 'same subject' and *-na* 'different subject'

---

4. From the different-subject marking on the clause, it seems that this example is being interpreted as 'Lynn asked where one can dance', with an arbitrary pronominal subject in the embedded clause.

in their complement clauses, as in the following examples:

(49) *Charles-at   im-ikallo-h   [abíika-cha].*
      Charles-NM   III-difficult-TNS sick:L-SS
      'It's hard on Charles that he got sick.'

(50) *Sa-nokoowa-chi-h   [Pam-at   hamburger a-hokóopa-na].*
      1sII-angry-CAUS-TNS Pam-NM hamburger 1sIII-steal:L-DS
      'It made me mad that Pam stole my hamburger.'

These clauses have not generally been recognized as complement clauses in previous accounts of Choctaw. Nicklas (1974) and Davies (1981), for example, treat -*cha* and -*na* as markers of coordination, so that example (50) would be comparable to the English sentence 'Pam stole my hamburger and it made me mad.'

It will be shown in section 16.3.1.2 below that -*cha* and -*na* generally occur in clauses translated by English 'and'. Despite their translation, they do not show the syntactic properties of coordinate clauses, but of adjunct clauses.

The -*cha* and -*na* that occur in the complements to psychological verbs, however, have a different status, and appear to mark complement clauses. There are two arguments for this conclusion. The first comes from paraphrases, and the second from word order.

Alternate phrasings of sentences with -*cha* and -*na* often have the clause in question marked for nominative case or with an uncontroversial subordinate complementizing suffixes (compare the preceding two examples):

(51) *[Pam-at   hamburger a-hokopa-mat]   sa-nokowa-chi-h.*
      Pam-NM hamburger 1sIII-steal-D:NM 1sII-angry-CAUS-TNS
      'It made me mad that Pam stole my hamburger.'

(52) *Charles-at   im-ikallo-h   [abiika-tokat].*
      Charles-NM   III-difficult-TNS sick-PT:COMP:SS
      'It's hard on Charles that he got sick.'

This is suggestive, but hardly convincing by itself.

A more important piece of evidence that -*cha* and -*na* clauses may serve as arguments comes from word order. In the most neutral word order, adjunct -*cha* and -*na* clauses come before a main clause. Complement -*cha* and -*na* clauses, on the other hand, follow the verb. Consider the following examples:

(53) *Illípa' kaniimi-ka   lowak apákna' aa-nonáachi-cha*
      food   some-COMP:DS   fire top   LOC-cook:L-SS
      apa-t   tahli-h.
      eat-PART complete-TNS
      'He cooked some food on the fire and ate it all.'

(54)   *Si-ataklama-tok* [*Charles-at   iskáli' habíina-na*].
       1sII-bother-PT   Charles-NM money receive:L-DS
       'It bothered me that Charles received the money.'

By the account here, (53) is an adjunct clause and (54) is a complement clause.

Speakers generally judge postposed adjunct clauses with -*cha* or -*na* as awkward or ungrammatical:[5]

(55)   ?*Bill-at hilha-h   [*John-at talóowa-na*].
       Bill-NM   dance-TNS John-NM sing:L-DS
       ('Bill danced and John sang.')

However, with psychological verbs that take -*cha* and -*na* clauses as complements, the preferred position is after the verb. Sentences with psychological verbs in which the -*cha* and -*na* clauses precede the verb are also acceptable, but rarely volunteered.[6]

There may also be some -*cha* and -*na* complements which normally precede the verb that subcategorizes for them. Such may be the case with verbs of perception *hákloh* 'to hear' and *písah* 'to see'.

(56)   <Himonna isuba nuchi ʋt samahanchi na haⁿkloli.>
       Himonna-h issóbah innochi-yat sammaháchi-na
       now-TNS   horse   collar-NM   jingle:HN-DS
       háklo-li-h.
       hear:N-1sI-TNS
       'I hear the horse collar jingling.' (Byington 1915:322)

(57)   *Bonnie-at   bookóshi'-ma issi' átta-na písa-tok   miyah.*
       Bonnie-NM creek-D:AC   deer be:L-DS see:N-PT HSAY
       'Bonnie saw the deer at the creek, they say.'

There is a distinct argument from word order for examples like (57). If we attempted to interpret this example with -*na* as an adjunct clause, 'The deer was at the creek and Bonnie saw it, they say', then the example would contain a center-embedded adjunct clause. However, such a word order is quite marked for adjunct clauses in general:

---

5. However, Munro (2005) includes a folkloric text in Chickasaw which ends with a postposed -*cha* clause, and she notes that this appears to be a rhetorical device in that language. I am not aware of such examples in Choctaw.

6. Linker (1987) mentions the fact that clauses marked with -*cha* and -*na* can be extraposed (i.e., occur to the right of the main verb). She takes this fact as more evidence that the switch-reference marking of -*cha* and -*na* clauses cannot be determined by linear order. However, she does not discuss whether extraposed clauses are complements or not. As stated in the text, I believe that in general extraposed word order is possible only for -*cha* and -*na* clauses which are complements of a psychological verb.

(58)   ??*John-at* [*Mary-at   taloowa-hma̲*] *hilha-tok   miyah.*
       John-NM   Mary-NM   sing-when:DS dance-PT HSAY
       'When Mary sang, John danced, they say.'

While center-embedding is highly marked for adjunct clauses, it is to be expected for complement clauses.

Since some verbs select complement *-cha* and *-na* clauses, it is clear that *-cha* and *-na* can be complementizing suffixes. But it is simpler to claim that they are always complementizing suffixes than to claim that they are complementizing suffixes in some instances and conjunctions in others.

The following verbs are those that take *-cha* and *-na* complements:

(59)   *nokoowachih*   'anger'
       naayoppah   'be glad'
       noklhaka̲chah   'be surprised'
       i̲kalloh   'be difficult for'
       i̲palammichih   'be difficult for'
       i̲taklamah   'bother'
       pi̲sah   'see'
       ha̲kloh   'hear'

16.2.3.1. *Tohnoh,* 'order', 'hire'

The verb *tohnoh* 'order, hire' is a special case. It appears with *-na* before the verb which corresponds to its complement in English:

(60)   *Aaron tóhno-li-na   iya-tok.*
       Aaron   order:L-1SI-DS   go-PT
       'I ordered Aaron to go (and he went).'

Some evidence for an analysis in which the 'order' clause is the main clause at some level of representation comes from the fact that an NP contained in the 'order' clause may be the antecedent for a reflexive in the following clause:

(61)   <Mihma tohno na yʊmmʊt ilapa apehʊt a̲ya cha, ʊbanumpa isht ahanta he . . .>
       Mihma tóhno-na   yamm-at ilaapa apiiha-t
       and   order:L-DS that-NM self   be:with-PART
       á̲ya-cha   abano̲pa' isht-aha̲tt-ahii-h.
       go:along:L-SS preach   INSTR-be:HN-IRR-TNS
       'He_i commanded them to go with him_i and preach.' (Mark 3:14)

The verb *tohnoh* may also appear with a complement bearing the morphology usual for purpose clauses, *-aachi̲* + *-h* + *-oo* + switch-reference.

(62)   *Chi-tohno-h-a̲   hoshi' híshi' patalhpo'*
       2sII-hire-TNS-Q bird   feather bed

isht   ish-im-on-aachị-h-ọ?
INSTR 2SI-III-arrive-IRR-TNS-PART:DS
'Did she hire you to bring the feather bed to her?'

It appears that the person hired is an argument of both clauses, given that it may occur marked either nominative or accusative:

(63)   *John-at/John-a̱   hashshok amoochi-h-ọ*
       John-NM/John-AC grass   mow-TNS-PART:DS
       tohno-li-h.
       hire-1SI-TNS
       'I hired John to mow the grass.'

16.2.4. Complement alternations with psychological verbs

As described in the preceding section, many psychological verbs take object complements marked with *-cha* or *-na*. There is another group of psychological verbs, however, that show an alternation in valence or complement type. These verbs have two arguments: an event (the *causal events*) which causes person (the *experiencer*) to have an emotion. The variation concerns which of these arguments is presented as the subject of the psychological verb.

In the experiencer object variant, the verb appears with an apparent clausal subject and the experiencer of the psychological state is the object of the verb. In the experiencer subject variant, the experiencer of the psychological state is the subject of the psychological verb and the clause is a complement marked with *-cha* or *-na*. Compare the following examples:

(64)   [*Ofi-it   wohwa-t*]   *Charles nokshoobli-h.*
       dog-NM bark-PART Charles frighten-TNS
       'The dog barking frightened Charles.'

(65)   *Charles-at nokshoopa-h*   [*ofi-it   wóhwa-na*]
       Charles-NM be:frightened-TNS dog-NM bark:L-DS
       'Charles is frightened by the dog barking.'

In example (64), *nokshooblih* 'to frighten' is a transitive verb with an apparent clausal subject and an NP object. The verb of the causal event is followed by the participial suffix *-t* (section 13.4). In example (65), however, the psychological verb is *nokshoopah* 'to be afraid', and the causal event clause is a complement marked with *-na*. Note that the form of the psychological verb changes as well. The experiencer object verb *nokshooblih* contains the suffix *-li*, which typically occurs on transitives, while the experiencer subject verb *nokshoopah* contains the suffix *-a*, which typically occurs on intransitives (section 8.1)

Another pair of verbs with similar properties is *ataklamah* 'to be bothered by', *ataklammih* 'to bother':

(66) *Pam-at ataklama-h [Charles-at talóowa-na]*.
Pam-NM bother-TNS   Charles-NM sing:L-DS
'Pam is bothered by Charles singing.'

(67) *[Charles-at taloowa-t] Pam ataklammi-h*.
Charles-NM sing-PART Pam bother-TNS
'Charles's singing bothers Pam.'

The syntactic properties of these two alternants are not well-understood, and need further study.

16.2.5. Complement clauses with -a̱ and -at

Adjectival complements to some verbs appear with the complementizing suffixes *-at* 'same subject' and *-a̱* 'different subject'.

(68) *Am-alla' nakni' lhampko-ya̱ sa-banna-h*.
1sIII-child male   strong-AC   1sII-want-TNS
'I want my son to be strong.'

These complementizing suffixes also appear on some verbal complements, and in this case they are apparently always preceded by the irrealis *-ahii*.[7]

(69) *Taloow-ahii-yat sa-komota-h*.
sing-IRR-COMP:SS 1sII-fear-TNS
'I'm afraid to sing.'

(70) <Holhpokuna ho̱ falamʋt Helot a̱ okla ik im ono ka hi a̱, Chihowa hʋt
i̱ miha hatuk o̱, . . .>
Holhpokonna-h-o̱   falaama-t   Herod-a̱   oklah
dream-TNS-PART:DS return-PART Herod-AC PLUR
ik-im-óon-ok-ahii-ya̱   Chihoowah-at
N-III-arrive:L-NEG-IRR-COMP:DS God-NM
i̱-miha-haatoko̱ . . .
III-say-because:DS
'Because God warned them in a dream that they should not return to Herod . . .' (Matt. 2:12)

16.2.6. Complement clauses without overt complementizing suffixes

A few verbs in Choctaw take clausal complements which have no accompanying complementizing suffix, as in the following examples:

7. There is a striking similarity in Koasati, where the cognate *-á:hi* 'intention' may be used with the same-subject switch-reference marker in the complement to certain verbs (Kimball 1991:181):
Há:lo-l-á:hi-k   ca-bàn.
hear-1sI-intent-SS 1sII-want
'I want to hear it.'

(71) *John-at   iya-tok   sa-yimmi-h.*
      John-NM go-PT   1sII-believe-TNS
      I believe John went.'

(72) *John-at   yopi-sh   átta-h   písa-li-tok.*
      John-NM swim-PART:SS be:N-TNS see:N-1sI-PT
      'I saw John swimming.'

The verbs that allow this kind of complement all have the semantics of thought, belief, or perception. This may correlate with a crosslinguistic tendency for complements of these verbs to be reduced or less than fully clausal.

16.2.7. Complements to verbs of speech

The syntax of quotation is particularly complex in Choctaw. There are two types of quoting constructions, which I will call the simple and the complex.

In simple quoting constructions there is one verb of saying and the quoted material is its complement. When the quote is indirect, it is usually followed by *miyah* 'say, hearsay' and a switch-reference marker (73); when the quote is direct it is not (74)–(75).[8]

(73) *John-at   chaah-a   miya-h-o̱   ish-maka-h.*
      John-NM tall-TNS hearsay-TNS-PART:DS 2sI-say-TNS
      'You said that John is tall.'

(74) *"Náni'-ma̱   kátak   ish-aa-hokli-tok?"   a̱t*
      fish-D:AC   where 2sI-LOC-catch-PT   come:and
      i̱-ponaklo-h.
      III-ask-TNS
      '"Where did you catch those fish?" he asked.' (T4:3)

(75) *"Táani-cha   oh-okaami-h!"   ópah   tíkchi-it*
      get:up:L-SS PL-wash:face-TNS owl   wife-NM
      aachi-ttook.
      say-DPAST
      '"Y'all get up and wash your faces!" the owl's wife said.' (T1:33)

The complex quoting construction uses two verbs of saying, one preceding the quoted material and the other following it.[9] The first verb of saying is subordinated to the second, and bears a same- subject switch-reference marker:

8. In these examples there are several distinct verbs glossed 'say'. So far as I know, there is no syntactic difference between them.
9. Pam Munro (p.c., 1986) has called this the frame construction, and notes that it is quite common crosslinguistically, especially in American Indian languages. Some other languages with this construction are Cree (Ahenakew 1987:145), Lahu (Matisoff 1973:468), and Yatzachi el Bajo Zapotec (Butler 1980).

(76) *Ishki-it   maka-hmat "Tamaaha' iya-li-h,"   i̱-maka-tok.*
  mother-NM say-SS   town   go-1SI-TNS III-say-PT
  'Her mother said, "I'm going to town."'

(77) *Chókfih-at i̱-maka-hmat "Okmocho̱-t   hilha-yo̱*
  rabbit-NM III-say-SS   close:eyes-PART dance-DS
  taloowa-l-aachi̱-h," aachi-ttook.
  sing-1SI-IRR-TNS   say-DPAST
  'The rabbit said, "Close your eyes and dance while I sing."' (T3:4)

The complex quoting construction can also be used with indirect quotations, in which case the quoted material is followed by *miyah* 'hearsay'. *Miyah* is followed by a switch-reference marker which is sensitive to coreference between the subject of the quoted material and the following verb of saying.

The switch-reference marker on the first verb of saying must always be same-subject, since it always has the same subject as the final verb of saying. However, the switch-reference marker that follows *miyah* may be either same-subject or different subject, since the subject of the quotation need not be the same as the subject of the verb of saying.[10]

(78) *Ishki-it   i̱-maka-hmat tamaaha' iya-h   miya-h-oosh*
  mother-NM III-say-SS   town   go-TNS say-TNS-PART:SS
  i̱-maka-tok.
  III-say-PT
  'Her mother$_i$ said that she$_i$ was going to town.'

(79) *Ishki-it   i̱-maka-hmat Charles-at   ahpali-tok*
  mother-NM III-say-SS   Charles-NM kiss-PT
  miya-h-o̱   i̱-maka-tok.
  say-TNS-PART:DS III-say-PT
  'Her mother said that Charles kissed her.'

Both the simple and complex constructions occur frequently in texts, with the complex one slightly more common.[11]

Both the simple and the complex constructions may also occur with the verb *ahnih* 'think':[12]

---

10. In sentences like (78), where there is a same-subject relation between the verb of saying and the quoted material, *miyah-oosh* may be phonologically reduced to *miyaash* or the same-subject marker may appear directly on the verb of the quoted material, yielding *iyaash* in one variant of (78).

11. For some reason, complex quoting constructions are rare in the Choctaw translation of the New Testament. Given their frequency in modern spoken Choctaw, this may suggest that the translation is unidiomatic in this respect.

12. *Ahnih* is a difficult verb to gloss in Choctaw, since it covers a broader range than any English verb. Its meanings include 'think', 'like', 'hope', 'wish', and 'intend'. For simplicity I gloss it 'think' wherever it occurs.

(80) *"Kátina   mato   niya-h-chi?"   ahni-ttook.*
      why   that:NM fat-TNS-wonder think-DPAST
      '"Why is that one fat?" she thought.' (T1:14)

(81) *"Apiisachi-li-kmato ikhána-l-ahina-h"   áhni-cha* . . .
      watch-1sI-if:SS   know:N-1sI-POT-TNS think:L-SS
      '"If I watch, I'll know," she thought and . . .' (T1:15)

(82) *Anokfilli-hmat, "Ilappak-akinih-o   illípa'-ma*
      think-SS   here-indeed-FOC:AC food-D:AC
      aay-ishi-li-kmat hopaaki' ak-íiy-ok-ahina-h,'   áhni-cha . . .
      LOC-get-1sI-if:SS far   1sN-go:L-NEG-POT-TNS think:L-SS
      '"If I get that food right here, I won't have to go far," he thought.'
      (T5:2)

Although the verb *anokfillih* also means 'think', there are no volunteered examples in which it occurs as the main verb with a direct quote. All cases of direct quotes of thoughts use the verb *ahnih*.

A subtype of the complex construction, or possibly a third construction type, consists of a quotation followed by two verbs of saying or thinking, the first of which is subordinated to the second.

(83) *"Alla-to   okla-kátihmi-haatoko?" aachi-t tíkchi'*
      child-NM2 PL-do:what-because:DS   say-SS wife
      i-ponaklo-h.
      III-ask-TNS
      '"What's wrong with the kids?" he asked his wife.' (T1:47–48)

(84) *Hihma " Shokani-ito illípa' yohmi-ka oklah*
      then   ant-NM2   food   do:so-DS PLUR
      ashaachi-tok," ahni-t   anokfílli-cha iya-tok.
      put:away-PT   think-SS think:L-SS   go-PT
      '"The ants put some food away," he thought, and went (away).'
      (T2:14–16)

16.2.8. Equi complements

Equi complements are those that lack person marking. They are somewhat comparable to English infinitivals. However, English infinitival complements lack both tense marking and person marking, while Choctaw equi complements lack only person marking. There are two types of equi complements in Choctaw, those with no overt complementizing suffix and those with the *-ka* complementizing suffix.

16.2.8.1. Equi complements without overt complementizing suffixes

This type of equi complement in Choctaw consists of a simple verb stem followed by the default tense marker *-h*. They are formally identical to the ordinary third person (citation) form, but they are used as the same-subject complement of another verb. The following verbs may take this type of equi complement:

(85)   *ahnih*   'to think'
       bannah   'to want'
       yimmih   'to believe'

The following sentences show equi complements. In each case, one might expect subject marking on the embedded verb, but it does not appear.

(86)   *Tamaaha' iya-h   sa-banna-h.*
       town   go-TNS 1sII-want -TNS
       'I want to go to town.'

(87)   *Hohchafo-h yimmi-li-h.*
       hungry-TNS believe-1sI-TNS
       'I believe I'm hungry.' (Davies 1986:32)

16.2.8.2. Equi complements with -*ka*

Some verbs take equi complements with the complementizing suffix -*ka*, as noted by Davies (1986:91). The verbs involved include the following:

(88)   *ikhánah*   'to know'
       anokfokah   'to intend'
       nokshoopah   'to be afraid'
       iponnah   'to be skilled at; to know how to'

The following sentences show examples of equi complements with -*ka*:

(89)   *Chi-sso-kat   ikhána-li-h.*
       2sII-hit-COMP:SS know:N-1sI-TNS
       'I know that I hit you.'

(90)   *Hilha-kat   sa-nokshoopa-h.*
       dance-COMP:SS 1sII-afraid-TNS
       'I am afraid to dance.' (Davies 1981:43)

(91)   *Baliil-aachi-kat ikhána-li-h.*
       run-IRR-COMP:SS know-1sI-TNS
       'I know I will run.'

(92)   *Tamaaha' iy-ahina-kat   si-anokfoka-h-ookakoosh,*
       town   go-POT-COMP:SS 1sII-intend-TNS-but:SS
       am-ihaksi-tok   aachiini-tok.
       1sIII-forget-PT EVID-PT
       'I intended to go to town, but I forgot.'

(93)   <huchim ulla ya̲ na hochukma isht ima kʋt huchimponna chatuk>
       Hachim-alla-ya̲   naa-hoochókma' isht   im-a-kat
       2PIII-child-AC   thing-good:PL   INSTR III-give-COMP:SS

hachim-ponna-hchaa-tok.
2PIII-skilled-generic-PT
'You [plural] are skilled at giving good things to your children.' (Matt.
7:11)

In all of these examples, the embedded verb lacks agreement for its
subject.

16.3. Adjunct clauses

16.3.1. Temporal clauses

16.3.1.1. Ordinary temporal clauses

The complementizing suffix -hma indicates 'when'. Its switch-reference
forms are -hmat 'same subject' and -hma 'different subject'.

(94) Mihmat   iskáli' oklah i-taha-h   fókkaali-hmat,
      and:when money PLUR III-complete-TNS about-when:SS
      alikchi-t   iskáli' kaniimi ittahobbi-hmat oklah miti-ttook.
      doctor-PART money some   gather-when:SS PLUR come-DPAST
      'And when their money was about gone, they earned some money by
      doctoring, and came.'

Unlike English 'when', Choctaw -hma cannot be used for events that
have not yet taken place. These events must use the irrealis
complementizing suffix -kma 'if':

(95) Aaittanáaha' ona-li-kmat,   chi-písa-l-aachi-h.
      church   arrive:1SI-if:SS 2SI-see:N-1SI-IRR-TNS
      'I'll see you when I get to church.'

The English distinction between 'if I get to church' and 'when I get to
church' cannot be directly translated in Choctaw. The English distinction
is one of degrees of certainty about future events. (Of course, it is possible
to express degree of certainty through other means in Choctaw.) In
Choctaw, all future events are irrealis, and so they must use the irrealis
complementizing suffix -kma.

Initial phrases that identify the time frame for a following event are
usually followed by -oo in modern Choctaw:

(96) Háshi'=kanálli' toklo-h fókkaali-h-o   ot   ii-nosi-ttook.
      clock   two-TNS about-TNS-PART:DS go& 1PI-sleep-DPAST
      'We went to sleep at about two o'clock.'

(97) Nittak ammona-m-∅-akili-h-o,   Chihoowah-at yakni'-pa
      day   first-DEM-COP-EMPH-TNS-PART:DS God-NM   world-D:AC
      ikbi-ttook.
      make-DPAST
      'In the beginning, God created this world.'

The suffix -*oo* is also appropriate for events that are simultaneous:

(98)   *Sa-nosi-h-ǫ*   *ǫba-tok.*
        1sII-sleep-TNS-PART:DS   rain-PT
        'It rained while I slept.' (Nicklas 1974:254)

In older Choctaw material, -*ka* is more frequent in these contexts:

(99)   <Mih nitak mak inli ka . . .>
        Mih   nittak-m-Ø-akịli-ka . . .
        same day-DEM-COP-EMPH-COMP:DS
        'On the same day . . .' (Matt. 22:23)

(100)   <Vmmona ka Anumpa hʋt ahanta mʋt, . . .>
        Ammona-ka   anǫpah-at   ahátta-mat, . . .
        first-COMP   word-NM   be:HN-D:NM
        'In the beginning was the word, . . .' (John 1:1)

The suffix -*ka* is still used with some initial temporal phrases in Choctaw, however:

(101)   *Tịkba-ka̠   tǫksáali-cha   anǫti' ịpa-h.*
        first-COMP:DS work:L-SS   and   eat-TNS
        'First he worked, and then he ate.' (Linker 1987:98)

16.3.1.2. Temporal sequence clauses

The switch-reference markers -*cha* and -*na* are used to link clauses in temporal sequence, and are often translated as 'and', as in the following examples:

(102)   *Okti-yat wiiki-t   tali'=anǫpoli' api' liwiilú-chi-na*
        ice-NM   heavy-PART telephone   pole break:L-CAUS-DS
        alla' alhtakla' pihlúichi'   anǫpa   il-ị-bóhl-ahii-kiiyo-na
        child orphan   leader:NML word   1PI-III-send:L-IRR-NEG-DS
        nowa-t   1PI-go:DU-DPAST
        walk-PART 1PI-go:DU-DPAST
        'The ice was heavy and broke the telephone phones and we couldn't send word to the superintendent of the orphanage, and so we walked.'

(103)   *Nashooba-yat nipi' toshaafa'-ma̠ hókli-cha apa-t   tahli-h.*
        wolf-NM   meat piece-D:AC   catch:L-SS eat-PART complete-TNS
        'The wolf caught the piece of meat and ate it up.' (T5:16-17)

The analysis of -*cha* and -*na* has been controversial. They have been cited by Davies (1981) and Nicklas (1974) as coordinating conjunctions. However, Linker (1987) has shown convincingly that they are better analysed as subordinate complementizing suffixes.

One of Linker's arguments is that clauses linked by the putative coordinators *-cha* and *-na* may not be independently marked for tense.[13] Instead, they must be interpreted with the tense of the following clause:

(104) *John-at taloowa-tok-na Bill-at hilh-aachi̱-h.
       John-NM sing-PT-DS   Bill-NM dance-IRR-TNS
       ('John sang and Bill will dance.')

(105) John-at talóowa-na Bill-at hilh-aachi̱-h.
       John-NM sing:L-DS Bill-NM dance-IRR-TNS
       'John will sing and Bill will dance.'

However, there is in general no restriction on conjoining sentences with different tenses, as the following sentences with a zero conjunction and with the conjunction *anó̱ti'* demonstrate:

(106) Robert-ato   Jackie ahpali-h; Heather-ato   Joe
       Robert-NM2 Jackie kiss-TNS   Heather-NM2 Joe
       itti-haalall-aachi̱-h.
       RCP-marry-IRR-TNS
       'Robert kissed Jackie, and Heather is going to marry Joe.'

(107) John-at   taloowa-tok anó̱ti' Bill-at hilh-aachi̱-h.
       John-NM sing-PT   and   Bill-NM dance-IRR-TNS
       'John sang, and Bill will dance.'

There is some additional evidence for the claim that clauses connected by *-cha* and *-na* are not coordinate beyond that mentioned by Linker. This evidence concerns the acceptability of questioning the subject of the second clause. As the following examples show, such questions are acceptable:

(108) John-at   talóowa-na Bill-at hilha-h.
       John-NM sing:L-DS Bill-NM dance-TNS
       'John sang and Bill danced.'

(109) Kátah-oosh John-at   talóowa-na hilha-h?
       who-FOC:NM John-NM sing:L-DS   dance-TNS
       'Who₁ did John sing and t₁ dance?'

If clauses linked by *-cha* or *-na* were coordinate, one would expect that extraction from one of the conjuncts would be ungrammatical, due to the Coordinate Structure Constraint (Ross 1968). However examples like (109) show that this is not the case. Additionally, we know that Choctaw does show effects of the Coordinate Structure Constraint in other environments, since clauses connected by the conjunction *anó̱ti'* obey the

---

13. Linker reports an exception to this general principle: a clause marked with different-subject *-na* may be preceded by the irrealis *-aachi̱*, but not by *-tok*. As noted in chapter 11, this follows under an approach that treats the irrealis as a modal element rather than a tense marker.

Coordinate Structure Constraint.[14]

(110) *John-at   taloowa-h aṉóti' Bill-at   hilha-h.*
      John-NM sing-TNS   and   Bill-NM dance-TNS
      'John sang and Bill danced.'

(111) *Kátah-oosh John-at   taloowa-h aṉóti' hilha-h.*
      who-FOC:NM John-NM sing-TNS   and   dance-TNS
      ('Who did John sing and dance?')

16.3.1.3. Temporal duration clauses

Clauses marked with *-na* are also used in expressions of duration. A clause marked with *-na* is followed by a temporal verb:

(112) *John-at   hiẖílha-na   onna-h.*
      John-NM dance:HN-DS   dawn-TNS
      'John danced until dawn.'

(113) *Óba-na   shohbi-h.*
      rain:L-DS day:pass-TNS
      'It rained all day.'

(114) *Híka'-m̱a ish-hop̱ása-na hopaaki-h.*
      gum-D:AC   2SI-chew:L-DS long:time:pass-TNS
      'You've been chewing that gum for a long time.'

(115) <Chi haksi na hopaki kʊt kátiohma chi̧ cho?>
      Chi-háksi-na   hopaaki-kat   katiohm-aachi̧-h-cho?
      2SII-drunk:L-DS   long:time:pass-COMP:SS how:much-IRR-TNS-Q
      'How long will you be drunk?' (1 Sam. 1:14)

The temporal verbs that occur in this construction include *onnah* 'to dawn', *shohbih* 'for a day to pass', *hopaakih* 'for a long time to pass'. Although the English translation does not suggest a verb, *biliiyah* 'forever' also belongs in this group:

(116) <. . . sa tikba a noho̱wa na bilia hi oke>
      . . . sa-tikba' aa-nohó̱wa-na   bílliy-ahii-okii.
      1SII-front   LOC-walk:HN-DS forever:G-IRR-EMPH
      '. . . [they] should walk before me forever.' (1 Sam. 2:30)

(117) <. . . yʊmmak o̱ ahanta na bilia hi o̱ isht ona la hi oke>
      yammak-o̱   ahátta-na   bílliy-ahii-o̱   isht
      there-FOC:AC live:HN-DS   forever-G IRR-PART:DS   INSTR

---

14. *Aṉóti'* seems to mean something like 'and then' for many speakers. It seems plausible that there might therefore be some restriction that the event in the second conjunct occur after the event in the first conjunct.
   Byington (1915:44) defines *aṉóti'* as both an adverb 'again, once more, a second time, further, and' and as a conjunction 'and'.

ona-l-ahii-okii.
arrive-1SI-IRR-EMPH
'I will bring him so that he can live there forever.' (1 Sam. 1:22)

A quantified noun referring to a time period may also serve as the second part of a duration expression.

(118) <. . . ile luyuhmi na hushi tahlapi tok.>
ili-lóyyohmi-na   hashi'   tálhlhaapi-ttook.
RFL-hide:Y-DS   month   five-DPAST
'She hid herself for five months.' (Luke 1:25)

The tense or mood appropriate to the verb of the clause preceding *-na* shows up on the temporal verb:

(119) *Óba-na   shohb-aachini-h   chim-ahwah?*
rain:L-DS   day:pass-IRR-TNS   2SIII-seem:Q:TNS
'Does it seem to you that it will rain all day?'

(120) *Hihilha-li-na   shohbi-tok.*
dance:HN-1SI-DS   day:pass-PT
'I danced all day.'

For most temporal verbs, it is ungrammatical to reverse the pattern and allow the temporal verb to precede *-na*:

(121) **Shohbi-na oba-tok.*
day:pass-DS   rain-PT
('It rained all day')

However, for unknown reasons, the reversed pattern is the norm for a few temporal verbs:

(122) *Poláka-na mihchi-li-tok.*
finally-DS   do-1SI-PT
'I finally did it.'

(123) *Chüki-na illi-h.*
early-DS   dic-TNS
'He died early.'

Temporal verbs seem transparent for purposes of switch-reference marking. That is, when a sentence with a duration clause is embedded, its switch-reference marker is coindexed with the subject of the clause preceding *-na,* as in the following example:

(124) *John-at [e [pro hihilha-na] onna-kat]*
John-NM   dance:HN-DS   dawn-COMP:SS
ikhána-h.
know:N-TNS
'John knows that he danced until dawn.'

Since temporal verbs like *onnah* 'to dawn' have expletive subjects, this is another example of the expletive transparency discussed above for interrogative yes-no complements.

16.3.2. Purpose clauses

Purpose clauses are generally indicated through use of the irrealis *-aachi* plus either *-ka* or *-oo*, generally followed by a switch-reference marker. In modern Choctaw, *-oo* is the more frequent complementizing suffix for purpose clauses, while both *-oo* and *-ka* are found in older Choctaw materials.

(125) <. . . isht ʋla chi ho, in tishu ʋhleha ha pit tilheli tok.>
 . . . *isht al-aachi̱-h-o̱*   *i̱-tishoh*   *alhiihah-a̱*
 INSTR   come-IRR-TNS-PART:DS III-servant group-AC
 pit   tilhiili-ttook.
 away   send:PLOBJ-DPAST
 'He sent his servants to bring them.' (Matt. 22:3)

(126) <. . . pisa chi̱ hosh mi̱ko ʋt ant chukowa mʋt, . . .>
 . . . *pis-aachi̱-h-oosh*   *mi̱kko-yat*   *a̱t*   *chokkowa-hmat, . . .*
 see-IRR-TNS-PART:SS chief-NM   come:and enter-when:SS
 'When the king entered to see them...' (Matt. 22:11)

The following passage from the Bible shows a purpose clause in *-ka*:

(127) <Kʋta chia hoh cho? achit ont i̱ ponakla chi̱ ka, Chu okla hʋt . . . pit tihleli na . . .>
 'Ká̱tah   chi-a-h-oh-cho?'   *aachi-t*   *o̱t*
 who   2SII-be-TNS-LINK-Q say-PART go:and
 i̱-ponakl-aachi̱-ka, Jew oklah-at . . . pit
 III-ask-IRR-COMP   Jew people-NM away
 tilhíili-na . . .
 send:L-DS
 The Jews sent (priests and Levites from Jerusalem) to ask him, "Who are you?", and . . .' (John 1:19)

Most speakers now prefer the complementizing suffix *-oo* in contexts like these:

(128) *Palláska' ikbi-l-aachi̱-h-oosh*   *bótta' chopa-li-tok.*
 bread   make-1SI-IRR-TNS-PART:SS flour   buy-1SI-PT
 'I bought flour to make bread.'

(129) *Ílhpak im-atahli-l-aachi̱-oosh*   *ala-li-h.*
 food   III-prepare-1SI-IRR-PART:SS arrive-1SI-TNS
 'I came to prepare food.'

In the Choctaw Bible, negative purpose clauses (or "lest" clauses) are often formed with a negative verb, the irrealis *-aachi-*, the complementizing suffix *-ka*, and the suffix *-ako̱*:

(130) <. . . itin lumaka iksho ka chi kak o, hatak moma kvt ilap tekchi ak
       inli ho ieshikma, . . .>
       . . . ittilomaaka' iksh-ok-aachi-k-ako,   hattak móma-kat
       fornication   not:exist-NEG-IRR-COMP-DS man   all-COMP:SS
       ilaap tikchi-akili-h-o   iishi-kma, . . .
       self   wife-EMPH-TNS-PART:DS take-IRR:DS
       'To avoid fornication, let every man take his own wife...' (1 Cor. 7:2)

More rarely, purpose clauses are shown with participles in -t:

(131) Hattak=shaali' chopa-t   tamaaha' iya-li-tok.
       car   buy-PART town   go-1SI-PT
       'I went to town to buy a car.'

In some cases, the idea of purpose or intention is merely implied by the
temporal sequence of the two actions.

(132) <Il im anumpuli na Chentail ʋt okchaya chi ka pim alʋmmi hoke.>
       Il-im-anopóoli-na Chentail-at   okcháy-aachi-ka
       1PI-III-talk:L-DS   Gentiles-NM   live:N-IRR-COMP
       pim-alammi-h-okii.
       1PIII-forbid-TNS-indeed
       'They forbid us to talk to the Gentiles that they might be saved.' (1
       Thess. 2:16)

16.3.3. Manner clauses

Manner clauses are generally expressed with the complementizing
suffix -oo:

(133) Nosi-kiiyo-h-oosh   ittóla-tok.
       sleep-NEG-TNS-PART:SS lie:N-PT
       'She lay there not sleeping.' (T1:17)

(134) Opah-at ik-nanokáay-o-h-oosh   hikíya-ttook.
       owl-NM   N-say:something:L-NEG-TNS-PART:SS stand:N-DPAST
       'The owl stood there saying nothing.' (T1:53)

There are also some cases of -ka on manner clauses:

(135) Hina' ichaapa-ka   aya-tokla-tok.
       road   opposite-COMP:DS go:along-DU-PT
       'They were walking along on opposite sides of the road.'

16.3.4. "According to" clauses

"According to" clauses precede a main clause and express the source
of evidence for the main assertion or the expectations with respect to
which the main assertion is made. These clauses are marked with the
complementizing suffix -ka.

(136) *Anokfilli-li-kano   chíhto-h.*
think-1SI-COMP:DS2 big:H-TNS
'He's bigger than I thought.'

(137) *Anokfilli-li-ka̲   John-at pisachokma-h.*
think-1SI-COMP:DS John-NM goodlooking-TNS
'I think John is goodlooking; according to what I think, John is goodlooking.'

(138) *J. P.-at ashshowa-ka̲   okhata' álhlhi' o̲t*
J. P.-NM smell-COMP:DS ocean   edge   go:and
atta-tok ahooba-h.
be-PT   seem-TNS
'J. P. smells like he's been to the beach.'

(139) *Ish-maka-tokano   ik-ó̲b-o-tok.*
2SI-say-PT:COMP:DS2 N-rain:L-NEG-PT
'It didn't rain as long as you said.'

As discussed in chapter 12, an initial "according to" clause licenses a shift in the interpretation of evidentials in the following main clause.

16.3.5. Reason clauses

Reason clauses are indicated through the complementizing suffix *-haatokoo-* or *-haatokooka-*. These complementizing suffixes are usually followed by a switch-reference marker.

(140) *Kaah sa-banna-haatokoosh, iskáli' ittahobli-li-tok.*
car   1SI-want-because:SS   money gather-1SI-PT
'Because I wanted a car, I saved money.'

(141) *Tákkon-at a̲-lawa-haatokoosh,   páska'=chapóli' ikbi-l-aachi̲-h.*
apple-NM 1SIII-many-because:SS pie   make-1SI-IRR-TNS
'Because I have lots of apples, I'm going to make a pie.'

Occasionally the switch-reference marker is omitted:

(142) *Kaniiya-li-tok [yakni' i̲la-h   pi̲sa-h*
leave-1SI-PT   land   different-TNS see-TNS
sa-banna-haatokoo].
1SI-want-because
'I left because I wanted to see different countries.'

The variant suffix *-haatokooka-* appears mainly in older materials:

(143) <. . . *yakni vt i̲ su̲ko keyo hatuk okvt, chekosi fehna offo tok.*>
. . . *yakni-yat   i̲-sokko-kiiyo-haatokookat,*
land-NM   III-thick-NEG-because:SS
chiikosi-fúhna offo-ttook.
little-indeed   come:up-DPAST

'Because the ground wasn't deep enough, little came up . . .' (Mark 4:5)

(144) <ʋlhpesa keyu, issish o isht ʋlhtoba hatuk oka>
   alhpiisah kiiyoh, issish-o   isht-alhtoba-haatokooka
   correct   not   blood-FOC:AC INSTR-be:paid-because
   'It isn't right, because it is the price of blood.' (Matt. 27:6)

Another complementizing suffix used for expressing reason is -*ooka*, 'for (this reason), because'. It is generally not followed by a switch-reference marker:

(145) *A̱-nokoowa-tok-ooka,   ik-átt-o-t   ahni-li-h.*
   1sIII-mad-PT-because N-be-NEG-PART think-1SI-TNS
   'Because he was mad at me, I hope he's not there.'

(146) <Yohmi kia ʋba pit hʋsh anumpuli hokʋt it ʋlbillit mihi̱ha kʋt, oklushi nan ik ithano ak okʋno hʋch ik chohmo kashke; yammak okʋto anumpuli fehna kako̱, hakla hinla, im ahoba cha tuk oka.>
   Yohmi-kia aba' pit   hash-ano̱poli-hookat itt-albilli-t
   do:so-but up   away 2PI-talk:COMP:SS   RCP-repeat-PART
   mihi̱ha-kat,   okl-oshi'   na̱n-ik-itháan-o-ak-ook-ano
   say:HN-COMP:SS people-DIM thing-N-know:L-NEG-OBL-COM-AC2
   hachik-chohm-ok-ashkii; yammak-ook-ato ano̱poli-fi̱hna-k-ako̱
   2PN-like-NEG-EXHORT   that-COM-NM2   talk-very-OBL-CONTR:AC
   hakl-ahi̱la-h   im-ahooba-hchaa-tok-ooka.
   hear-POT-TNS III-seem-always-PT-for
   'But when ye pray, use not vain repetitions, as the heathens do; for they think that they shall be heard for their much speaking.' (Matt. 6:7)

(147) <. . . himonasi kʋno ihst ai pi okcha̱ya yokʋt pi bili̱ka kʋt pi yimmi hatok ano i̱ shahli hoka.>
   . . . himmonasi-kano isht-aa-pi-okcha̱ya-yook-at
   now-COMP:DS2   INSTR-LOC-1PII-live-COMPAR-NM
   pi-bili̱ka-kat   pi-yimmi-h   a-ttook-ano
   1PII-near-COMP:SS 1PII-believe-TNS COP-DPAST-AC2
   i̱-shahli-h-ooka.
   III-exceed-TNS-for
   '[Now it is time to awake out of sleep,] for now our salvation is nearer than we believed.'[15] (Rom. 13:11)

The suffix -*ooka* is frequently used in the biblical formula "as it is written." In Choctaw, this phrase is frequently translated with an initial "according to" clause and a final verb of saying, followed by -*ooka*.

---

15. Literally 'The closeness of our salvation to us exceeds what we believed.'

(148) <Holihiso kʋt, Chekob ano i̱ hullo li tok: amba Esau yokʋno ak i̱ hullo
       ki tok, ahanchi hatok oka.>
       Holihísso-kat,   Jacob-ano i̱-hollo-li-tok;
       write:HN-COMP:SS Jacob-AC2 III-love-1sI-PT
       amba Esau-yook-ano   ak-i̱-hóll-o-kii-ttook,
       but   Esau-COMPAR-AC2 1sN-III-love:L-NEG-NEG-DPAST
       ahá̱chi-h   a-ttook-ooka.
       say:HN-TNS COP-DPAST-for
       'For it is written, I love Jacob, but hate Esau.' (Rom. 9:13)

(149) <Yʋmmak okʋt hopoyuksa ya̱ ilap nan isht imponna ak inli ho̱ isht
       ishi yoke, achi hosh holisso tok oka.>
       Yammak-ook-at hopoyoksa-ya̱ ilaap
       that-COMPAR-NM wise-AC   self
       na̱n-isht-i̱-ponna-aki̱lih-o̱
       thing-INSTR-III-clever-indeed-FOC:AC
       isht   ishi-yokiih, aachi-h-oosh   holisso-ttook-ooka.
       INSTR take-indeed say-TNS-PART:SS write-PT-for
       'For it is written, He taketh the wise in their own craftiness.' (1 Cor.
       3:19)

This suffix also appears with the pro-verbs *yakohmih* and *yamohmih*
in the sense 'therefore':

(150) <Yʋmohmi hoka himak a pilla kʋno nan it im apesʋt kil ahanto
       kashke.>
       Yamohmih-ooka himmaka pilla-kano   na̱n
       PROV-for   now   from-COMP:DS thing
       itt-im-apiisa-t   kil-ahá̱tt-ok-ashkii.
       RECIP-III-judge-PART 1PN-be:HN-NEG-EXHORT
       'Therefore, let us not judge each other from now on.' (Rom. 14:13)

16.3.6. Conditional clauses

Conditional clauses are indicated with the complementizing suffix
-kma, as in the following examples:

(151) *Tiballichi-li-kma̱, am-anooli-h.*
       err-1sI-IRR:DS 1sIII-tell-TNS
       'If I make a mistake, tell me.'

(152) *Chi-hohchafo-hoo-kmat, pállaska-kia ponaklo-h.*
       2sII-hungry-LINK-IRR:SS bread-too   ask-TNS
       'If you're hungry, ask for bread.'

As discussed in section 16.3.1.1 above, *-kma* is more generally the
complementizing suffix for adverbial irrealis events and corresponds
to certain senses of English *when* as well as *if*, as in the following
example:

(153) *Aaittanáaha' ona-li-kmat,   chi-písa-l-aachi-h.*
church   arrive:1SI-if:SS 2SI-see:N-1SI-IRR-TNS
'I'll see you when I get to church.'

16.3.7. Parallel clauses

When two clauses present parallel but contrasting information, the
first clause typically ends with *-kma*. This is a somewhat unexpected
usage of this complementizing suffix, since in all other contexts it
shows the irrealis. Consider the following examples:

(154) *Goodland aay-achókma' ii-pisa-h   kaniimi-kma,*
Goodland LOC-good:NML 1PI-see-TNS sometimes-IRR
ik-achókm-o'   ayna-h   ii-pisa-ttook.
N-good:L-NEG-NML and-TNS 1PI-see-PT
'We sometimes saw good times at Goodland, but we also saw bad
times.'

(155) *Nittak oshta holísso' ii-pisa-kmat,   nittak achaffa-kano*
day   four   book   1PI-see-IRR:SS day   one-COMP:DS2
ii-tóksali-ttook.
1PI-work-DPAST
'We went to school for four days, and worked one day.'

(156) *John-at   tolobli-kma an-ak-kia tolobli-h.*
John-NM jump-IRR:DS I-OBL-too jump-TNS
'John jumped and I did too.'

None of these examples describe irrealis situations, but *-kma* is used
nevertheless.

This complementizing suffix *-kma* is also used in situations where
English would use 'or'. When noun phrases are in parallel with each
other, they are typically followed by the determiner *-ak*, then the
copula *oo* followed by the irrealis *-kma*. In the traditional
orthography, this ending is written <-kmá>.

(157) <... tʊli holisso lakna yak okmá, keyukmʊt tempel a tʊli holisso lakna
yʊt isht a holitopa kak okmá, nanta hosh i shahli ho?>
... táli'=holísso'=lákna-yak oo-kma, kiiyo-kmat tempel-a
gold-OBL   COP-IRR NEG-IRR:SS temple-AC
táli'=hólisso'=lákna-yat isht   aa-holiitopa-k-ak oo-kma
gold-NM   INSTR LOC-holy-CON-OBL COP-IRR
náta-h-oosh   i-shahli-h-o?
what-TNS-PART:NM III-exceed-TNS-Q
'Which is greater—the gold or the temple where the gold is
sanctified?' (Matt. 22:17)

(158) <Pi haknip ak okmá, keyukmʊt pi shilombish ak okmá, katimampo
       kak osh, Chihowa ha holba fiehna ho?>
       Pi-haknip-ak   oo-kma,   kiiyo-kmat pi-shilobish-ak oo-kma,
       1PII-flesh-OBL COP-IRR   NEG-IRR:SS 1PII-soul-OBL   COP-IRR
       kátimapo-k-akoosh Chihoowah-a holba-fúhna-h-o?
       which-TNS-CON:NM God-AC   resemble-very-TNS-Q
       'Which is most like to God, our body or our soul?' (Catechism 21–22)

16.3.8. Concessive clauses

Concessive clauses are shown through the use of the complementizing
suffix *-makoo*:

(159) *Iya-li-h-makoosh   sa-nayopp-aachi-k   kiiyo-h.*
       go-1SI-TNS-CONCESS:SS 1SII-happy-IRR-TNS NEG-TNS
       'Even if I go, I won't be happy.'

(160) *Qba-h-mako,   iya-l-aachi-h.*
       rain-TNS-CONCESS:DS go-1SI-IRR-TNS
       'Even if it rains, I'll go.'

Some speakers allow the use of the N markers in place of the
ordinary agreement markers when a verb is marked in the
concessive. In such cases, the verb is followed by the potential *-ahila-*:

(161) *Ik-ob-ahila-h-mako,   iya-l-aachi-h.*
       N-rain-POT-TNS-CONCESS:DS go-1SI-IRR-TNS
       'Even if it rains, I'll go.'

(162) *Ik-si-abiik-ahila-h-makoosh,   iya-l-aachi-h.*
       N-1SII-sick-POT-TNS-CONCESS:SS go-1SI-IRR-TNS
       'Even if I get sick, I'll go.'

16.3.9. "Tough" complements

Choctaw has a few predicates that resemble the English adjectives
tough, difficult, and *easy* in their complementation possibilities. In
English, these adjectives have either an expletive subject and a
clausal object which is complete, or else an NP subject and a clausal
object with a gap corresponding to the subject:

(163a) It is easy to play this sonata.

(163b) This sonata is easy to play.

Choctaw shows very similar contrasts:

(164) *Issóbah ilapp-a o-biniil-ahii-ya kallo-h.*
       horse   this-AC on-sit-IRR-DS   hard-TNS
       'It is hard to ride (lit., "sit on") this horse.'

(165) *Issóbah   ilapp-at   o̲-biniil-ahii-ya̲   kallo-h.*
      horse   this-NM   on-sit-IRR-DS   hard-TNS
      'This horse is hard to ride.'

In Choctaw, the contrast between the two sentences is not signalled by a word order change, but by the change in the case marking of 'horse'.

To explain the different-subject switch-reference marking on the embedded verb in a sentence like (164), we can posit an expletive subject. Since the subject of the matrix verb is an expletive, and the subject of the embedded verb is an arbitrary pronominal, the two subjects are different from each other.

The predicates that are known to show this variable complementation are shown in table 16.2. Sometimes the meaning of the predicate in the "tough" construction is slightly different from its ordinary sense.

Table 16.2. Predicates allowing "tough" complements

PREDICATE	MEANING IN TOUGH CONSTRUCTION	ORDINARY MEANING
kalloh	'to be difficult'	'to be hard (in texture)'
ola̲sih	'to be easy'	'to be near (in space)'
achokmah	'to be easy'	'to be good'
chiikosih	'to be easy'	'to be near (in time)'

Some further examples of these constructions follow:

(166a) *Charles-a̲   haksich-aana-ka̲   ola̲si-h.*
       Charles-AC   trick-POT-COMP:DS   easy-TNS
       'It's easy to trick Charles.'

(166b) *Charles-at   haksich-aana-ka̲   ola̲si-h.*
       Charles-NM   trick-POT-COMP:DS   easy-TNS
       'Charles is easy to trick.'

(167a) *Issóbah   ilapp-a̲   o̲-biniili-ka̲   achokma-h.*
       horse   this-AC   ON-sit-COMP:DS   good-TNS
       'It's easy to ride this horse.'

(167b) *Issóbah   ilapp-at   o̲-biniili-ka̲   achokma-h.*
       horse   this-NM   ON-sit-COMP:DS   good-TNS
       'This horse is easy to ride.'

When the nonexpletive NP is marked nominative, we would expect it to behave like an ordinary subject for switch-reference. This expectation is realized in some examples:

(168) *Issóbah ilapp-at o̱-biniili-ka̱   kállo-cha pisokpolo-h.*
horse   this-NM   on-sit-COMP:DS hard:L-SS ugly-TNS
'This horse is hard to ride and ugly (too).'

However, there are also examples that show unexpected variability in the switch-reference marking:

(169) *Charles-at   im-anopol-ahii-ya̱   kallo-kat/kallo-ka̱*
Charles-NM III-talk-IRR-DS   hard-COMP:SS/hard-COMP:DS
ikhána-h.
know:N-TNS
'Charles knows that he's hard to talk to.'

It is not clear what is responsible for such variation. The interaction of the tough construction with switch-reference marking requires more investigation.

16.4. Relative clauses

16.4.1. Introduction

The following example shows a relative clause in Choctaw.

(170) [*Mary-at   páska' chapóli' ikbi-toka̱*]
Mary-NM bread sweet   make-PT:COMP:DS
apa-li-tok.
eat-1SI-PT
'I ate the cake that Mary made.'

In this example, *páska' chapóli'* 'cake' is contained within the relative clause that modifies it. Such relative clauses are labelled "internally headed" in the typological literature. All Choctaw relative clauses are best analyzed as internally headed; Choctaw does not have any relative clauses in which the head is external to the relative clause.

Any common noun phrase within the relative clause may be interpreted as its head, leading to potential ambiguity in some cases. Consider the following example:

(171) *John-at   [cholhkan-at hattak kopooli-tok-ma]   písa-tok*
John-NM spider-NM   man   bite-PT-D:AC   see:N-PT
'John saw the spider that bit the man.'
'John saw the man that the spider bit.'

In this example, either noun phrase within the relative clause may be interpreted as the head, and so the sentence is ambiguous. In context there is rarely any confusion, but any Choctaw relative clause with more than one common noun is potentially ambiguous.

The following are more examples of relative clauses:

(172) [*Jan im-ofi-yat   illi-k-aash*]   *písa-li-h.*
Jan   III-dog-NM   die-TNS-PREV   see:N-1SI-TNS
'I saw Jan's dog that died.'

(173) [*Hishi' isht ala-k-akọ*]   *písa-li-biika-tok.*
feather INST arrive-TNS-CON:AC   see:N-1SI-PT
'I used to see the feathers she brought'

(174) *Ofi-it* [*John-at kaah chọpa-tok-a̲*] *notaaka' aa-nosi-tok aachiini-tok.*
dog-NM John-NM car buy-PT-AC   under LOC-sleep-PT EVID-PT
'The dog apparently sleeps under the car that John bought.'

While there seems to be a preference for overt mention of the head of the relative clauses, there are some instances in which a null pronominal may also be interpreted as the head:

(175) <. . . mihma sholi tuk ʋt lumvt hieli tok.>
. . . *mihma* [*shooli-tok-at*] *lohma-t   hiili-ttook.*
and   carry-PT-NM   quiet-PART stand:DU-DPAST
'and those that bore him stood quietly.' (Luke 7:14)

More common in this context is the use of either a generic noun like *hattak* 'man, person', *ohóoyo'* 'woman', *alla'* 'child' or the use of an indefinite such as *kánah* 'someone':

(176) <. . . kʋna hosh Chisʋs a̲ ibafoyukʋt nusi tok okʋno Chihowa hʋt iba tanicha hi oka.>
. . . [*kánah-oosh   Chisaas-a̲ ibafóyyooka-t*
someone-FOC:NM Jesus-NM   be:with:Y-PART
nosi-tok-ook-ano]   *Chihoowah-at ibaa-taani-ch-ahi-ooka.*
sleep-PT-COMPAR-AC2 God-NM   COM-wake-CAUS-IRR-for
'For God will cause those who sleep with Jesus to wake with him.'[16]
(1 Thess. 4:14)

16.4.2. Relative clause morphology

A relative clause is shown through morphology that follows the verb. There are four types of marking for relative clauses in Choctaw: with demonstratives; with the previous-mention marker *-aash*; with the complementizing suffix *-ka*; and with simple case marking.

Marking with a demonstrative is shown in example (177), where the demonstrative *-ma* has been suffixed to the verb of the relative clause.

---

16. There seems to be a discrepancy between the Choctaw and the text of the King James Bible at this point. The Choctaw, as shown above, seems to say "God will cause those who sleep with Jesus to *wake with him.*" The King James Version says "them also which sleep in Jesus will God *bring with him.*"

(177) [*Ofi' chópa-li-tok-mat*] *homma-h.*
       dog buy:N-1SI-PT-D:NM red-TNS
       'The dog that I bought is red.'

Marking with /-aash/ is shown in (178):

(178) [*Ofi' ipiita-li-k-aash*]   *balii-t   kaniiya-h.*
       dog   feed-1SI-TNS-PREV run-PART go:away-TNS
       'The dog I fed ran away.'

As noted in chapter 5, the previous-mention marker -*aash* is a clausal
determiner, and must always be preceded by the tense marker -*k*.
    It is possible to have both a demonstrative and -*aash*:

(179) [*Ofi' ipiita-li-k-aash-ma̱*]   *balii-t   kaniiya-h.*
       dog   feed-1SI-TNS-PREV-D:DS run-PART go:away-TNS
       'That dog I fed ran away.'

A third option for relative clauses is the complementizing suffix -*ka*:

(180) *Harry-at* [*kaah cho̱pa-li-toka̱*]   *ik-ayoppách-o-tok.*
       Harry-NM   car   buy-1SI-PT:COMP:DS N-like:L-NEG-PT
       'Harry doesn' t like the car that I bought.'

(181) Ohoyo hʋt i̱ hatak a̱sha kʋt i̱nlai a ahnit a̱ya hoka, ik achukmo ak
       inlishke.
       [*Ohooyoh-at i̱-háttak   a̱sha-kat*] *i̱la-ya̱   ahni-t*
       woman-NM   III-husband have-COMP:NM other-AC think-PART
       a̱ya-h-ooka,   ik-achókm-o Ø-aki̱li-shkii.
       go:around-TNS-for N-good:L-NEG COP-indeed-EXHORT
       'It is not good for a woman who has a husband to go around thinking
       about others.' (Byington 1827:58)

Finally, there are a few relative clauses in the Choctaw Bible with
simple case markers suffixed to the verb without a preceding
demonstrative:

(182) <. . . micha auet chin tihleli tuk a̱ tvli ishit boli chia ma!>
       Micha [*awiit   chi̱-tilhiili-tok-a̱*] *tali' ishit   bóoli'*
       and:SS toward 2SIII-send-PT-AC rock INSTR throw:NML
       chi-ya-h-ma'!
       2SII-be-TNS-VOC
       'And you are a thrower of stones at those who are sent to you.'[17]
       (Luke 13:34)

(183) . . . <mihma sholi tuk vt lumvt hieli tok.>
       Mihma [*shooli-tok-at*] *looma-t   hiili-ttook.*
       and   carry-PT-NM hide-PART stand:PL-DPAST
       'And those that had carried him stood silently.' (Luke 7:14)

---

17. *Tali' ishit bóoli'* must be a nominalization meaning 'thrower of stones', rather
than a relative clause, due to the lack of verbal morphology on *bóoli'*.

This last possibility seems the least frequent option for relative clauses.

16.4.3. Alternation between case and switch-reference

Gordon (1987) has shown that Choctaw relative clauses may be marked for either case or switch-reference, regardless of which of these four marking options is chosen. Recall that -*t* functions as both nominative case and same-subject switch-reference, while vowel nasalization is both accusative and different-subject. In most instances, it is not difficult to tell what the function is; when these affixes appear on noun phrases they are case markers, and when they appear on verbs they are switch-reference markers.

From this perspective, relative clauses present a difficulty because they are noun phrases that end with a verb. Consider the following example again:

(184)   [*Ofi' ipiita-li-k-aash-ma*]   *balii-t   kaniiya-h.*
        dog   feed-1SI-TNS-PREV-D:DS   run-PART go:away-TNS
        'That dog I fed ran away.'

In this case, should the nasalization at the end of *ipiitalikaashma* be interpreted as case marking or switch-reference marking? In this case only the switch-reference interpretation is reasonable; the main clause and the relative clauses have different subjects, so the nasalization can be interpreted as different subject marking. It cannot be interpreted as case marking because the relative clause is in subject position and requires the nominative case, while nasalization is a mark of the accusative.

Example (184) shows a relative clause with switch-reference marking. It is also grammatical to case-mark the relative clause, as in the following example:

(185)   [*Ofi' ipiita-li-k-aash-mat*]   *balii-t kaniiya-h.*
        dog   feed-1SI-TNS-PREV-D:NM   run-PART go:away-TNS
        'That dog I fed ran away.'

Here the -*t* at the end of *ipiitalikaashmat* must be the nominative case marker, not the same-subject marker, since the relative clause and matrix clause have different subjects.

In many instances, the right case marker and the right switch-reference marker will turn out to be the same morpheme, and in this instance, no variation is allowed:

(186)   [*Ofi' ipiita-li-k-aash-ma*]   *ish-písa-tok.*
        dog   feed-1SI-TNS-PREV-D:AC/DS 2SI-see-PT
        'You saw the dog I fed.'

(187) *[Ofi' ipiita-li-k-aash-mat]   ish-písa-tok.
       dog   feed-1SI-TNS-PREV-D:NM/SS 2SI-see-PT
       'You saw the dog I fed.'

In several of the relative clauses, an element -hoo- appears
between the verb stem and the complementizing suffix. Its precise
function is unknown, but I gloss it as 'linker'.[18]

(188) <Yakni moma hvch iyi pvtha yvt ai o̱ hika he puta hokvno . . .>
       Yakni' mo̱ma hach-iyyipatha-yat
       land   all   2PII-foot-NM
       aay-o̱-hik-ahii-h   pootta-hoo-kano . . .
       LOC-on-step-IRR-TNS all-LINK-COMP:DS2
       'Every place that your foot treads on . . .' (Josh. 1:3)

16.4.4. Extraction from relative clauses

Broadwell (1990a) shows that Choctaw allows extraction of
interrogatives from relative clauses, as in the following example:

(189) Kátomma-h John-at [ofi' aa-písa-tok-at] cho̱pa-tok?
       where-TNS   John-NM dog LOC-see-PT-SS buy-PT
       Where₁ did John₂ buy [the dog [he₂ saw t₁]]?'
       ('What is the place such that John bought the dog he saw at that
       place?')

While the English translation is interpreted with main clause
interrogation, the Choctaw sentence involves interrogation from the
relative clause. This is made clear by the presence of the locative
prefix on the embedded verb. The following example also shows
extraction from a relative clause:

(190) Náta-h-oosh   Bill-at [ohooyo'-ma̱ kobli-tok-ma̱] afaama-tok?
       what-TNS-PART:SS Bill-NM woman-D:AC bite-PT-D:AC meet-PT
       'What₁ did Bill meet that woman [that t₁ bit]?'
       ('What is the thing such that Bill met that woman that the thing bit?')

As these examples show, extraction is permitted both from relative
clauses marked for switch-reference (189) and from relative clauses
marked for case (190). The presence of elements like demonstratives
does not affect the extraction possibilities.

Since relative clauses are "islands" in most languages, not
allowing constituents to be extracted from them, Broadwell (1990a)
suggests that the grammaticality of examples like (189) and (190) is
evidence that internally headed relative clauses in Choctaw are not
NPs in surface syntax, but have a syntactic status like that of
complement clauses.

18. It is reminiscent of a -hoo- that occurs as a form of the copula in Chickasaw
(Munro 1987bc).

16.4.5. Extraposed relative clauses

It is also common for Choctaw relatives to be extraposed to the end of the clause, leaving the head of the relative clause in situ:

(191) *Ofi-it   balii-t   kaniiya-h   [ipiita-li-k-aash-m-at]*
dog-NM   run-PART   go:away-TNS   feed-1SI-TNS-PREV-NM
'The dog that I fed ran away.'

(192) *Hattak-ma̱ pi̱sa-li-tok   [yopi-sh   á̱tta-ka̱]*
man-D:AC   see:N-1SI-PT   swim-PART:SS   be:N-COMP:DS
'I saw the man that was swimming.'

If extraposition is thought to be the result of movement, then the extraposed relative clauses in Choctaw are surprising, because they would seem to be derived from a structure in which the relative clause forms a constituent distinct from the head. But Choctaw has internally headed relative clauses, and the head of the relative clause is inside the clause that modifies it. Choctaw does not have any externally headed relative clauses.

A second surprising fact about constructions of this sort is that the head of such relative clauses sometimes retains the case marking appropriate for its role in the subordinate clause:

(193) *Ofi' balii-t   kaniiya-h   [ipiita-li-k-aash-m-at]*
dog   run-PART   go:away-TNS   feed-1SI-TNS-PREV-NM
'The dog that I fed ran away.'

In this example, it appears that *ofi'* 'dog' may appear without the nominative marker because it is the object of the relative clause. Compare the version without extraposition:

(194) *[Ofi' ipiita-li-k-aash-m-at]   balii-t   kaniiya-h*
dog   feed-1SI-TNS-PREV-NM   run-PART   go:away-TNS
'The dog that I fed ran away.'

16.4.6. Positioning of quantifiers and demonstratives in relative clauses

In relative clauses, quantifiers and demonstratives associated with the head of the relative clause tend to appear to the right of the verb, while the head remains in situ:

(195) *[Mary-at paska' cha̱póli' ikbi-tok]-ma̱   chopa-li-tok*
Mary-NM bread sweet   made-PT-DEM:AC   buy-1SI-PT
'I bought that cake that Mary made.'

(196) *[Mary-at paska' chapoli' ikbi-tok]-a̱   mo̱ma-ka̱   chopa-li-tok.*
Mary-NM bread sweet   made-PT-AC   all-COMP:AC   buy-1sI-PT
'I bought all the cakes that Mary made.'

(197) <Chihowa hʊt nana il a kaniohmi poyutta ka̱, ithana ho̱? Chihowa hʊt
       nana il a kaniohmi poyutta ka̱, ithana hoke.>
       Chihoowah-at [*na̱nah il-akaniohmi*]   *póyyootta-ka̱*
       God-NM   thing   1PI-do:something   all:Y-COMP:DS
       ithá̱na-h-o̱?   *Chihoowah-at* [*na̱nah il-akaniohmi*]
       know:N-TNS-Q God-NM   thing   1PI-do:something
       póyyootta-ka̱   ithá̱na-h-okii?
       all:Y-COMP:DS know:N-TNS-indeed
       'Does God know everything we do? Indeed, God does know everything
       we do.' (Catechism 22)

17. Subject and object changing rules

Choctaw does not have a passive, but there are two other rules that have the effect of creating new subjects and objects: possessor raising and dative raising.[1] The closely related language Chickasaw has analogous rules, which have been extensively investigated by Munro and Gordon (1982) and Carden, Gordon, and Munro (1982); at several points in this chapter, the Choctaw data are compared with data from Chickasaw.

17.1. Possessor raising

17.1.1. General properties

Choctaw has a construction in which an NP that is the possessor of the subject or object may appear with nominative or accusative case.

Instances in which the possessor of the subject appears in the nominative case are labelled "subject possessor raising", as in the following examples:

(1) *John im-ofi-yat illi-h.*
     John III-dog-NM die-TNS
     'John's dog died.'

(2) *John-at ofi' im-illi-h.*
     John-NM dog III-die-TNS
     'John's dog died.'

Example (1) is an ordinary sentence, while (2) shows possessor raising. Notice that there are three differences between (1) and (2). First, in (1), nominative case appears on the possessum 'dog', while in (2), nominative is on the possessor 'John'. Second, the possessive (III) prefix *im-* appears on the noun 'dog' in (1), but not in (2). Third, there is a dative (III) applicative *im-* on the verb in (2).

We can think of the construction in the following schematic terms:

(3) NP_1-$case_1$ $prefix_1$-$Noun_2$(-$case_2$) $prefix_2$-Verb

The syntactic structure that most accurately seems to capture the syntax of possessor raising in Choctaw may be something like that in figure 17.1.

---

1. For information on the transitive-intransitive alternation, see chapter 8.

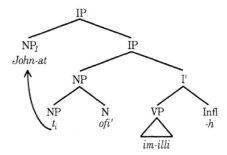

Figure 17.1.

In this structure, the possessor, NP_1, has moved out of the subject, NP_2, and adjoined to the clause. There is evidence from adverb placement that supports the idea that the possessor and possessum form a constituent in (1), but not in (2). In the example with possessor raising, an adverbial may intervene between the two elements, but this is not possible in (1):

(4a)   *John piláashaash im-ofi-yat illi-h.
       John yesterday   III-dog-NM D-die-TNS
       'John's dog died yesterday.'

(4b)   John-at piláashaash ofi-yat im-illi-h.
       John-NM yesterday   dog-NM III-die-TNS
       'John's dog died yesterday.'

17.1.2. Variability in the subject possessor raising construction

The subject possessor raising construction is somewhat variable from speaker to speaker.[2] One point subject to variation is the sort of case marking which the possessum may bear. Some speakers object to multiple instances of the neutral nominative case marker -at. Both Mr. Henry Willis and Mrs. Edith Gem found (5) perfectly acceptable, but (6) somewhat odd.

(5)   John-at ofi' im-illi-h.
       John-NM dog III-die-TNS
       'John's dog died.'

(6)   ??John-at ofi-yat im-illi-h.
       John-NM dog-NM III-die-TNS
       'John's dog died.'

However, both agreed that sentences of this sort are considerably better

---

2. It is unclear whether the differences speakers report in these sentences can be attributed to regional dialects or whether they represent idiolectal variation. It is also unclear whether some of the reported differences between Chickasaw and Choctaw represent idiolectal differences between individual speakers of these languages.

if the possessor bears contrastive nominative case:

(7)   *John-akoosh ofi-yat   im-illi-h.*
       John-CON:NM dog-NM III-die-TNS
       'It was John whose dog died.'

(8)   *Mary-akoosh   im-oshi-yat   i̱-kaniiya-tok.*
       Mary-CON:NM III-uncle-NM III-go:away-PT
       'It was Mary whose uncle passed away.'

In contrast, Chickasaw seems to allow multiple instances of the neutral nominative more freely (Munro and Gordon 1982):

(9a)   *Jan im-ofi'-at   impa*   (Chickasaw)
       Jan III-dog-NM eat
       'Jan's dog is eating.'

(9b)   *Jan-at   ofi'-at   im-impa.*
       Jan-NM dog-NM III-eat
       'Jan's dog is eating.'

    A second area of variation is in the occurrence of III prefixes on the possessum, the verb, or both. For Henry Willis, the III prefix generally occurs on both the possessum and the verb in a possessor raising construction:

(10)   *Mary-akoosh   im-oshi-yat   i̱-kaniiya-tok.*
       Mary-CON:NM III-uncle-NM III-go:away-PT
       'It was Mary whose uncle passed away.'

Other speakers, such as Mrs. Edith Gem, generally add the III prefix only to the verb.
    In Chickasaw, however, the III prefix generally occurs on either the possessum or the verb, but not both. The choice of noun or verb appears to be lexically based (Carden, Gordon, and Munro 1982).

17.1.3. Object possessor raising

There is also a rule of object possessor raising (Munro 1984b) that makes possessors of objects into objects, as shown in the following example:

(11a) *A̱-shokha' nipi' apa-tok.*
       1sIII-pig   meat eat-PT
       'He ate my bacon.'

(11b) *Shokha' nipi' am-apa-tok.*
       pig   meat 1sIII-eat-PT
       'He ate my bacon.'

In this example, the signal of object possessor raising is the lack of the expected III-prefix showing possession of the object noun and an additional III-prefix on the verb.

Object possessor raising may consist of moving a possessor NP from [Spec, NP] position to an VP-adjoined position as represented in figure 17.2.

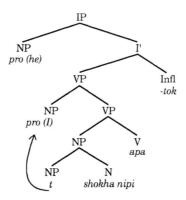

Figure 17.2.

The same rule occurs in Chickasaw:

(12a) *Ofi'-at   ihoo   im-pask-a   apa-tok.*   (Chickasaw)
     dog-NM woman III-bread-AC eat-PT
     'The dog ate the woman's bread.'

(12b) *Ofi'-at   ihoo-a   paska im-apa-tok.*
     dog-NM woman-AC bread III-eat-PT
     'The dog ate the woman's bread.'

The III prefix that appears on the verb in object possessor raising is somewhat different in position from the ordinary dative III marker. Ordinary IIIs follow the negative (N) prefixes:

(13)   *Ik-im-áach-o-tok.*
     N-III-say:L-NEG-PT
     'He didn't say it to her.'

However, the III prefix associated with a raised object precedes the N prefix:

(14)   *Ofi am-ik-hálhlh-o-tok.*
     dog III-N-kick:L-NEG-PT
     'He didn't kick my dog.'

17.1.4. A transitivity restriction on subject possessor raising

Subject possessor raising is restricted to intransitive verbs. While a sentence like (15) is grammatical in Choctaw, a transitive counterpart like (16) is not:

(15) *Mary-akoosh im-oshi-yat i-kaniiya-tok.*
Mary-CON:NM III-uncle-NM III-go:away-PT
'It was Mary whose uncle passed away.'

(16) **Mary-akoosh im-oshi-yat ofi' i-chopa-tok.*
Mary-CON:NM III-uncle-NM dog III-buy-PT
('It was Mary whose uncle bought the dog.')

Baker (1985) has suggested that the fact that subject possessor raising in Choctaw and Chickasaw is only allowed when the verb is intransitive may be evidence that all the putative examples of possessor raising from subjects actually are unaccusative, and that the possessum is thus an object in deep structure.

This position is difficult to maintain. In Choctaw, Davies (1981, 1986) has argued that the type of subject agreement a verb takes indicates whether its subject is underlyingly accusative. Specifically, verbs with I subject marking are unergative and verbs with II subject marking are unaccusative. Assuming this argument to be correct, then the existence of verbs which take I subject agreement and allow subject possessor raising is evidence against Baker's hypothesis.

There appear to be some verbs of this sort. Consider the following examples:

(17) *John-akoosh im-ofi-yat balii-t kaniiya-h.*
John-CON:NM III-dog-NM run-PART go:away-TNS
'John's dog ran away.'

(18) *Pam-at katos-at i-baliili-h.*
Pam-NM cat-NM III-run-TNS
'Pam's cat is running.'

Because the verbs *baliilih* 'to run' and *kaniiyah* 'to go away' both take I agreement, they should be unergatives. However, they may occur with possessor raising, showing that the process is not restricted to unaccusatives.

The Choctaw rule of subject possessor raising is, however, more lexically restricted than has been widely recognized in previous work (Gordon 1986; Broadwell 1990a). Table 17.1 lists some verbs that allow or disallow possessor raising, along with the kind of subject agreement they occur with. It is difficult to see what semantic generalization covers the classes of verbs that do and do not allow possessor raising.

Table 17.1. Lexical restrictions on subject possessor raising

POSSESSOR RAISING ALLOWED		POSSESSOR RAISING BARRED	
illih	'to die' (II)	*nokoowah*	'to be angry' (II)
baliilih	'to run' (I)	*howiitah*	'to vomit' (I)
hohchafoh	'to be hungry'(II)	*yopih*	'to swim' (I)
nokshilah	'to be thirsty' (II)	*taloowah*	'to sing' (I)
tasiboh	'to be crazy' (II)		
lakshah	'to sweat' (II)		
hotilhkoh	'to cough' (I or II)		

Carden, Gordon, and Munro (1982) demonstrate that possessor raising is less restricted in Chickasaw and applies to a wider range of intransitives.

17.1.5. The interaction of possessor raising and switch-reference

Since possessor raising creates structures with two nominative-marked NPs, questions about which serves as subject for switch-reference marking naturally arise. There seems to be a certain amount of variability in whether speakers consider the raised possessor a subject for the purposes of switch-reference.

For Mr. Henry Tubby (Mississippi Choctaw) and Mr. Henry Willis (Oklahoma Choctaw), the second of the nominative-marked NPs (i.e., the 'original' subject) continues to act as the subject for switch-reference.

(19) *Harry-at   ofi-it   illi-hma,   yaaya-tok.*   (Mississippi Choctaw)
      Harry-NM dog-NM die-when:DS cry-PT
      'When Harry$_i$'s dog$_j$ died, he$_i$ cried.'[3]

(20a) *Mary-akoosh   im-oshi'   im-illi-h-ookako*   (Oklahoma Choctaw)
      Mary-CON:NM III-uncle III-die-TNS-but:DS
      ik-l-o-tok.
      N-come-NEG-PT
      'It was Mary whose uncle died, but she didn't come (to the funeral).'

(20b) ?*Mary-akoosh   im-oshi'   im-illi-h-ookakoosh ik-l-o-tok.*
      Mary-CON:NM   III-uncle III-die-TNS-but:SS   N-come-NEG-PT

---

3. It is unclear to me why there is no III prefix in this example.

In these examples, although the raised possessor is the same as the subject of the matrix sentence, the switch-reference marker is nevertheless different-subject. This seems to show that possessor raising does not create subjects that are relevant to switch-reference.

However, some speakers have the opposite judgment. For Mrs. Edith Gem, possessor raising in a subordinate clause does affect switch-reference:

(21) *John-at im-ofi' im-illi-tok-oosh,*   *nokhåklo-sh   bínniili-h.*
      John-NM III-dog III-die-PT-PART:SS,   sad:N-PART:SS sit:G-TNS
      'Because John's dog died, he's sad.'

The following example from the Choctaw New Testament shows a passage where lower clause possessor-raising does affect switch-reference:

(22) <. . . noshkobo hʊt im o̠ hlipia hokmʊt, ilap noshkobo ha̠ hofahyali hoke.>
      . . . noshkoboh-at im-o̠-lhipiiya-hoo-kmat, ilaap noshkoboh-a̠
      head-NM   III-on-cover-LINK-IRR:SS self   head-AC
      hofahyali-h-okii.
      dishonor-TNS-INDEED
      '[Every man whose] head is covered, dishonors his head.' (1 Cor. 11:4)

In this example, we can tell that 'every man' has been possessor-raised in the first clause because of the III prefix on the verb. 'Every man' is also the subject of the second clause, and the switch-reference marker connecting the two clauses is SS.

In Chickasaw, the possessor does show subject properties for switch-reference (Gordon 1986):

(23) *Jan-at ofi'-at im-illi-hmat/*-hma̠,*   (Chickasaw)
      Jan-NM dog-NM III-die-when:SS/*-when:DS
      yaa-tok.
      cry-PT
      'When Jan's dog died, she cried'

The interaction of switch-reference and possessor raising is discussed in more detail by Gordon (1986) and Broadwell (1990a).

17.2. Dative raising

17.2.1. General description

The rule of dative raising[4] makes a dative argument into a subject, as in the following examples:

---

4. Munro and Gordon (1982) call this rule III-subjectivalization.

(24) *John-at   iskali-yat   im-ásha-h.*
      John-NM money-NM III-be:PLUR:N-TNS
      'John has money.'

(25) <Pin tikba Eblaham ʋt . . . Chihowa holitopa yʋt ant i̱ haiaka tok.>
      Pi̱-tikba'   Abraham-at . . . Chihoowa
      1PIII-front Abraham-NM   God
      holiittopa-yat a̱t   i-hayaaka-ttook.
      holy-NM   come:and III-appear-DPAST
      'Holy God appeared to our forefather Abraham.' (Acts 7:2)

Unlike possessor raising, there are sometimes no alternatives to the
dative-raised version of the sentence. *Áshah* means 'be, exist' in its
ordinary usage but is only interpreted as a possessive in the presence
of dative raising.

(26) *John im-iskali-yat   ásha-h.*
      John III-money-NM be:PLUR:N-TNS
      'John's money exists.'

Similarly, *hayaakah* means 'to be visible' in its normal usage, but
'appear to' when used with dative raising. The characteristic syntax
of dative raising clauses is the following:

(27) NP_1-NM NP_2-NM III-Verb

Dative raising is most often found in expressions of possession and
with verbs of appearance. Clauses with dative raising look much like
possessor raising clauses, but there are some differences.

    Choctaw speakers such as Mr. Henry Willis (Oklahoma Choctaw)
are reluctant to accept possessor raising examples with two instances
of the neutral nominative marker (although examples where the
possessor bears contrastive nominative are fine). Dative raising
examples with two neutral nominatives are fine, however:

(28a) Possessor raising
       John-at   ofi' im-illi-h.
       John-NM dog III-die-TNS
       'John's dog died.'

(28b) ??*John-at ofi-yat   im-illi-h.*
       John-NM dog-NM III-die-TNS

(29) Dative raising
      John-at   iskali-yat   im-ásha-h.
      John-NM money-NM III-be:PL:N-TNS
      'John has money.'

Another clear difference between possessor raising and dative raising
is that in possessor raising there is always a relationship of
possession between the first two NPs. This is not true for examples

like (25) above.

17.2.2. Dative raising and switch-reference

As was the case with possessor raising, a rule like dative raising creates the possibility of interaction with the switch-reference system. For speakers I consulted, the dative-raised NP acts as the subject for switch-reference marking. Thus in (30) and (31) the dative raised null pronominal (*pro*) is coreferential with the subject of the matrix clause, and this induces same-subject marking.

(30) *John-at   nayoppa-h* [pro *ofi-yat   im-átta-haatokoosh/*-haatoko*].
      John-NM happy-TNS   dog-NM III-be:N-because:SS/*because:DS
      'John is happy because he has a dog.'

(31) [pro *Akaka'   lawa-h-o   i-máya-tokoosh*],
      chicken   many-TNS-PART:DS III-be:PL:N-because:SS
      ábi-h-oosh   atta-h.
      kill:N-TNS-PART:SS be-TNS
      'He has lots of chickens, so he's killing them (from time to time, frequently).'

The following textual example shows again that the dative-raised NP possessor may control the switch-reference marking:

(32) *Yamm-ako   shokhatta-at míchci-cha nashooba' áabi-cha*
      that-CON:AC possum-NM   do:L-SS   wolf   kill:L-SS
      ilapp-ato nokshóopa-at ik-im-iksh-o-h-oosh
      this-NM2   fear-NM   N-III-not:exist-NEG-TNS-PART:SS
      itti' akkóowa-cha i-chokka' iya-tok.
      tree descend:L-SS III-house go-PT
      'That's how Possum did it, and killed the wolf, and he had no fear, and he went down the tree and went home.' (T5:35–37)

In this example, the clause marked in boldface shows dative raising, and has two nominative case arguments. *Ilappato* 'this one' refers to Possum. Possum is the subject of the preceding clause '(he) killed the wolf' and is also the subject of the following clause 'went down the tree', and same-subject switch-reference marking is used on both the verb *áabicha* 'killed and' and *ikimikshohoosh* 'not having'.

Munro (1986) reports that in Chickasaw either same-subject or different-subject marking is available in the embedded clause:

(33) *Ihoo-at   nokhanglo* [*ofi'-at   in-kaniya-toka/tokat*]. (Chickasaw)
      woman-NM sad   dog-NM III-lost-PT:DS/PT:SS
      'The woman is sad that she lost her dog.'

18. Adverbs and their equivalents

Choctaw adverbials can be divided into two large groups: those that are independent words (section 18.1) and those that are verbal suffixes (section 18.2). A number of classes of English adverbials correspond not to adverbials but to other parts of speech in Choctaw; section 18.3 describes a number of such alternatives to adverbs.

18.1. Independent adverbials

18.1.1. Temporal

There are two groups of temporal adverbs that are distinguished from each other by morphology and word order. External temporal adverbs situate the time of an event with respect to some sentence-external perspective, such as the time of speech or the calendar. Examples include the Choctaw equivalents of *yesterday* and *at 4 o'clock*. Internal temporal adverbs situate the time of an event before or after subparts of that same event. Examples include the Choctaw equivalents of *finally* (which means 'after a preparatory stage'), *twice* ('after an initial repetition') and *just now* ('during the event which led to the current resultant state').

18.1.1.1. External temporal adverbs

External temporal adverbs are generally clause-initial. Those that refer to times in the past are frequently followed by the suffix *-aash*:

(1)   *Tuesday-aash iya-li-tok.*
      Tuesday-PREV go-1SI-PT
      'I went on Tuesday.'

(2)   *Mishsh-aash chǫpa-li-tok.*
      two:days-PREV buy-1SI-PT
      'I bought it two days ago (the day before yesterday).'

When the adverbial phrase contains a verbal element, it must also be marked with a tense marker, and the suffix *-aash* requires that the preceding tense be *-k*:

(3)   *Háshi'=kanálli' oshta-k-aash John-at baliili-h.*
      o'clock   four-TNS-PREV John-NM run-TNS
      'John was running at four o'clock.'

Piláashaash 'yesterday' presumably includes the past time suffix -*aash*, but there is no independent word *pilaash*. The suffix -*aash* also functions as a previous-mention marker on noun phrases (see chapter 5).

Another possibility for past-time adverbials is the suffix -*hma̱* 'when:DS':

(4) *Háshi'=kanálli' oshta-hma̱   John-at   baliili-t   tahli-tok.*
     o'clock   four-when:DS John-NM run-PART complete-PT
     'John finished running at four o'clock.'

The difference between -*k-aash* and -*hma̱* here appears to be that -*k-aash* is used with events that occur over time spans and -*hma̱* with events that that occur at particular points in time. So in (4), the sentence specifies that at a particular time point (four o'clock), John ended his running. In (3), by contrast, John's running occupied a time span that included four o'clock.

Adverbs that refer to times in the future are generally followed by -*kma̱*, the irrealis different-subject marker:

(5) *Tuesday-kma̱   iya-l-aachi̱-h.*
     Tuesday-IRR:DS go-1SI-IRR-TNS
     'I will go on Tuesday.'

'Tomorrow' is expressed through use of the verb *onnah* 'to dawn', followed by -*kma̱*:

(6) *Onna-kma̱   chi-pi̱sa-l-aachi̱-h.*
     dawn-IRR:DS 2SII-see:N-1SI-IRR-TNS
     'I'll see you tomorrow.' (Lit., 'I'll see you when it dawns.')

As mentioned above, external temporal adverbs are best in sentence-initial position. Occasionally they also appear after the subject or in sentence-final position. They may not appear between the verb and the object:

(7a) *Piláashaash Mary-at   sholosh cho̱pa-tok.* (best order)
     yesterday   Mary-NM shoe   buy-PT
     'Yesterday Mary bought shoes.'

(7b) *Mary-at   piláashaash sholosh cho̱pa-tok.*
     Mary-NM yesterday   shoe   buy-PT

(7c) *Mary-at   sholosh cho̱pa-tok piláashaash.*
     Mary-NM shoe   buy-PT   yesterday

(7d) **Mary-at   sholosh piláashaash cho̱pa-tok.*
     Mary-NM shoe   yesterday   buy-PT

This distribution can be accounted for if we assume that Choctaw has a verb phrase, as argued in chapter 3. We can account for this distribution if posit a structure like that in figure 18.1. In this structure, an external temporal adverb occurs as a daughter of IP, but is freely ordered with respect to other daughters of IP.

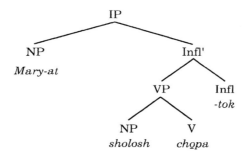

Figure 18.1.

18.1.1.2. Internal temporal adverbs

Internal temporal adverbs differ from external temporal adverbs in morphology and word order. They are followed either by no overt subordinator or by participial *-oo*, and they typically occur between the subject and the verb phrase:

(8)   *John-at pol<u>a</u>ka-h   shokha'-m<u>a</u> abi-tok.*
       John-NM finally-TNS hog-D:AC   kill-PT
       'John finally killed that hog.'

(9)   *John-at pállammi-h-<u>o</u>   shokha'-m<u>a</u> abi-tok.*
       John-NM after:difficulty:G-TNS-PART:DS hog-D:AC   kill-PT
       'John finally killed that hog after several tries.'

Pállammih appears to be the g-grade of the verb *ipalammih*, which means 'to suffer'. It implies that the event was preceded by some number of unsuccessful attempts, and is often translated 'finally'. *Pol<u>a</u>kah* also corresponds approximately to English 'finally', but implies that there was some delay in the start of the event.

Other members of this group are *hitokloh* 'twice', *himmonasi'* 'just now', and *himo'/homo'* 'just now'.

Unlike the external temporal adverbs, internal temporal adverbs are best after the subject. They may be fronted to sentence-initial position, but they may not occur after the verb or between the verb and its object:

(10a) *Mary-at homo' sholosh ch<u>o</u>pa-h.*   (best order)
      Mary-NM just shoe buy-TNS
      'Mary just bought some shoes.'

(10b) *Homo' Mary-at   sholosh ch<u>o</u>pa-h.*
      just   Mary-NM shoe   buy-TNS

(10c) *Mary-at sholosh homo' chopa-h.
       Mary-NM shoe   just   buy-TNS

(10d) *Mary-at sholosh chopa-h homo'.
       Mary-NM shoe   buy-TNS just

Using the same phrase structure shown above, we can describe the distribution of internal temporal adverbs as follows:

(11)   Internal temporal adverbs appear on the left edge of an extended maximal projection of the verb (i.e. on the left edge of VP or the IP).

18.1.2. *piih* 'just, only'

The adverb *piih* means 'just, only, merely' and it appears to have different word-order properties than any of the other adverbs.[1] It may occur either before the VP or before the verb, but not before the subject and not after the verb.

(12a) John-at piih na=chapoli' pisa-tok.
       John-NM only cake   see-PT
       'John only looked at the cake.'

(12b) John-at na=chapoli' piih pisa-tok.
       John-NM cake   only see-PT

(12c) *Piih John-at na=chapoli' pisa-tok.
       just   John-NM cake   see-PT

(12d) *John-at na=chapoli' pisa-tok piih.
       John-NM cake   see-PT   only

There does not seem to be any difference in the interpretation of *piih* that correlates with its word order. It is possible for both (12a) and (12b) to be interpreted with focus on either the verb or the object.

Etymologically, *piih* seems related to the verb *pilah* 'to cause to move away, to send, to throw' and to the incomplete path modifier *pilah* (see chapter 15). Consider the following larger context for *piih*, where I have supplied an English translation that captures some of the sense of Choctaw *piih*:

(13)   John-at na=chapoli' ik-p-o-h;   piih na=chapoli' pisa-tok.
       John-NM cake   N-eat-NEG-TNS   only cake   see-PT
       'John didn't eat the cake; he only went so far as to look at the cake.'

The idea is that John's actions did not go as far as they might have; they only went up to a certain point. In this respect, *piih* is like the path

---

1. Its positioning seems to be like that of the plural preverb *oklah* (see chapter 3).

modifier *pilah*, which says that the path did not reach its goal, but only went some portion of the distance.[2]

We can describe the distribution of *piih* as follows:

(14)   *Piih* appears on the left edge of a projection of the verb (i.e., on the left edge of V or VP).[3]

18.2. Adverbial suffixes

Adverbials may occur in the verbal suffix complex. The adverbials fall into four groups: the action modifiers -*moma* 'still, again', -*fiihna* 'intensifier', and -*fokka* or -*fokkaali* 'approximately'; the temporal modifiers -*hchaa* 'always' and -*isha* 'yet'; the truth modifiers -*naaha*- 'almost' and -*malhlhi* 'truly'; and the speaker evaluations -*akili* 'indeed', -*kiiyo* 'negative', and -*polla* 'must'.

18.2.1. Positions for adverbials

There are three positions in the verbal suffix complex where adverbials may appear, shown in the following schema as Adv_1, Adv_2, and Adv_3:

(15)   [Verb+Agreement] + Adv_1 + Modals + Adv_2 + Tense + Adv_3 + Complementizer/Illocutionary Force

For ease of reference, I will refer to these respectively as the pre-modal, pre-tense, and post-tense positions.[4] Apparently none of the adverbials felicitously occur in all three positions. They are all restricted to one or two of the positions. The generalizations are the following:

(16)   Action modifiers appear in Adv_1 or Adv_2.
        Temporal modifiers appear in Adv_2 only.
        Truth modifiers appear in Adv_2 only.
        Speaker evaluations appear in Adv_2 or Adv_3.

There appear to be no adverbials that occur exclusively in Adv_3.

18.2.2. Action modifiers

18.2.2.1. -*moma* 'still, again'

The adverbial suffix -*moma* occurs in the following examples with the meaning 'still' or 'again'. It occurs in pre-modal and pre-tense positions.

---

2. Evans (1995) points out a similar relationship between a verb of uncompleted motion and the expression of the concept 'only' in the Australian language Mayali.

3. It is unclear whether there is any evidence for a V' projection in Choctaw.

4. Since complementizers and markers of illocutionary force will not appear in all the examples, in general I will take any occurrence of an adverbial after a tense marker to indicate that it can appear in the post-tense (Adv_3) position.

(17) *Ot   chokkowa-li-hma taloowa-sh   hikiya-moma-tok.*
      come:and enter-1SI-when:DS sing-PART:SS stand:N-still-PT
      'When I came in, he was still singing.'

(18a) *Taloowa-mom-aachi-h.*
       sing-again-IRR-TNS
       'They're going to sing again.'

(18b) *Taloow-aachi-moma-h.*
       sing-IRR-again-TNS

(19a) *Taloowa-moma-tok.*
       sing-still-PT
       'They were still singing.'

(19b) **Taloowa-tok-moma.*
       sing-PT-still
       ('They were still singing.')

(20) *Hattak-ma piláashaash afaama-li-tokat,*
      man-D:AC yesterday   meet-1SI-PT:COMP:SS
      himmah nittak afaama-li-moma-tok
      now   day   meet-1SI-still-PT
      'That man that I met yesterday, I met again today.'[5]

The adverbial *-moma* 'still' looks like the quantifier *momah* 'all' (discussed in chapter 14), but it is unclear whether there is any semantic connection between the two.

18.2.2.2. *-fíìhna* 'intensifier'

The suffix *-fíìhna* is usually translated 'very much', 'often', or 'a lot'.

(21) *Káfi-ya   ishko-li-fíìhna-kiiyo-h.*
      coffee-AC drink-1SI-much-NEG-TNS
      'I don't drink coffee very much.'

(22) <. . . alta chito fehna ho ikbi tok.>
      Alta   chito-fíìhna-h-o   ikbi-ttook.
      altar big-very-TNS-PART:DS make-DPAST
      'He made a very big altar.' (Josh. 22:10)

The suffix *-fíìhna* may appear in pre-modal and pre-tense positions. There are slight differences between its glosses in these positions probably due to difference in the relative scope:

(23) *Ob-aachi-fíìhna-h.*
      rain-IRR-really-TNS
      'It's really going to rain.'

5. Since *piláashaash* does not normally occur between the verb and its object, we must assume that the object NP serving as head of this relative clause has been fronted to some clause-initial position.

(24)   <u>O</u>ba-fǔhn-aach<u>i</u>-h.
       rain-really-IRR-TNS
       'It will really rain.'

The suffix -fǔhna also occurs on noun phrases, as discussed in chapter 5.

18.2.2.3. -fokka, -fokkaali 'approximately'

-fokka and the apparently identical -fokkaali are usually translated into English as 'about' or 'approximately'. In my data, they appear most frequently following interrogatives and quantifiers.

(25)   Hashi' kanalli' toklo-fokkaali-h-<u>o</u>   <u>ot</u>   ii-nosi-ttook.
       sun   move   two-about-TNS-PART:DS go:and 1PI-sleep-DPAST
       'We went to sleep at about two o'clock.'

(26)   <Nan-ithʋnanchi ma katiohmi fokak mak <u>o</u> ilʋppa puta kʋt ai
       yʋmohma hi oh cho?>
       N<u>an</u>=ithan<u>á</u>chi-' ma' k<u>á</u>tiohmi-fokka-km-ak<u>o</u> ilappa potta-kat
       teacher-NML   VOC INT-about-IRR-CON:DS   this   all-COMP:NM
       aa-yamohm-ahii-oh-cho?
       LOC-happen-IRR-LINK-Q
       'Master, when will all these teachings be fulfilled?' (Luke 21:7)

18.2.3. Temporal modifiers

18.2.3.1. -hchaa 'generic'

This morpheme indicates that the action is generically true, or true over some extended period of time.[6] It is often translated into English as 'always' in the affirmative or 'never' in the negative. This suffix always appears in the pre-tense position, and in main clauses is always immediately followed by -tok 'past' or -ttook 'distant past':

(27)   Pisa si-achokma-kat   ikh<u>á</u>na-li-hchaa-tok.
       see   1SII-good-COMP:SS know:N-1SI-generic-PT
       'I always know when I look good.'[7]

(28)   Hih<u>í</u>lha-li-hchaa-tok.
       dance:HN-1SI-generic-PT
       'I always dance.'

---

6. Byington notes that -hchaa- is "used with verbs to express general truths or common usage, custom, etc., and when used in reference to persons it is implied that they are alive. For the dead bekatok is used instead of chatok" (1915:100). This seems to need some modification, given examples like (30) below, where the Saducees were presumably dead at the time of writing. Perhaps Byington's statement needs to be relativized to the point of view of the quoted speaker.

7. See chapter 11 for discussion of -tok in examples like this.

(29) *Káfi' ishko-l-ahii-baano-hchaa-tok.*
     coffee drink-1SI-IRR-really-generic-PT
     'I'm usually able to really drink (a lot of) coffee.'

(30) <Satusi ʋlheha hʋt, illi yʋt falamʋt tana he keyu achi chatuk>
     Satusi   alhiihah-at illi-yat   falaama-t   taan-ahii-kiiyo-h
     Sadducee group-NM   dead-NM return-PART rise-IRR-NEG-TNS
     aachi-hchaa-tok
     say-generic-PT
     'the Sadducees, who say that there is no resurrection' (Matt. 22:23)

(31) <. . . nana kʋt ai ʋlhpesa keyu, kashofa keyu hokʋno himmona kia,
     ʋpa li chatuk keyu hokʋt achi tok.>
     . . . *náṉa-k-at aay-alhpiisa-kiiyo-h,*
     thing-TNS-NM LOC-right-NEG-TNS
     kashoofa-kiiyo-h-ook-ano   himmona-kia apa-li-hchaa-tok
     clean-NEG-TNS-COMPAR-AC2 now-too   eat-1SI-generic-PT
     kiiyo-h-ookat,   aachi-ttook.
     NEG-TNS-but:SS say-DPAST
     '"Until now, I have never eaten anything common or unclean," he
     said.' (Acts 10:14)

The following example shows that it is ungrammatical for *-hchaa* to
appear in the pre-modal position before the irrealis *-aachi̱*.

(32a) *Pisa si-achokma-h bílliy-aachi̱-h.*
      see   1SII-good-TNS forever:G-IRR-TNS
      'I'll always be good looking.'

(32b) **Pisa si-achokma-hch-aachi̱-h.*
      see   1SII-good-always-IRR-TNS

Adverbial *-hchaa* can also be followed by the previous-mention
marker *-aash* (chapter 5). This combination appears in a conventional
opening of Choctaw folktales:

(33) *Hopaaki-hchaa-sh issi-yat   ko̱wi'   chito-h ano̱ka-ma̱*
     long-always-PREV deer-NM woods big-TNS in-DEM:AC
     átta-ttook.
     be:N-DPAST
     'Long ago, Deer was in a big woods.'

(34) *Hopaaki-hchaa-sh lowak-at achaffa-h illa-ttook.*
     long-always-PREV fire-NM   one-TNS   only-DPAST
     'Long ago, there was only one fire.'

18.2.3.2. *-i̱sha-* 'yet'

This affix does not occur with any of the modals, so it is not possible to
determine whether it is in pre-modal or pre-tense position. I have
included it with the temporal modifiers based on its meaning. It only

occurs on verbs that are negative, and is thus a polarity item, like English 'yet'.[8]

(35) *Ik-oklhilúl-ok-isha-h.*
      N-dark:L-NEG-yet-TNS
      'It wasn't dark yet.'

(36) *Is-sa-halali-haatoko,   ik-sa-ll-ok-isha-shkii.*
      2SI-1SII-hold:N-because:DS   N-1SII-die-NEG-yet-EXCLAM
      'Because you're holding on to me, I'm not dead yet.'[9]

The idea 'before X' is frequently expressed as 'when X hasn't happened yet' in Choctaw, as in the following example:

(37) <Nana a huchi bunna puta hokut huch ik im asilhho kisha kak inli ho, huch Iki ut ithana hoke.>
      Nána-h   hachi-banna-h potta-ho-kat,
      thing-TNS 2PII-want-TNS all-LINK-COMP:SS
      hachik-im-asilhlh-ok-isha-k-Ø-akili-h-o,
      2PN-III-ask-NEG-yet-TNS-COP-indeed-TNS-PART:DS
      hachi-ki-yat   ithána-h-ookii.
      2PIII-father-NM know:N-TNS-indeed
      'Whatever you want, before you have even asked him, your Father knows it.' (Lit., 'Whatever you want, when you still haven't asked him, your Father knows it.') (Matt. 6:8)

Unlike English, the negation must occur on the same verb that -*isha* occurs on. The negation of a verb in a higher clause is not sufficient to license the occurrence of -*isha*.

(38) *Ak-itháan-o-h   ik-talóow-ok-osha-kma nana-ka.*
      1SN-know:L-NEG-TNS N-sing:L-NEG-yet-IRR   whether-COMP:DS
      'I don't know whether he has sung yet.'

(39) *Ak-ithaan-o-h   taloowa-osha-kma nana-ka.*
      1SN-know:L-NEG-TNS sing-yet-IRR   whether-COMP:DS
      ('I don't know whether he has sung yet.')

18.2.4. Truth modifiers

18.2.4.1. -*malhlhi*- 'truly'

This adverbial appears in pre-tense position.[10] It may not precede a modal.

---

8. There is an idiolectal or dialectal variant of this suffix, -*osha*.

9. This is a line from a traditional Choctaw hymn.

10. Diachronically, it must be related to the independent stative verb *alhlhih* 'to be true'.

(40) *Aka̲ka' nipi'-m-ak   álla-h-o̲   apa-li-malhlhi-tok.*
      chicken meat-DEM-OBL only-TNS-PART:DS eat-1SI-truly-PT
      'I really did only eat chicken.'

(41a) *Aká̲ka' nípi'-m-ak   álla-h-o̲   apa-l-aachi̲-malhlhi-h.*
      chicken meat-DEM-OBL only-TNS-PART:DS eat-1SI-IRR-truly-TNS
      'I'm really only going to eat chicken.'

(41b) **Aká̲ka' nípi'-m-ak   álla-h-o̲   apa-li-malhlh-aachi̲-h.*
      chicken meat-DEM-OBL only-TNS-PART:DS eat-1SI-truly-IRR-TNS

It is fairly frequent in the Choctaw Bible, as in the following examples:

(42) <Sal ʋt ʋla chi̲ mʋhli cho?>
      Saul-at   al-aachi̲-malhlhi-h-cho?
      Saul-NM arrive-IRR-truly-TNS-Q
      'Is it true that Saul will come?' (1 Sam. 23:10)

(43) <Hatak okʋto ʋm ʋla mʋhli tuk . . .>
      Hattak-ook-ato   am-ala-malhlhi-tok.
      man-COMPAR-NM2 1SIII-come-truly-PT
      'It is true that two men came to me.' (Josh. 2:4)

The adverbial *-malhlhi* seems to be appropriate in approximately the same contexts as the English "It is true that . . ."—namely, in situations where the truth of a proposition is being questioned or contrasted with the falsity of another proposition.

In some cases, it seems that *-malhlhi* must be attached to a null copula. In (44), it appears after a noun in the accusative case, while in (45) it follows a verb with a different subject marker.

(44) <Ilʋppak osh Klaist fehna mako̲ mʋhli kʋno, hatak pehlichi ʋhleha hʋt akostininchi hoh chishba?>
      Ilappak-oosh Christ-fúhna-mak-o̲   Ø-malhlhi-kano
      this-FOC:NM   Christ-very-DEM-FOC:AC COP-truly-COMP:DS2
      hattak pihlíchi' alhiihah-at akostiní̲chi-h-o̲   chishba?
      man   leader   group-NM   understand-TNS-Q doubt
      'Do the rulers understand that this is truly the very Christ?' (John 7:26)

(45) <Elias ak osh ti̲kba ʋla chah, nan okluha ka falaminchit achukmalit taiyahla he tuk o̲ mʋhli.>
      Elias-akoosh ti̲kba' áala-cha   ná̲n-okloha-ka falammi̲chi-t
      Elias-CON:NM first   arrive:L-SS thing-all-COMP return-PART
      achokmali-t táyyahl-ahii-tok-o̲   Ø-malhlhi-h.
      do:well-PART complete:Y-IRR-PT-PART:DS COP-truly-TNS
      'It is truly the case that Elias will come first and completely restore all things.' (Matt. 17:11)

The following example is puzzling in showing -*malhlhi* after the tense marker. Perhaps it also involves a null copula:

(46)   <. . . i̱ haiaka li tuk mvhli keyu cho?>
        . . . *i̱-hayaaka-li-tok ∅-malhlhi-kiiyo-h-cho?*
        III-appear-1SI-PT   COP-truly-NEG-TNS-Q
        'Did I not truly appear to (them)?' (1 Sam. 2:27)

18.2.4.2. -*naaha* 'almost'

This adverbial is incompatible with modals, and always appears immediately before the tense morpheme:[11]

(47)   *Sa-bikiili-naaha-tok.*
        1SII-stifle-almost-PT
        'I almost feel like I can't breathe.'

(48)   *Sa-lli-naaha-tok.*
        1SII-die-almost-PT
        'I almost died.'

(49a)   *Sa-yyi' okpani-li-naaha-tok.*
        1SII-leg break-1SI-almost-PT
        'I almost broke my leg.'

(49b)   **Sa-yyi' okpani-li-naah-aachi̱-h*
        1SII-leg break-1SI-almost-IRR-TNS
        ('I will almost break my leg.')

18.2.5. Speaker evaluations

18.2.5.1. -*kiiyo* 'negative'

The negative -*kiiyo* may appear in pre-tense or post-tense position, but it may not appear in pre-modal position. The pre-tense position is far more common in texts:

(50a)   *John-at shókha' abi-kiiyo-tok.*
        John-NM hog   kill-NEG-PT
        'John didn't kill the hog.'

(50b)   *John-at shókha' abi-tok-kiiyo(-h).*
        John-NM hog   kill-PT-NEG(-TNS)

(51a)   *John-at shókha' ab-aachi̱-kiiyo-h.*
        John-NM hog   kill-IRR-NEG-TNS
        'John isn't going to kill the hog.'

---

11. Nicklas (1974:186) lists several other variants of this suffix: -*ahǫsi*, -*ahǫsi*, -*na̱ha*, -*naha̱ǫsi*, and -*na̱ǫsi*.

(51b) *John-at shókha' abi-kiiyo(k)-aachi̱-h.
John-NM hog   kill-NEG-IRR-TNS

(52) <. . . chʋch atuk ma, i̱ haponakla he keyu hokmʋt, . . .>
. . . church aa-tok-ma i̱-haponakl-ahii-kiiyo-h-oo-kmat . . .
church   COP-PT-IRR III-listen-IRR-NEG-TNS-LINK-IRR:SS
'If he won't listen to the church . . .' (Matt. 18:17)

When -kiiyo is in post-tense position, it has some properties of an independent word. The verb preceding it sometimes shows the participial -oo, generally marked for different subject.

(53) <ibbak achifa ha yo̱ keyukmʋt, impa keyu beka tuk>[12]
ibbak achiif-ahii-yo̱   kiiyo-kmat, ipa-kiiyo-biika-tok
hand wash-IRR-PART:DS NEG-IRR:SS eat-NEG-extent-PT
'If they haven't washed their hands, they don't eat.' (Mark 7:33)

(54) <Iskʋli ont isht aiyopi fehna ka ish atobbi ho̱ keyukmʋt . . .>
Iskáli' o̱t   isht   áyyopi-fíhna-ka   ish-atobbi-h-o̱
money go:and INSTR last-exactly-COMP 2SI-pay-TNS-PART:DS
kiiyo-kmat . . .
NEG-IRR:SS
'If you haven't paid the last bit of the money . . .' (Luke 12:59)

(55) <nan ashʋchi tok o̱ keyu hoke>
ná̱n=asháchchi-ttook-o̱ kiiyo-h-okii
sin-DPAST-PART:DS   NEG-TNS-INDEED
'. . . they did not sin . . .' (John 9:3)

(56) <Vba yak o̱ auet ai ima ho̱ keyukma, hatak ʋt nana ho̱ ilap inli kʋt isha he keyu hoke.>
Aba-yako̱   awiit   aay-ima-h-o̱   kiiyo-kma,
above-CON:AC toward LOC-give-TNS-PART:DS NEG-IRR
hattak-at ná̱na-h-o̱   ilaapi̱li-kat
man-NM   thing-TNS-PART:AC do:by:oneself-COMP:SS
ish-ahii-kiiyo-h-okii.
get-IRR-NEG-TNS-INDEED
'If he does not get it from heaven, a man gets nothing by himself.'
(John 3:27)

Another property of post-tense -kiiyo that makes it seem like an independent word is the occasional appearance of a second tense marker following -kiiyo:

(57) <Vno ak osh chim apesa li tuk keyu cho?>
Ano-akoosh chim-apiisa-li-tok   kiiyo-h-cho?
I-CON:NM   2SIII-command-1SI-PT NEG-TNS-Q
'Have I not commanded you?' (Josh. 1:9)

12. The Choctaw text here says <achifa ha yo̱>, which is unintelligible to speakers I asked. It is probably a misprint for <achifa he yo̱>.

(58) *Taloowa-tok-kiiyo-h-o̱?*
      sing-PT-NEG-TNS-Q
      'Didn't she sing?'

We might treat these last two facts as evidence that there is an auxiliary verb *kiiyoh*, but there are several puzzles for this approach. Unlike the uncontroversial auxiliaries, *-kiiyo* is never followed by irrealis morphemes or by the first person agreement *-li*. Also unlike the other auxiliaries, it is preceded by a verb explicitly marked for tense. Possibly there are different classes of auxiliaries, so that *tahlih/tahah* and *kiiyoh* are both auxiliaries but belong to different classes.

18.2.5.2. *-polla* 'must'

Polla or *-polla* is a poorly understood element in Choctaw which can be glossed as 'must' or 'because' (Nicklas 1974:141). It may appear either before or after tense.

(59) *O̱ba-polla-tok.*
      rain-must-PT
      'It must have rained.'

(60) *O̱ba-tok-polla.*
      rain-PT-must
      'It must have rained.'

(61) *Ala-polla-haatokoosh, ala-t   a̱-binaachi-tok.*
      come-must-because   come-PART 1sIII-camp-PT
      'He had to come, so he came and camped with me.'

(62) *M-ak-Ø-polla-kiiyo-kiya,   i̱lachi-h-oosh*
      that-OBL-COP-must-NEG-but do:differently-TNS-PART:SS
      ish-mihchi-kma̱, alhpiis-aki̱li-h.
      2sI-do-if:DS   okay-indeed-TNS
      'It mustn't be that way; if you do it differently, it will be okay.'

In main clauses with an irrealis modal, *-polla* implies that the speaker is sure of the outcome:

(63) *Oktosh-aachi̱-polla-h.*
      snow-IRR-must-TNS
      'It *will* snow.'

When the clause is past tense, the sentence is generally translated as 'must have':

(64) *O̱ba-polla-tok.*
      rain-must-PT
      'It must have rained.'

The element -*polla* also appears in exhortations:

(65)   *Ish-la-polla-shkii!*
        2SI-come-must-EXHORT
        'You must come!'

When *polla* is a separate word, it is most likely that it is a verb. Some evidence that *polla* may be a main verb comes from examples in which it takes a clausal complement:

(66)   *Oktosh-aachi̱-ka̱   polla-h.*
        snow-IRR-COMP:DS must-TNS
        'It *will* snow.'

When embedded, *polla* usually occurs in reason clauses, where it has the gloss 'because'. The relationship between 'because' and 'must' is less than clear. Perhaps the common semantics has to do with the presupposition that the preceding clause is true.

(67)   <Huchim anukfila hʊt ik hlampko pulla kak o̱, hatak anumpuli chatuk
        mak o̱ chiyuhmit anumpuli lishke>
        Hachim-anokfilah-at   ik-lhápk-o-polla-k-ako̱,
        2PIII-mind-NM   N-strong:L-NEG-because-OBL-CON:DS
        hattak anópoli-hchaa-tok-mak-o̱   chóyyohmi-t
        man   talk-generic-PT-DEM-FOC:AC   be:like:Y-PART
        anópoli-li-shkii
        talk-1SI-EXHORT
        'Because your minds are not strong, I speak like men speak.' (Rom. 6:19)

(68)   <. . . ilap ʊt anumpa kʊllo ikbi tuk pulla, micha apehat binohma̱ya
        hatuk pulla mak o̱ ik im ai a̱hlo ka hi a̱ ik ahno ki tok.>
        Ilaap-at anno̱pa' kállo' ikbi-tok-polla,   micha
        self-NM word   strong make-PT-because and
        apiiha-t   binohmáya-h aa-tok-polla   m-ako̱
        with-PART   sit:PL-TNS   be-PT-because that-CON:AC
        ik-im-aay-álh-ok-ahii-ya̱   ik-áhn-o-kii-ttook.
        N-III-LOC-true:L-NEG-IRR2-DS N-think:L-NEG-NEG-DPAST
        'Because of the oath he took, and because of those that were sitting with her, he would not refuse her.' (Mark 6:26)

In a few instances, *polla* occurs, but it is unclear what it contributes to the meaning of the sentence as a whole:

(69)   <. . . ilʊppak osh Klaist, yakni okchalinchi mak atuk pulla ka il
        akostininchishke . . .>
        Ilapp-akoosh Klaist, yakni' okchalíchi'
        this-CON:NM   Christ land   save:NML
        mak aa-tok-polla-ka   il-akostini̱chi-shkii.
        DEM be-PT-must-COMP 1PI-believe-EXHORT
        'We believe that this is Christ, the savior of the world . . .' (John 4:41)

Perhaps *polla* ought to be translated 'must be' in this example.

The use of *polla* as a determiner in noun phrases is discussed in chapter 5.

18.2.5.3. -*akilih* 'indeed'

The emphatic particle -*akilih* is quite frequent in spoken Choctaw.[13] It ends in an *h* which appears only when there is a following vowel. There are two possibilities for the analysis. The final *h* could be the default tense marker -*h*. However, since this *h* appears in cases where tense is already marked elsewhere, that suggests that there is an additional verbal element present—either a null copula or -*akili* itself. Alternately, the underlying form may be -*akilih*.

(70)   <Nana a huchi bunna puta hokut huch ik im asilhho kisha kak inli ho, huch Iki ut ithana hoke.>
        Nana   hachi-banna-h   pootta-hoo-kat,
        thing 2PII-want-TNS   all-LINK-COMP:SS
        hachik-im-asílhlh-ok-isha-k-akilih-o,
        2PN-III-ask:L-NEG-yet-TNS-indeed-PART:DS
        hachi-ki-yat   ithána-h-ookii.
        2PIII-father-NM   know:N-TNS-indeed
        'Whatever you want, before you have even asked him, your Father knows it.' (Lit. 'Whatever you want, when you still haven't asked him, your Father knows it.') (Matt. 6:8)

The element -*akilih* appears in pre-tense and post-tense positions.

(71)   *Miti-akili-tok.*
        come-indeed-PT
        'He sure did come.'

(72)   *Mit-aachi-kili-h*
        come-IRR-indeed-TNS
        'He sure will come.'

(73)   *Oba-tok-akilih.*
        rain-PT-indeed
        'It did also rain.'

(74)   *Ob-akili-tok.*
        rain-indeed-PT
        'It also rained.'

In the Choctaw testament, -*akilih* is customarily written as two words and Byington (1915) glosses it as 'also, likewise, too, that again'. He

13. This morpheme is often pronounced [agēli], that is, with a lowering of the second vowel. This pronunciation is somewhat puzzling. [e] is not phonemic in Choctaw, and there is no rule that predicts that *i* should be pronounced [e] in this context.

suggests that it is composed of -*ak* 'that' and *ili* 'self, also'. In the terms of this description, Byington's demonstrative -*ak* should probably be equated with -*ak* 'oblique' (discussed in chapter 5).[14] This suffix should be compared to the suffix -*akilih*- which appears on nouns.

18.3. Concepts not expressed by adverbials

Several classes of adverbials that are common in other languages are absent in Choctaw. These include adverbs of manner, speaker evaluation, and quantification. The follow sections briefly discuss how Choctaw expresses these concepts.

18.3.1. Manner expressions

Manner is not expressed by adverbials in Choctaw, but by verbs. The most frequent combination is a verb of manner subordinated to another verb.

(75) <Oh ia cha, ʋlosi atukma achukmalit hʋsh hoyashke.>
      Oh-íiya-cha   allọsi' aa-tok-ma   achokmali-t   hash-hoy-ashkii.
      PLUR-go:L-SS child   COP-PT-DEM do:well-PART 2PI-search-EXHORT
      'Go and search diligently for the child.' (Matt. 2:8)

(76) <Pit ʋlhpesʋchit ish anukfilli mʋhlishke.>
      Pit   alhpiisachi-t   ish-anokfilli-malhlhi-shkii.
      away   do:correctly-PART   2SI-think-truly-EXHORT
      'You have judged correctly.' (Luke 7:43)

Also possible are constructions where the verb of manner is the main verb and the verb of action is subordinate:

(77) *Pihlichi-kat   achokma-h.*
      lead-COMP:SS good-TNS
      'He leads well.'

(78) *Chahta' annọpa'   anọpoli-li-kat*
      Choctaw language speak-1sI-COMP:SS
      alhpisaali-li-akili-h-ọ?
      do:correctly-1sI-indeed-TNS-Q
      'Am I speaking Choctaw correctly?'

18.3.2. Speaker-oriented adverbs

English adverbs that express a speaker's attitude towards a proposition or evidence for a proposition are expressed by evidential suffixes and auxiliaries, discussed in chapters 12 and 13:

14. The identification of *ili* is more difficult, but it is perhaps related to a morpheme *illa* which means 'only'.

(79)   _Ǫb-aachi̱-h-a._
       rain-IRR-TNS-GUESS
       'It's probably going to rain.'

18.3.3. Quantificational adverbs

English adverbs like _completely, totally, utterly_ are expressed in Choctaw through auxiliaries, which are discussed in chapter 13:

(80)   _Itti-yat   kobaafa-t   taha-h._
       wood-NM   broken-PART   complete-TNS
       'The wood is completely broken up.'

19. Lexical semantics and special semantic fields

This chapter outlines the lexical semantics of several complex semantic fields in Choctaw: kinship terminology, verbs of location, verbs of possession, and verbs of physical and metaphorical motion. I also include data on the special semantic fields of baby talk and personal names.

19.1. Kinship terminology

Choctaw kinship terminology is in the process of change. This section discusses the most traditional terminology and some of the ways in which the system seems to be changing.

As discussed in chapter 4, some nouns show agreement with a possessor through the use of class II prefixes, while other nouns use class III prefixes. Although class II prefixes are primarily found with kinship terms and body part terms, many kinship terms nevertheless show possession through class III prefixes. In the following discussion, I have shown the first person singular possessed forms as an indication of the possessor agreement type; *sa-* or *si-* is the first person singular class II prefix and *am-* or *a̲-* is the first person singular class III prefix.

Many kinship terms vary according to the sex of the ego. For example, *-tiik* is the word used for speaking of sister of a man, as in the following:

(1) *John i̲-tiik*   'John's sister'
     a̲-tiik   'my sister' (said by a man)
     chi̲-tiik   'your sister' (said to a man)

As this example shows, it is not the sex of the *speaker* that is relevant, but the sex of the person whose relationship is being spoken of.

19.1.1. Relationships within the immediate family

The full set of sibling terms that are differentiated by sex or ego is as follows:

(2) *sa-nakfish*   'my younger brother [male ego]; my younger sister [female ego]'
     am-anni'   'my older brother [male ego]'
     a̲-tiik   'my sister [male ego]'
     a̲-nákfi'   'my brother' [female ego]'

Some speakers of Oklahoma Choctaw no longer have the same gender restrictions on these kinship terms.

The following terms can be used for either male or female egos:

(3a)   *sa-ttiabishi'*   'my brother or sister'[1]
        sa-ttibaapishi'   'my brother or sister'

(3b)   *sa-tikba'*   'my older brother or sister'
        a̱-tikba'   'my older brother or sister'

(3c)   *am-akni'*   'the oldest child in my family'

Ittiabishi' is a contraction of *ittibaapishi'*, composed of *itti-* 'reciprocal', *ibaa-* 'comitative', and *pishi* 'suck', literally 'one who sucked with'. For speakers I have consulted, this noun takes a II or III prefix. However, Byington (1915:214) lists forms like the following:

(4a)   *itti-baa-pishi-li'*
        RCP-COMIT-suck-1SI
        'my brother' (lit., 'I sucked with him')

(4b)   *ish-itti-baa-pishi'*
        2SI-RCP-COMIT-suck
        'your brother' (lit., 'you sucked with him')

(4c)   *chi-tti-baa-pishi'*
        2SII-RCP-COMIT-suck
        'your brother' (lit., 'he sucked with you')

Since nouns do not normally receive class I marking for possessives, it seems clear that these expressions are deverbal. *Ittibaapishi'* is the normal translation for 'brother' and 'sister' in the Choctaw translation of the Bible (perhaps to avoid difficulties in determining relative ages of siblings mentioned in the Bible).

Munro and Willmond (1994) report that the Chickasaw cognate *ittibaapishi* is normally used with II possession, but that I is possible, though rare.

The following terms for parents are used:

(5)   *sa-shki'*   'my mother'   ·
       a̱-ki'   'my father'

Some speakers also use the English terms *mama* and *daddy*, with varying degrees of assimilation to Choctaw phonology.

(6)   *a̱-mamah*   'my mother'
       a̱-daddy, a̱-taatih   'my father'

In terms for children, sex of the relative is marked only optionally.

---

1. For some speakers I have recorded *sa-tiabishi'* with simple *t* rather than a geminate.

(7a) *si-oshi'*   *(nakni')*
      1sII-child male
      'my son'

(7b) *si-oshi'*   *(tiik)*
      1sII-child female
      'my daughter'

The Choctaw Bible uses another word, *sa-sso'* for 'my son', but this term is now obsolete.

The terms for 'husband' and 'wife' are simply the terms for 'man' and 'woman' with the appropriate possessive prefix.

(8a) *am-ohóoyo'*
      1sIII-woman
      'my wife'

(8b) *a-háttak*   .
      1sIII-man
      'my husband'

However, as Nicklas (1974:50) notes, in these words the pitch accent is on the penult, in contrast to their normal final accent (*ohooyó', hatták*).

To be polite, husbands and wives do not call each other by name, and they may also avoid the terms 'husband' and 'wife'. It is common for husbands and wives to refer to each other by their relationship to their children. For example, if a man and his wife have a son named John, then the husband may call his wife *John ishki'* 'John's mother', and the wife may call her husband *John iki'* 'John's father'.

19.1.2. Aunts and uncles

Terms for aunts and uncles by blood are as follows:

(9a) *am-oshi'*
      1sIII-mother's:brother
      'my mother's brother'

(9b) *a-ki'*   *acháffa'*
      1sIII-fatheother
      'my father's brother'

(10a) *a-hokni'*
      1sIII-father's:sister
      'my father's sister'

(10b) *sa-shki'*   *acháffa'*
      1sII-mother other
      'my mother's sister'

Swanton (1931:85–87) notes that at one time *-hokni'* was used only for male egos, with females using the term *ippókni'*. However, this is no longer the case for speakers I consulted. *Hokni'* is used for both male and female egos.

Aunts and uncles by marriage get a different set of terms in the traditional usage, as in (11a)–(14a) these are now generally replaced by the compound terms in (11b)–(14b). In the traditional terminology, we see the generational skewing associated with the Crow type of kinship terminology. Note that the term for the mother's brother's wife, *saháyya'*, is the same as the term for a brother's wife, and that the term for the father's sister's husband, *amaafo'*, is the same as the term for grandfather.

(11a) *sa-háyya'*
       1sII-(mother's):brother's:wife
       'my mother's brother's wife' (traditional term)

(11b) *am-oshi'*   *im-ohóoyo'*
       1sIII-mother's:brother III-wife
       'my mother's brother's wife' (current term)

(12a) *sa-shki'*
       1sII-mother
       'my father's brother's wife' (traditional term)

(12b) *a-ki'*   *achaffa' im-ohóoyo'*
       1sIII-father other   III-wife
       'my father's brother's wife' (current term)

(13a) *am-aafo'*
       1sIII-grandfather
       'my father's sister's husband' (traditional term)

(13b) *a-hokni'*   *i-háttak*
       1sIII-father's:sister III-husband
       'my father's sister's husband' (current term)

(14a) *a-ki'*
       1sIII-father
       'my mother's sister's husband' (traditional term)

(14b) *sa-shki'*   *acháffa' i-háttak*
       1sII-mother other   III-husband
       'my mother's sister's husband' (current term)

(15)   *am-oshi'*   *acháffa'*
       1sIII-mother's:brother other
       'my stepmother's brother'

19.1.3. Nieces and nephews

Terms for nieces and nephews vary according to the sex of the ego. Children of a same-sex sibling are called 'half-children', while children of opposite-sex siblings receive special terms.

(16)   *Sa-bbayyi'*   'my sister's son [male ego]; my brother's son
                              [female ego]'
        sa-bbi' tiik   'my sister's daughter [male ego]; my brother's
                             daughter [female ego]'

(17a)   *si-oshi'   iklanna'*
        1sII-son   half
        'my brother's son [male ego]; my sister's son [female ego]'

(17b)   *si-oshi'   tiik   iklanna'*
        1sII-son   female   half
        'my brother's daughter [male ego]; my sister's daughter [female ego]'

19.1.4. Grandparents and grandchildren

The following terms are used for grandparents and grandchildren:

(18)   *am-aafo'*   'my grandfather'
        sa-ppókni'   'my grandmother'

(19)   *sa-ppok   (nakni'/tiik)*
        1sII-grandchild male/female
        'my grandchild'

19.1.5. Relatives by marriage

The following terms are used for in-laws belonging to one's own generation:

(20a)   *am-aalakosi'*   'my wife's brother'
        a̱-lakos²

(20b)   *am-aalakos   ohooyo'*
        1sIII-wife's:brother female
        'my wife's sister'

(21a)   *sa-ppo'*   'my husband's brother' (rare)

(21b)   *am-o̱balaaha'*   'my husband's sister' (rare)

(21c)   *am-alla'   i̱-hokni'*
        1sIII-child III-father's:sister
        'my husband's sister' (= 'my child's paternal aunt')

(22a)   *am-aalak*   'my sister's husband'

(22b)   *sa-háyya'*   'my brother's wife'

---

2. Mississippi Choctaw men sometimes use this word more widely as an affectionate term of address to friends. Speakers of Oklahoma Choctaw that I consulted were unfamiliar with this usage.

It is considered impolite for a woman to call her husband's brothers and sisters by name, and this may be related to the rarity of the traditional terms for these relationships. As the term *amalla' ihokni'* shows, the strategy of referring to certain relatives in terms of the relation they bear to your children (seen above in terms for 'husband' and 'wife') is also operative in this area.

Terms for parents-in-law are as follows:

(23)   *sa-ppochi'*   'my father-in-law'
        sa-ppoch-ohooyo'   'my mother-in-law'

19.1.6. The *halooka'* relationship

In addition to the terms for in-laws given above, there is also a special term, *halooka'*, which has no equivalent in English. Roughly, *halooka'* are the close male relatives of a spouse. More specifically, a woman's *halooka'* are her husband's brother and her husband's father. A man's *halooka'* are his wife's brother and father. These relatives are due special respect, and Choctaws sometimes refer to such relatives as *halooka'*. This term is fairly common among the Mississippi Choctaws, but several Oklahoma Choctaws I consulted were unfamiliar with it.

When Mississippi Choctaws are asked the names for in-law relations like 'husband's brother', they tend to be puzzled that they do not know the name for this relative and then mention that this person is *halooka'*. It seems to be the case that the rules of politeness required towards this class of relations tend to make direct reference to them rather rare; circumlocutions and references to the rela-tionship that such people bear to children are the norm.

Byington says that the word *halooka'* means 'sacred, beloved, dear' and defines *halooka'* as "father-in-law; son-in-law; an appelation proper only for those who sustain this marriage relation, and not even used by others in speaking of them; a man who sustains the relation of uncle calls his niece's husband *haloka*, and the latter calls this uncle *haloka* in return" (1915:134–35).

19.1.7. Cousins

The earliest records of the Choctaw kinship system show that different kinds of cousins had different names (Swanton 1931), but this system is no longer in use, with one exception. Speakers of Choctaw call their father's sisters *ahokni'* 'my aunt', and some Mississippi Choctaw also use this word in referring to the daughters of the father's sister. Swanton (1931:85) confirms that this is a conservative feature in the kinship system. The preservation of an extended sense of the word *ahokni'* may be related to the important role that the father's sister plays in the Choctaw family. She is a figure of authority who is due respect from her nieces and nephews.

The general way of referring to cousins in modern Choctaw is to use the correct word for 'brother' or 'sister' (depending on the sex and age of the ego) and follow this with the Choctaw word *iklanna'* 'half'.

19.1.8. Half-relatives and step-relatives

Step-relatives are those who are related through the remarriage of a parent. A step-relative bears no blood relationship to the ego. In Choctaw, these relatives are called by the regular name for that relative, followed by the word *toba'* 'make'. So *sashki' toba'* is 'my stepmother'; *sanakfish toba'* is 'my younger stepbrother [male ego]; my younger stepsister [female ego]'; and so on.

Half-relatives are those who are related through only one parent, as is the case when a parent has children with a second spouse. There is no special word for such relatives in Choctaw. They are simply called by the ordinary terms for 'brother' and 'sister'.

The difference between the English and Choctaw words for these relatives tends to be confusing to speakers of both languages. The Choctaw term *tiabishi' iklanna'* is literally 'half brother', but it refers to the relative that is called 'cousin' in English. The English word 'half-brother' is simply *tiabishi'* 'brother' in Choctaw.

19.2. Verbs of position

As noted in chapter 3, Choctaw has a special set of verbs of position. These are displayed in table 19.1. As Nicklas (1974:59) and Heath (1980) discuss, all the verbs of position in Choctaw show three-way suppletion for the number of the subject (singular, dual, and plural). This pattern of suppletion is peculiar to this set of verbs; most Choctaw verb stems show no number alternations. Note that most of the plural forms show two forms, one ending in *-ohlih* and another ending in *-ohmáyah*. The latter form seems more common, and it may include a form of the independent verb *máyah* 'to sit, dwell (pl.)'. The verb 'to lie' is exceptional in that its plural has only one form.[3]

---

3. There is a verb *kahlih* 'to place a bet', which may be historically related to this verb of position.

Table 19.1 Verbs of position

SINGULAR	DUAL	PLURAL	GLOSS
attah	ashwah	ayyaashah áashah, áshah, máyah[4]	'to sit, dwell'
biniilih	chiiyah	binohlih, binohmáyah	'to sit'
talaayah	taloohah	talohlih, talohmáyah	'to lie, sit'
hikiiyah	hiilih	hiyohlih, hiyohmáyah	'to stand'
ittolah	kahah	kahmáyah	'to lie'
takaalih	takoohah	takohlih, takohmáyah	'to hang'

All of these verbs may be used to describe the position of an animate subject, but inanimate objects are classified according to the verb of position that they occur with. Nicklas describes this classification as follows:

> All of these verbs can be used to tell what posture something is in. Their meanings when the actor is animate (a human or animal) are those given in the list. *Atta* is used only in speaking of humans and birds, for the most part. *Talaya* is used only when speaking of inanimate objects. In speaking of inanimate objects, *hikiya* is used if the major dimension is vertical, *ittola* is used if the major dimension is horizontal, and *talaya* is used for globular objects. (1974:59)

A few points here require some discussion.

The semantics of *talaayah* 'to sit, lie' are difficult for many Choctaw speakers to explain. Prototypical instances include containers like coffee cups, pans, vases, buckets, and baskets, as in the following example:

(24) *Káfi' aayíshko-yat aayi̱pa' talá̱ya-h.*
      coffee cup-NM   table   lie:N-TNS
      'The coffee cup is on the table.'

Talaayah is also used in describing the location of cities, countries, and buildings:

(25) <Atuk osh Katalenes okla i̱ yakni Kalili auet i chapa ka talaia ka, okla ont ataiya tok.>
      Aa-tok-oosh   Gadarenes oklah i̱-yakni' Galilee awiit
      be-PT-PART:SS Gadarenes people III-land Galilee toward

---

4. See discussion in text for differences between these verbs.

ichaapa-ka   talaaya-ka   oklah ot   atayya-ttook.
beside-COMP lie-COMP   PLUR go:and land-DPAST
'And they arrived at the country of the Gadarenes, which is over towards Galilee.' (Luke 8:26)

(26) *Los Angeles-ma   Dodgers aa-washóoha'-mat taláya-h.*
Los Angeles-D:AC Dodgers LOC-play-D:NM   lie:N-TNS
'Dodger Stadium (lit., "where the Dodgers play") is in Los Angeles.'

Talaayah is also sometimes used for the location or possession of water or food:

(27) <Oka' kapʋssai ʋt chin talaia? An talaiʋshke.>
Oka   kapassa-yat chi-talaayah? A-talaaya-shkii.
water cold-NM   2sII-lie   1sIII-lie-indeed
'Have you any fresh water? Yes, I have.' (Byington 1827:117)

(28) *Ilhpak-at itikba' talohmáya-h.*
food-NM   front   lie:PL-TNS
'The food is in front of it.'

Mrs. Edith Gem suggested that the reason *talaayah* is appropriate for water is that the water is almost certainly contained in something.

Choctaws sometimes use *talaayah* to describe a person lying on his back, but this is considered a humorous description (perhaps because a human is being compared to an object).[5]

Hikiiyah 'to stand' is used for things like tables, chairs, beds, cars, corn, trees, and horns.

(29) *Waanota' kaah-at hikíya-h.*
yard   car-NM   stand:N-TNS
'There is a car in the yard.'

(30) *Osaapa' tachi-yat hiyohmáya-h.*
field   corn-NM stand:PL-TNS
'There's corn in the field.'

(31) *Aahopóoni'-ma aabinüli' hikiya-h.*
kitchen-D:AC   chair   stand:N-TNS
'There's a chair in the kitchen.'

A rather surprising use of *hikiiyah* describes the position of boils, warts or moles on the skin:

(32) *Tali' lósa' sa-bbak pa   hikíya-h.*
rock black 1sII-arm here stand:N-TNS
'There's a mole here on my arm.'

---

5. Munro and Willmond (1994) note that the Chickasaw cognate *tálla'a* is also used as a joking description of people.

In the Choctaw Bible, *hikiiyah* is also used for grass, but speakers I consulted thought this sounded odd. Some idiomatic uses of *hikiiyah* as an auxiliary verb are discussed in chapter 13.

Ittolah 'to lie' is used (a) with relatively small inanimate objects that are not in containers, such as pencils, apples, and books or, (b) with larger items that have a horizontal orientation:

(33) *Isht=holissóchi-yat aaı̨́pa' ittǫ́la-h.*
      pencil-NM   table   lie:N-TNS
      'The pencil is lying on the table.'

(34) *Tákkon-at aaı̨́pa' paknaka' ittǫ́la-h.*
      apple-NM   table   on   lie:N-TNS
      'There is an apple on the table.'

(35) *Itti'-ma   oklah bashli-tok-o ittǫ́la-h.*
      tree-DEM   PLUR   cut-PT-DS   lie:N-TNS
      'The tree they cut is lying there.'

Takaalih 'to hang' describes the position of things located off the ground.

(36) *Tákkon-at itti'-ma̲   takohmáya-h.*
      apple-NM   tree-D:NM   hang:PL-TNS
      'Apples are hanging on the tree.'

(37) *Hashi'=kanálli-it wall-ma̲   takáli-tok.*
      clock-NM   wall-D:AC hang:N-PT
      'The clock is on the wall.'

Scars and tattoos are described as 'hanging' on the body:

(38) *Mı̨sa-yat sa-bbak   takáli-h.*
      scar-NM   1sII-arm   hang:N-TNS
      'There's a scar on my arm.'

Takaalih seems to be the correct positional verb for scars and tattoos regardless of where they appear on the body; the orientation of the affected body part does not seem to affect the choice of verb.

There are some special difficulties associated with describing the use of the verbs *áyyaashah*, *áashah* and *ą́shah*. All are used to describe the location of plural subjects. *Áashah* and *áyyaashah* appear to be reduced and unreduced forms, respectively, of the y-grade of an unattested root *ashah*. *Ą́shah* appears to be the n-grade of the same verb. *Áashah* implies purposeful staying in a place, or having a certain place as a residence, and requires an animate subject:

(39) *Ofi-yat waanota' áasha-h.*
      dog-NM   yard   be:PL-TNS
      'The dogs stay in the yard, live in the yard.'

(40) *Hattak okloshi'-mat yakni'-m-ako̱   áasha-h.*
      man   tribe-D:NM   land-that-CON:AC be:PL-TNS
      'That tribe lives in that land.'

A̱*shah* tends to imply simple location, without the same durative or purposeful sense:

(41) *Itti' kobóhli'   waanota' ásha-h.*
      tree broken:PL yard   be:PL-TNS
      'There are sticks in the yard.'

In general, á*shah* is not used with animate things; one of the other verbs describing position is better:

(42) *Ofi-yat waanota' ásha-h.*
      dog-NM   yard   be:pl-TNS
      'There are dogs in the yard.'

(43) *Ofi-yat waanota' ma̱ya-h.*
      dog-NM   yard   be:PL-TNS
      'There are (three or more) dogs in the yard.'

All of the positional verbs may also be used as auxiliaries. This usage is described in chapter 13.

19.3. Verbs of possession

19.3.1. Possession with *ishih*

There are two ways that possession may be indicated. The first is to use the n-grade of the verb *ishih* 'to take, get', as in the following example:

(44) *Shapo' ish-i̱shi-h-o̱?*
      hat   2SI-have:N-TNS-Q
      'Do you have a hat?'

The n-grade is a durative aspectual form, discussed in more detail in chapter 10.

I̱*shih* is an ordinary verb with a nominative subject and an accusative or unmarked object:

(45) *John-at skali'   i̱shi-h.*
      John-NM money have:N-TNS
      'John has money.'

However, possessive sentences with i̱*shih* are somewhat restricted in their use. Some conservative speakers of Choctaw say that the verb i̱*shih* is comparable to a verb like *hold* in English, and it is best used with objects that are actually in a person's hands. Such speakers would find a sentence like the following odd or ungram-matical (if used to mean 'have'), since it implies that the person is holding the dog in his or her arms:

(46)   % *Ofi' ish-įshi-h-ǫ?*
       dog   2SI-have:N-TNS-Q
       'Do you have a dog?'

However, many speakers do use the verb in wider contexts. I suspect that possessive sentences with *įshih* are becoming more common among younger speakers of the language, since they allow speakers to avoid some of the semantic and syntactic complexities associated with the alternative construction described below.

19.3.2. Possession with positionals

A second, more conservative, way of forming possessive sentences is to use the III (dative applicative) prefix with the same positional verbs found in positional sentences. Both the possessor and the possessed NP typically appear with nominative case. However, either of the nominative cases may be omitted. When the possessed item is animate, the verbs *áttah/áshwah/máyah* 'to be [sigular/dual/plural]' are used.[6]

(47)   *John-at   ofi-yat   im-átta-h.*
       John-NM dog-NM III-be:SG:N-TNS
       'John has a dog.'

(48)   *John-at   ofi'   toklo-h-oosh   im-áshwa-h.*
       John-NM dog   two-TNS-PART:SS III-be:DU:N-TNS
       'John has two dogs.'

(49)   *John-at   ofi'   tóchchiina-h-oosh   i-máya-h.*
       John-NM dog   three-TNS-PART:SS III-be:PL:N-TNS
       'John has three dogs.'

Áshah may be used for three or more possessed inanimate objects. If the possessed item is singular or dual, some other positional verb must be used.

(50)   *Isht=holissóchi'   am-ásha-h.*
       pen   1sIII-be:PL:N-TNS
       'I have (three or more) pens.'

(51)   *Holisso'=annópa'   achaffa-h-oosh*
       book   one-TNS-PART:SS
       *am-ittóla-h/*am-ásha-h.*
       1sIII-lie:SG:N-TNS/1sIII-be:PL:N-TNS
       'I have one book.'

---

6. These verbs are in the n-grade, which is typically used in possessives of this kind.

(52) *Holisso'=annópa' toklo-h-oosh*
    book   two-TNS-PART:SS
    *a̲-kaaha-h/*am-ásha-h.*
    1sIII-lie:DU-TNS/1sIII-be:PL:N-TNS
    'I have two books.'

Despite the fact that, strictly speaking, *áshah* is only used with count nouns referring to three or more entities, certain kinds of mass nouns do cooccur with it:

(53) *Skali-it   am-ásha-h.*
    money-NM   1sIII-be:PL:N-TNS
    'I have money.'

(54) *Hapi-yat am-ásha-h.*
    salt-NM   1sIII-be:PL:N-TNS
    'I have salt.'

(55) <Ilhpak ʋpa la chi̲ kʋt ʋm a̲sha . . .>
    Ilhpak apa-l-aachi̲-kat   am-a̲sha-h . . .
    food   eat-1sI-IRR-COMP:SS 1sIII-be:PL:N-TNS
    'I have food to eat . . .' (John 4:32)

When positionals are used in possessive constructions, the selectional restrictions described above for locative constructions apply to the possessed item. For example, when the location of a container is stated, the positional verb *talaayah* is used. Similarly, the possession of a container is expressed through the use of *talaayah* plus a dative prefix:

(56) *Káfi' aayíshko-yat aayípa' talá̲ya-h.*
    coffee cup-NM   table   lie:N-TNS
    'The coffee cup is on the table.'

(57) *Káfi' aayíshko-yat a̲-talá̲ya-h.*
    coffee cup-NM   1sIII-lie:N-TNS
    'I have a coffee cup.'

Some other examples of positional verbs used in possessive constructions follow:

(58) *John-at   aayípa' i̲-hikiiya-h.*
    John-NM table   III-stand-TNS
    'John has a table.'

(59) *John-at aayípa' toklo-h-oosh   i̲-hiili-h.*
    John-NM table   two-TNS-PART:SS III-stand
    'John has two tables.'

(60) *Hashi' kanálli' anóoli a̲-taká̲li-h.*
    sun   move   tell   1sIII-hang-TNS
    'I have a clock.' (said of a clock hanging on the wall)

(61)   *Holisso'=annópa' achaffa-h-oosh   am-ittóla-h*
       book   one-TNS-PART:SS 1sIII-lie:SG:N-TNS
       'I have one book.'

19.3.3. The syntax of possessive expressions

Either or both of the noun phrases in a possessive sentence may be marked nominative. All of the following sentences were judged acceptable:

(62)   *John-at   skali-yat   im-áshah.*
       John-NM money-NM III-be:PL:N
       'John has money.'

(63)   *John-at   skali'   im-ásha-h.*
       John-NM money III-be:PL:N-TNS
       'John has money.'

(64)   *John skali-yat   im-ásha-h.*
       John money-NM III-be:PL:N-TNS
       'John has money.'

However, it is not acceptable to omit nominative case from both of the noun phrases:

(65)   **John skali   im-áshah.*
       John money III-be:PL:N
       'John has money.'

When the possessed item is quantified, the quantifier may serve as the predicate of the sentence, taking a III prefix to indicate the possessor.

(66)   *Ofi-yat   a-tóchchiina-h.*
       dog-NM 1sIII-three-TNS
       'I have three dogs.'

(67)   *Anopa'=holisso(-yat) a-laawa-h.*
       book-(NM)   1sIII-many-TNS
       'I have many books.'

(68)   *Tachi' am-iklanna-h chim-aa-l-aachi-h.*
       corn 1sIII-half-TNS   2sIII-give-1sI-IRR-TNS
       'I'm going to give you half the corn I have.'

The negatives of all the possessives use the verb *ikshoh* 'to not exist' with a dative prefix, regardless of the verb that they appear with in the affirmative possessives:[7]

(69)   *Ofi-yat   ik-sam-iksho-h.*
       dog-NM   N-1sIII-not:exist-TNS
       'I don't have a dog.'

(70)   *Aayípa-at   ik-sam-iksho-h.*
       table-NM   N-1sIII-not:exist-TNS
       'I don't have a table.'

(71)   <. . . ai ashʋchika yʋt ik pim iksho.>
       aayashshachika-yat   ik-pim-iksho-h.
       sin-NM   N-1PIII-not:exist-TNS
       'We have no sin.' (1 John 1:18)

(72)   <Oka p<u>a</u>ki ʋt okla ik im ikshoshke.>
       Okap<u>a</u>kki-yat   oklah   ik-im-iksho-shkii.
       wine-NM   PLUR   N-III-not:exist-EXHORT
       'They have no wine.' (John 2:3)

Negation of the verb of position is unusual:

(73a) ??*Aayípa-at   ik-s<u>a</u>-hikíiy-o-h.*
       table-NM   N-1sIII-stand:L-NEG-TNS
       ('I don't have a table.')

(73b) ??*Aayípa-at   <u>a</u>-hikiiya-kiiyo-h.*
       table-NM   1sIII-stand-NEG-TNS
       ('I don't have a table.')

19.4. Verbs of physical and metaphorical motion

As discussed in chapter 15, the single-event directionals *pit, iit,* and *awiit* are used when the following verb includes a motion component. Verbs

---

7. *Ikshoh* looks as if it is the negative of verb of the form *VCV*, since verbs of this shape lose the initial vowel following a class I or N prefix. Nicklas (1974:69) suggests a derivation from the verb *ashah* 'to be (plural)'. This seems plausible as a diachronic analysis. However, difficulties for this as a synchronic analysis are presented by the occurrence of an extra *ik-* prefix when the verb appears with person markers, e.g.:

    Ik-sa-kshoh.   'I'm not there.'
    Ik-sam-ikshoh.   'I don't have any.'

Since there is no reason for the negative prefix *ik-* to appear twice, this seems to show that the root of the verb is actually *iksho*. However, under this analysis one must explain why the third person forms of the verb (without II or III prefixes) do not show a *ik-* prefix:

    Ikshoh.   'He's not there.'
    Ik-ikshoh.

The likeliest possibility seems to be that Choctaw has a rule of morphological haplology, which deletes the prefix *ik-* when it appears immediately before the verb stem.

with a motion component contrast with stative predicates, and the single-event directionals are inappropriate with statives:

(74)   *Ofi-yat pit   homma-h.
       dog-NM away red-TNS
       ('The dog is red.')

Broadwell (2000) gives a formal analysis of the lexical semantics of verbs which may appear with the single-event directionals. This section lists some of the semantic classes that are compatible with these directionals.

19.4.1. Physical motion and sending

It is unsurprising that verbs in which there is actual physical motion of objects or people through space count as motion predicates in Choctaw. The following is a partial list of verbs of physical motion that may be used with the group A directionals:

(75)   *iyyakayyah*   'to follow'
       atohnoh   'to send, order'
       tilhiilih   'to send [plural object]'
       oyyah   'to go up, climb'
       tanablih   'to cross over'
       ilhkolih   'to go [plural]'
       kanallih   'to move'
       ḳachih   'to send; to sell'
       pilah   'to throw, send'
       itokaahah   'to throw in the fire'
       kochchah   'to go out'
       ashaachih   'to gather'
       okaachih   'to throw in the water'
       lhayah   'to throw away'
       abachakaalih   'to lift the head'

Some examples of these verbs used with directionals follow:

(76)   *Iit   pila-h.*
       toward throw/send-TNS
       'He threw it (toward me).'

(77)   *Pit   pila-h.*
       away throw/send-TNS
       'He threw it [away from me].'

(78)   *Chokka' ila-h   pit   kanalli-tok.*
       house   other-TNS away move-PT
       'They moved to a different house.'

(79) <Atuk osh okhʋta hash mish tʋnnʋp pit tanʋblit Katalenes yakni a
okla ona tok.>
Aatokoosh okhatah-aash tanap   pit   tanabli-t
and:SS   ocean-PREV   other:side away cross-PART
Gadarenes yakni-ya̲ oklah ona-ttook.
Gadarenes land-AC PLUR arrive:there-DPAST
'And they came over unto the other side of the sea, into the country of
the Gadarenes.' (Mark 5:1)

(80) <Shukha laua ak o̲ pit ish pi on tihleli na yʋmmak o̲ ont il abehashke
. . .>
Shókha' lawa-ako̲   pit   ish-pi-o̲-tilhúili-na   yamm-ako̲
hog   many-CON:AC away 2SI-1PII-on-send:L-DS that-CON:AC
o̲t   il-abiiha-shkii.
go:and 1PI-be:in-EXHORT
'Send us into the swine, that we may enter into them.' (Mark 5:12)

19.4.2. Giving

Verbs of giving also appear with the directional particles.

(81) *imah*   'to give'
      ipiitah   'to give [to several], to distribute'

(82) <Nana kʋt holitompa hokʋno ofi puta ma pit hʋch ik imokmʋt, . . .>
Ná̲na-kat   holitópa-h-ook-ano   ofi' pootta-ma pit
thing-COMP:SS holy:N-TNS-COMPAR-AC2 dog all-that   away
hachik-úim-o-kmat . . .
2PII-III:give:L-NEG-IRR:SS
'Give not that which is holy unto the dogs . . .' (Matt. 7:6)

(83) <. . . pit ipeta tok.>
. . . *Pit ipiita-ttook.*
away give-DPAST
'he gave them [to his disciples]' (Matt. 14:19)

19.4.3. Perception

The directional particles also show that the following verbs of perception
are also treated by the grammar as containing a component of motion.

(84) *pisah*   'to see'
      hopo̲koyoh   'to look here and there'
      hakloh   'to hear'

Consider the following examples:

(85)   <Yohmi tok kia Chisʋs ʋt mishema ho̱ minti na pit pisa mʋt, malelit
ont aiokpʋchit, . . .>
Yohmi-ttook-kia   Jesus-at   mishiima-h-o̱   mı́ti-na
do:so-DPAST-but   Jesus-NM   far:off-TNS-PART:DS   come:L-DS
pit   pisa-hmat,   maliili-t   o̱t   ayokpachi-t . . .
away   see-when:SS   run-PART   go:and   worship-PART

'But when he saw Jesus [coming] afar off, he ran and worshipped him,
and . . .' (Mark 5:6)

(86)   <ʋba pilla ha̱ pit ish hopo̱koyo cha>
aba' pillah-a̱   pit   ish-hopo̱kóoyo-cha
up   toward-AC   away   2SI-look:L-SS
'Look now towards heaven.' (Gen. 15:5)

Verbs of perception show a further degree of abstraction from
physical motion, for what is the moving object in perception? In the folk
physics of vision implied by English semantics, this object is an abstract
gaze, conceived of as moving from the perceiver to the perceived object.
The Choctaw *pisah* 'to see' shows that a similar abstract gaze is
conceived of as moving along a path from the seer to the thing.

However, Choctaw and English show somewhat surprisingly
different conceptions of hearing. In English, sounds are conceived as
moving from their sources to arrive at the ear of the perceiver, and the
perceiver is the goal of the abstract motion.[8] In Choctaw, however,
hearing is like sight—an auditory equivalent of the gaze is conceived of
as moving away from the hearer, and the particle *pit*, showing motion
away from the reference point, is used:

(87)   <Mihma mı̱ko Helot ʋt yʋmma pit haklo . . .>
Mihma mı̱ko' Herod-at   yamma pit   há̱klo . . .
and   king   Herod-NM   that   away   hear:N
'And King Herod heard of him.' (Mark 6:14)

19.4.4. Speech and thought

Directional particles appear with verbs of speech and thought, including
at least the following:

---

8. *A noise came from the garage* shows this pattern. In English, the volitional
counterpart *I listened to the noise* shows a reversal, with the sound source treated as
a goal. In Choctaw, *há̱kloh* means both 'hear' and 'listen', and the sound is treated as
the goal in both volitional and nonvolitional contexts.

(88)   *anǫpolih*   'to say'[9]
       ithanah   'to know, recognize'
       hoyoh   'to call'
       mihah   'to say'
       anoolih   'to tell'
       yimmih   'to believe'
       anokfillih 'to think, consider'

Consider the following examples:

(89)   *Pit   im-anooli-h!*
       away   III-tell-TNS
       'Tell him!'

(90)   <Kυna hosh υm anumpa ha̱ haklo cha, auet sa kanchi tok a̱ pit i̱
       yimmi hokυto, aiokchayυt bilia ya̱ ahayuchi . . .>
       Kanah-oosh   am-anǫpah-a̱   hǎklo-cha
       who-FOC:NM   1SIII-word-AC   hear-L-SS
       awiit   sa-ka̱chi-ttook-a̱   pit   i̱-yimmi-h-ook-ato
       toward   1SII-send-DPAST-AC   away   III-believe-TNS-COMPAR-NM2
       aay-okchǎya-t   bílliya-ya̱   aa-hayoochi . . .
       LOC-live:N-PART   forever:G-AC   LOC-find
       'Whoever hears my words and believes him who sent me shall have
       eternal life.' (John 5:24)

(91)   <. . . pυska yatuk ash okla pit ik anukfillo kak a tok.>
       . . . paska-yaa-tok-aash   oklah   pit
       bread-COP-TNS-PREV   PLUR   away
       ik-anokfíll-ok-ak   a-ttook.
       N-think:L-NEG-OBL   be-DPAST
       '. . . they did not consider the [miracle of the] bread.' (Mark 6:52)

(92)   <. . . mih makinli ho̱ yυmmak ash okla pit ithana tok.>
       . . . mih-m-aki̱li-h-o̱   yammak-aash
       same-DEM-indeed-TNS-AC   that-PREV
       oklah   pit   ithana-ttook.
       PLUR   away   know-DPAST
       '[Immediately] they knew him.' (Mark 6:54)

19.4.5. Emotions

Choctaw emotion terms fall into two groups, which we might call
"directed" and "nondirected" emotions. Directed emotions seem to be
spoken of as if moving along a path from the experiencer to the cause of
the emotion, while nondirected emotions do not employ this metaphor.

---

9. *Aba pit anǫpolih*, literally 'talk upwards' is idiomatic for 'pray'.

(93) Some directed emotions
    i̱holloh   'to love'
    i̱nokhakloh   'to be sad about, to grieve over'
    ayokpa̱chih   'to like'

(94) Some nondirected emotions
    noklhaka̱chah   'to be startled'
    i̱nokshoopah   'to be afraid of'

Speakers have variable judgments on the following emotions:

(95) Variable emotions
    i̱nokoowah   'to be angry at'
    i̱noktalhah   'to be jealous of'

The following examples are accepted by some speakers but not others.

(96) %_John-at Bill pit i̱-nokoowa-h._
    John-NM   Bill   away   III-angry-TNS
    'John is mad at Bill.'

(97) %_John-at Bill pit i̱-noktalha-h._
    John-NM   Bill   away   III-jealous-TNS
    'John is jealous of Bill.'

The lexical semantics of Choctaw emotion terms are not well understood and deserve more careful investigation.

19.5. Baby talk

A distinctive baby talk is found in Mississippi Choctaw, but speakers of Oklahoma Choctaw I consulted generally did not remember any baby talk. One Oklahoma Choctaw speaker recalled _chi̱chi'_ 'milk' and _choocho'_ 'pig', but none of the other words in table 19.2.

19.6. Personal names

In some communities on the Mississippi Choctaw reservation, Choctaw personal names are still used, in addition to conventional English names. Some women's names are listed in table 19.3, and some men's names in table 19.4. These lists are not exhaustive, but give a representative sample of personal names.

19.6.1. Phonology of personal names

The phonology of personal names diverges in some ways from that of other words in Choctaw. Some names display apparently phonemic units not otherwise found in Choctaw. A phoneme /d/ appears in the name _Danas_, and /ʤ/ in the name _Joowit_.

Table 19.2. Mississippi Choctaw baby talk vocabulary

ORDINARY CHOCTAW	BABY TALK	TRANSLATION
holaafah	*wawah*	'to defecate'
hosho̱wah	*o̱wah*	'to urinate'
hosho̱wah	*púpiih*	'to urinate'
hattak lósa'	*kóssa'*	'black person'
nahóllo'	*lóolo'*	'white person'
afo'	*paapa'*	'grandfather'
pishókchi'	*chúchi'*	'milk'
ippókni'	*pónni'*	'grandmother'
imo̱shi'	*o̱shi'*	'mother's brother'
nakfi'	*akfi'*	'brother'
apah	*paapah*	'to eat'
ishkoh	*ikkoh*	'to drink'
ofó̱sik	*ó̱sik*	'puppy'
katos	*tikih*	'cat, kitten'
shokha'	*choocho'*	'pig'
waak	*muumu'*	'cow'

A phoneme /æ/ appears in the names *Læ̍æch* and *Læ̍æsh*. In ordinary Choctaw words, [æ] is found as a variant pronunciation of the sequence /ayi/. For instance, *sayimmih* 'I believe' may be pronounced [sayimmih] or [sæmmih]. However, I do not believe that the name *Læ̍æsh* has an alternate pronunciation as [layish], which suggests that /æ/ here has phonemic status.

Ordinary Choctaw words do not have *ch* in syllable-final position, but this appears in the three of the attested personal names: *Illich*, *Læ̍æch*, and *Naach*. The sound *m* is extremely rare in word-final position in ordinary Choctaw words, but appears in the name *Hatom*.

19.6.2. Etymology of personal names

Swanton (1931) is the best source for traditional Choctaw naming practices. In the system described there, men received a war name based on some characteristic or memorable action in battle. This action is named by a verb, followed by the same-subject switch- reference marker *-t* and a nominalized form of the verb *abih* 'to kill'. For example, the name *Falaamatábi'* has the following etymology:

(98) *falaama-t ábi'*
     return-PART kill:NML
     'He returns and kills it; one who returns and kills it'

Several of the men's names in the list below conform to this traditional pattern. The very common Choctaw surname *Tubby* is based on the final two syllables of a traditional man's name.

Women's names traditionally followed a similar pattern, with the final verb being *imah* 'to give', preceded by a verb that describes a characteristic or memorable way of giving. For example, the name *Hootima'* is etymologically as follows:

(99) *hoo-t   íma'*
     search-PART give:NML
     'She searches and gives; one who searches and gives'

Several of the women's names on the list also follow the traditional pattern.

Of the remaining names, some appear to be loans from English or possibly French, while the remainder have no known etymology. Some show similarity to Koasati personal names recorded by Kimball (1991).

Table 19.3. Women's names

CHOCTAW	ETYMOLOGY (IF KNOWN)
achaakanonáachi'	'cooks next to it'
achokmatíma'	'is good and gives'
anooli'	'tells'
awiita'	
biima'	
chiliifa'	from English *Geneva*?
chokmahabi'	
chooni'	
choosi'	from English *Josie*?
chooti'	
chopa'	'buys'
hatom	
hootanna'	'weaving woman'
hootíma'	'searches and gives'
hopoocho'	
hopooni'	'cooks'
iisan	
iita'	

Table 19.3. Women's names, *continued*

CHOCTAW	ETYMOLOGY (IF KNOWN)
iyakatíma'	'goes and gives'
kạchi'	'sells'
kiliihonna'	
kola'	
liisan	
liyaama'	
lootíma'	
maachi'	from English *Martha* ?
maasi'	
maat	
maatíma'	
miila'	
mitíma'	
mạtíma'	
mạyatíma'	
naach	
niisan	
niiwi'	
nili'	from English *Nellie*?
okchatíma'	'wakes up and gives'
oloos	
ona'	'gets there' (?)
onaali'	'I have arrived' ?
onatíma'	'arrives and gives'
ooli'	
pocho'	
saali'	
saami'	
samaachi'	
samiiha'	

Table 19.3. Women's names, *continued*

CHOCTAW	ETYMOLOGY (IF KNOWN)
satíma'	
silli'	
sillin	
shimmi'	
sokkot	sound of hitting a rock
sooni'	
soot	
sootíma'	
tassa'	
o̲tíma'	'goes and gives'
tonna'	
yimmi'	'believes'

Table 19.4. Men's names

CHOCTAW	ETYMOLOGY (IF KNOWN)
abit	'hunter'
achaaka̲tábi'	'kills next to it'
achaffa' tonooli'	'rolls one thing' (?)
bichchi'	
biich	from English *Bates*?
biisan	
chaan	from English *John*?
chahta'	'Choctaw'
chaliis	
chashwi'	
daanas	from English *Thomas*?
falaamatábi'	'returns and kills'
finaachi'	from *French*?
halli'	
hilooha'	'thunder'
hokta'	
hopaayi' osi'	'little prophet'
iilis	

Table 19.4. Men's names, *continued*

CHOCTAW	ETYMOLOGY (IF KNOWN)
illich	
isht aya'	'brings'
joowit	
kachaábi'	
kanootábi'	
kochos	
koti'	
lawiisman	
lææch, lææsh	
liita'	
likman	
liyaat	
lohmi'	'hides'
lhotaklo'	'hummingbird'
malit	
massin	
momat ábi'	'kills them all'
motábi'	'kills them all' (?)
nita'	'bear'
noowi'	
oliis	
oloosman	
pasli'	'slices'
pilla'	
pitwi'	
saan	
shaatikli'	
sachi'	
silwi'	
sat	

Table 19.4. Men's names, *continued*

CHOCTAW	ETYMOLOGY (IF KNOWN)
s_ata'	
shtábi'	'kills with'
isht'bi'	'gets it and kills'
tashka'	'warrior'
tiich	
tokábi'	
toona'	
waalis	from English *Wallace*?

20. Texts

The following stories were told by Henry Willis, of Moore, Oklahoma during the summer of 1993. Mr. Willis grew up in the area of Stratford, Oklahoma, and he is a speaker of Oklahoma Choctaw. The text shown here was not produced spontaneously, but was carefully prepared by Mr. Willis, and repeatedly revised to arrive at the version below.

The text is first presented in modified traditional orthography, with the morphological analysis of each word indicated. The second line shows a morpheme by morpheme gloss, while a third gives a free translation in English.

An additional line of analysis is added when compound words in Choctaw correspond to a single word in English. The first gloss line shows the literal sense of the compound (enclosed in square brackets), while the second gloss line shows the usual single word translation in English. An example of this is shown for the word 'west' in sentence (1) below. Each sentence of the text is numbered separately.

My first days in school

(1) *Si-alla-h   moma-ka   a-ki'   anoti'*
     1SII-child-TNS still-COMP:DS 1SIII-father and
     ha-shki-yat   kowi' toklo-h   mahli-mma'   kowi'
     1SII-mother-NM mile two-TNS south-towards mile
     toklo-h   hashi' okattola-imma   tamaaha' bilika'
     two-TNS [sun   go:down]-towards town   near
              [west]-towards
     hohchifo-kat   Stratford-ako   ashwa-ttook.
     named-COMP:SS Stratford-CON:AC live:DU-DPAST
     'When I was a child, my father and mother lived two miles west and
     two miles south of a town called Stratford.'

(2) *Nittak ámmoona holísso' aa-pisa'*
     day   first   [book   LOC-see:NML]
                        [school]
     ibaachaffa-li-ka   nána' il-ikhána-kat   pi-hohchifo-ako
     enter-1SI-COMP:DS thing 1PI-learn:N-COMP:SS 1PII-name-CON:AC
     il-aach-aachi-h   miya-h-o   il-ikhána-ttook.
     1PI-say-IRR-TNS say-TNS-PRT:DS 1PI-learn:N-DPAST
     'The first day that I went to school, what we learned was how to say
     our names.'

(3)	*Ámmoona-ka holísso' pisá-chi-ya*
	first-COMP:DS [book see-CAUS:NML]-ACC
			[teacher]-ACC
	*im-ikhana-li-fúhna-kiiyo-kiya			ánnopa' tikba-ka*
	III-understand-1SI-really-NEG-although word first:N-COMP:DS
	nána' ponaklo-kat, "Wakáaya-cha chi-hohchifo makaachi-h"
	thing ask-COMP:SS stand:up:L-SS 2SII-name say-TNS
	aachi-ttook.
	say-DPAST
	'Although I didn't understand the teacher, the first thing she said
	was, "Stand up and say your name!"'

(4)	*Im-ikhana-li-fúhna-kiiyo-kiya*
	III-understand-1SI-really-NEG-although
	*a-holísso' itt-ibaa-písa'	 alhiiha-yat oklah si-apiila-ttook.*
	1SIII-[book RCP-COM-see:NML group]-NM PLUR 1SII-help-DPAST
	1SIII-[classmates]-NM
	'Although I didn't understand her, my classmates helped me.'

(5)	*Oklah am-ikhána-akili-ttook	 naahollo' anópa'*
	PLUR 1SIII-know:N-indeed-DPAST [white:people language]
						[English]
	anopoli-li-ahii-kiiyo-ka
	speak-1SI-IRR-NEG-COMP:DS
	'They knew that I didn't speak English.'

(6)	*Holísso' pisá-chi-yat	 hikiiya-l-aachi-h-o*
	[book see-CAUS:NML]-NM stand-1SI-IRR-TNS-PRT:DS
	[teacher]-NM
	*a-ponaklo-hma	 holísso' sa-baa-písa'*
	1SIII-ask-when:DS [book 1SII-COM-see:NML]
			[my classmate]
	achaffa-kat ibbak aba wakiili-t
	one-COMP:SS hand up raise-SS
	*hikiiya-l-aachi-h-o	 im-ikhána-t hikiiya-li-ttook.*
	stand-1SI-IRR-TNS-PRT:DS III-know:N-SS stand-1SI-DPAST
	'When the teacher asked me to stand up, one of my classmates lifted
	her hand, and I understood that I was to stand up, and I stood.'

(7)	*A-hma híkkiya-t naa sa-yoppa-ttook.*
	be-when stand:G-SS [thing 1SII-happy-DPAST]
			[I was happy]
	'I stood up proudly.'

(8)	*Holísso' pisá-chi-yat	 si-hohchifo' maka-l-aachi-h-o*
	[book see-CAUS:NML]-NM 1SII-name say-1SI-IRR-TNS-PART:DS
	[teacher]-NM
	ponaklo-ttook
	ask-DPAST
	'The teacher asked me to say my name.'

(9) *Alla' alhiiha' įla-kat   hohchifo'*
child group   other-COMP:NM name
ima-ka̱   há̱klo-li-ttook.
give-COMP:DS hear:N-1SI-DPAST
'I had heard the other kids give their names.'

(10) *Aa-tok-o̱   an-ak-kia nokshópa-h*
be-PT-PART:DS I-OBL-TOO afraid:N-TNS
chóyyohmi-h-oosh   si-hohchifo' ló̱hma-t   anooli-li-ttook.
sort:of-Y-TNS-PART:SS 1SII-name quiet:N-SS tell-1SI-DPAST
'So I also said my name, timidly and softly.'

(11) *A-hma̱   holísso' pisá-chi-yat   ató̱kla-t*
be-when:DS [book   see-CAUS:NML]-NM again:N-SS
          [teacher]-NM
si-hohchifo' aachi-ttook.
1SII-name   say-DPAST
'And then the teacher repeated my name.'

(12) *Hi-cha biniili-l-aachi̱-h-o̱   maka-ttook.*
do-SS sit-1SI-IRR-TNS-PART:DS say-DPAST
'And she told me to sit down.'

(13) *Naa yoppa-h-oosh   bínnili-li-ttook.*
thing happy-TNS-PART:SS sit:G-1SI-DPAST
'I sat down happily.'

(14) *Nittak ató̱kla-hma̱,   ofi' hohchifo' ano̱ti'*
day   second:N-when:DS dog name   and
ká̱nimma' atta-ka̱   il-anool-aachi̱-h miya-h-o̱
where   live-COMP:DS 1PI-tell-IRR-TNS say-TNS-PART:DS
maká̱achi-na oklah il-anooli-ttook.
say:L-DS   PLUR 1PI-tell-DPAST
'The second day, she said we were supposed to say the names of (our)
dogs and where they lived, so we said them.'

(15) *Anooli-l-aachi̱-h miya-ka̱   ona-hma̱,*
tell-1SI-IRR-TNS say-COMP:DS arrive-when:DS
il-itt-ibaa-písa'   alhiiha-yat si-apí̱la-na   anooli-t
[1PI-RCP-COM-see:NML group]-NM 1SII-help:L-DS tell-SS
[my classmates]-NM
lhopolli-li-ttook.
through-1SI-DPAST
'When the time came that I had to say it, my classmates helped me
and I got through it.'

(16) *Yak michi-h-oosh   anooli-li-ttook.*
this do-TNS-PART:SS tell-1SI-DPAST
'This is how I told it.'

(17) *Alla' alhiiha-yat ofi' hohchifo' makaachi-kma,*
      kid   group-NM   dog name   say-IRR:DS
      hohchifo kánimma' achokmali-li-kmat   sa-noshkobo'
      name   whatever like-1SI-IRR:SS   1SII-head
      akoshchonnoli-li-ttook.
      nod-1SI-DPAST
      'When the other kids said a dog's name, I nodded my head at
      whatever name I liked.'

(18) *Anoti' kánimma' imma' kánimma'*
      and   whatever toward where
      atta-h   pit bilhibli-kma, achokmali-li-kmat,
      live-TNS DIR point-IRR:DS like-1SI-IRR:SS
      akoshchonnoli-li-ttook.
      nod-1SI-DPAST
      'And when they pointed towards a direction where it lived, I nodded
      if I liked it.'

(19) *Nittak atóchchiina-hma holísso' aa-písa-yat   lowa-t*
      day   third:G-when:DS [book   LOC-see-NML]-NM burn-SS
                             [school]-NM
      táaha-na   falaama-t ak-íiy-o-kii-ttook.
      complete:L-DS return-SS 1SN-go:L-NEG-NEG-DPAST
      'On the third day, the school burned down, so I didn't go back.'

Life at the orphanage

(20) *Stratford holisso' aa-písa-yat   lowa-t   táaha-na,*
      Stratford [book   LOC-see-NML]-NM burn-PART complete:L-DS
               [school]-NM
      alla' alhtakla' aay-aasha-'   ha-shki'   anoti' a-ki-yat
      [child orphan LOC-exist-NML] 1SII-mother and   1SIII-father
      [orphanage]
      pi-pila-ttook,
      1PII-send-DPAST
      'When the Stratford school burned down, my mother and father seat
      us to an orphanage.'[1]

(21) *Hugo bilika-ako   Goodland alhtakla' aay-asha-'*
      Hugo near-CON:AC Goodland [orphan   LOC-exist-NML]
      talaaya-haatoko, hattak laawa shaali-'   ii-fokka-h-oosh,
      lie-because:DS   [people many carry-NML] 1PI-get:on-TNS-PART:SS
                       [bus]

---

1. At the time Mr. Willis attended Goodland, it was known as Goodland Indian
Orphanage. Although it began as a school for orphans, during the years of the
depression it had become a boarding school for Native American children, and accepted
both orphans and children with living parents. The institution is now called Goodland
Presbyterian Children's Home, and it is located near Hugo, Oklahoma.

Stratford hikiiya-t   Hugo il-ona-ttook.
Stratford stand-PART 1PI-arrive-DPAST
'Because the Goodland orphanage was near Hugo, we rode the bus
from Stratford to Hugo.'

(22) *Ma   hikii-t   Goodland on-aachi-ka   kowi' oshta-ttook*
      there stand-SS Goodland arrive-IRR-COMP:DS   mile   four-DPAST
      'It was four miles to Goodland from there.'

(23) *Tali'   aay-anopoli-yat toksali-kiiyo-ttook.*
      [metal LOC-talk]-NM   work-NEG-PAST
      [telephone]-NM
      'The telephones didn't work.'

(24) *Okti-yat wiiki-t   tali' anopoli' api' liwiilüichi-na*
      ice-NM   heavy-PART [metal talk stalk] break:L-DS
                            [telephone pole]
      alla' alhtakla' pihlüichi' ánnopa' il-i-bóhl-ahii-kiiyo-na
      [child orphan   lead:NML] word   1PI-III-SEND:L-IRR-NEG-DS
      [orphanage superintendent]
      nowa-t il-ittiyaachi-ttook.
      walk-PART 1PI-go:DU-DPAST
      'The ice was heavy and broke the telephone poles, and we couldn't
      send word to the superintendent of the orphanage, so we walked.'

(25) *Kániimi-h-o   ik-pi-afámm-o-toka*
      why-TNS-PART:DS N-1PII-meet:L-NEG-PT:COMP:DS
      ak-ikháan-o-h.
      1sN-know:L-NEG-TNS
      'I don't know why someone didn't meet us.'

(26) *Chiikosi-na sa-tikáhbi-t   taha-h.*
      soon-DS   1sII-tired:H-PART complete-TNS
      'Soon I got tired out.'

(27) *Hihma, am-annih-at   sa-shaali-h-oosh*
      and   1sIII-older:sibling-NM 1sII-carry-TNS-PART:SS
      sa-sht-iya-h;   ninak hopaaki' il-ona-ttook.
      1sII-INST-go-TNS night late   1PI-arrive-DPAST
      'Then my older brother carried me; we got there late at night.'

(28) *Hashi' kanalli' toklo-fokkaali-h-o   ot   ii-nosi-ttook.*
      [sun   move]   two-about-TNS-PART:DS go:and 1PI-sleep-DPAST
      [o'clock]
      'We went to sleep at about two o'clock.'

(29) *Afammi' awahchákkaali' pókkooli' tóchchiina'   akochcha'*
      year   nineteen   [ten   three]   out
                              [thirty]

tálhlhaapi' mak fokkaali-hma̱,   ilhpak aahooch-aachi̱-ka̱
five   then about-when:DS food   find-IRR-COMP:DS
kallo-ttook.
hard-DPAST

'It was about 1935, and food was hard to find.'

(30) *Mak-ookako̱   alhtakla' aay-asha-'   holisso'*
      that-because:DS [orphan LOC-exist]-NML book
                        [orphanage]
      ii-pis-aachi̱-h-o̱   pi-pila-ttook.
      1PI-see-IRR-TNS-PART:DS 1PII-send-DPAST
      'That's why they sent us to the orphanage to learn to read.'

(31) *Goodland aay-achokma-' ii-pisa-h   kaniimi-kma,*
      Goodland LOC-good-NML 1PI-see-TNS sometimes-IRR
      ik-achókm-o-'   ayna-h ii-pisa-ttook.
      N-good:L-NEG-NML and-TNS 1PI-see-DPAST
      'We sometimes saw good times at Goodland, but we also saw bad
      times.'

(32) *Holisso' hochiifo-h il-ikhana-ttook.*
      book   read-TNS   1PI-learn-DPAST
      'We learned to read.'

(33) *Alla' alhtakla' i̱la-h-at   laawa-ttook.*
      child orphan   other-TNS-NM many-DPAST
      'There were lots of other orphans.'

(34) *A̱-kana'   lawaa-t   afaama-li-ttook.*
      1sIII-friend many-PART meet-1sI-DPAST
      'I met many friends.'

(35) *Holisso' aa-pisa-yat   nan-a<lh>powa-at   im-áyyaasha-ttook.*
      [book   LOC-see]-NML [thing-tame:INTR]-NM III-exist:PL-DPAST
      [school]-NM   [livestock]-NM
      'The school had a lot of livestock.'

(36) *Hikmat, naa-waaya-'   ilaapi̱li-h-oosh*
      and:SS [thing-grow-NML] do:for:self-TNS-PART:SS
      pim-atahli-ttook.
      1PIII-prepare-DPAST
      'And they grew their own vegetables and prepared them for us.'

(37) *Nittak oshta' holisso ii-pisa-kmat, nittak achaffa-kano*
      day   four   book   1PI-see-IRR:SS day   one-COMP:DS
      ii-to̱ksali-ttook
      1PI-work-DPAST
      'We went to school for four days, and worked one day.'

References

Ahenakew, Freda

1987   *Cree language structures: A Cree approach.* Winnipeg: Pemmican Publications.

Baker, Mark

1985   Incorporation: A theory of grammatical function changing. Ph.D. diss., Massachusetts Institute of Technology.

1991   On some subject/object asymmetries in Mohawk. *Natural Language and Linguistic Theory* 9:537–76.

Booker, Karen M.

1980   Comparative Muskogean: Aspects of Proto-Muskogean verb morphology. Ph.D. diss., University of Kansas.

Boynton, Sylvia S.

1982   Mikasuki grammar in outline. Ph.D. diss., University of Florida.

Bresnan, Joan

1995   Linear order, syntactic rank, and empty categories: On weak crossover. In *Formal issues in Lexical-Functional Grammar,* edited by Mary Dalrymple, Ronald M. Kaplan, John T. Maxwell III, and Annie Zaenen, 241–74. CSLI Lecture Notes 47. Stanford, Calif: Center for the Study of Language and Information.

Broadwell, George A.

1987a   Nominal *-ka in Proto-Muskogean. In *Muskogean linguistics,* edited by Pamela Munro, 9–20. UCLA Occasional Papers in Linguistics. Department of Linguistics, University of California, Los Angeles.

1987b   A Mississippi Choctaw–English dictionary, with an English–Choctaw index. Manuscript.

1988a   Multiple θ-role assignment in Choctaw. In *Thematic roles,* edited by Wendy Wilkins, 113–27, Syntax and Semantics 22. New York: Academic Press.

1988b   Reflexive movement in Choctaw. *Proceedings of the North East Linguistic Society* 18:53–64. Graduate Linguistic Student Association, University of Massachusetts, Amherst.

1990a   Extending the binding theory: A Muskogean case study. Ph.D. diss., University of California, Los Angeles.

1990b   Choctaw texts. Manuscript.

1991a   Speaker and SELF in Choctaw. *International Journal of American Linguistics* 57:411–25.

1991b   The divorce of Amos and Molsey Yale: A 19th century Choctaw court case. Manuscript.

1992   The glottal stop in Mississippi Choctaw of Oklahoma. Manuscript.

1993   Subtractive morphology in Southern Muskogean. *International Journal of American Linguistics* 59:416–29.

1995   1990 census figures for speakers of American Indian languages. *International Journal of American Linguistics* 61:145–50.

1996   Causation and affectedness in Choctaw. *1994 Mid-America Linguistics Conference,* edited by Frances Ingemann, 483–93. Lawrence: University of Kansas.

2000   Choctaw directionals and the syntax of complex predication. In *Argument realization,* edited by Miriam Butt and Tracy Holloway King, 111–34. Stanford, Cal.: CSLI Publications.

Broadwell, George A., and Jack B. Martin.

1993   The clitic/agreement split: Asymmetries in Choctaw person marking. *Proceedings of the Annual Meeting of the Berkeley Linguistic Society* 19S:1–10.

Brugger, Gerhard

1997   Event time properties. Manuscript, copy in Broadwell's possession.

Bushnell, David I., Jr.

1909   *The Choctaw of Bayou Lacomb, St. Tammany Parish, Louisiana.* Bureau of American Ethnology Bulletin 48. Washington, D.C.

Butler, Inez

1980   *Gramática zapoteca: zapoteco de Yatzachi el Bajo.* Mexico City: Instituto Lingüística de Verano.

Byington, Cyrus

1827   *A spelling book, written in the Chahta language, with an English translation.* 2nd ed. Cincinnati: Morgan, Lodge, and Fisher.

1852   *Holisso Anumpa Tosholi, an English and Choctaw definer: For the Choctaw academies and schools.* New York: S. W. Benedict.

1870   *Grammar of the Choctaw language,* edited by Daniel G. Brinton. Philadelphia: McCalla and Stavely. [Also published in *Proceedings of the American Philosophical Society* 11: 317-67, 1871.]

1915   *A dictionary of the Choctaw language,* edited by John R. Swanton and Henry S. Halbert. Bureau of American Ethnology Bulletin 46. Washington, D.C.

Carden, Guy, Lynn Gordon, and Pamela Munro

1982   Raising rules and the projection principle. Manuscript, copy in Broadwell's possession.

Chomsky, Noam

1975   Conditions on rules of grammar. In *Current issues in linguistic theory,* edited by Roger Cole, 3–50, Bloomington: Indiana University Press.

1981   *Lectures on government and binding.* Dordrecht: Foris.

Cline, David M.

1987   Oklahoma Seminole and the Muskogean H-Grade. In *Muskogean linguistics,* edited by Pamela Munro, 36–50. UCLA Occasional Papers in Linguistics. Department of Linguistics, University of California, Los Angeles.

Crawford, James

1978   *The Mobilian trade language.* Knoxville: University of Tennessee Press.

Davies, William

1981   Choctaw clause structure. Ph.D. diss., University of California, San Diego.

1986   *Choctaw verb agreement and universal grammar.* Dordrecht: Reidel.

Debo, Angie

1961   *The rise and fall of the Choctaw republic.* Norman: University of Oklahoma Press.

Derrick-Mescua, Maria

1980   A phonology and morphology of Mikasuki. Ph.D. diss.. University of Florida.

Drechsel, Emmanuel

1979   Mobilian Jargon: linguistic, sociocultural, and historical aspects of an American Indian lingua franca. Ph.D. diss.. University of Wisconsin.

Evans, Nicholas

1995   A-quantifiers and scope in Mayali. In *Quantification in Natural Languages,* edited by Emmon Bach, Eloise Jelinek, Angelika Kratzer, and Barbara Partee, 207–70. Dordrecht: Kluwer.

Foley, William

1986   *The Papuan languages of New Guinea.* Cambridge: Cambridge
          University Press.

Fortune, Jim

1986   *Choctaw demographic survey 1986.* Philadelphia, Miss.: Choctaw
          Heritage Press, Mississippi Band of Choctaw Indians.

Georgopoulos, Carol

1991   Canonical government and the specifier parameter: An ECP
          account of weak crossover. *Natural language and linguistic
          theory* 9:1–46.

Gordon, Lynn

1986   Possessor raising and switch-reference in Chickasaw.
          Manuscript, copy in Broadwell's possession.

1987   Relative clauses in Western Muskogean languages. In
          Muskogean linguistics, edited by Pamela Munro, 66–80. UCLA
          Occasional Papers in Linguistics. Department of Linguistics,
          University of California, Los Angeles.

Gordon, Matthew, Pamela Munro, and Peter Ladefoged

1997   The Phonetic Structures of Chickasaw. *UCLA Working Papers
          in Phonetics* 95 (Fieldwork Studies of Targeted Languages 5),
          41–67. Los Angeles: Department of Linguistics, University of
          California, Los Angeles.

Haag, Marcia

1995   Lexical categories in Choctaw and universal grammar. Ph.D.
          diss., Stony Brook University, State University of New York.

1997   Continuous and Discrete Adjectival Scales. *Lingua* 103:113–26.

Haas, Mary R.

1941a   The classification of the Muskogean languages. In *Language,
          culture and personality: Essays in memory of Edward Sapir,*
          edited by Leslie Spier, A. Irving Hallowell, and Stanley S.
          Newman, 41–56. Menasha, Wisc.: Banta Publishing.

1941b   Noun incorporation in the Muskogean languages. *Language*
          17:311–15.

1951   The Proto-Gulf word for *water* (with notes on Siouan-Yuchi).
          International Journal of American Linguistics 17:71–79.

1952   The Proto-Gulf word for *land* (with a note on Proto-Siouan).
          International Journal of American Linguistics 18:238–40.

Haiman, John

1983   On some origins of switch-reference marking. In *Switch-reference and universal grammar*, edited by John Haiman and Pamela Munro, 105–28. Amsterdam: John Benjamins.

Hale, Kenneth

1983   Warlpiri and the grammar of nonconfigurational languages. *Natural language and linguistic theory* 1:5–47.

1989   On nonconfigurational structures. In *Configurationality: The typology of asymmetries*, edited by László Marácz and Pieter Muysken, 293–300. Dordrecht: Foris.

Hardy, Donald E.

1988   The semantics of Creek morphosyntax. Ph.D. diss. Rice University.

Hardy, Heather K., and Timothy Montler

1986   Alabama radical morphology: H-infix and disfixation. In *In Honor of Mary Haas*, edited by William Shipley, 377–410. Berlin: Mouton de Gruyter.

Haspelmath, Martin

1993   More on the typology of inchoative/causative verb alter-nations. In *Causatives and transitivity*, edited by Bernard Comrie and Maria Polinsky, 87–120. Studies in Language Companion Series, 23. Amsterdam: Benjamins.

Heath, Jeffrey

1980   Choctaw suppletive verbs and derivational morphology. *Kansas Working Papers in Linguistics* 5(2):1–24. Lawrence: Linguistics Graduate Student Association, University of Kansas.

Jelinek, Eloise

1984   Empty case, categories, and configurationality. *Natural language and linguistic theory* 2:39–76.

1989   The case split and configurationality in Choctaw. In *Configurationality: The typology of asymmetries*, edited by László Marácz and Pieter Muysken, 117–41. Dordrecht: Foris.

Kenaston, Monte Ray

1972   Sharecropping, solidarity, and social cleavage: The genesis of a Choctaw sub-community in Tennessee. Ph.D. diss., Southern Illinois University.

Ketcham, William H.

1916   *Kiahlik iksa nana-aiyimmika i̱ katikisma : Chahta anumpa isht
        a toshowa hoke. (A catechism of the Catholic religion translated
        into the Choctaw language).* Washington, D.C.: Bureau of
        Catholic Indian Missions.

Kimball, Geoffrey

1985   A descriptive grammar of Koasati. Ph.D. diss., Tulane
        University.

1987   A grammatical sketch of Apalachee. *International Journal of
        American Linguistics* 53:136–74.

1988   An Apalachee vocabulary. *International Journal of American
        Linguistics* 54: 387–98.

1991   *Koasati grammar.* Lincoln: University of Nebraska Press.

Koopman, Hilda, and Dominique Sportiche

1982   Variables and the bijection principle. *Linguistic Review*
        2:139–60.

Kuno, Susumo

1973   *The structure of the Japanese language.* Cambridge, Mass:
        M.I.T. Press.

Kwachka, Patricia

1981   The acquisition of English by Choctaw-speaking children. Ph.D.
        diss.,University of Florida.

Levin, Beth

1993   *English verb classes and alternations: A preliminary
        investigation.* Chicago: University of Chicago Press.

Linker, Wendy

1987   On the co-ordinating status of -chah and -nah in Choctaw. In
        Muskogean linguistics, edited by Pamela Munro, 96–110. UCLA
        Occasional Papers in Linguistics. Department of Linguistics,
        University of California, Los Angeles.

Lupardus, Karen J.

1982   The language of the Alabama Indians. Ph.D. diss., University of
        Kansas.

Martin, Jack

1991   The determination of grammatical relations in syntax. Ph.D.
        diss., University of California, Los Angeles.

Matisoff, James

1973   *The grammar of Lahu.* University of California Publications in
        Linguistics 75. Berkeley: University of California Press.

Munro, Pamela

1983.   When "same" is not "not different." In *Switch-reference and universal grammar*, edited by John Haiman and Pamela Munro, 223–44. Amsterdam: John Benjamins

1984a   Auxiliaries and auxiliarization in Western Muskogean. In *Historical syntax*, edited by Jacek Fisiak, 332-62. Trends in Linguistics, Studies and Monographs 23. Berlin: Mouton.

1984b   The syntactic status of object possessor raising in Western Muskogean. *Proceedings of the Berkeley Linguistic Society* 10:634–49.

1985   Chickasaw accent and verb grades. In *Studia linguistica diachronica et synchronica: Werner Winter sexagenario*, edited by Ursula Pieper and Gerhard Stickel, 581–93. Berlin: Mouton.

1986   Subject-creating rules in Chickasaw. Manuscript, copy in Broadwell's possession.

1987a   Some morphological differences between Chickasaw and Choctaw. In *Muskogean linguistics*, edited by Pamela Munro, 119–33. UCLA Occasional Papers in Linguistics. Department of Linguistics, University of California, Los Angeles.

1987b   A brief sketch of Chickasaw structure. Manuscript, copy in Broadwell's possession.

1989   Chickasaw applicative verb prefixes. Manuscript, copy in Broadwell's possession.

2005   Chickasaw. In *Native Languages of the Southeastern United States: Representative studies*, edited by Heather Hardy and Janine Scancarelli, 114–56. Lincoln: University of Nebraska Press.

Munro, Pamela, George A. Broadwell, David M. Cline, Abigail C. Cohn, Emanuel J. Drechsel, Heather K. Hardy, Geoffrey D. Kimball, Jack Martin, and D. J. West

1992   Muskogean cognate sets. Manuscript, copy in Broadwell's possession.

Munro, Pamela, and Lynn Gordon

1982   Syntactic relations in Western Muskogean: a typological perspective. *Language* 58:81–115.

Munro, Pamela, and Catherine Willmond

1994   *Chickasaw: An analytical dictionary*. Norman: University of Oklahoma Press.

Napoli, Donna Jo

1989   *Predication theory: A case study for indexing theory.* Cambridge:
        Cambridge University Press.

Nathan, Michele

1977   Grammatical description of the Florida Seminole dialect of
        Creek. Ph.D. diss., Tulane University.

Nicklas, Thurston Dale

1974   The elements of Choctaw. Ph.D. diss., University of Michigan.

Payne, Doris

1979   Switch-reference in Chickasaw. In *Studies of Switch-reference,*
        edited by Pamela Munro, 89–118. UCLA Papers in Syntax.
        Department of Linguistics, University of California, Los
        Angeles.

Roberts, Charles

1986   The second Choctaw removal, 1903. In *After Removal: The
        Choctaw in Mississippi,* edited by Samuel J. Wells and Roseanna
        Tubby, 94–111. Jackson: University of Mississippi Press.

Roche, Joan Marie

1982   Sociocultural aspects of diabetes in an Apache-Choctaw
        community in Louisiana. Ph.D. diss., Catholic University of
        America.

Ross, John R.

1968   Constraints on variables in syntax. Ph.D. diss., Massachusetts
        Institute of Technology.

Safir, Ken

1984   Multiple variable binding. *Linguistic Inquiry* 15:603–38.

Speas, Margaret

1990   *Phrase structure in natural language.* Dordrecht: Kluwer.

Stassen, Leon

1985   *Comparison and universal grammar.* Oxford: Blackwell.

Swanton, John R.

1931   *Source materical for the social and ceremonial life of the
        Choctaw Indians.* Bureau of American Ethnology Bulletin 103.
        Washington, D.C.

1946   *The Indians of the southeastern United States.* Bureau of
        American Ethnology Bulletin 137. Washington, D.C.

Sylestine, Cora, Heather K. Hardy, and Timothy Montler

1993   *Dictionary of the Alabama language.* Austin: University of Texas
        Press.

Ulrich, Charles

1986   Choctaw morphophonology. Ph.D. diss., University of California, Los Angeles.

1993   The glottal stop in Western Muskogean. *International Journal of American Linguistics* 1993:430–41.

1994   A unified account of Choctaw intensives. *Phonology* 11:325–39.

Wasow, Thomas

1979   *Anaphora in generative grammar.* Ghent: E. Story.

Watkins, Ben

1892   *Complete Choctaw definer: English with Choctaw definition.* Van Buren, Ark.: J. W. Baldwin.

Whitman, John

1982   Configurationality parameters. In *Issues in Japanese Linguistics,* ed. by Takashi Imai and Mamoru Saito, 352–74. Dordrecht: Foris.

Wierzbicka, Anna

1992   *Semantics, culture, and cognition.* Oxford: Oxford University Press.

Williams, Loring S.

1835   *Family education and government: A discourse in the Choctaw language.* Boston: American Board of Commissioners for Foreign Missions.

Williams, Robert Scott

1995   Language obsolescence and structural change: the case of Oklahoma Choctaw. Ph.D. diss., University of California, Los Angeles.

Wright, Alfred

1852a   *A book of questions on the gospel of Mark, in the Choctaw language; for the use of Bible classes and sabbath schools.* New York: S.W. Benedict.

1852b   *A book of questions on the gospel of Luke, in the Choctaw language; for the use of Bible classes and sabbath schools.* New York: S.W. Benedict.

Wright, Allen

1880   *Chahta leksikon.* St. Louis: Presbyterian Publishing Co.

Index

In *Studies in the Anthropology of North American Indians*

The Medicine Men: Oglala Sioux Ceremony and Healing
By Thomas H. Lewis

A Dictionary of Creek / Muskogee
By Jack B. Martin and
Margaret McKane Mauldin

Wolverine Myths and Visions: Dene Traditions from Northern Alberta
Edited by Patrick Moore and Angela Wheelock

Households and Families of the Longhouse Iroquois at Six Nations Reserve
By Merlin G. Myers
Foreword by Fred Eggan
Afterword by M. Sam Cronk

Ceremonies of the Pawnee
By James R. Murie
Edited by Douglas R. Parks

Archaeology and Ethnohistory of the Omaha Indians: The Big Village Site
By John M. O'Shea and
John Ludwickson

Traditional Narratives of the Arikara Indians (4 vols.)
By Douglas R. Parks

Osage Grammar
By Carolyn Quintero

They Treated Us Just Like Indians: The Worlds of Bennett County, South Dakota
By Paula L. Wagoner

A Grammar of Kiowa
By Laurel J. Watkins with the
assistance of Parker McKenzie

Native Languages and Language Families of North America
(folded study map and wall display map)
Compiled by Ives Goddard